FARM HOUSE

C·O·O·K·B·O·O·K

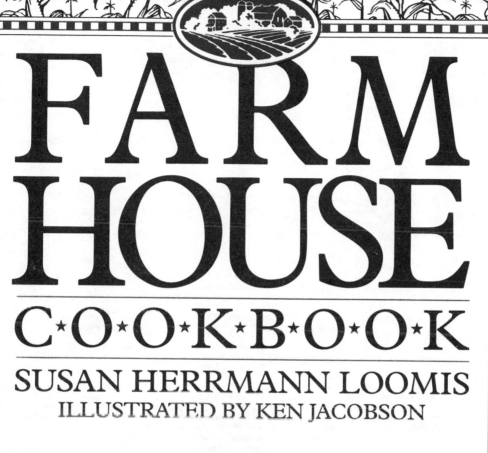

FARM HOUSE

C·O·O·K·B·O·O·K

SUSAN HERRMANN LOOMIS

ILLUSTRATED BY KEN JACOBSON

WORKMAN PUBLISHING ▪ NEW YORK

Versions of some of the material contained in this book were previously published: "Maytag Blue," Blue Cheese and Onion Tart,
and Blue Cheese Spread, *New York Times*, January 3, 1990; "Seattle's Pike Place Market," *Food & Wine*, November 1988; "A Slippery Harvest,"
Seafood Business Magazine, November–December 1990; "Rosey's the Name, Produce Is the Game," *Food & Wine*, November 1988;
"Hazelnuts by Any Other Name," *Boston Globe*, May 3, 1989; "An Education in Blueberries," Nate Pennell's Mulligan
Stew with Blueberry Dumplings, Blueberry Syrup, and Blueberry Glacé Pie, *New York Times Magazine*, September 15, 1991;
"Oh, Those Flavorful Apples," Best-Ever Apple Pie, Meringue-Topped Baked Stuffed Apples, Apple Crisp, and Apple
Sorbet, *Eating Well*, October 1991; Arkansas Barbecue, Bobbie Clark's Baked Beans, Eureka Farm Chicken with Garbanzos,
Six-Layer Dinner, Pulla, and Alice Berner's Apple Pancake, *Gourmet*, April 1991.

Library of Congress Cataloging-in-Publication Data
Loomis, Susan Herrmann.
Farmhouse cookbook / by Susan Herrmann Loomis.
p. cm.
Includes index.
ISBN 1-56305-125-7 ISBN 0-89480-772-2 (pbk.)
1. Cookery, American. I. Title.
TX715.L844 1991
641.s973—dc20 91-50390
CIP

Front cover design by Charles Kreloff
Book design by Lisa Hollander and Charles Kreloff
Chapter logos by Jo Tomallo

Books are available at special discounts when purchased in bulk for premiums and sales promotions as
well as for fund-raising or educational use. Special editions or book excerpts can also be created to specification.
For details, contact the Special Sales Director at address below.

Workman Publishing Company, Inc.
708 Broadway
New York, N.Y. 10003

Manufactured in the United States of America

First printing October 1991
10 9 8 7 6 5 4 3

DEDICATION

With gratitude to Barney Smith,
who exemplifies all the farmers in America who plan their crops,
pray for rain, and risk their fortunes
to keep food on our tables.

With love to Joseph Kip.

ACKNOWLEDGMENTS

Acknowledging all of the people who help in the writing of a book seems an almost impossible task because the help comes from so many directions, in so many different ways. Nonetheless, here is an attempt.

The best place for me to start is by thanking the most important person involved in this book, my husband, Michael. Together we traveled more than twenty thousand miles across America while researching. He not only participated in the adventures with gusto but also drove a good share of the miles, navigated, helped out with chores on farms, often asked the questions that brought an interview together, and was moral and entertaining support throughout the entire process.

A VERY SPECIAL THANK YOU

I want to thank Daniel Johnnes, sommelier at Montrachet and the Tribeca Grill in New York and friend of long standing, for his fine wine choices. He tasted and tested and understood completely the spirit of the book, and the recipes.

All of the recipes in this book have been tested many times in my kitchen, then tested a final time to be sure they are reliable. I am lucky enough to have had help from the finest for those final tests. Many, many thanks go to my loyal and efficient chief tester Mary Kay Sisson in Washington, whose eagerness never faltered. Thanks, too, to Cathy Burgett, who acted as pastry troubleshooter, ironing out the kinks in troublesome recipes and making herself available as a skilled expert, and to Barbara Leopold, whose willingness and comments were invaluable.

There would have been no reason to do this book without the farmers who till the soil and provide us with our abundance of food, an essential freedom we should never take for granted. Their lives and culture drew me to this book. The farmers you will meet in these pages welcomed me with astonishing generosity and frankness. They willingly took precious time to teach and talk, and we had many a merry evening around farm tables.

Special thanks, not only for information and assistance but for unforgettable hospitality to Alice and Bud Berner and Aili and Bill Takala in Montana; Li and Jon Ochs in Washington; Caryl, Barney, and Nelson Smith in Iowa; Betty and Larry Yaeger and Linda and Amos Stoltzfus in Pennsylvania; Irene and Pete Yamamoto in California; Juanita and Rufino Hormachea in Idaho; Martha and Phil Byrnes in Nevada; the Carpenter Family

and Mark Cain and Mike Crain in Arkansas; Elizabeth Ryan and Peter Zimmermann and Lillian and Miles Cahn in New York; and Velma and Walter Williams in Texas. There were many others who extended themselves well beyond what I expected, and I thank them all.

We moved from Seattle to New York a third of the way through this project and there are people who helped in both venues. Thanks to Cynthia Nims in Seattle, who was in on the start and who worked with her typical efficiency and enthusiasm, and again to Barbara Leopold in New York, who began working with me at a crucial moment and was invaluable in everything from researching to recipe testing, as well as being a sheer pleasure to work with. Thanks also to Gayle Herrmann for her thorough research help, and to Hedi Levine for hers.

Thanks to our friends who either steered us to farming relatives or welcomed us when we visited their neighborhoods: Al and Diane McClane, Jerry

Lyman, Marie and Andy Keech, Kip Brundage and Tracy Lord, Barbara Tropp, Julia and Paul Child, Stuart Yatsko, Hal Hendler, Harry and Debbie Putnam, Tom Putnam, Karen and Chuck Malody, and Dodie Fredericks.

Thanks to Mark Musick in Seattle, who, when I told him about this book, opened his valuable files and started me on my way. Thanks, too, to Elizabeth Schneider in New York for her generous information, and to August Schumacher in Massachusetts for his.

I wouldn't have been able to do this book without the support of Peter and Carolan Workman and the friendship and careful attention of my wonderful editor Suzanne Rafer. Thank you, too, to Kathie Ness for her precise copy editing, and to everyone at Workman for their enthusiastic support including Andrea Glickson, Janet Harris, Lisa Hollander, Lori S. Malkin, Shannon Ryan, Bert Snyder, Ina Stern, and all the other Workman people who make this process such fun.

My literary agents Susan and Bob Lescher have been a profound source of support, friendship, and assistance, and I am forever grateful to them and their daughter Susannah for the respite and calm environs of Woodstock, which helped me complete this book. I am also grateful to my friend Patricia Wells, who is a continual source of support and good times.

Thanks to the experts who reviewed

portions of this book including Garth Youngberg, Executive Director of the Institute for Alternative Agriculture, and his colleagues there; Fred Kirschenmann, grain farmer; Roger Blobaum of the Center for Science in the Public Interest; and Steve Curran, Associate Professor at the Department of Grains Science of Kansas State University.

Thanks to several editors who responded with enthusiasm and assignments when they learned of the nature of this book including Carole Lalli, Pamela Mitchell, Rux Martin, Penelope Green, Eric Asimov, Evelynne Kramer, and Zanne Zakroff.

For the meals they shared, the comments they made, and the leftovers they took home I'd like to thank Pat Mowry and Eric Rutter, Rosemary Ellis and Jim Anderson, Carole Fahrenbruch, Danny Peary, Anne Hurley, Ellen Cole and Michael Daum, and Suzanne and Ned Hamlin.

Finally, thanks to my parents, Doris Bain and Joseph Herrmann, for their constant support. They, and my dear grandmother, who was the best farm cook I ever met, instilled in me a respect for good food and the best possible ingredients, and a deep curiosity in the people who make them possible.

CONTENTS

GARDEN SALADS
• 265 •

A FULL LARDER
• 311 •

CRUSTY BREADS
• 349 •

COOKIES AND CAKES
• 373 •

MILE-HIGH PIES
• 427 •

FRUITS, DESSERTS
• 469 •

WHAT'S DOING DOWN ON THE FARM

When I began the odyssey that became this book, I went in search of my idea of farming, of what I imagined to be the soul of the American family farm.

Never having lived on a farm, I had citified notions, replete with visions of irresistibly soft newborn lambs, air so clean and fields so green that every moment in them was pure pleasure. I expected hearty meals of mouthwatering soups, stews, and roasts with slabs of fresh-from-the-oven bread dripping with butter and honey to restore energy after hard work in the fields and orchards.

I wanted to meet farmers on their turf, smell the richness of the soil and let it run through my fingers, walk through waist-high wheat, eat an ear of corn right from the stalk, sit around a laden farm table.

Over the course of more than two years I did all of those things, along with my husband, Michael who was photographer, driver, and invaluable companion. Any notions I had—or call them fantasies—were fulfilled.

We spent hours in the fields—helping fill seed bins, riding in tractors, following harvesting crews, and dodging broccoli stems as they were sliced off, before a rubber band was put around the remaining bunch. We munched organically grown carrots fresh from the soil, sucked just-cut sugar cane, and crunched incomparable apples straight from the orchard.

I spent many hours in the kitchens of those farms, gleaning tips about pastry-making, bread-baking, noodle-making, and chicken-stewing. We sampled cookies, cakes, pies, and doughnuts; ice creams, custards, puddings, and crisps; and ate soups and stews with more flavor than I had ever imagined possible. We watched goat's milk being transformed into cheese, and ate tortillas fresh from the griddle.

I doubt I'll ever taste a better barbecue than the one we had with the Carpenter family at their farm in Arkansas, nor savor anything quite as delicate as the new almonds from Pete Yamamoto's orchard.

I was constantly reminded of how much flavor food can have when it's grown nearby and hasn't sat in a box, traveled for miles, or languished on a refrigerated shelf.

I've become an even more ardent supporter of farmer's markets than I was before. Every idea I've ever had about seasonal eating has been reinforced a hundred times over.

I no longer wince at the price of organic produce, because I know what it costs to grow it. I bypass the fat, garish red tomatoes at the supermarket in favor of smaller, softer, warmer tomatoes from the farmer, and if it's October and I can't find a good tomato, I eat something else.

While much of my idealized image was satisfied, other parts of it were shattered as I came to realize what's involved in the day-to-day life, and business, of a farmer. For every golden moment, happy card game, and luscious meal there are long working hours, the vagaries of weather, the loans from the bank.

I understand that driving a tractor along straight rows from dawn into the night can be mind-bendingly dull, that watching a hailstorm destroy a crop can break a heart as well as a year's budget, that having a barn full of lowing cattle means shoving your warm feet into icy cold boots every morning.

From many farm cooks I learned that, given their druthers, they'd prefer to be in the fields because it's less work. Many of the women I met had once had time to cook but were now pressed into farmwork on a full-time basis. Where that was the case, a farm meal was too often microwaved frozen foods, Spam sandwiches eaten on the run, pop-up biscuits baked in a flash.

I learned the true meaning of deception as farmers recounted having been encouraged, even pushed, by the government to get bigger and more modern, to "plant fencerow to fencerow." But when the time came for the farmers to sell the fruits of their labor and recoup their investment, the market promised by the government had, mysteriously, disappeared.

The effect on small and mid-size family farms, and on their communities, has been tragic. Banks foreclose on farms, farmers are out of work, small towns crumble when no one has the money to buy or the spirit to participate. Big corporate farms have moved in to snatch what they can.

Though the 1980s saw a tremendous decline in the number of small farms, the trend has actually been steady since the 1930s. In 1935 there were more than 6 million farms; now there are slightly more than 2 million. While nearly all of those are classified as family farms (owned by a family group or family corporation), the actual number of farms owned and worked by families is just under 500,000.

What this points out is that fewer, larger farms are producing an increasing amount of food in America. The agricultural base of our society is becoming ever

smaller and the food supply is becoming controlled by ever fewer numbers of large corporate hands. There are many reasons for this situation including the low prices paid to the farmer, the high cost of land, and the enormous expense of all that is necessary to run a farm.

The fact that any small farms survive is a testament to incredibly hard work, good planning, smart marketing, and general dedication.

The farmers who have survived are not easily sold on government planning. They exhibit determination, independence, and often blatant mistrust of those fancy government deals. They go their own way, seek their own markets, look for more satisfying alternative farming methods.

DOING THE RESEARCH

■■■■

There are some 2 million farms in America, and as I began planning my research, I was daunted by what I'd set out to do. I immediately narrowed my choices to family farms, where the owner might actually be the farmer. I looked for farmers who were progressive, successful, and good at what they do.

I listed the foods I love to eat—artichokes and almonds, corn and avocados, lettuces and grapes—and lined up farms specializing in those. Then I looked for farms that represent an area, such as a hog farm in Iowa, a dairy farm in Wis-

consin, an apple farm in New York.

Once I started the research, it seemed that everyone I encountered was related to a farmer: "Oh, you've got to visit my aunt in Iowa," or "I've got relatives on the farm in Montana—why don't you give them a call." I often followed their suggestions, with delightful results. I got other names from county extension offices, from going to farm conferences, and from tips I picked up here and there.

Catching a farmer at home wasn't easy unless I called late in the evening or before dawn. Once I reached them, however, I was surprised at their willingness to talk and their wide-open encouragement to "come by and see us" despite their busy schedules.

I was seduced by farming on our first visit to Eureka Farm in eastern Washington, the home of Jon and Li Ochs and their five children. The Ochses are passionate farmers with a single driving mission: They want to make the earth a better place to live, and to that end they raise lentils, wheat, and chick-peas almost entirely without the use of chemicals. One of the most enjoyable evenings of my life was spent around their dining table, because as well as being enthusiastic about their joint endeavors they are funny, vibrant, and sophisticated, and Li is a gifted cook.

With that happy beginning we went on to visit almond, grape, vegetable, and artichoke farms in California, wheat and oat farms and cattle ranches in Montana, small grain farms in North Dakota, and bean and turkey farms in South Dakota. We visited cheese makers and hog farmers in the Midwest, herb and citrus growers in the Southwest, greens and specialty vegetable farmers in the South, sugar cane, corn, mango, and avocado farmers in the Southeast, and apple growers, sea vegetable farmers, and goat farmers in the Northeast.

No matter what the season or the chores needing to be done, we found that farmers were willing to take time to answer questions. Fred Kirschenmann couldn't stop planting his field, so he asked me to hop in the tractor and we talked as he drove steadily along.

Everywhere we stopped we were greeted with hospitality, generosity, and even open arms. We were prepared for camping because many farms are far from towns and accommodations. But we rarely pitched our tent, and instead were offered a bed.

At the Berner farm in Montana,

we were invited to stay over Memorial Day weekend so we could get in on all the festivities. Bud Berner took us on his regular Sunday drive to check the progress of his fields. I felt like a kid breaking the rules when he turned off the road right into an oat field, then remembered that he was the farmer and could do what he liked. "No matter how many years you plant it, when it comes up and looks good, you never get tired of looking at it," he said, touching the oats outside the window.

In Iowa, Caryl and Barney Smith came out of the house to greet us with huge hugs and cold glasses of iced tea. We are friends with their niece, but never expected such warmth. Caryl treated us to many of her culinary specialties, like her rich posole, sweet apple pie, lively rolled tacos, and the fresh garden tomatoes that found their way into all the meals while we were there.

I went to Texas on my own, and there Velma and Walter Williams took me in and insisted I stay not just one night but several. Velma produced every favorite dish she knew, introduced me to her cattle individually, by name, and sat beside me at a cattle auction easily as excited as I was, though she goes at least once a month. Walter instructed me about pecans, taught me how to shoot a rifle, and regaled me with tales of his childhood, when his family was dirt-poor but always had plenty of pepper sauce to make their food palatable.

We drove 20,000 miles, zigzagging across the country to visit farms I'd chosen, camping out when the miles were too many to make in a day, visiting country antique stores to break the tedium, eating in small country cafés when we passed a likely candidate.

OUR ETHNIC DIVERSITY

The farmers we met made me understand, deeply, the open-heartedness and energetic spirit of America. Through them we also got a close-up look at the many ethnic communities and influences alive in farm country today.

Many of the farmers we met were first-generation Americans. Aili and Bill Takala, in Montana, came from Finland and both speak with a distinct Finnish accent gentled by their many years in America. Pauline and Theodore Kirschenmann are of Russian-German extraction, and they too have the edge of an accent that comes from their native language.

Pete Yamamoto spoke Japanese with his parents, who came to farm in this country before the Second World War. Chew Chang, in Seattle, is an even more recent arrival, having come ten years ago after fleeing her native Laos. They have all brought their own farming methods and ideas to this land and have blended them with all they've learned here.

Ethnic influences were strong in the foods we sampled and in the recipes I gathered. Helen Pavich's dishes reflect her Hungarian heritage, and the recipes from Mike and Ron Rosella leave no doubt

about their Italian origin.

It was astonishing to realize, when talking with these farmers, that in many cases just a single generation has elapsed since parts of this country were settled. The farmers we met, or their parents, were the ones who broke the sod, homesteading in remote areas and establishing communities where none had existed.

This country is so young to have come so far, and nowhere was that more apparent to me than when I was talking with the people who till the soil. As a country we are developing an agricultural system, and fortunately our farmers are willing and ready to change as they can and to hold fast when they must.

Our visits were sometimes bittersweet as we listened to tales of struggle, of adversity brought on by government programs, agribusiness, freak weather. There was never a feeling of hopelessness, just a sad realization that farmers must fight tooth and nail for the privilege of doing what they love and need to do.

Along with the bittersweet was the optimism of farmers who've seen that they must be businesspeople, and marketing and public relations experts, too. They read the market, find a niche, and plant to fill a specific need.

The face of farming in America is clearly changing, evolving as it always has to meet the needs of a demanding, trend-conscious populace. For the past several years, grain farmers planted their fields in oats as the oat bran craze swept the country. Now rice farmers are hopping with excitement at the discovery of rice bran's possibilities. Sun-dried tomatoes keep some farmers in business, while minced garlic makes others a success. It's a fascinating profession, a multi-faceted, complex industry.

Farming is essential to a healthy, balanced society, and to the health of each individual in the country. If we lose our farms, we lose the ability to produce our own food, which is a vital measure of our independence and our quality of life.

The people you will meet in these pages are keeping these values alive for us through their work. I'm grateful to all of them for their openness and generosity, their ideas and stories, and the recipes that warm and satisfy us. To all of them, and to their colleagues I haven't met, a hearty thank-you for much more than the help they gave me on this book.

Susan Herrmann Loomis

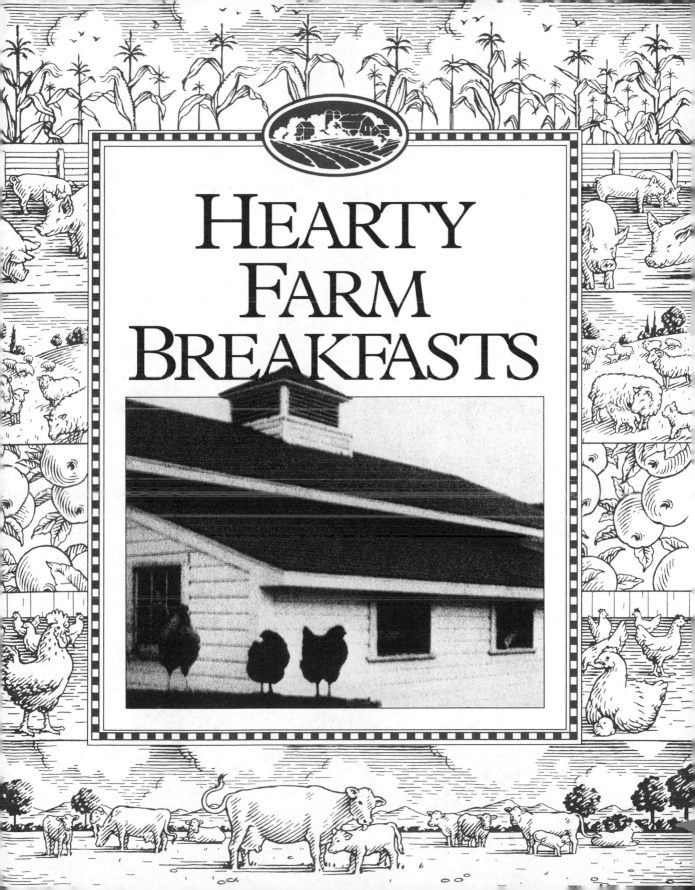

HEARTY FARM BREAKFASTS

WARM STARTS ON A COLD MORNING

Farmers get up early, and once the first chores of the day are done, they are ready to sit down in a big, cozy kitchen to a huge, hearty breakfast.

Well, while many farmers fit right into that scenario, today many others, whose spouses have headed off to their own jobs, go to the town café, which by 8 A.M. is loud with conversation and camaraderie.

I never saw so many slices of pie ordered for breakfast as I did at Cooky's Cafe in Golden City, Missouri. At the Loveless Cafe in Nashville, Tennessee, the order of the early morning was fried chicken with chicken-fat biscuits, delivered in their cast-iron skillet, and in Indiana it was biscuits-'n'-gravy with a side of buckwheat cakes and a log boom of sausages. On a bitter morning in Idaho, I followed the other customers' example and ordered up some sweet, sticky, cinnamon-rich rolls to help me brave my way through the day.

In farm kitchens I ate my share of eggs and fresh ham, steak strips and potatoes, and leftover chicken stew. But what I loved best were the baked goods—the pancakes, the granola, and the sweet rolls and buns. They start the morning off right and give a glow to the day.

CREAMED EGGS

Morning comes early on the farm, and breakfasts are usually hearty affairs. In winter they're eaten well before dawn. In summer the sky is lightening as the last bit of egg is sopped off the plate with a piece of toast.

This recipe was inspired by many of my farm visits, where eggs appeared at the breakfast table in all manner of ways. Sometimes they were fried, sometimes poached, sometimes hard-cooked. Here they are baked in cream with a touch of cheese and chives. The result is silken, filling, and flavorful.

Check on the eggs at least once to be sure they don't over-cook—unless, like many of the farmers I visited, you like your yolks hard. If that is the case, let them cook longer than the time called for.

These eggs can be served for any meal, and the herbs can be varied.

1 tablespoon unsalted butter, at room
    temperature
8 large eggs
⅓ cup finely grated Romano or Parmesan cheese
1 large bunch fresh chives, minced
1 cup heavy (whipping) cream
Salt and freshly ground black pepper

1 Preheat the oven to 325°F. Lightly butter eight ½-cup ramekins or other ovenproof dishes.

2 Break 1 egg into each ramekin, and sprinkle them with the cheese and the chives. Pour 2 tablespoons cream over each, and season with salt and pepper to taste. Place the ramekins on a baking sheet and transfer to the oven.

3 Bake until the eggs are set and the cream is bubbling lightly around the edges, about 10 minutes. Remove from the oven and serve immediately.

8 servings

FRIED EGG-IN-A-HOLE SANDWICHES

Fried eggs, crisp bacon, and toast are still a pretty standard breakfast on the American farm. This version is one my husband, who was raised on a horse farm in Virginia, grew up eating. He still loves it on a cold morning when there is a good day's work ahead. It's fun, tasty, and pretty on the plate, too.

8 slices good-quality white bread, preferably
  homemade or Pepperidge Farm Distinctive
  White sandwich bread
8 strips bacon
8 large eggs
Salt and freshly ground black pepper

1 Cut a small round out of the center of each slice of bread, using a 2-inch cookie cutter. Set aside the rounds and the slices of bread.

2 Fry the bacon in a large skillet over medium-high heat until crisp, about 7 to 8 minutes. Drain the bacon on a plate lined with paper towels. Keep warm. Drain all but ¼ inch of fat from the pan.

3 Return the pan to the heat and add the bread slices and the bread rounds. You will probably have to do this in batches. Break an egg into each "hole" in the bread,

season with salt and pepper to taste, and cook until the egg white is set on the bottom and the yolk begins to get firm, about 1 minute. With a spatula, carefully flip the bread slices with the egg, and the separate bread rounds. Cook until the bread is golden and the eggs are cooked to your liking. If you like the eggs nearly cooked through, they will take an additional 2 to 3 minutes. If you like them soft, they will take an additional 1 minute.

4 To serve, arrange 2 slices of bread and eggs on a plate, place a bread round at an angle over each egg, and garnish with 2 slices of bacon.
Serve immediately.

4 servings

BETTER THAN BRAN

This basic granola is toasty, crunchy, and lightly sweet. It won't win any low-fat contests, but its flavor is tough to beat and a small amount goes a long way.

Try granola in the morning with milk and fresh fruit, sprinkled over ice cream for dessert, or added to muffins, quick breads, or cookies in place of rolled oats.

If you can't find unsweetened coconut use the sweetened variety, but first rinse it with boiling water and drain it. Leave the almonds whole if you like, or chop them in half—not much smaller, or they will brown too much in the oven.

12 tablespoons (1½ sticks) unsalted butter
½ cup mild honey
½ teaspoon salt
1 teaspoon vanilla extract
4½ cups rolled oats
1 cup wheat germ
1 cup unsweetened shredded coconut (available at natural foods stores)
1 cup almonds, whole or halved

1 Preheat the oven to 300°F.

2 Combine the butter, honey, and salt in a heavy medium-size saucepan over medium heat, stirring occasionally so the salt dissolves. When the mixture is warm and well blended, remove the pan from the heat and stir in the vanilla.

3 In a large bowl mix together the oats, wheat germ, coconut, and almonds. Pour in the butter mixture, and stir well so all the ingredients are moistened. Spoon the mixture into two 12½ x 8½-inch baking dishes, and bake in the center of the oven until the granola is toasty brown, 35 to 40 minutes, stirring about every 15 minutes so it browns evenly.

4 Transfer the dishes to wire racks to cool. Stir the granola occasionally as it cools, so it doesn't form large clumps. The granola will keep for at least 1 week in an airtight container.

About 8 cups (16 servings)

JUST WHAT IS ORGANIC FARMING?

Deciding just what organic farming methods are, and who is an organic farmer, is difficult in part because there is no accepted definition for the term organic. "Ten years ago we defined organic as 'farming systems that avoid or largely exclude synthetic pesticides,'" says Dr. Garth Youngberg, who helped write the USDA definition of organic and who now heads the Institute for Alternative Agriculture. "Then, farmers who occasionally used pesticides or fertilizers called themselves organic. Now, for marketing purposes, organic tends to mean complete abstention from synthetic chemicals, though it differs from state to state."

In general, organic farming relies on crop rotation, biological pest controls, botanical pesticides made from plants, and animal manure and plant residues and debris for fertilizers. Twenty-six states have organic standards, and all of them are different. What is allowed in one state may not be allowed in another. The Organic Foods Production Association of North America, the trade association, has recommended national standards to serve as guidelines for the federal government, and a Senate bill has funds earmarked for a national organic standards board.

Senator Patrick Leahy introduced an Organic Foods Production Act into Congress which calls for a national standard for organic products and legal restrictions on the use of the term organic. This was included in the 1990 Farm Bill and signed into law in November 1990.

By establishing a standard, this bill encourages organic farming and a better environment. It also calls for a program to investigate a "transitional" label on low-input farming products.

The bill also includes a provision for a national list of approved substances that may be used in organic production. It states that a natural substance may not be included on the list if it is shown to be harmful to the environment or to human health, and it provides for the inclusion of synthetic substances if they are shown to be beneficial, consistent with organic farm practices, without a natural substitute, and harmless to human health or the environment. This act covers not only produce but all animal products and by-products, as well as post-harvest processing and handling of food products.

ALICE BERNER'S MOM'S PANCAKES

A lice Berner, a farmer in northern Montana, has an awe-inspiring amount of energy and exuberance. Small, with brown eyes and a halo of curly brown hair, she doesn't walk, she runs, and when she talks her hands move as fast as her mouth.

Though she spends just about as much time in the fields as her husband, Bud, she loves to cook, and manages to prepare three solid meals a day. The Berners raise their 3,000-plus acres of grains without any synthetic chemicals, and they are as conscious of what they put in their mouths as they are of what they put in the ground.

We were sitting at the Berners' round kitchen table, keeping warm inside as snow piled up outside the windows. Alice was going through her recipe box, and I was writing as fast as I could. "These are easy to make and you won't believe the flavor," she said, tossing a handwritten recipe card my way. This recipe for pancakes—more accurately really thin, tender griddlecakes—was on it, and she was right.

Alice comes from a long line of women who love to cook, and most of her favorite recipes are those her mother prepared. She tends to adapt recipes, adjusting them to fit her more up-to-date concerns about lower fat, less salt, and quicker cooking—but these griddlecakes she has left as is. They need no adaptation, refinement, or tinkering.

The secret is the buttermilk, which gives them a near-sourdough tang. I cook them in a nonstick pan, though a well-blackened cast-iron skillet is more traditional. If you prefer the traditional route, you will need to cook the pancakes in a small amount of oil. Serve them smothered in Rhubarb Preserves or Blueberry Syrup (see Index).

2 cups all-purpose flour
1 teaspoon baking soda
½ teaspoon baking powder
½ teaspoon salt
2 tablespoons sugar
2⅓ cups buttermilk
2 eggs
3 tablespoons peanut oil

1 Sift the dry ingredients together into a medium-size bowl. In a small bowl, whisk together buttermilk, eggs, and oil. Pour the liquid into the dry ingredients, whisking just until they are incorporated. Don't overwhisk the mixture, or the pancakes will be tough.

2 Place a nonstick skillet over medium heat. When the skillet is hot, pour in ⅓ cup batter for each pancake. Cook until bubbles form on the top of the pancakes, about 3 minutes. Then turn and cook until the bottom is golden and cooked, about 30 seconds. Serve immediately.

About 1 dozen (3 to 4 servings)

GOLDEN CORN PANCAKES

I have a passion for fresh corn in just about any form. Once summer arrives—often even before, when good corn from Florida is in the market—I'm putting it in salads, eating it by the ear for lunch and dinner, and generally making it a major part of my diet.

The idea for these pancakes came to me on an early summer morning when I was hankering after corn. My husband and I love pancakes, and it didn't take much to make me combine the two. We like them so much that I even make them in winter with frozen corn, since corn is one vegetable that survives the freezing process very well. Serve corn pancakes with honey, butter, and maple syrup for breakfast, or at dinner as an accompaniment to fried chicken.

1 to 1¼ cups milk

4 tablespoons (½ stick) unsalted butter

1 cup fresh corn kernels or good-quality frozen

1¼ cups all-purpose flour

2 teaspoons baking powder

¾ teaspoon salt

2 large eggs

1 to 2 teaspoons mild vegetable oil, such as safflower

1 Combine 1 cup milk, the butter, and the corn in a small saucepan over

medium heat. When the butter has melted, remove the pan from the heat and let the mixture cool to lukewarm.

2 Sift the dry ingredients together onto a piece of waxed paper.

3 In a large bowl, beat the eggs until they are well mixed. Add the milk mixture. Then gently stir in the flour mixture, mixing just until it is moistened and thoroughly combined. It should be the consistency of cake batter. Add the remaining milk if the batter is very thick.

4 Brush a large heavy skillet or griddle with the oil, and place it over medium-

high heat. When a drop of water sizzles in the pan, pour the batter, ¼ cup for each pancake, into the skillet. Cook the cakes until bubbles cover the surface and begin to burst, 2 to 3 minutes. Flip the cakes and cook for about 30 seconds on the other side. Serve immediately if you can, or keep them warm in a single layer on a platter in a low (200°F) oven.

About 1 dozen
(3 to 4 servings)

DUNDEE ORCHARDS FRENCH TOAST

This recipe was given to me by Marlyce Tolvstad, owner of Dundee Orchards in Dundee, Oregon. Marlyce has about an acre of hazelnut trees on her property, which overlooks the lush Willamette Valley with its vineyards, nut orchards, and berry vines. She has built up a successful business in flavored hazelnut butter—made from her own hazelnuts and those of a farming friend, Ben Mitchell—which she markets nationwide. Marlyce serves this French toast dusted with confectioners' sugar and heaped with fresh fruits, or simply with maple syrup. It's so quick you could make it on a weekday, but it's ideal for a lazy weekend morning or a Sunday brunch with friends and family.

½ cup cream cheese, at room
   temperature
6 tablespoons Hazelnut Butter, at room
   temperature (see page 346)
2 teaspoons sugar
12 slices good-quality white bread,
   such as Pepperidge Farm Distinctive
   White sandwich bread
¾ cup milk
3 large eggs
1 teaspoon vanilla extract
2 to 4 tablespoons unsalted butter

1 Mix the cream cheese and the hazelnut
butter together in a small bowl. Add the
sugar, mix well, and set aside.

2 Cut about four small (½-inch-long) slits
in each slice of bread. Spread the hazelnut mixture on one side of each of the
slices.

3 In a shallow bowl, whisk together the
milk, eggs, and vanilla until thoroughly
combined.

4 Melt 2 tablespoons butter in a large
heavy skillet over medium-high heat
until hot but not smoking. Dip a slice of
bread completely in the milk mixture. Let
the excess drip off, then place it in the skillet and cook until it is golden on each side,
2 to 3 minutes per side. Repeat with the remaining bread, adding more butter as
needed. As they are cooked, transfer the
pieces of French toast to a warmed serving
platter or individual plates.

5 Serve immediately, hazelnut side up,
with confectioners' sugar, maple syrup,
or honey alongside.

6 servings

WAKE-UP BREAD-AND-BUTTER PUDDING

V ersions of this recipe came from a number of farm women, who called
it everything from Strata to Wake-Up Bread Pudding. It is a quirky,
delicious dish that is perfect for breakfast because its fullness of flavor
wakes you up gently without bogging you down.

Its savor rests largely on the bread, which must be very good quality. I like to make my own, but if there isn't time I use a good brand such as Pepperidge Farm Distinctive White.

This can sit overnight in the refrigerator once it is prepared, to be cooked the following morning. If you aren't that organized, let it sit for at least 2 hours before baking; this allows the bread to soak up the custard and the flavors of onion and bacon. I like to leave just the corners of the bread sticking above the custard so they bake up crisp and golden, giving the pudding a varied texture.

For those watching their butter intake, all but 1 tablespoon of the butter can be omitted. The results will be lighter, the flavor only slightly less rich. The 1 tablespoon should be used to butter the pan.

15 thin (⅜-inch) slices white bread,
  with crusts
6 tablespoons (¾ stick) unsalted butter,
  at room temperature
8 ounces slab bacon, rind removed, cut into
  ¼-inch squares
6 large eggs
4 cups milk
Salt and freshly ground black pepper
4 ounces sharp Cheddar cheese, finely grated
4 scallions (green onions), trimmed and cut
  diagonally into ¼-inch-thick slices

1 Spread 1 side of each slice of bread with softened butter.

2 Sauté the bacon in a medium-size heavy skillet over medium-high heat until it is crisp and golden, 5 to 7 minutes. Drain, and set aside.

3 In a large bowl, whisk together the eggs and the milk until thoroughly combined. Season generously with salt and pepper.

4 Arrange the buttered bread in two rows in an 8½ x 12½ inch oval baking dish, turn the slices and overlapping them so that a corner is sticking up. Sprinkle the cheese, scallions, and bacon between the slices of bread. Whisk the egg mixture once to mix in the seasonings and pour it over the bread, making sure you moisten all the slices. Gently press the slices down so they soak up the custard, and let the dish sit, covered, at room temperature for at least 2 hours or overnight in the refrigerator.

5 Preheat the oven to 350°F.

6 Bake the pudding in the center of the oven until the top is deep golden brown and puffed well above the edges of the baking dish, about 50 minutes. To be sure it is cooked through, shake the dish gently. It should shake slightly, but as one piece, not just in the middle.

7 Remove from the oven and serve immediately.

6 to 8 servings

BREAKFAST BISCUITS 'N' GRAVY

Biscuits and gravy is a culinary signpost of rural America. Once the city is far behind, this homey dish becomes part of the landscape, served at every roadside café and restaurant, in as many different ways as there are license plates on the cars out front.

As my husband and I drove from farm to farm, we often found ourselves on the road in the early morning, hunger gnawing at our stomachs. We would pull into the most likely looking café, opting for the small homey kind. We always ordered a serving of biscuits and gravy, eager to see what would appear. Sometimes the biscuits were crisp outside, steaming hot inside, and obviously just out of the oven, the gravy toasty brown with chunks of seasoned sausage meat in it. Other times the biscuits were like hockey pucks, left over from ages past, the gravy milky white and flavorless. There was rarely anything in between.

The dish seemed to reflect the spirit of an area. In towns where farms were prospering, where the hardware store was still family-owned and the café was the heart and soul of the community, the biscuits and gravy were good. In towns where economic hard times had fallen, where agribusiness had scooped up not only the family farms but the family business as well, the café was a shell, the service listless, the conversation nonexistent, and the biscuits and gravy dull, day old, and just plain awful.

This recipe is my version of good-times biscuits and gravy. Instead of using just the fat and flavoring from pork sausage, the way it is done in most cafés and the way the dish was originally devised, I include the sausages, which makes it a full meal. I've added some spicing, relied heavily on black pepper the way most cafés do, and sprinkled it all with fresh sage, which is not essential but gives it a lilt.

The biscuits in this dish are tender but they aren't light and feathery, because they need some texture to stand up to the gravy.

FOR THE BISCUITS

1¾ cups unbleached all-purpose flour

2 teaspoons baking powder

1 teaspoon salt

4 tablespoons (½ stick) unsalted butter,
  chilled

⅓ cup plain yogurt

½ cup plus 2 tablespoons milk

FOR THE SAUSAGES

1½ pounds pork sausage

1½ tablespoons minced fresh sage leaves,
  or 1 teaspoon dried

¾ teaspoon salt

Freshly ground black pepper

½ teaspoon paprika

¼ teaspoon ground allspice

FOR THE GRAVY

3 tablespoons unsalted butter, or
  as needed

3 tablespoons all-purpose flour

2¼ cups milk

Salt and freshly ground black pepper

2 tablespoons fresh sage leaves,
  for garnish

1 Preheat the oven to 425°F. Cover a baking sheet with a piece of parchment paper.

2 Make the biscuits: Sift the flour, baking powder, and salt together into a large bowl. Using two knives or a pastry blender, cut in the butter until the texture ranges from cornmeal to the size of small peas. (These two steps can be done quickly in a food processor.) Using a fork, gradually mix in the yogurt, then the milk, until the dough is quite soft and somewhat sticky. Work quickly without overworking the dough. Turn it out onto a lightly floured surface and knead it briefly, just long enough to get it to hold together. Roll it out so it is about 1¼ inches thick, and cut it into 2-inch rounds. (You will have 10 biscuits.) Arrange the rounds on the prepared baking sheet, and bake in the center of the oven until they are deep golden, puffed, and cooked through, 18 to 20 minutes.

3 While the biscuits are baking, prepare the sausages: Place all the sausage ingredients in a large bowl and mix thoroughly, using your fingers. Shape into eight small patties. To test the seasoning, fry a tiny patty and taste; adjust if necessary.

4 Place the patties in a large heavy or nonstick skillet over medium-high heat, and cook until they are crisp and brown on the outside and cooked through inside, about 8 minutes per side. Transfer the sausage patties to a warmed platter and keep warm.

5 Make the gravy: Add enough of the butter to the skillet so the bottom is covered with ⅛ inch of fat. Stir, scraping up the browned bits from the bottom of the skillet. Reduce the heat to medium and add the flour slowly, stirring until it has absorbed the butter. Cook, stirring constantly, until it turns golden brown, at least 2 minutes. Then slowly pour in the milk, stirring constantly, and cook until the gravy thickens to the consistency of very heavy cream. Season to taste with salt and a generous amount of black pepper.

6 To serve, split two biscuits in half. Place the bottom halves on a warm plate, top them with sausage patties, and pour a generous amount of gravy over the sausage. Mince the fresh sage and sprinkle some over the sausage and gravy. Set the biscuit tops at an angle, partially covering the sausages, and serve immediately.

4 servings (with extra biscuits)

EARLY MORNING BRAN MUFFINS

I've been a fan of bran muffins ever since my sister went on a muffin-making jag many years ago. Like the ones she made, these are rich and moist. I developed them from several farm recipes I picked up during my travels. They are hearty in flavor and have just the right touch of sweetness.

The other bonus from these, and from all other muffins, is that they are quick to make. I assemble the ingredients the night before, then mix up the batter and bake them in the morning so they are on the table for breakfast. It's a good way to start the day, and a great way to maintain the affection of family and friends!

1 cup unprocessed bran

1¼ cups milk

¼ cup honey

¼ cup molasses

¾ cup whole-wheat flour

¾ cup cake flour

2 teaspoons baking powder

½ teaspoon baking soda

1 teaspoon salt

8 tablespoons (1 stick) unsalted butter, melted

1 large egg

1 teaspoon vanilla extract

Zest of 2 oranges, minced

¾ cup finely chopped pitted dates, or whole raisins

1 Preheat the oven to 400°F. Butter 12 muffin cups.

2 In a large bowl, or the bowl of an electric mixer, combine the bran, milk, honey, and molasses. Mix well, and then let stand for at least 2 minutes, but not longer than 20 minutes.

3 Mix together the flours, baking powder, baking soda, and salt.

4 Add the butter, egg, vanilla extract, and orange zest to the bran mixture, and

mix well. Then add the dry ingredients, mixing just until they are combined. Fold in the dates. Fill the prepared muffin cups two-thirds full with the batter.

5 Bake until the muffins are golden and puffed, about 17 minutes. Remove the muffin tins from the oven, and turn the muffins out onto wire cooling racks to cool for about 5 minutes before serving.

12 muffins

OATMEAL-BLUEBERRY MUFFINS

When I asked Arkansas vegetable farmer, Bobbie Clark (see page 81), for some of her family's favorite recipes, she marked this one with exclamation points. It's a relatively recent find for her, made possible by the increasing quantity of blueberries being raised in Arkansas. A particular variety has been specially developed for the heat there, and while they lack the spice of a lowbush berry from a cooler climate, they are ideal for muffins and cobblers.

These muffins have a nice toothsome difference because of the rolled oats, and they're so full of berries they are almost blue inside. I make them for breakfast often during blueberry season, and once in a while at other times of the year with frozen berries when I'm hankering for a taste of summer. They're quick, not too sweet, and full of flavor.

If you use frozen berries, add them to the batter in the frozen state. If you are using fresh berries, don't worry about rinsing them (it often does more harm than good). Just pick them over carefully.

1½ cups all-purpose flour
6 tablespoons sugar
1 tablespoon baking powder
½ teaspoon salt
½ teaspoon freshly grated nutmeg
1½ cups rolled oats
1 cup milk
1 teaspoon vanilla extract
1 large egg
4 tablespoons (½ stick) unsalted butter, melted
1 heaping cup blueberries

1 Preheat the oven to 425°F. Lightly oil 12 muffin cups.

2 Sift the flour, sugar, baking powder, salt, and nutmeg together onto a piece of waxed paper. Mix in the oats.

3 In a large bowl stir together the milk, vanilla, egg, and melted butter. Add the dry ingredients and mix just until they are thoroughly moistened. Don't overmix or the muffins will be tough. Fold in the blueberries.

4 Fill the prepared muffin cups two-thirds full with batter, and bake in the center of the oven until the muffins are golden and spring back when lightly touched, 12 to 15 minutes. Remove the tins from the oven, turn the muffins out on a wire rack, and let them cool for 5 minutes before serving.

12 muffins

BLUEBERRY MUFFINS

This is a distillation of recipes from several places where blueberries are a thriving industry—the Pacific Northwest, central Texas, and of course Maine. From traveling the country and eating blueberries coast to coast, I now know which are my favorites: the wild lowbush berries from Maine.

The Maine blueberry industry has a slight inferiority complex. It produces flavorful, high-quality wild berries in abundance, yet where do most of them go? Into the freezer, into the little cans that come with blueberry muffin mix, into sauces and cake mixes. It's a shame, because wild blueberries rival tiny wild strawberries or wild cherries in the exquisite complexity of their flavor, which hovers between sweet and tart, with a spiciness that makes your eyes open wide.

The most common blueberries in the market are domestic hybrids. Sometimes they can be tasty, but too often they have as much flavor and juice as a cotton ball. The only way to tell is by tasting, so taste until you find a grower who produces berries with flavor, or a frozen brand that suits your palate.

Big hybrid berries tend to bleed more, flooding the foods they are baked in with a bluish gray color. If the berries have flavor, however, the color doesn't matter.

These muffins are cakey rather than dense, and they are seasoned with cinnamon, which is the common blueberry spice in Maine. The lemon zest adds sprightly flavor, and a tinge of bright color as well.

If you are using frozen berries, make sure they rattle in the box or bag before you buy them. If they don't, chances are they've been thawed and refrozen, and won't be worth much. Never thaw frozen berries before adding them to the batter—they will lose all their juice and turn to a tasteless purple mass.

1¼ cups all-purpose flour
2 teaspoons baking powder
½ teaspoon ground cinnamon
½ teaspoon salt
1 large egg
½ cup sugar
4 tablespoons (½ stick) unsalted butter, melted
½ cup milk
Zest of 1 lemon, minced
1½ cups blueberries, fresh or frozen

1 Preheat the oven to 400°F. Lightly oil 12 muffin cups.

2 Sift the flour, baking powder, cinnamon, and salt together onto a sheet of waxed paper.

3 In a medium-size bowl, whisk together the egg and sugar until the mixture is pale yellow. Add the melted butter and the milk, and mix well. Then beat in the lemon zest. Fold in the dry ingredients, and finally fold in the berries just enough to thoroughly moisten them. Don't overmix or the muffins will be tough.

4 Fill the prepared muffin cups half full with batter and bake until the muffins are golden and spring back when pressed lightly, about 20 minutes. Turn the muffins out onto a wire rack, and let them cool for 5 minutes before serving.

12 small muffins

CRANBERRY-PUMPKIN MUFFINS

These cheerful-looking golden muffins are perfect for breakfast because they wake up your mouth with a subtle spicy tang. They're tender and light, and will disappear quickly from the table.

You can make these year-round if you have a cache of frozen cranberries in the freezer. Don't thaw them before you stir them into the batter, because they maintain their shape and texture better when frozen. Also, freezing cranberries makes them juicier, so you'll get an extra hit of tart juice if the berries are frozen.

2 cups all-purpose flour
2½ teaspoons baking powder
1 teaspoon salt
½ teaspoon ground cinnamon
½ teaspoon ground allspice
¼ teaspoon freshly grated nutmeg
¾ cup sugar
⅓ cup mild vegetable oil, such as safflower
2 large eggs
1¼ cups canned pumpkin purée
½ cup milk
½ cup walnuts, coarsely chopped
2 cups cranberries, fresh or frozen, coarsely chopped

1 Preheat the oven to 400°F. Heavily butter 12 muffin cups.

2 Sift together the flour, baking powder, salt, cinnamon, allspice, nutmeg, and sugar, and set aside.

3 In a medium-size bowl, whisk together the oil, eggs, pumpkin, and milk until thoroughly combined. Add the dry ingredients and mix with a wooden spoon, just until they are moistened. Don't overmix or the muffins will be tough. Fold in the nuts and the cranberries. Fill the prepared muffin cups two-thirds full with batter.

4 Bake in the center of the oven until the muffins are puffed and golden and spring back when touched, 20 to 25 minutes. Check them after 20 minutes, as overbaking will result in dry muffins. Remove the muffin tins from the oven, and let cool for at least 5 minutes before unmolding and serving the muffins.

12 muffins

HOT CROSS BUNS

Sometimes there's nothing better in life than a tender, buttery hot cross bun. Eating one is sort of like sinking into a pillow of goodness, a pleasure one should afford oneself several times a year. I ate many wonderful sweet yeasty buns on the farms I visited, and I took elements from each of them to put into this recipe.

I always make hot cross buns for Easter, though I don't reserve them for just one day a year. Instead, I follow my own advice and make them whenever a real breakfast treat is in order.

2 packages active dry yeast
½ cup warm water
1 cup lukewarm milk
½ cup sugar
½ teaspoon salt
1 heaping teaspoon freshly ground cardamom
   (seeds from about 10 pods)
½ teaspoon ground allspice
¼ teaspoon ground cinnamon
3 large eggs, beaten
6 to 6½ cups sifted unbleached all-purpose
   flour
4 tablespoons (½ stick) unsalted butter,
   melted
1 cup dried currants
1 egg mixed with 2 teaspoons water

ICING
¾ cup confectioners' sugar
1 tablespoon plus 1 teaspoon freshly squeezed
   lemon juice

1 Dissolve the yeast in the warm water in a large mixing bowl or the bowl of an electric mixer. Stir in the milk and sugar. When there are some bubbles on top of the liquid, after about 2 minutes, add the salt, cardamom, allspice, cinnamon, eggs, and 3½ cups flour. Mix the batter until it is smooth and elastic, about 5 minutes. Add the melted butter and mix well. Add 2½ cups flour, 1 cup at a time, mixing well after each addition. The dough should be soft but it shouldn't stick to your fingers. If it does, add the remaining ½ cup flour. Turn the dough out onto a lightly floured surface and knead until it is smooth and glossy. This will take about 10 minutes. Add the currants and knead until they are incorporated. Cover the dough with a cloth, and let it rest for 15 minutes.

2 Turn the dough out onto a lightly floured surface, and knead just until it is satiny and any air bubbles are released, which should take just 3 to 4 minutes.

3 Transfer the dough to a mixing bowl, cover lightly with a cloth, and let rise in

a warm spot (68° to 70°F) until it has doubled in bulk, 1½ to 2 hours. Punch the dough down, return it to the bowl, cover, and let rise until it is doubled again, about 1 hour.

4 Line one or two baking sheets with lightly buttered parchment paper.

5 Turn the dough out onto a smooth work surface, and punch it down. Divide the dough into 24 equal pieces. Roll the pieces between your hands to form balls, and place them on the prepared baking sheets, leaving about ½ inch between them. Cover lightly with a cotton towel and let rise until doubled in bulk, about 30 minutes.

6 Meanwhile, preheat the oven to 375°F.

7 Brush the buns lightly with the egg wash, and bake in the center of the oven until they are golden and puffed, about 20 minutes. Remove from the oven, remove to a wire rack, and let cool.

8 To make the icing, mix the confectioners' sugar and lemon juice in a small bowl, and drizzle it over the buns forming a cross pattern. Serve immediately.

24 buns

DOUGH HOOKS

I f your electric mixer has a dough hook, use it in any recipe in this chapter calling for kneading the dough. It will certainly shorten kneading time and make your life a bit easier.

APPLE CREAM SWEET ROLLS

This recipe comes from Pauline Kirschenmann, whose husband, Theodore, and son, Fred, farm 3,100 acres near Windsor, North Dakota.

I spent a day with Fred, which proved a real education in farming (see page 116). Spending time in Fred's mother's kitchen was no less an education. In her eighties, Pauline Kirschenmann still cooks three meals a day for her husband, son, and the farm crew—which can number a dozen. The Kirschenmann's are Russian-German, and Pauline's cooking speaks of that ancestry.

I serve these rolls for breakfast at our house. I make the dough the night before, let it rise overnight in the refrigerator, and then allow about 1½ hours in the morning before I want to pull them steaming from the oven. They are yeasty and rich, and just sweet enough to get the day going.

FOR THE DOUGH

¼ cup milk

2 tablespoons unsalted butter

½ teaspoon salt

1 package active dry yeast

¼ cup lukewarm water

2 tablespoons granulated sugar

2¼ to 2½ cups all-purpose flour

2 large eggs

FOR THE APPLE MIXTURE

2 tablespoons unsalted butter, melted

½ cup packed brown sugar

1 small tart apple

1 teaspoon ground cinnamon

½ cup raisins

3 tablespoons heavy (whipping) cream

1 Prepare the dough: Combine the milk, butter, and salt in a small heavy saucepan, and heat just to the boiling point. Remove from the heat and cool to lukewarm, stirring occasionally so the butter melts.

2 In a large mixing bowl, or the bowl of an electric mixer, dissolve the yeast in the lukewarm water. Mix in the sugar, and add the cooled milk mixture.

3 When there are some bubbles on top of the liquid, add 1 cup of the flour and mix well. Then add the eggs, one at a time, beating well after each addition. Stir in another cup of flour and mix vigorously for several minutes. (If you are making this dough in an electric mixer, mix on high speed for about 3 minutes. If mixing by hand, mix for at least 5 minutes.) The dough will become elastic, but it will still be rather sticky.

4 Turn the dough out onto a heavily floured surface, and knead in the remaining flour. The dough will be quite soft, but it should be elastic and should not stick to your fingers when you touch it. If you need to do so, add a bit more flour, but not enough to make the dough firm. Place the dough in a bowl, cover with a towel, and set aside in a warm spot (68° to 70°F) to rise until doubled in bulk, about 1 hour. (If you want to save the dough for the next morning, place it in a bowl, cover it tightly, and refrigerate.)

5 Preheat the oven to 375°F. Butter a 7 x 11 x 1½-inch baking dish, using 1 table-

spoon of the melted butter. Sprinkle it with ¼ cup of the brown sugar.

6 Peel and halve the apple. Cut out the core, then slice each half very thin (¹⁄₁₆-inch slices). Arrange the slices in the baking dish in neat rows, overlapping them if necessary, so they completely cover the bottom of the dish.

7 Roll the dough out to form a 9 x 16-inch rectangle, and brush it with the remaining 1 tablespoon melted butter. Sprinkle the dough evenly, out to the very edges, with the remaining ¼ cup brown sugar, the cinnamon, and the raisins. Beginning at one long side, tightly roll up the dough jelly-roll fashion, pushing back any raisins that fall out. With the seam down on the work surface, cut the roll into sixteen 1-inch-thick slices. Place the slices on their sides in the prepared pan, so the concentric circles of filling show. The rolls will fit in the pan with room between them to rise.

8 Loosely cover the rolls with a towel, and let them rise in a warm spot until they have filled out the pan but haven't quite doubled in bulk, about 20 minutes.

9 Drizzle the cream over the rolls, and bake in the center of the oven until they are golden and cooked through, 20 to 25 minutes. To test for doneness, place the blade of a knife between two rolls in the center of the pan, and pull back on it to look into the dough.

10 Remove the pan from the oven, and let the rolls cool for 5 minutes before serving. Cut the rolls, removing them carefully from the pan with a spatula so you get the apples too. Serve apple side up. For a more dramatic presentation, invert the rolls onto a warmed serving tray.

16 rolls

PAULINE'S KUCHEN

This is one of Pauline Kirschenmann's specialities. Her granddaughter requests *kuchen* each time she visits, and the farm crew looks forward to the days when it appears on the kitchen table too.

Pauline uses whatever fruit is in season, sometimes mixing varieties, and when fruit is scarce she tops it with raisins. I've tried it with nectarines, peaches, plums, grapes, raisins, prunes, and berries, and each give a tender, sweet result.

I've adjusted Pauline's recipe by reducing the sugar a bit, using unsalted butter instead of lard in the dough, and adding a touch of vanilla to the cream.

FOR THE DOUGH

1 package active dry yeast

1 cup lukewarm milk

3 tablespoons sugar

1 teaspoon salt

3 to 3¼ cups unbleached all-purpose flour

1 large egg

2 tablespoons unsalted butter or lard, melted and cooled

FOR THE CUSTARD

1 cup sour cream

2 eggs

½ cup milk

3 tablespoons sugar

1 teaspoon vanilla extract (optional)

1 tablespoon unbleached all-purpose flour

FOR THE TOPPING

4 tablespoons (½ stick) unsalted butter, at room temperature

7 tablespoons sugar

¼ cup unbleached all-purpose flour

4 cups fresh or 3 cups dried fruit, such as grapes, cherries, plums, apricots, raisins, figs, or prunes (see Note)

1 Prepare the dough: Combine the yeast, milk, and sugar in a large mixing bowl or in the bowl of an electric mixer. Stir to dissolve the yeast. When there are some bubbles on top of the liquid, after about 2 minutes, add the salt and mix well. Add 1 cup of the flour, then the egg and the melted butter, and mix thoroughly. Continue adding the flour, 1 cup at a time, mixing well after each addition. When the dough is too stiff to mix, turn it out onto a well-floured surface and knead in enough flour so the dough doesn't stick (it should still be soft). Return the dough to the mixing bowl, cover with a towel, and let rise in a warm spot (68° to 70°F) until doubled in bulk. (If you are preparing the dough the night before, place it in the bowl, cover tightly with aluminum foil, and refrigerate overnight.)

2 Prepare the custard: Whisk the sour cream and the eggs together in a medium-size bowl until combined. Then add the milk, sugar, and the vanilla if you are using it, and mix well. Whisk in the flour, and set aside. (If you are making this the night before, refrigerate, covered, until ready to use.)

3 In a small bowl, mix together the butter, sugar, and flour for the topping until combined. (The mixture will be crumbly.) Set aside. (If you are making this the night before, refrigerate, covered, until ready to use.)

4 Preheat the oven to 400°F. Lightly butter a 10 x 15-inch baking pan.

5 Turn the dough out onto a floured surface. Roll it out to form a rectangle slightly larger than the baking pan, and then transfer it to the pan. Using your fingers, crimp the edges to make a border ½-inch-higher than the bottom of the dough.

6 Pour the fruit into the pan, and then pour the custard over the fruit. Crumble the topping over all.

7 Bake in the center of the oven until the dough is puffed and golden around the edges and the custard is lightly set, 25 minutes. Remove from the oven and cool on a wire rack for 10 minutes before cutting.

8 to 10 servings

Note: Cut fresh fruit, such as plums and apricots, in quarters. If you are using dried fruit, such as figs or prunes, coarsely chop them.

JERILYN'S NORTHWEST BLACKBERRY COBBLER

Jerilyn Brusseau is the owner of brusseau's, a friendly café-restaurant in Edmonds, Washington, about 40 minutes north of Seattle. Ever since she opened the café more than a decade ago, it's been popular with locals and visitors alike. I know Seattle residents who make the drive to brusseau's on a Sunday morning just for the mountainous cinnamon rolls, the omelets, and the slices of well-seasoned quiche. They rarely leave, I've heard, without taking a portion of this cobbler to eat when they get home.

When it comes to fresh berries, Jerilyn is pickier than anyone I know, and she buys all she uses from local organic farms. This cobbler is on the menu year-round, and to make sure she has enough berries for it, and for the home-made jam her father makes for the restaurant, she freezes them. I like to serve the cobbler for breakfast. It bakes a long time, but is simple and quick to put together.

FOR THE FILLING

6 cups blackberries, raspberries, or rinsed,
    hulled strawberries
1¼ cups sugar
¼ cup all-purpose flour

FOR THE BATTER

2 cups all-purpose flour
1 cup plus 1 tablespoon sugar
1 tablespoon baking powder
1 teaspoon salt
1 cup milk
8 tablespoons (1 stick) unsalted butter, melted
¼ teaspoon freshly grated nutmeg

1 cup heavy (whipping) cream, for garnish

1 Preheat the oven to 350°F.

2 Make the filling: Mix the berries, sugar, and flour together in a large bowl, and pour into a 15-inch nonreactive oval baking dish.

3 Make the batter: Combine the flour, 1 cup of the sugar, the baking powder, and the salt in a food processor. Process to combine. Then add the milk and the melted butter, and beat until smooth.

4 Spoon the batter over the berries, making sure you spread it to the edges of the dish (to prevent any excess juice from boiling over). Sprinkle the remaining 1 tablespoon sugar and the nutmeg over the batter.

5 Bake the cobbler in the center of the oven until the crust is brown and crisp on the outside and cooked all the way through, and the berries are bubbling up through it, about 1 hour.

6 Remove the cobbler from the oven and let it cool for 10 minutes before serving. Serve the cream alongside.

8 to 10 servings

DANISH PUFFS

I got this recipe from Wayne Boynton, a sugar cane grower in Belle Glade, Florida. He spent the day giving my husband and me a tour of his sugar plantation, taking us out to talk with the cane cutters, cutting lengths of sugar cane for us to chew on, and generally filling us in on the history of Florida sugar cane.

Wayne provided not only a lifetime's worth of information about sugar but also a half dozen favorite family recipes using everything they grow on their farm, from sugar to corn. This is one his wife makes often, and at his insistence once entered in a baking contest. It won first prize in two categories, and Wayne is as proud as if he'd made it up himself.

The first time I made it I couldn't imagine what it would be until I'd gotten it assembled. I was thrilled with the result, which is something between a Danish pastry and a coffee cake. I like to serve it for a late breakfast with fresh fruit as an accompaniment.

You can vary the flavor of the frosting to change the taste of the pastry—add cinnamon or nutmeg, or make the Caramel Frosting on page 414.

Don't be put off by the substantial amount of almond extract in the filling. Baking takes the edge away, leaving a gentle, mellow flavor.

*FOR THE PASTRY AND
THE FILLING*

2 cups all-purpose flour

¼ teaspoon salt

1 cup (2 sticks) unsalted butter, chilled, cut into pieces

1 cup plus 2 tablespoons cold water

3 large eggs

2 teaspoons almond extract

FOR THE FROSTING

1 cup confectioners' sugar

⅛ teaspoon salt

1 tablespoon unsalted butter, at room temperature

2 tablespoons heavy (whipping) cream

2 teaspoons vanilla extract

1 Preheat the oven to 425°F. Line a baking sheet with parchment paper.

2 Make the pastry: Place the flour and the salt in a food processor, and process to mix. Add the butter and process until the mixture resembles coarse meal. Add 2 tablespoons of the water, and process until the dough is mixed and nearly holds together but doesn't form a ball.

3 Remove a scant 2 cups of the dough and set it aside. Form the remaining dough into a ball, and divide it in half. Working on a well-floured surface, roll out each half to form a 12 x 3½-inch rectangle, and transfer them to the prepared baking sheet. Cover with waxed paper and refrigerate until ready to bake. (This dough may be prepared the night before you plan to bake it. If you are holding it overnight, wrap and refrigerate the reserved dough too.)

4 Make the filling: Bring the remaining 1 cup water to a boil in a large heavy saucepan over high heat. When the water is boiling, remove the pan from the heat and whisk in the reserved dough. (If this dough was refrigerated, it needs to come to room temperature before proceeding with this step.) It will be stiff, but with persistent whisking it will absorb the liquid and become smooth. Whisk in the eggs, one at a time, until you have a very smooth, soft mixture. Then whisk in the almond extract.

5 Spread the filling over the two pastry rectangles. (You will think it is too much filling, but it isn't. Just pour and spread it evenly, and it will hold its shape.)

6 Bake in the center of the oven until the filling is puffed and has cracked along the top, 30 to 40 minutes.

7 While the pastries are baking, make the frosting: Place the confectioners' sugar and the salt in a food processor, and process to mix. With the processor running,

add the butter, cream, and vanilla. Mix until the ingredients are smooth and thoroughly combined.

8 Remove the pastries from the oven and transfer them to wire cooling racks. While they are still hot, spread the frosting over the top. Serve immediately.

Two 12-inch pastries (12 to 14 servings)

BREAKFAST CRANBERRY CAKE

T his is a version of the cranberry cake made by LaRene Morrison for her restaurant, The Dunes, in Grayland, Washington, near the state's cranberry bogs. It's hearty, homey, and popular beyond belief–I don't think I've ever made a cake that has been as universally loved as this one.

I serve this for breakfast and for dessert. It works well either way–with crème fraîche for break-

fast, with fresh vanilla ice cream for dessert.

FOR THE CRANBERRY SAUCE

1½ cups granulated sugar
2 cups water
4 cups cranberries, fresh or frozen
Grated zest of 1 orange

FOR THE CAKE

2½ cups all-purpose flour
1 teaspoon freshly grated nutmeg
1 teaspoon ground cinnamon
1 teaspoon salt
1 teaspoon baking powder
1 teaspoon baking soda
3 large eggs
1 cup granulated sugar
½ cup packed light brown sugar
12 tablespoons (1½ sticks) unsalted butter,
    melted
1 cup buttermilk

1 Preheat the oven to 350°F. Oil a 9 x 13 x 2-inch baking pan.

2 Make the sauce: Combine the sugar, water, and cranberries in a large heavy saucepan over medium-high heat. Bring to a boil, stirring occasionally. Then reduce the heat to medium and cook until the sauce has thickened and darkened, about 10 minutes. (The cranberries will sound a bit like popcorn as they explode in the sauce.) Stir in the orange zest, remove the pan from the heat, and let cool.

3 Prepare the cake batter: Sift the flour, spices, salt, baking powder, and baking soda together onto a piece of waxed paper.

4 In a large bowl, or the bowl of an electric mixer, combine the eggs with the sugars and mix until they are thoroughly blended; then add the melted butter and mix well. Add the dry ingredients in thirds, alternating with the buttermilk, beginning and ending with the dry ingredients. Mix quickly, stirring just until the ingredients are thoroughly blended. Be careful not to overmix, or the cake will be tough.

5 Spread the cooled cranberry sauce in the prepared baking pan. Pour the cake batter over it, and smooth it out evenly. Bake in the center of the oven until the cake is golden and springs back when touched, about 35 minutes. Let cool at least 10 minutes. Cut the cake, removing the pieces carefully from the pan with a spatula so you get the cranberries too. Serve cranberry side up.

1 cake (10 servings)

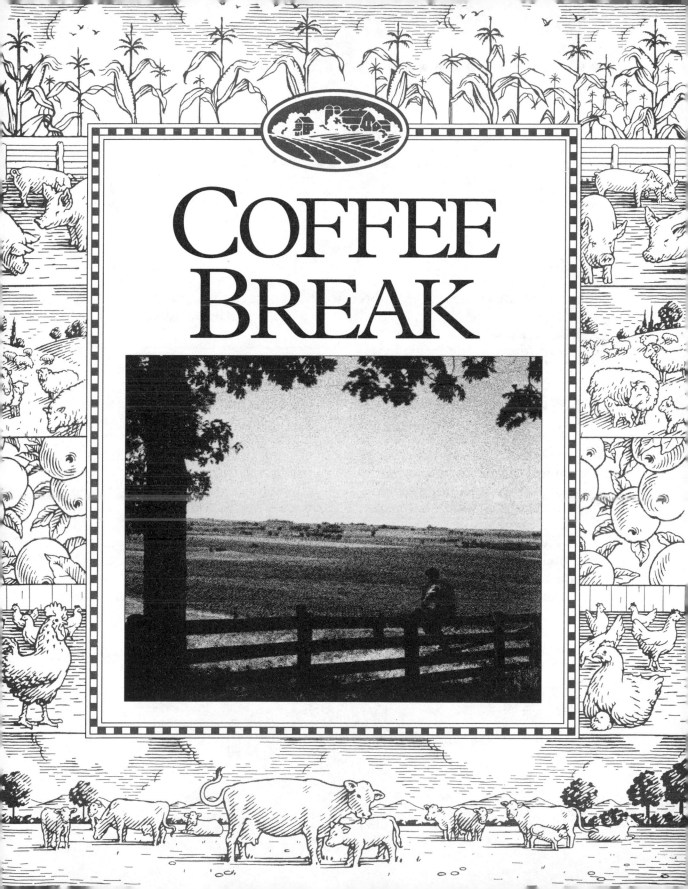

COFFEE
BREAK

SNACKS TO KEEP THE ENERGY UP

Snacks and little bites to nibble are a big part of the farmhouse eating scheme. The work is hard, the hours long, and three meals a day just aren't enough.

On many of the farms I visited, main meals were taken in the house, then the men and women returned to the fields with a bag of snacks to keep them going. While doughnuts and coffee help the urban worker through a long day, a handful of cheese pennies or a sandwich oozing with pimiento cheese helps the farmer meet nature's deadlines.

Farm work often goes on way into the night, and when the farmer arrives home there is usually a small meal waiting to quell hunger. These little meals are surprisingly varied, and include dishes like a farmhouse tomato pie, hummus with toast or crackers, and cucumber rounds with egg. The seasons dictate their appearance, and during the summer, vegetables prevail in the form of cooling salsas or fresh corn on the cob in many different guises. In winter flavors deepen into spiced chicken liver nibbles or a blue cheese and onion tart.

I loved these snack-like foods, and carefully collected recipes to re-create at home as appetizers, which I do often. I've gone on to create some of my own, based on the notion of fresh and hearty snacks from the farm.

CUMIN-SPICED CORN ROUNDS

I love corn season, when green-husked ears, strands of silk straying out the ends, are piled at farm stands, on roadside tables, and in supermarket produce sections. Corn says "summer" without hesitation, and I eat it, and serve it, every chance I get.

Corn is a major part of the American diet, whether it's in the form of the corn sweeteners used in processed foods, the corn fed to fatten livestock destined for our tables, or the corn that is made into flakes, meal, and puffs. But despite its pervasive presence, it never loses its appeal—particularly when it is served on the cob.

This dish was inspired by my travels from the West Coast to the East during corn season, visiting farms all along the way. Growers convinced us to eat it uncooked, right out of the husk, and it was deliciously sweet and tender. We also cooked it over campfires, ate it at backyard barbecues and family picnics, and came to appreciate its every variety.

One of my favorite ways to serve corn is in these spicy rounds. They're an easy finger food and a good prelude to a casual summer meal.

4 medium ears fresh corn
4 tablespoons (½ stick) unsalted butter
¼ teaspoon cayenne pepper
½ teaspoon ground cumin
1 tablespoon fresh oregano leaves, or
  1 teaspoon dried
¼ teaspoon salt, or to taste

1 Cut the ears of corn into 1½-inch rounds. Bring a large pot of water to a boil over high heat, and cook the corn just until it begins to soften, 3 to 4 minutes. Drain and reserve.

2 Melt the butter in a large heavy skillet over medium-high heat. Add the spices, and stir so they are evenly distributed in the butter. Then add the rounds of corn and cook, tossing so they are covered in butter, until they are heated through, 2 to 3 minutes. Transfer to a platter or a shallow bowl, and serve. Eat these rounds with your fingers, the same way you'd eat a full ear of corn.

4 to 6 appetizer servings

SAVORY EGGPLANT AND PEANUTS

When I traveled through the South, I nibbled on freshly roasted peanuts, boiled peanuts, raw peanuts, and more. I stood knee deep in peanut plants inhaling the perfume of their tiny yellow flowers and was surrounded by the toasty aroma of the nuts in a processing plant. I came to think of peanuts as something more than the better half of a peanut butter and jelly sandwich, and once home, began using them in salads, soups, and sauces.

This salad, based on a recipe I stumbled on in *The African News Cookbook*, edited by Tami Hultman, has become a favorite way to use peanuts. It is zesty and unusual, yet the familiar flavor of the nuts and the luscious texture of the eggplant make it a combination that appeals to many.

My favorite way to serve this is as an appetizer or snack, with toasted triangles of pita bread. It is also delicious atop a green salad or alongside roasted chicken, fish, or lamb.

Because the eggplant is salted before draining, the salad should be amply seasoned. If you want to adjust the seasoning, it's best to increase the amount of lemon juice, rather than adding more salt. Try this with a lightly chilled ale alongside.

2 eggplants (1 pound each), peeled and cut
  into ¾ x ¼ x ¼-inch pieces
1½ tablespoons salt
3 tablespoons extra-virgin olive oil
2 tablespoons freshly squeezed lemon juice
¼ cup Spanish peanuts, with skins, toasted
  (see Note)
1 clove garlic, peeled and minced
½ jalapeño pepper, with seeds and
  membrane, minced
Salt and freshly ground black pepper

1 In a large bowl, toss the eggplant with the salt so it is evenly mixed, and place in a colander. Allow the eggplant to drain for 35 minutes. Rinse thoroughly, then gently squeeze the eggplant in small batches in a cotton tea towel to remove as much liquid as possible.

2 Heat the oil in a large heavy skillet over medium-high heat. When the oil is hot

and a wisp of smoke comes off the surface, add the eggplant and sauté, stirring frequently, until it is golden, about 8 minutes. Transfer the eggplant to a medium-size bowl and add the remaining ingredients. Season to taste if necessary, and chill, covered, for at least 1 hour before serving.

8 to 10 appetizer servings (4 to 6 salad servings)

Note: To toast peanuts, preheat the oven to 350°F. Place the nuts in a baking pan large enough to hold them in a single layer, stirring once, until they give off a toasted aroma, 10 to 15 minutes.

CUKES AND DILLED EGGS

This recipe was inspired by a stroll through the Pike Place Market in Seattle, where long, thin European cucumbers abound in summer and fresh eggs are to be had for the asking at one of the permanent market stalls.

I love cucumber anytime because it gives a summery lilt to whatever it touches. But I particularly like it when temperatures soar and the appetite drops, when cool, refreshing little bites sustain and restore. These tidbits are a perfect addition to a big family reunion where barbecue or fried chicken is on the menu because they act as both a snack and a salad—and they are small, light, and attractive enough to appeal to all ages.

1 European cucumber or 4 to 5 Kirby
  (pickling) cucumbers
6 large hard-cooked eggs
3 tablespoons sour cream
1 teaspoon heavy (whipping) cream
1¼ teaspoons Dijon mustard
⅓ cup gently packed fresh dill sprigs
Salt
Cayenne pepper to taste
1 small handful fresh dill sprigs, for garnish

1 Using the tines of a fork, score the cucumber down its length so that when you cut it in rounds, they will be somewhat

scalloped. Cut the cucumber into thick (¼-inch) rounds.

2 Mash the eggs in a large bowl, using a fork or a potato masher, until the whites are finely crumbled. Mix in the sour cream, heavy cream, and mustard until thoroughly combined. Mince the dill and add it. Then season to taste with salt and cayenne pepper.

3 Place a mounded teaspoon of the egg mixture atop each cucumber round, and garnish with a dill sprig. These can be made up to 2 hours in advance; cover them

with waxed paper and keep refrigerated. Remove them from the refrigerator about 30 minutes before serving, so they aren't chilled.

40 pieces

Variation: Mix the sour cream, 2 teaspoons heavy cream, and 1½ teaspoons best-quality curry powder into the mashed eggs. Season to taste with salt. Place a mounded teaspoon of the egg mixture atop each cucumber round, and garnish with a leaf of Italian (flat-leaf) parsley.

PRUNE BITES

I talian prune plums are a big crop in the Pacific Northwest, particularly in Oregon, where mild summer temperatures bring out their sugary sweetness. Though I love fresh plums, I love them dried even more, and I slip them into meals when I can.

Try to use good-size plump prunes for this recipe. Though prepitted prunes are simplest to work with, they are generally not the best quality and tend to be small and shriveled. I prefer to pit my own, which takes some time but is well worth it.

Kasseri, a Greek cheese, is not always easy to find. Very sharp Cheddar makes a fine substitute.

1 pound dried prunes, pitted
4 to 6 ounces kasseri or sharp Cheddar cheese,
  cut in ¾ x ¼ x ¼-inch sticks
Freshly squeezed juice of 1 lime (2½ to
  3 tablespoons)

1 Preheat the oven to 350°F.

2 Stuff each prune with a piece of cheese, and place the prunes in a 9 x 13-inch baking dish.

3 Bake the prunes until the cheese has softened but not entirely melted, about 10 minutes. Remove the prunes from the oven, drizzle with the lime juice, and serve immediately.

40 to 50 stuffed prunes
(8 to 10 servings)

SPICED CHICKEN LIVER NIBBLES

E very restaurant in rural America offers fried chicken, it seems, and often fried chicken livers too. They come to the table steaming hot, with a thick crust that crunches into tender, flavorful liver.

While I can take or leave most liver, chicken livers are delectable, and I love to prepare them in any number of ways. This is a favorite because it's crisp, pleasantly seasoned, and perfect as an appetizer or for a little nibble in the afternoon. I actually like to serve these before a meal of fried chicken—they are a tasty complement.

Depending on the size of the chicken livers you use, these are either a good-size mouthful or one that takes two bites. If you prefer something to pop in your mouth, cut the livers in half and adjust the amount of bacon accordingly. (I prefer the hearty two-bite version.)

⅓ cup all-purpose flour
1 teaspoon ground ginger
⅛ to ¼ teaspoon cayenne pepper
¼ teaspoon salt
1 pound chicken livers, rinsed and patted dry
About 8 strips good-quality thick-sliced bacon, cut in half crosswise
¼ cup lard or mild cooking oil, such as safflower

1 Mix the flour and spices together in a shallow bowl or on a piece of waxed paper.

2 Dredge the livers in the flour mixture, shaking off any excess. Then wrap a bacon strip around each liver, holding it in place with a toothpick. Dredge the bacon-

wrapped livers again, and set aside.

3 Heat the lard or oil in a large heavy skillet over medium heat. When it is hot but not smoking, add the livers, leaving plenty of room in the pan so they aren't crowded. Cook until they are crisp and brown on the outside and cooked through on the inside, 5 to 6 minutes per side. Transfer to a plate lined with paper towels to drain, and then serve immediately, with or without the toothpick.

12 appetizers (6 to 8 servings)

BLUE CHEESE SPREAD

The walnuts and blue cheese make this spread rich, silken, and addictive. I love to have it on hand to serve as a snack or as an appetizer, along with freshly made toast cut into small triangles, or good-quality crackers.

The best way to serve it, since it does not turn out a gorgeous color, is to pack it into two small ramekins, smooth the top, and cover it with the minced walnuts. Once your guests try it, they won't care what color it is.

This will keep up to 10 days, tightly covered and refrigerated.

½ cup walnut pieces
½ cup Maytag, Oregon, or Danish
   blue cheese
¼ cup cream cheese
1 teaspoon cognac
1 tablespoon minced walnuts, for garnish

1 Process the walnuts in a food processor until they are finely chopped, using short pulses to avoid overprocessing.

2 Add the blue cheese and cream cheese, and process until they are thoroughly combined. Add the cognac, process until well mixed, and then transfer the mixture to one large or two small ramekins. Sprinkle with the minced walnuts, and serve.

¾ cup (8 to 10 appetizer servings)

MAYTAG BLUE

All too often, an impersonal processing plant lurks behind the quaint image of a specialty food producer. But Maytag Dairy Farm, the home of Maytag blue cheese, is the real thing.

Maytag, in the small community of Newton, Iowa outside Des Moines, is a rambling clapboard dairy in the yard of a lovely old farmhouse, smack in the middle of a pasture dotted with black-and-white Holstein cattle. The dairy began producing in 1941 and is still owned by the Maytag family. The acting president, Donn Campbell, is the son of the original dairy herd manager, and the current dairy manager, James Stevens, has worked there for more than 40 years.

The palpable aroma of sweet milk wafts through the screen door of the dairy, where a crew makes the cheese the old-fashioned way—by hand. They use raw milk from a local cooperative; some of it comes from the herd outside the dairy windows.

What draws cheese lovers to Maytag blue is its creamy tang, which is similar to, though sharper than, the flavor of Roquefort cheese. Those at Maytag are, modestly, loath to make such a comparison, though there is some basis for it.

"As the story goes," James Stevens said, "Iowa State University isolated one pure mold spore from Roquefort cheese to make their mold." For years the University supplied the dairy with mold; now it is manufactured commercially.

Maytag blue, as it is called, has been made by the same method since 1941. It is aged for a minimum of 6 months in a cool, moist underground "cave," or aging room. It emerges rich and creamy, and riddled with deep blue veins. Determined to remain small, Maytag produces only 250,000 pounds of cheese a year.

▶ ▶ ▶

A CHEESE HOBBIEST

■ ■ ■ ■ ■

The Maytag dairy farm began as a wealthy man's hobby. Elmer H. Maytag, son of the founder of the Maytag Washing Machine Company, loved Holstein cattle and developed a prize-winning herd and the dairy in the 1920s. He left the herd to his sons, one of whom, Frederick L. Maytag 2nd, wanted to turn the dairy into a money-making proposition. He went to the dairy industry department at Iowa State University for advice, and they recommended their newly patented blue cheese process. Soon after, the first batch of Maytag blue was produced.

The mail-order dairy business expanded steadily throughout the 1940s and '50s, with a hiatus during World War II. And though Maytag blue cheese has been championed by a number of American food writers, including James Beard and Clementine Paddleford, it has remained a well-kept secret because until recently it was sold exclusively through mail order.

HOW THE CHEESE IS MADE

■ ■ ■ ■ ■

The small warm dairy, awash in the aroma of rich fresh milk, is in full production by 7 A.M. each weekday morning. "Full production" means four men making cheese, another painstakingly washing salt off partially aged wheels, and still another in the windowless "cave," turning hundreds of cheeses a quarter revolution so they age evenly.

To make a day's production of blue cheese, about 1,000 gallons of milk are heated to 90°F and separated so the cream can be homogenized to break down the size of its butterfat particles.

"Blue-veined cheese," Stevens said, referring to Roquefort, "is traditionally made with sheep's or goat's milk, which has smaller butterfat particles than cow's milk. It's very important to get the cow's milk so it physically resembles goat's or sheep's milk."

The cream is mixed back into the milk, then poured into long stainless steel vats. A lactic culture is added to create a certain acidity level, then rennet is added to develop the curd. Twenty minutes later, when a Jell-O-like curd has formed, two men cut it with wire "knives" into ½-inch cubes, which sink to the bottom of the vat. After 15 minutes the curds are gently stirred with a large acrylic fork that looks like part of a Claes Oldenburg sculpture.

Two long wooden boxes, called racks, are set across the vat at either end and are lined with cotton cloth. A worker stands at each end of one of the racks, and as one scoops the curd into it, the other throws a handful of coarse

salt over it, then dusts it with a dark gray powder. The powder is the mold that will creep through the cheese as it ages and give it its characteristic color and flavor.

The amount is gauged by eye. "It's kind of like adding pepper to your mashed potatoes," Stevens said. "When you think it's enough, you stop."

The workers lift up the corners of the cloth and energetically roll the blubbery curd back and forth between them to mix in the powder and salt. The curd is transferred to two hundred wide metal cylinders called hoops, which are turned every half hour until early evening, then left to drain overnight.

The next day the cheeses, which when aged will weigh about 4 pounds apiece, are removed from the hoops. Coarse salt is strewn on a heavy wooden table, and the cheeses are rolled in it before being put in the cave. The salting is repeated each day for four days. On the fifth day, the wheels are pierced with holes, which encourages the mold to penetrate evenly.

In the moist, refrigerated cave, the ivory wheels of cheese rest on floor-to-ceiling wooden shelves, with the youngest toward the front. The narrow shelves, cupped to hold the cheeses on their sides, are made of cypress wood, which doesn't deteriorate in moisture,

and many of them have been there for more than 20 years.

After a month, the wheels of cheese, already sweetly aromatic, are scrubbed with fresh water, dipped in golden wax, transferred to another cave, and aged for at least 6 months at 49°F.

EXPANDING THE LINE

Five years ago Maytag began making a white Cheddar and a creamy Edam cheese in a room adjacent to the one where the blue cheese is made. In doing so it defied the experts, who contend that no other cheese can be made in proximity to blue cheese without being infected with the mold. "We've never had a problem yet," Stevens said, patting a fat square of white Cheddar. Their signature cheese, however, remains Maytag blue.

Being a well-kept secret is fine for those in on the secret. If you can't find Maytag blue at your cheese shop, you can obtain a mail-order catalog by calling the Maytag Dairy Farms at 1-800-247-2458 (in Iowa 1-800-258-2437).

MAYTAG BLUE CRISPS

Donn Campbell, president of Maytag Dairy (described on page 43), says this intriguing savory nibble is one of his favorite recipes. I like to serve them before a meal, with a glass of wine or sherry.

Baked, they keep very well— up to a couple of weeks—if stored in an airtight container. Unbaked, the dough will keep for 2 weeks in the refrigerator. You can also freeze the dough. Shape it into logs first, and thaw it for 30 minutes before slicing it. Frozen, the dough will keep for 2 months.

1¾ cups all-purpose flour
1 teaspoon freshly ground black pepper
8 ounces Maytag, Oregon, or Danish blue cheese, at room temperature
8 tablespoons (1 stick) unsalted butter, at room temperature
1 large egg
¾ cup toasted pecans (see Note), coarsely chopped

1 Prepare these the day before you plan to bake them. Sift the flour and pepper together into a bowl.

2 In a medium-size bowl, cream together the blue cheese and butter until light. There will be some lumps of cheese, which is fine. Add the egg and mix well.

3 Add the flour to the cheese mixture, mixing quickly but thoroughly. Add the nuts, and mix just until they are evenly distributed throughout the dough, which will be quite firm.

4 Shape the dough into two long logs about 1½ inches in diameter. Wrap in waxed paper and refrigerate overnight.

5 Preheat the oven to 375°F.

6 Cut the logs into thin rounds (about ⅛ inch thick) and place them on ungreased baking sheets. Bake in the center of the oven until the rounds are golden and crisp, 10 to 15 minutes.

10 dozen

Note: To toast the pecans, preheat the oven to 350°F. Place the pecans in a baking pan large enough to hold them in a single layer, and toast, stirring once, until they give off a toasted aroma, 10 to 15 minutes.

CHEESE PENNIES

When I was growing up, this was one of my favorite Christmas "cookies." I still love their piquant, savory contrast to the oceans of sweets that circulate at that time of year. They're good any time, of course, to serve with a pre-dinner drink or glass of wine, or to have on the cookie tray for those who would rather eat something savory. I like to have a roll or two of these on hand in the freezer, for those unexpected moments when a tasty treat is in order.

These "pennies" rely on the cheese for their flavor, so be sure to choose a good-quality extra-sharp Cheddar. And refrigerate the dough overnight because the pennies won't bake evenly if they haven't been chilled through. You may also freeze them; they will keep for 2 months. Take them out of the freezer about 30 minutes before you plan to bake them, so they can be sliced easily.

1 cup unbleached all-purpose flour
½ teaspoon salt
½ teaspoon cayenne pepper
8 ounces extra-sharp Cheddar cheese
8 tablespoons (1 stick), unsalted butter,
  at room temperature

1 Prepare these the day before you plan to bake them. Sift the dry ingredients together into a small bowl or onto a sheet of waxed paper. Grate the cheese, using the smaller holes in a cheese grater, into another small bowl.

2 In a large mixing bowl, cream the butter until it is soft and pale yellow. Add the cheese and mix well; then gradually stir in the flour. The mixture will be quite stiff.

3 Shape the dough into two 9-inch-long logs about 1 inch in diameter. Wrap them first in waxed paper, then in aluminum foil, and refrigerate overnight. (Alternatively, you may freeze these for several hours to speed up the process.) These will keep in the refrigerator for up to 1 week.

4 Preheat the oven to 375°F.

5 Slice the rolls into rounds ⅛ to ¼ inch thick, and place them about ½ inch apart on an ungreased baking sheet. Bake until they are golden, about 12 minutes. Transfer the cheese pennies to a wire cooling rack. They will keep for several days in an airtight container.

About 70

SALLY WALSTON'S PIMIENTO CHEESE SPREAD

I had a vague childhood memory of pimiento cheese spread, and I was thrilled to rediscover it at Jim and Sally Walston's Rocky Branch Farms in Mexia (pronounced Ma-hay-a in Texan, Meh-hee-ya in Spanish), Texas. After a tour around the farm's fruit orchards, Sally offered lunch—cold roast beef sandwiches or a Texas specialty, pimiento cheese sandwiches. Before I could answer, Jim said, "Sally makes the best darned pimiento cheese in Texas," so my choice was clear.

Sally set to grating Cheddar, using the large vintage grater she's used for 50 years. When I bit into the sandwich put in front of me—thick slices of white bread with pale pink and orange pimiento spread oozing out the sides—the moist piquancy of good sharp cheese, sweet peppers, and crunchy sweet bits of pecan flooded my mouth, and I ate that sandwich in record time. I could easily have eaten two, but I refrained and asked, instead, for her recipe.

Pimiento cheese makes a wonderful sandwich, a delicious spread on crackers, and an unusual dip for fresh vegetables. I like to have a supply in the refrigerator for impromptu occasions. It will keep well for up to a week.

1 jar (4 ounces) pimientos, undrained
1 pound medium-sharp or sharp Cheddar
   cheese, grated
1 cup mayonnaise
½ cup coarsely chopped pecans
Salt and freshly ground black
   pepper

1 Coarsely chop the pimientos. Reserve the juice.

2 Place the cheese in a medium-size mixing bowl. Combine the pimientos, reserved juice, and the mayonnaise in another bowl, and then toss with the cheese until all the ingredients are thoroughly combined. Stir in the pecans, and season to taste with salt and pepper.

4 cups (8 sandwiches)

HUMMUS

This light, tangy purée is a traditional dish in the Middle East, where it is made with freshly cooked garbanzo beans (chick-peas) and served with pita bread hot from the oven. Li Ochs, who with her husband, Jon, farms 800 acres of garbanzo beans in eastern Washington, makes it often for their family, which includes five children ages six through eighteen.

Li's hummus is more flavorful than any I've ever had, due in large part to the freshly cooked garbanzos and the generous amount of garlic. I make it often to have on hand as a dip with vegetables, as a spread on sandwiches, or as a cool sauce with grilled or broiled meats and fish. This keeps well, refrigerated, for at least a week.

If you can't find dried garbanzo beans, use the canned variety, but be sure to rinse them thoroughly first.

2 cups cooked garbanzo beans (chick-peas; page 167)
¼ cup freshly squeezed lemon juice
3 large cloves garlic, peeled
1 cup tahini (sesame paste; available at most health and gourmet food stores)
¼ to ½ cup cold water (optional)
Salt
1 tablespoon olive oil (optional)
Paprika (optional)

1 Place the garbanzos and ¼ cup of the lemon juice in a food processor, and process until the garbanzos are mashed but not completely puréed. Add the garlic, the remaining ½ cup lemon juice, and the tahini, and process until the mixture is a smooth puree. With short on-and-off pulses, add water to thin out the hummus if it seems too thick. Season to taste with salt.

2 To serve, spoon the hummus into a shallow bowl or a rimmed plate. Drizzle it with the olive oil and sprinkle with paprika, if desired. Serve slightly chilled or at room temperature.

3½ cups (10 to 12 servings)

BILL KROME AND THE FLORIDA AVOCADO

Bill Krome has been a major player in the Florida avocado industry for more than sixty years, and once he starts talking about avocados, in a soft voice that deepens with emphasis, his knowledge and devotion show with an intensity that has never faded.

Success with avocados is in Bill's genes, a direct inheritance from his father, who was a pioneer in the Florida groves and who helped lay the groundwork for the Florida industry. The elder Mr. Krome's contributions were recognized when one of the main streets in Homestead, Florida, a town in the heart of avocado country, was named Krome Avenue.

Bill's father wasted no time training his son. "When I was in my early teens, he had me going out to the groves to look at trees, grade them, and estimate the harvest," he said. The training proved invaluable because his father died when Bill was only fourteen, leaving him in charge. Except for his college years, Bill has been in charge ever since.

Even before the avocado industry became established soon after the turn of the century, it had enemies. The two greatest (discounting the Depression of the 1920s and '30s) were hurricanes and rock. The soil around Homestead isn't anything one can pick up and let run through the fingers. Rather, it's a hard, calcium-rich rock covered with a thin layer of topsoil.

At first dynamite was used to blast planting holes for the avocado trees, which proved highly ineffective in such porous rock and gave the trees shallow footing. Every time a hurricane blew, the trees went down like dominoes. "We'd have to hire a crew to stand the trees back up," Bill said, laughing at the memory.

FOLLOWING A DREAM

Despite the seeming unfriendliness of the Florida rock, the early avocado pioneers, who had seen avocados growing in similar subtropical conditions, persisted in their dream to create a Florida avocado industry.

"It wasn't until World War II that we started to get better," he continued. What changed things then was the invention of the rock plough, whose manganese steel blade

digs right through the rock. The 18-inch-deep trenches form a grid pattern, and the trees are planted at the intersections.

The avocados don't get much from the rock, and so they are irrigated and fertilized regularly. It's almost hydroponic agriculture, because the trees live off water and fertilizer. Nevertheless, they remain productive for up to 80 years.

Hurricanes are still a threat to the groves, though according to Bill they occur less often than when he was growing up. And the new planting methods mean that when they do occur, fewer trees go down. Nonetheless, to safeguard the trees, which will grow to 60 feet if left alone, they are trimmed to about 20 feet.

Florida avocado varieties are legion and their characteristics are as numerous. Each has its signature fat content—always lower than the popular California Haas—and its own texture, water content, and flavor. While some Florida varieties like the Booth 7's and 8's can compete with the Haas in every way except its year-round season, others like the Lula and the Monroe are watery and thin-tasting. During the season, which ranges from June through February, any one of the varieties might be available, but there isn't any way to tell the difference without taking a bite.

FASCINATING BUT FICKLE

Avocado trees are complex and fickle, and Bill's fascination with them is easy to understand. "All avocado flowers are female when they first open," he said as he drove us through his grove. "They close, and when they reopen, they're male."

There are two flowering patterns on avocado trees, referred to as A and B. Half the trees will open in the morning, the other half in the afternoon. The first batch opens, closes, and reopens on the afternoon of the following day, when the second group is opening for the first time. That's when the flowers are fertilized.

Trees are either A's or B's, and some are self-pollinating. "The self-pollinating are the most reliable bearers, and the sorry bearers have to be helped by cross-pollination," Bill said.

The most a tree in his groves has ever yielded (over its lifetime) is thirty 50-pound bushels. A grove needs to yield between two and three hundred bushels to be profitable. "The good groves have always paid," he said loyally. But he, like most growers, has had bad groves. "One of my credentials is that I've made all the mistakes," he said, laughing and referring to a situation when he thought it was time to expand and nearly lost everything he had. "To be an avocado farmer it's not enough to be intelligent," he said. "You've got to know the business."

BILL KROME'S GUACAMOLE

Bill Krome might be considered one of the grandfathers of Florida's avocado industry (see page 50). He bought his first grove when he was only fifteen, in 1929, and has shepherded the growing of avocados, and limes and mangoes, since then.

This is his special guacamole recipe, which he serves at every opportunity. It's a natural combination of his two major crops, avocados and limes, with the unusual addition of blue cheese. "People just can't get over how good it is," he said. Florida avocados have a relatively low fat content compared with the Haas avocados from California, and they are the better choice for this recipe. The blue cheese adds an edge and a creamy richness, the lime its tart tang. I like to serve this with crackers, freshly toasted bread, or fresh vegetables.

½ ounce Maytag, Oregon, or Danish
blue cheese (about 2 tablespoons),
at room temperature
2 tablespoons freshly squeezed lime juice
2 cups diced avocado
Juice of ½ small onion (see Note)
Salt
¼ teaspoon Tabasco sauce, or to taste

Place the blue cheese and the lime juice in a medium-size bowl, and whisk until they are combined. Add the avocado and crush it, using a fork or a potato masher, until the mixture forms a chunky purée. Add the onion juice, then season to taste with salt and Tabasco. Stir well, and serve immediately, as it won't keep.

2 cups (4 to 6 appetizer servings)

Note: To extract the juice from an onion, grate the onion on the small holes of a hand grater, place the gratings in a square of cheesecloth, and squeeze out the juice. Alternatively, you can simply mince the onion and add it as is.

PIQUANT GUACAMOLE

Although avocados are delicious just about any way they are prepared, guacamole appears to be America's favorite way of eating them. It makes sense—their rich, buttery quality is a perfect foil for pungent spicy flavors. Guacamole is delicious on its own as a dip or slathered on sandwiches, and it is a must with Fajitas (see Index).

This version of guacamole is very Southwestern.

3 avocados, pitted and peeled
2 scallions (green onions), trimmed and sliced
   into thin rounds
1 clove garlic, peeled and minced
3 tablespoons freshly squeezed lemon juice
2 small plum tomatoes, coarsely chopped
1 small handful cilantro leaves
⅛ teaspoon cayenne pepper
Salt

Place the avocados in a medium-size bowl and mash them with a fork or a potato masher until you have a coarse purée. Add the scallions, garlic, lemon juice, and tomatoes, and stir well. Mince the cilantro and stir it into the guacamole. Season with the cayenne pepper and salt to taste. Let the guacamole ripen at room temperature, covered, for about 30 minutes before serving.

2 cups (4 to 6 servings)

CILANTRO

Cilantro (sometimes called Chinese parsley) has a dusky flavor that some love and some dislike. It can overpower a dish, but used judiciously it is delectable, and it enhances spicy, tangy mixtures. Try it in fresh tomato sauces and tropical fruit salsas. Sprinkle it over chicken, shellfish, and meaty fish such as swordfish, mahi-mahi, and tuna. Combine it with lime juice, ginger, hot peppers, and avocado. Add it to cornmeal stuffings and polenta, to a marinade for pork spareribs, and to zesty summer squash sautés. Dried cilantro is not worth bothering with.

DRIPPING SPRINGS SALSA

We arrived at Dripping Springs Garden in the Ozarks outside of Fayetteville, Arkansas, on an August afternoon after traveling what seemed like many miles over a rutted dirt road that wound into the mountains like a corkscrew. In reality the miles had been only six, but in our trusty but not overly springy Honda, it felt like a long, long journey.

Owners Mark Cain and Michael Crain welcomed us, and after a look at their impeccably landscaped gardens, we went into the cool of their home. Inside, we were offered an impressive array of fresh vegetables and corn chips to dip into a bowl of zesty homemade salsa. Mike Crain pointed to a shelf of jars filled with the red sauce. "That's our winter supply," he said, laughing, for there seemed to be enough to feed a whole neighborhood. This salsa is addictive, though, and filled with the vivid flavors of summer. It pays to have some on hand, as an unequaled antidote to the chill of winter. When I asked Mark for the recipe, he gave it with ease until he got to the garlic. "Garlic, hmmm," he said. "I use lots, and that's as definite as I can get."

This wonderful salsa has myriad uses: to spice up sandwiches, add to soups, give tomato juice a zing, or serve as a dip for fresh vegetables or corn chips.

2 pounds fresh tomatoes, peeled and cored
1 large onion, peeled and coarsely chopped
2 cups lightly packed cilantro leaves, rinsed and
   gently dried
½ fresh jalapeño pepper, with seeds
2 tablespoons freshly squeezed lemon juice
3 cloves garlic, peeled

Place all the ingredients in a food processor or blender, and process until the mixture is a thick purée. Let it sit at room temperature for about 30 minutes before serving, to allow the flavors to mellow. Serve the salsa chilled or at room temperature, or process in a water bath to preserve.

About 3 cups (15 to 20 appetizers)

BLUE CHEESE AND ONION TART

Blue cheese and onions is a marriage made in heaven. After I'd visited the Maytag Dairy in Newton, Iowa, and returned home with a wheel of blue cheese in my bag, I could hardly wait to use some in this tart. (For more on the dairy, see page 43.)

I like to serve this in very thin wedges as an hors d'oeuvre or in thick wedges as a main course with a crisp green salad, bread, and a lightly chilled Alsatian Riesling 1989.

1½ tablespoons unsalted butter
2 large onions, peeled and thinly sliced, (4½ cups)
1 cup (6 ounces) blue cheese
Salt and freshly ground black pepper
3 large eggs
½ cup milk
¼ cup heavy (whipping) cream
2 shallots, peeled and thinly sliced
1 prebaked 9-inch pastry shell (page 431)

1 Preheat the oven to 400°F.

2 Melt the butter in a large skillet over medium heat. When it foams, add the onions and stir until they are coated with the butter. Cover the skillet, reduce the heat to medium-low, and cook the onions, stirring occasionally, until they turn soft and golden, about 20 minutes.

3 Add the blue cheese to the onions, and stir just until it melts. Season to taste with salt and pepper, and set aside.

4 In a small bowl, whisk together the eggs, milk, and cream. Season with salt and pepper.

5 Pour the onion-cheese mixture into the tart shell and spread it out evenly. Pour the milk mixture over the onions, spreading them out so the custard is mixed all through them. (The amount of custard you use may vary slightly, depending on how much the onions cook down.) Arrange the shallot slices over the top, and bake until the tart is golden and puffed, 25 to 30 minutes.

6 Remove the tart from the oven and let it cool for 5 minutes. Then remove the ring of the tart pan, and cool the tart to room temperature on a wire rack. Serve at room temperature or slightly chilled.

12 appetizer servings

SUMMER TOMATO PIE

This pie is inspired by the lush ripe tomatoes of summer. Cut in thin slices, the pie makes a good appetizer—or it can be served as a main course, along with a green salad and fresh bread.

1 recipe Buttery Pastry (page 431)
1 cup heavy (whipping) cream
2 large eggs
3 teaspoons fresh thyme leaves or 1 teaspoon
  dried
1 small clove garlic, peeled and minced
½ cup finely grated Swiss-type cheese,
  such as Gruyère
½ cup finely grated sharp Cheddar cheese
Salt and freshly ground black pepper
2½ pounds ripe tomatoes, peeled and
  cored

1 On a lightly floured surface, roll out the pastry to fit a 9-inch pie plate. There will be quite a bit extra; leave it hanging over the edges of the pan. Refrigerate for at least 30 minutes.

2 Preheat the oven to 425°F.

3 Prebake the pastry: Place the pan on a baking sheet in the center of the oven, and bake for 10 minutes. Using a very sharp knife held at a slight angle to the edge of the cake pan, trim off the edges of the pastry flush with the pan, letting the scraps fall onto the baking sheet. Continue baking until the pastry is pale gold, another 10

minutes. Remove it from the oven, and let the pastry cool completely.

4 Whisk together the cream and the eggs in a large bowl until combined. Add the thyme and garlic, and mix well. Then stir in the cheeses. Season generously with salt and pepper.

5 Coarsely chop the tomatoes and add them to the mixture. Mix, set aside.

6 When the pastry has cooled, fill it with the tomato mixture. The tomatoes will mound slightly in the center of the pan, which is fine. Bake in the center of the oven for 10 minutes. Reduce the heat to 350°F and continue baking until the custard is set and the pie is golden on top, about 55 minutes.

7 Let the pie cool for at least 10 minutes. Serve it immediately, or let it cool to room temperature before serving.

12 appetizer servings

WARMING SOUPS

A BIG POT OF SOUP

I ate soup after soup on the farms that I visited, each one so good I'd swear it was better than the one before it. Every bowlful was like a mirror of what was being grown locally—if I was visiting a bean farm, the soup was chockful of beans; a vegetable farm, then it was more vegetables than anything else.

Soups are perfect for farm life. There is never a lack of a hungry audience. After a wintry day working in the fields or in the barn, or attending an auction, a warming hearty soup is a restorative elixir. If it's hot out and haying time, a cool soup replenishes with fresh bright flavor. There is also always an abundance of fresh ingredients to pop into a pot, and plenty of time to slowly let their luscious flavors blend and build.

But not all soups are slow-cooked. Some are made and meant to be eaten quickly, like Broccoli Parsnip Soup, or Basque Potato and Green Bean Soup with Garlic.

Others like Sweet Cream of Tomato Soup capture flavor at the height of the season and can be kept to savor all year. Still others, like the Chilled Honeydew Soup are delicately flavored and intended for a formal affair.

Soups are great for a crowd, and ideal for entertaining. They're versatile and are easily made and served. So the next time you've got a hungry group to feed, whether it's family, friends, or farmhands, bring out the pot, ladle up the soup, and sit down to a good rousing meal.

PENNSYLVANIA CHICKEN CORN SOUP

During the Linebach Produce Auction in Shippensburg, Pennsylvania, I talked with Mary Linebach, a cheerful, sweet-faced Mennonite woman whose hair was pulled into a tight knot and hidden under a sheer bonnet. She has a ready laugh, which undoubtedly stands her in good stead, because she works nearly full-time at the auction and still cooks meals for her family of seventeen.

As we looked over the produce, she talked about her family's favorite dishes—the things she can practically make with her eyes closed, like apple grunt, the Amish Tomato Ketchup (see page 335) she serves with pancakes in the mornings, beef and vegetable soup, and the traditional Pennsylvania Dutch chicken and corn soup. When I asked for the recipe she looked at me in astonishment, as though it was unthinkable I didn't make it all the time myself. "It's served at every gathering around here," she said.

She gave me her recipe, which was really just a list of ingredients, and I went from there to create this warm, hearty soup that will tempt you time and again. It tastes so good that you know it will cure what ails you, and if nothing ails you, it will make you feel better than you already do! I love to make it in fall, when the last of the corn is still at the market and the air snaps with a chill that calls for a hot, hearty meal.

Don't be put off by the addition of saffron, a spice that is often ignored because of its reputed expense. By the ounce, saffron is expensive, but an ounce would last a neighborhood a lifetime. The amount of saffron used here will hardly set you back, so please buy some, use what you need, and carefully store the rest in a dark, dry place (it lasts virtually forever).

Serve a Silverado Chardonnay 1989 alongside.

1 chicken (3½ to 4 pounds) cut into
 serving pieces
1 large onion, peeled and diced
Salt
8 black peppercorns
1 bay leaf
Several sprigs fresh thyme, or ½ teaspoon
 dried
1 teaspoon saffron threads, or ¾ teaspoon
 saffron powder
Freshly ground black pepper
2 cups corn kernels, preferably fresh
2 cups Alice's Mother's Noodles
 (recipe follows), or 6 ounces dried
 egg noodles

1 Rinse the chicken well. Place it and the
 onion in a large heavy saucepan or soup
pot. Cover with water, and add salt, the
peppercorns, bay leaf, and thyme. Bring to
a boil over high heat. Reduce the heat to
medium-low, cover, and cook until the
chicken is tender and nearly cooked
through, about 30 minutes. Remove the
pan from the heat, and remove the chicken
pieces from the broth. Allow the chicken
to cool.

2 When the chicken is cool enough to
 handle, remove and discard the skin,
and pull the meat from the bones. Cut the
meat into bite-size pieces, and set aside.

3 Remove the thyme sprigs, bay leaf, and
 the peppercorns from the chicken broth,
and then bring it to a boil over medium-high
heat. Add the saffron, season generously with
salt and pepper, and cook for 15 minutes.
Add the reserved chicken and the corn. Bring
back to a boil. Add the noodles, and cook
until they are just tender, 5 minutes. Season
to taste, and serve immediately.

6 servings

CORN

*Corn is the most important grain in
the western hemisphere. Sweet
corn, or that destined for human consumption, is picked underripe, before the
kernels harden. That used for animal feed
is left on the stalk until the kernels harden
and dry. Old, or "heirloom," varieties,
which are considered to have more depth
of flavor than those common today, are
experiencing a revival and can sometimes
be found at farmers' markets.*

*When choosing sweet corn, look for
husks that are tightly closed, silk that is
golden and clean, not mushy or blackened,
and a stem end that looks newly cut and
isn't brown or dried out. If you can, peel
back the husk and pierce a kernel with
your fingernail—if juice spurts out, you're
onto something good. If there is no juice,
the corn is old, starchy, and won't be tasty.
Use corn as soon as possible after buying it.*

ALICE'S MOTHER'S NOODLES

■■■■■■

Alice Berner's family noodle recipe is put to much good use at the Berner farm. They are quick to make, and they cook within minutes. I like to add them to chicken soup, or to cook and serve them plain, tossed with butter and seasoned with salt and pepper.

Because these noodles contain baking powder, they increase slightly in size when cooked, so cut them accordingly. They need to sit to relax the gluten in the flour, so make them a couple of hours before you plan to cook them. Toss them lightly in flour and place them on a platter or work surface, covered with a cotton towel to keep them from drying out.

The reason for the range in the amount of cream needed is because it depends on how humid it is the day you make the noodles, the type and brand of flour you use, and a host of other variables. Begin with 1 tablespoon and work judiciously from there. As it says in the directions, the dough should be moist but not wet.

1 cup unbleached all-purpose flour
1 teaspoon baking powder
¼ teaspoon salt
1 large egg
1 to 4 tablespoons heavy (whipping) cream

1. Place the flour, baking powder, and salt in a small bowl. Make a well in the center, and add the egg and 1 tablespoon of the cream. Using a wooden spoon, mix the egg and cream until they are somewhat blended. Then quickly incorporate the flour mixture, mixing just until the ingredients are combined. If the mixture is quite dry and crumbly, add more cream. The dough should hold together; it can be moist but it shouldn't be wet. Cover the dough and let it sit for 30 minutes.

2. Roll the dough out on a lightly floured work surface to form a rectangle about 10 x 17 inches and ⅛ inch thick. Roll the rectangle up jelly-roll fashion. Then cut the roll into ¼-inch-thick strips. Unroll the strips, toss them with about 2 teaspoons of flour so they don't stick together, cover with a towel, and let them sit until you are ready to use them, at least 30 minutes.

3. To cook the noodles, bring a large pot of salted water or chicken stock to a boil, add the noodles, and cook until they are tender but not soggy, about 5 minutes. Drain and serve immediately.

2 cups uncooked noodles

THE INDOCHINESE FARM PROJECT

The Indochinese Farm Project was established in the Samamish Valley near Seattle, Washington, more than a decade ago. Its purpose was to help a community of Hmong, Laotians from the hill country of Laos, support themselves. A tract of land was donated, and each Hmong who was interested was given a section to farm.

Sam Shirasago, a retired farmer, got involved with the project after a group of Hmong came to his church to sell their produce.

"Their produce wasn't too good and they didn't know enough English yet to make change. I'd been thinking of joining the Peace Corps but my wife convinced me that I should try to help these farmers," he said.

When Sam visited the project, he was distressed with what he saw. "The farmers had a bunch of victory gardens, but their vegetables just didn't look good. They didn't know how to farm here," he said.

In Laos, farmers burn down a patch of jungle, farm it until the soil is depleted, then move onto another patch in a cycle called slash-and-burn farming. Sam taught the Laotians he worked with how to use land differently, how to plant in rows, stagger plantings through the season for a constant crop, and how to maintain the quality of the soil.

The Laotian farmers had also been trying to grow crops they were unfamiliar with, but which they thought would sell well. Sam convinced them to grow crops they knew, like baby bok choy, peas (which they harvest for just the tender tips of the plant), radishes (which they let go to seed so they can harvest the seed pods), cilantro, and a variety of Asian greens, like Chinese broccoli.

The combination of their hard work and a booming market for Asian greens has made many of these farmers more prosperous than they imagined possible. While Sam used to work with them in the fields, he now supervises and believes that the families in the project are just about ready to form their own cooperative and manage it without his help. He's confident they will survive and prosper. And though he claims he's going to retire a second time, chances are he'll be right back out in the field, surveying and giving directions whenever he's asked.

CHEW CHANG'S CHICKEN AND CHINESE MUSTARD GREEN SOUP

Chew Chang is the best of the farmers in the Indochinese Farm Project, according to Sam Shirasago (see facing page); she's always ready and willing to learn something new. Chew grows tall, sturdy sweet corn, *gai lan* (Chinese broccoli), bok choy, Chinese mustard cabbage, and cilantro—all crops that she grew in Laos. She loves to cook for her family, and shared recipes with me in lively but broken English, gesturing to make sure I understood. We laughed as I tried to decipher her instructions, but when I tasted this soup, I knew I'd gotten it right!

Chew makes this with chicken, but I've also tried it with seafood and with leftover Thanksgiving turkey, both of which are delicious. It's almost endlessly versatile. If you can't find fresh lemon grass, buy dried lemon grass, which is often sold as a tea, and use about ¼ cup.

If you want to maintain the Asian theme, serve hot green tea with the soup. Otherwise, I suggest a chilled crisp German Mosel Riesling Kabinett 1988.

FOR THE CONDIMENT
2 serrano chiles, trimmed and minced
1¼ cups fresh cilantro leaves
1 tablespoon freshly squeezed lime juice

8 cups water
2 stalks fresh lemon grass, cut into 2-inch lengths, or ¼ cup dried, tied in a bundle or in cheesecloth
1½ teaspoons salt
1½ pounds dark and light chicken meat (the meat from a 2½-pound chicken), uncooked
1 medium onion, peeled and coarsely chopped
1½ pounds gai lan (Chinese broccoli or Chinese kale) or gai choy (Chinese mustard cabbage), coarsely chopped
Salt and freshly ground black pepper

1 Make the pepper and cilantro condiment: Mince the chiles and the cilantro together until they are almost a purée. Add the lime juice and stir. Transfer the mixture to a small serving bowl and set aside.

2 Bring the water, lemon grass, and salt to a boil in a large stainless steel saucepan over high heat. Reduce the heat to medium, cover, and simmer for about 20 minutes.

3 Add the chicken to the broth, cover, and cook until it is almost opaque, about 4 minutes. Then add the onion and the greens, pushing the greens down into the liquid. Cover and bring back to a boil. Cook, pushing the greens down into the liquid occasionally so they cook evenly, until they have wilted and turned bright green, 5 to 8 minutes.

4 When the greens are bright green, remove the lemon grass. Season the soup to taste, and serve immediately, with the pepper and cilantro condiment on the side, for spooning atop the soup.

6 servings

MARMITAKO

M iren Artiach, the assistant secretary of state of Idaho, mentioned this as one of the dishes she loved best when she visited relatives in the Spanish Basque country. She said it was a common dish there, made with freshly caught tuna, and described it with her eyes closed, as though she could smell and taste it right then.

I followed her directions, which called for throwing everything in a pot together and flavoring it with chiles, and came up with this recipe which I love more each time I try it. It's hearty, earthy, yet elegant, with a gentle peppery background from the chile purée. I like to make it with tuna, but you could substitute an equal amount of veal or even, in a pinch, pork.

It calls for a full-bodied red such as a Côtes du Rhône Villages 1988, or a Rioja.

1¾ pounds tuna steaks, 1 inch thick
2 pounds Russet potatoes, peeled and cut into
    1½-inch chunks
5 cups water
1 tablespoon salt
2 medium onions, peeled and cut into large
    pieces
6 cloves garlic, peeled and halved lengthwise
7 tablespoons Ancho Chile Pepper Purée
    (page 315)
¼ cup minced fresh parsley, for garnish (optional)

1 Rinse the tuna steaks and pat them dry.
Cut them into 1½-inch cubes (as much
as possible), and refrigerate until right before cooking.

2 Place the potatoes, water, and salt in a
large heavy saucepan over medium-
high heat. Bring to a boil, reduce the heat

to medium, and cook until the potatoes are
nearly soft, 15 minutes. Add the onions
and garlic, and cook until the potatoes are
thoroughly soft and the onions and garlic
are cooked through, another 15 minutes.
Stir in the chile purée; then add the tuna
chunks and cook until they are opaque, 10
to 15 minutes. (If you are using veal or
pork, the cooking time will be somewhat
longer, an additional 5 to 10 minutes.
Check it frequently and cook until it is
done to your liking).

3 Garnish with the chopped parsley if
desired, and serve
immediately.

6 servings

CIOPPINO

I love this cioppino—it's rich and flavorful with herbs, wine, and lots of
succulent fresh seafood. One of the best touches, suggested by Helen
Pavich (see page 448), is the green grapes that are added at the last
minute. They heat right through and their translucent color is a gorgeous
contrast to the deep red of the soup.

I make this soup year-round,
and find it refreshing and soul-satis-
fying no matter what the season.
Vary the fish according to what is
fresh, using some that are meaty and

some that are less firm.
Try a full-bodied red, such as
Pesquera 1985, with this cioppino.

1 shark or swordfish steak (12 ounces to
   1 pound), skin removed, cut into 1-inch
   diamond shapes
1 snapper fillet (8 ounces), with skin, cut
   diagonally into 1½-inch-thick slices
1 pound small (28 per pound) shrimp, shelled
   and deveined
1 pound squid, cleaned and rinsed, mantle
   cut into thick (½-inch) rings, tentacles
   left whole
12 clams or mussels
¼ cup extra-virgin olive oil
1 large onion, peeled and diced
3 cloves garlic, peeled and minced
2 pounds plum tomatoes, peeled, or 2 cans
   (1 pound each) whole plum tomatoes
3 tablespoons tomato paste
½ cup dry white wine
1 cup Fish Stock (page 88) or Herbfarm
   Deluxe Chicken Stock (light version, page
   86)
2 cups hearty red wine, such as a
   Côtes du Rhône or a California
   Pinot Noir
2 tablespoons white wine vinegar
1 tablespoon fresh summer savory leaves, or
   1 teaspoon dried
1 large bunch fresh oregano, or 2 teaspoons
   dried
1 cup loosely packed fresh basil leaves, or
   1 tablespoon dried
½ cup fresh Italian (flat-leaf) parsley
   leaves
⅛ teaspoon cayenne pepper, or to taste
1 strip (¾ x 1 inch) orange zest
1½ cups seedless green grapes, preferably
   Thompson seedless, rinsed and patted dry
8 ounces crabmeat (optional)
Salt to taste
¼ cup minced fresh chives

1 Rinse the fish, the shrimp, and the squid,
  and pat dry. Refrigerate the seafood, covered, until just before using.

2 Place the clams or mussels in cold
  salted water (about 2 tablespoons salt
per gallon of water), and refrigerate for 1
hour. Drain, rinse, cover with a damp
towel, and reserve in the refrigerator until
ready to use.

3 Heat the olive oil in a large saucepan or
  stockpot over medium heat. Add the
onion and cook, stirring, until it turns
translucent, 3 to 5 minutes.

4 Stir in the garlic, and then the tomatoes
  and the tomato paste. Add the white
wine, stock, red wine, vinegar, savory,
oregano, ½ cup of the fresh basil or all the
dried, parsley, cayenne, and the orange zest,
and stir. Bring to a boil, reduce the heat,
cover, and simmer until the mixture has
thickened somewhat and mellowed, about
40 minutes. The soup can be made ahead
to this point.

5 To finish the cioppino, add the shark
  or swordfish and the clams or mussels.
Stir, and cook until the fish is nearly
opaque, about 2 minutes. Add the snapper
and the shrimp, stir gently, and cook an
additional 2 minutes. Add the squid, the
grapes, and the crabmeat if desired, stir
gently, and continue cooking until the
clams are open, the fish is opaque through,
the shrimp are pink and slightly curled,
and the squid is white through, 3 to 5 minutes. Season to taste with salt. (Cooking
times for the seafood will vary depending

on how cold it is when it goes into the soup, so watch it carefully to avoid overcooking.) Finely chop the remaining ½ cup basil leaves, and garnish the cioppino with the basil and the minced chives. Serve immediately.

6 to 8 servings

*A*lways buy fish according to the way it looks and the way it smells. It should look fresh enough to jump right off of the fish counter, bright and firm. If it has the least hint of a fishy odor pass it by and consider making something else for dinner. When you get home, immediately place the fish on the bottom shelf of the refrigerator, and use it the day you buy it, if possible.

CAULIFLOWER OYSTER SOUP

This soup speaks of the Northwest, especially the Skagit Valley just north of Seattle. There fields of plump cauliflower reach practically all the way to oyster-rich bays. It is perfect for late fall—the season to take advantage of sweet, delicately flavored cauliflower and briny oysters fattened after the summer spawn. It is mild and rich, yet full of satisfying flavor, and very quick to make.

*1 cauliflower (2 pounds), florets removed and
   rinsed, stem and leaves discarded
1 cup water
2½ cups milk
1 cup heavy (whipping) cream
Salt and freshly ground white pepper*

*¼ teaspoon turmeric
16 to 24 oysters (about 8 ounces), with their
   liquor (see Note)
1 tablespoon minced fresh chives and chervil,
   mixed, for garnish
Turmeric, for garnish*

1 Place the cauliflower florets in a large heavy casserole, and add the water. Bring to a boil over medium-high heat, reduce the heat to medium-low, and cook until the cauliflower is very tender, about 20 minutes. Check occasionally to be sure there is still enough water, and add a tablespoon or two if necessary. It is fine for the water to evaporate somewhat, but you don't want the pan to dry out completely or the cauliflower will brown.

2 Transfer the cauliflower to a food processor, add ½ cup of the milk and purée. Return the purée to the pan.

3 Whisk the remaining 2 cups milk and the cream into the cauliflower purée until it is smooth. Heat the mixture gently over medium heat until it is very hot. Don't let it boil, or it may curdle. Season to taste with salt and white pepper, and stir in the turmeric. Add the oysters and their liquor, and leave the pan on the heat just until they are hot, 3 to 5 minutes. Do not let the soup come to a boil, and do not allow the oysters to overcook, or they will become chewy and tough.

4 Ladle the soup into warmed bowls, garnish with the herbs and a sprinkling of turmeric, and serve.

6 servings

Note: Separate the oysters from their liquor, and strain the liquor through cheesecloth to remove any bits of shell.

SWEET CREAM OF TOMATO SOUP

This traditional Amish recipe was given to me by Linda Stoltzfus, whose husband Amos, at one time grew tomatoes commercially. Amos has switched to processing onions, but Linda maintains a small farm's worth of tomatoes in her garden.

If you're going to make this soup, get the best, ripest, most flavorful tomatoes you can. You'll be thrilled with the result, because good tomatoes make this what cream of tomato soup should be.

Linda makes gallons of the

tomato soup base and cans it; then she pulls it out throughout the year, adds milk, and serves it to her family as a potent reminder of summer. I follow her example, choosing tomatoes toward the end of the season when they are plentiful and full of summer sun, though I freeze the base instead of canning it. The results are the same.

The sugar in this recipe is optional—it depends on the acidity of the tomatoes. If they aren't naturally sweet, add sugar to taste. In any case add a pinch—it smooths out the taste. Linda makes hers very sweet, but I prefer just a touch of sugar. Serve this with a loaf of fresh bread and a cucumber salad or a simple green salad.

Try a Tavel Rosé de Provence with this soup.

3 medium onions, peeled and chopped
¼ cup water
½ bunch celery (about 6 ribs), trimmed and chopped
6 pounds fresh ripe tomatoes, quartered
2 tablespoons coarse (kosher) salt
1 to 2 tablespoons sugar (optional)
8 tablespoons (1 stick) unsalted butter, at room temperature
½ cup all-purpose flour
4 cups milk

1 Place the onions and the water in a large heavy soup pot over medium heat, and bring to a boil. Reduce the heat to low, cover, and cook, until the onions have softened and have begun to turn translucent,

JUST WHAT IS A "VINE RIPENED" TOMATO?

W hen Amos Stoltzfus was a tomato farmer, he specialized in "vine-ripened" tomatoes, which, contrary to what one might think, doesn't mean a tomato that has been left on the vine to ripen, but rather one with a bit of pink on the skin. What he sent to market were green tomatoes with a slight pink blush, referred to as "pinks," and those with more red, referred to as "reds," because they are still firm and will arrive at their destination in good condition. A tomato that has achieved its full red color and sweet ripe flavor won't transport well, so a farmer can't afford to ship truly vine-ripened tomatoes. Any that reached that stage at the Stoltzfus farm were sold right there.

Tomato tip: Don't refrigerate any tomatoes. Cold temperatures stop the ripening process dead in its tracks and kills flavor. If you have unripe tomatoes, leave them on the counter, instead, where they will ripen and turn a beautiful tomato red.

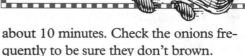

about 10 minutes. Check the onions frequently to be sure they don't brown.

2 Add the celery, tomatoes and salt to the onions, stir, and raise the heat to

medium. Cook, covered, until the tomatoes are tender, about 1 hour. Taste and add enough sugar to smooth out the flavor. Cook another 5 minutes.

3 In a small bowl mix together the butter and the flour until thoroughly combined.

4 Strain the soup, discarding the solids. Return the soup to the saucepan and bring to a boil over medium-high heat. Stir 1 cup of the soup into the flour and butter mixture, whisking until there are no lumps; then whisk that mixture into the soup. Lower the heat and gently cook, stirring frequently, until the soup has the consistency of a medium-thick gravy, about 8 minutes. Let it come just to the boiling point, but do not boil.

5 Heat the milk in another small saucepan over medium heat until it is almost at the boiling point. Slowly add the milk to the soup (do not let the soup boil, or it may curdle). Stir well, and serve.

12 cups (8 to 10 servings)

Note: The soup base (through step 4) may be canned or frozen. After thawing (if necessary) and reheating, add 1 cup hot milk to each 2 cups of soup base, as described in step 5.

CHUNKY PEANUT SOUP

This is a lively variation on a recipe I got from Bonnie Schimelpfening, whose husband, Bob, raises peanuts near Pleasanton, Texas. The thought of peanut butter in a soup may seem odd and unappealing, but I urge you to try this. Peanuts can actually give a very smooth, subtle, delicate flavor to foods, which is exactly what they do here. The result is surprisingly refreshing, and I've found it to be universally popular.

This recipe is for a large quantity, so make it for a crowd. You can substitute chicken, pork, beef, or even scallops for the fish.

Try this with a full-bodied Chardonnay such as Raymond California Select 1989.

2 tablespoons unsalted butter
1 medium onion, peeled and diced
2 medium carrots, peeled and diced
8 cups Herbfarm Deluxe Chicken Stock
 (page 86) or good-quality canned
 broth
1 cup unsalted crunchy peanut
 butter
1 small tomato, diced
4 small potatoes, peeled and cubed
1 small green pepper, roasted
 cored, seeded, peeled, and diced
 (see box, page 322)
3 tablespoons minced fresh parsley
1 large zucchini, trimmed and diced
1 cup button mushrooms, stems trimmed,
 caps diced
1 pound firm white fish such as halibut
 or snapper, bones removed, cut into
 bite-size pieces
1 cup fresh peas
3 tablespoons freshly squeezed lemon
 juice
Salt
Cayenne pepper

1 Melt the butter in a large stockpot over medium heat. When it is hot, add the onion and carrots and cook, stirring constantly, until the onion begins to turn translucent, about 5 minutes.

2 Meanwhile, mix 1 cup of the stock with the peanut butter in a medium-size bowl until smooth.

3 Add the remaining 7 cups chicken stock to the vegetables. Stir, and add the tomato, potatoes, roasted pepper, and 2 tablespoons of the parsley. Pour in the peanut butter mixture, and stir. Cover and bring almost to a boil. Simmer, partially covered, until the potatoes are cooked through, about 15 minutes. Then add the zucchini and the mushrooms, stir, and continue cooking until the zucchini is tender but still has texture, about 10 minutes. Stir in the fish and the peas, and cook until the fish is opaque and the peas are still bright green, 5 to 7 minutes. Add the lemon juice, stir, and season to taste with salt and cayenne pepper.

4 Ladle the peanut soup into warmed soup bowls, garnish with the remaining 1 tablespoon parsley, and serve immediately.

8 to 10 servings

A JAR' A JELLY OR A COLD BEER

Americans consume 3.25 billion pounds of peanuts each year. More than half of those are in the form of peanut butter, which is consumed at the rate of 3.3 pounds per capita per year.

Consumption figures like those please Bob Schimelpfening, who farms 230 acres of peanuts in Pleasanton, the heart of Texas peanut country. His wife, Bonnie, grew up on the farm, and they returned there nineteen years ago. Bob had never farmed a day in his life, but under the tutelage of his father-in-law, he's learned the ways of a peanut farmer. He has developed an obvious love for and sense of satisfaction from the profession as he's learned its tricks and vagaries.

Although Bonnie isn't wild about farming, she loves peanuts and everything about them. When I visited, she was putting the fin-

ishing touches on some handmade peanut-shaped mugs, and a pile of freshly made peanut brittle sat by the stove.

The couple's four sons—Steven, Chris, Tom, and Sean—are willing members of their father's farming crew, and seemingly well on their way to becoming peanut farmers themselves. During planting and harvest they come straight home from school to work in the fields, which they all profess to enjoy.

FRAGRANT FIELDS

Bob and I walked gingerly through a corner of one of his flat peanut fields on a hot, dry July day. There still were scattered yellow blooms on the plants, and the heady, almost cloying perfume of even so few of the puffy little flowers, which resemble tiny sweet-peas, was intoxicating. "Talkin' 'bout smell," he said as we tiptoed between rows. "When you're digging those nuts you get that peanut smell and all you want to do is grab a jar'a jelly or a cold beer."

The plants are delicately anchored into the soil by one long taproot. Bob stooped over

a bushy plant and pulled it easily from the warm, loose ground. Hanging from the base along with the snaky taproot was a profusion of narrow woody shoots covered with little white nodules, peanuts in the making. "We call these peanut pegs," he said, holding a shoot away from the plant. Sixty days after the nut is planted, the blossoms fall off and the stem drops to the soil and works its way in, just like a peg.

YIELD VS. FLAVOR

As anyone addicted to peanuts knows, there are several varieties, and Bob prefers a large, fairly whitish nut called the Florunner, a favorite among peanut farmers because they give a high yield. Other farmers in the area plant Spanish peanuts, which are small and have reddish papery skin, or long, narrow Virginia peanuts. The once-popular Virginia peanut is less used now, however, because it falls off the plant during harvest. The Spanish peanut is out of favor because its yields are low. A new peanut called the Tamrun 88 is in an experimental stage, and if it works, Bob may decide to plant it in upcoming years.

"The Spanish peanut and the Virginia peanut taste better, but the Florunner yields better and it's disease-resistant, so I plant that because I'm concerned about yield," Bob said. He needs to be concerned about yield, and he is particularly careful with his choice of peanut variety and farming techniques be-

cause he sells the bulk of his crop to other farmers for seed. He is paid a premium, but in exchange he must provide healthy, good-size, disease-free nuts.

Bob's vigilance includes checking the peanuts every week for disease, which he does by pulling up and inspecting a plant. If he sees suspicious signs, he may apply a spray though he's increasingly less inclined to use chemicals. "I try to stay away from chemicals as much as possible," he said. He fertilizes according to soil samples, and a huge pivot irrigation system, which is programmed to roll slowly across the fields, sprays liquid nitrogen along with water.

HARVESTING PEANUTS

The harvest begins in October, and in the early morning chill Bob pilots the combine through the field. It cuts the taproot, pulls up the peanut plant, and flips it over, leaving the pegs up in the air.

Bob waits until about noon the same day, when the chill and dampness have worn off, to run the combine through the same field. "The peanuts come out of the soil wet, at about 25 percent humidity," he said. "I don't run them through the combine to separate the nuts from the plant until they've dried down to about 16 percent humidity."

Like a giant monster inhaling its feed, the combine picks up the plants, and a conveyor belt drops them onto huge rolling cylinders that pull the nuts off the plants and then run

▶ ▶ ▶

them by a blower that propels them high up into a trailer.

It's dark before he parks the combine and heads for home. "You know that if you don't make it down the row and back before the day is over, you've got a good crop," Bob said.

The peanuts need more drying before they can be sold, and Bob and his father-in-law have patented the design of a screen-sided semi trailer that holds ten tons. The hot October air blows through and dries the nuts naturally, which allows the Schimelpfenigs to avoid the $30 per-ton fee they would have to pay someone to dry them artificially. "You want the nut to dry enough to separate from the shell, which takes about two days in our trucks," Bob said. "After that the shell acts like a blanket and protects the peanut inside from light frost damage."

After the peanut harvest, while the nuts are drying, Bob plants a rotation crop of either oats or coastal grass, both of which are used for animal feed. This contributes to the soil's health, as well as keeping the insect population down.

When the nuts are field-dry, Bob delivers them to a nearby processing plant. There they go through another dryer, then into big drums that rattle them from their shells. They are sized by electronic eyes, then graded. Number one's, or jumbos, the queen of peanuts, are those that are large and not split. They're bagged in 110-pound bags and stored at 42°F for up to three years. They are sold as edible nuts, later to be salted or dry-roasted. Any small or shriveled nuts are squeezed for oil, and regulars and mediums are used for seed, to be planted the following year.

The government has put a quota on the amount of peanuts that can be raised in the U.S. "We can only raise a certain amount for domestic use, and we get paid $600 a ton," Bob said. "If we sell them for export, we only get $140 a ton, so it isn't worth it to sell them. We're better off just disking (plowing) them into the ground at that price."

Bob thinks the peanut program is the only government agricultural program that works, because it gives him an assurance few other farmers have: He knows each year, barring freak weather, what he'll sow, what he'll reap, and what he'll be paid.

Bob never thought he'd find himself worrying about the viability of a peanut, or taking pleasure in the American passion for the small toasty nut. Now and then he thinks it might be fun to get back into his original field, which was electronics. But then he gets out there in that tractor, the smell of peanuts surrounds him, and off he goes, wishing for a jar'a jelly.

HEARTY VEGETABLE SOUP

This soup, packed with fresh vegetables and flavored with sweet apples, is a blend of many different recipes from farm kitchens. It is water-based, which I like as a change from a chicken or beef stock base because the result is a bit lighter, a bit more fresh and tasty.

Serve the soup with a salad of Winter Greens and LaRene Reed's Idaho Potato Rolls (see Index).

1 pound leeks, well-rinsed and cut into
   1½-inch pieces
1 pound Russet potatoes, peeled and cut into
   1¼-inch chunks
12 ounces carrots, peeled and cut into 1½-inch
   chunks
8 ounces sweet apples, such as Jonagold,
   peeled, cored, and cut into 1½-inch chunks
10 cups water
1 teaspoon coriander seeds
¼ teaspoon black peppercorns
3 bay leaves
1 tablespoon salt
2 cups fresh parsley leaves
2 cloves garlic, peeled
½ cup olive oil

1 Place the vegetables, apples, and water in a large soup pot over medium-high heat. Tie the coriander seeds and the peppercorns together in a cheesecloth bag, and add it to the pot. Add the bay leaves and the salt, reduce the heat to medium, cover, and cook until the vegetables are tender, about 45 minutes.

2 When the vegetables and apples are tender, remove them from the broth with a slotted spoon. Remove the bay leaves and cheesecloth bag. Reserve the broth. Purée the vegetables and apples, and transfer the purée to a medium-size soup pot. Add enough of the broth to make a soup that is thick, but not as thick as a purée (about 2½ cups). Bring almost to a boil over medium heat, so the soup is hot through.

3 Finely mince the parsley and garlic cloves together. Transfer to a small bowl, add the olive oil, and stir well.

4 To serve the soup, ladle it into heated soup bowls and add 1 tablespoon of the parsley mixture, swirling it on the top. Serve immediately.

6 to 8 servings

BASQUE POTATO SOUP

T his aromatic soup—which comes from Juanita Hormachea, in Boise, Idaho—is bursting with the flavors of potatoes, tomatoes, and fresh thyme, and it makes a quick, sustaining meal.

While the traditional sausage is *chorizo*, a spicy Spanish-style sausage, I vary the kinds I add. Sometimes I use sweet Italian sausages; at others I like something more highly spiced with fennel, paprika, or hot peppers. (If I use hot pepper sausages, I omit the red pepper flakes in the soup.)

If you don't have stock on hand, use water and double the amount of herbs and spices to add flavor. Serve this with freshly made cornbread and a crisp salad. Try a bottle of Spanish red wine, such as Marques de Caceras 1986, or a Côtes du Rhône.

1 pound chorizo or Italian sausage, cut into ½-inch-thick rounds
1 small onion, peeled and cut into ½-inch chunks
2 pounds tomatoes, cut into 1-inch chunks
4 medium Russet potatoes, peeled and cut into ½-inch chunks
¼ cup coarsely chopped fresh parsley
1 cup diagonally sliced celery (3 to 4 ribs; ½-inch-thick slices)
2 tablespoons chopped fresh celery leaves
4 cups Rich Beef Stock or Herbfarm Deluxe Chicken Stock (pages 87 or 86), good-quality canned broth or water
1 bay leaf
4 large sprigs fresh thyme, or ½ teaspoon dried
1 tablespoon freshly squeezed lemon juice
½ teaspoon dried red pepper flakes (optional)
Salt and freshly ground black pepper

1 Brown the sausages in a large heavy saucepan over medium-high heat, about 4 minutes. Add the onion and cook, stirring, until it begins to turn translucent, 5 minutes. Do not let it burn, but don't be concerned if it turns golden at the edges.

2 Add the remaining ingredients through the red pepper flakes (if desired), stir, and cover. Bring to a boil. Reduce the heat to medium-low and simmer, covered, until the potatoes are tender and the sausage is cooked through, about 30 minutes. Stir the

soup accasionally as it simmers. Season to taste with salt and pepper, and serve immediately.

6 servings

BASQUE POTATO AND GREEN BEAN SOUP WITH GARLIC

My collection of Basque recipes, gleaned from Juanita Hormachea and the Idaho Basques I met through her, could go on forever. I've included only my favorites here, and this soup ranks high. Simple and quick to make, it is finished off with the rich flavor of garlic lightly browned in olive oil. The recipe takes only 30 minutes, yet it produces a hearty soup with the flavor of a whole day's worth of cooking.

Try a chilled amber beer, such as Anchor Steam with this.

1½ pounds Russet potatoes, peeled and cut
  into 2-inch chunks
1 tablespoon coarse (kosher) salt
6 cups water
1 pound green beans, trimmed and cut
  diagonally into 2-inch pieces
6 tablespoons olive oil
6 large cloves garlic, peeled and thinly sliced
Salt
Freshly ground black pepper (optional)

1 Place the potatoes, salt, and water in a large saucepan over medium-high heat. Cover and bring to a boil. Cook until the potatoes are nearly soft through, about 15 minutes. Add the green beans and cook until they start to turn tender and lose their bright green color, about 15 minutes.

2 While the beans and potatoes are cooking, heat the olive oil in a small saucepan over medium-high heat. When the oil is hot but not smoking, add the

sliced garlic and cook, stirring constantly, until it turns golden brown, about 8 minutes. Remove from the heat and set aside.

3 When the beans and potatoes are cooked, add the garlic and oil to the soup, and stir. Season to taste with salt, and pepper if desired, and serve immediately.

6 servings

ROOT VEGETABLE AND LEEK SOUP WITH GOUDA CHEESE

There is nothing better on a chilly winter evening than a steaming bowl of fortifying soup made with the root vegetables that are at their best when the ground is cold, the air snappy.

Sadly, root vegetables are too often neglected because of their knobby, gnarly, ropy looks. But to ignore them is to do oneself a disservice, because their flavors are incomparably deep and subtle.

Ron Zimmerman, the chef and owner of the Herbfarm (see page 85) has a particular fondness for root vegetables, which he grows in a continually expanding kitchen garden alongside the restaurant. After a muddy foray out there, shovel in hand, he turned a handful of them into this soup, which made a lasting impression on me. The garnish of cheese adds just the right touch of creamy richness.

Ron wisely chooses to use local ingredients at their peak, rather than import pallid unseasonal imitations. They give his food a depth and harmony that comes only with seasonal cooking, and it is a good lesson to follow.

Try this soup—it will surprise you with its elegance. Serve a chilled Côtes du Rhône alongside.

2 tablespoons unsalted butter

1 small onion, peeled and finely chopped

3 leeks, white part only, well rinsed and finely chopped

3 cups Herbfarm Deluxe Chicken Stock (page 86)

1 large carrot, peeled and grated

3 good-size Jerusalem artichokes, peeled and grated

6 medium potatoes (preferably Yellow Finn), peeled and cut into large chunks

Salt and freshly ground black pepper

2 cups whole milk

1 cup grated Gouda cheese

2 heaping tablespoons minced fresh chives

1 In a large pot, melt the butter over medium heat. Add the onion and leeks and cook, stirring frequently, until the onion turns translucent and the leeks soften, about 10 minutes.

2 Add the chicken stock, carrots, and Jerusalem artichokes. Stir and bring to a simmer. Add the potatoes (do not stir), cover, and cook until the potatoes are very tender, about 25 minutes.

3 Lift out the cooked potatoes with a slotted spoon, and push them through a coarse sieve. Return them to the soup, stir, and season to taste with salt and pepper.

4 Bring the soup to a boil over medium-high heat. Stir in the milk, and when the soup returns to a simmer, stir in the cheese. Allow the cheese to melt, but do not boil again. Season to taste.

5 Divide the soup among six shallow soup bowls, garnish with the chives, and serve immediately.

6 servings

BROCCOLI PARSNIP SOUP

T hough broccoli (one of America's favorite vegetables, according to consumption statistics) is tasty, it can lack excitement and elegance. I love broccoli, but I tire of it steamed, stir-fried, or tossed in vinaigrette, and long to take advantage of its subtleties. This recipe, conceived

on a wintry day when I was re-membering an afternoon in the broccoli field at Purepak Farm in Oxnard California, does just that. It highlights broccoli's mild nutti-ness, combines it with the sweet-ness of parsnips—a neglected root vegetable—and rounds it off with smooth cream.

This rich soup makes an appetizing first course. Divided among six people, the cup of cream amounts to less than 3 tablespoons a serving—hardly an untoward in-dulgence. Try a young white French Burgundy such Macon Vil-lages Duboeuf 1988 with the soup.

1 pound broccoli, trimmed, stems
    peeled
1 tablespoon unsalted butter
1 medium onion, peeled and diced
4 medium parsnips, peeled and cut
    into thin rounds
2⅔ cups Herbfarm Deluxe Chicken Stock
    (page 86), good-quality canned broth,
    or water
⅔ cup milk
1 cup heavy (whipping) cream
Salt and freshly ground black pepper

1 Cut the stems from the broccoli, and slice them into thin rounds. Separate the florets into the smallest possible sections, trying to keep them a nice shape.

2 Melt the butter in a medium-size heavy saucepan over medium heat. Add the onion and cook, stirring frequently, until it begins to turn translucent, about 5 minutes.

3 Add the parsnips, the broccoli stems, and enough chicken stock to cover. Bring to a boil. Reduce the heat to medium-low, cover, and cook until the parsnips and broccoli are soft, about 20 minutes.

4 Bring a large pot of salted water to a boil (2 teaspoons salt for 3 quarts of water is a good amount). Add the broccoli florets and blanch them, leaving them in the water just until it returns to a boil. Transfer them to a bowl filled with ice water, to stop the cooking. When the florets are cooled, drain them and set aside.

5 Purée the parsnips and broccoli stems in a food processor, and return the purée to the pan. Stir in the remaining chicken stock, and bring to a boil over medium-high heat. Reduce the heat to medium, and slowly stir in the milk and the cream. Heat the soup through, stirring frequently, making sure it does not return to a boil. Season to taste. Add the broccoli florets and stir. When they are thoroughly hot, about 5 minutes, serve the soup im-mediately.

4 to 6 servings

THE CARPENTERS OF GRADY, ARKANSAS

Bobbie Clark has a smile as wide as Broadway, a laugh wrapped around every word. She is the ringleader of the 25-member extended family that runs the 400-acre Carpenter farm in Grady, Arkansas, near Pine Bluff. Though not the eldest, Bobbie calls herself the "second mama" of the gang. She's the one who rouses everyone out of bed in the middle of the night to harvest vegetables for an unexpected order, then sings and jokes out loud to keep them awake. She does the farm books, plans the color-coordinated outfits for herself and her sisters to wear at the Pine Bluff farmers' market, and along with "first mama" Katie Carpenter, the mother of Bobbie and the eight other Carpenter children, cooks huge meals each day for the crew.

"Oh yeah, we love our jobs, we love being together, and we eat together every day for lunch," Bobbie says, flashing her gorgeous smile. "And sometimes we even eat together for dinner too."

The Carpenters are mavericks in a part of Arkansas where the land is "flat as a pine floor" and covered with acre after acre of soybeans and corn. "My husband, he had 800 acres of beans and corn,"

Katie Carpenter says. "I had 3 acres of vegetables, and when Mr. Carpenter saw how the vegetables made the money to pay the bills, feed and clothe us, and how he was losing money every year, he gave it up and bought him a little ol' tractor. Now we have three tractors and 400 acres."

HOME-GROWN FAVORITES

The Carpenters grow the vegetables that have always been common in the diet of southeastern Arkansas, but were either grown just in home gardens or imported from elsewhere. "They grow greens and peppers, and eggplants and cucumbers," says Thomas Vaughn, a Vista volunteer and former county extension agent who helped the Carpenters make

▶▶▶

the change on their farm. "These are traditional foods here, but nontraditional as far as the farms go." They also grow squash, turnips, tomatoes, onions, hot peppers, lettuce, sweet potatoes, and dozens more vegetables, depending on

what they've discovered and how the weather goes.

Too many farmers in and around Grady and Pine Bluff are still going the route Abraham Carpenter was with his beans and corn. They're losing money every year, getting deeper and deeper into debt. Thomas Vaughn is actively involved in helping them make the transition to produce, to get them out of the "bean and corn trap" through a program he helped establish specifically for low-income farmers. "It helps them get on their feet and into something that will pay," he explains. The large farmers' market at Pine Bluff is an integral part of his program, because it gives these farmers a ready, eager, nearly bottomless market for their produce.

His work with the Carpenters has been an astonishing success. They've devised their own refrigeration system and ice house for produce, they repair all their own machinery, and if something needs inventing, they invent it. Not only do the 400 acres feed and clothe the entire Carpenter family, give them all full-time jobs

and most of them their own homes, but it does so in style.

"Why, we built a new house near here and I've got one closet just for my hats," exclaims Bobbie, who wears a different hat to market every day. "If I feel sassy, then I wear a sassy hat, and if I don't, I wear something else. We do have a lot of fun."

Despite the fun and laughter, they're very serious, very good businesspeople, and completely dedicated to serving their customers.

They work until the work is done, from the tiniest—who take time for naps under the shaded truck canopy—to the eldest. When they gather for the midday meal, they clown around and talk and eat with gusto.

Once lunch is finished and the dishes have been washed and put away, they're all business again. Those designated for field work—from Katie and Abraham on down—pile into the truck and head out. The automotive contingent goes out to the barn to work on the tractors, and Bobbie takes a minute to decide which job needs her the most before she goes to the fields or the house. "Yeah, we've got our troubles just like anybody, but we keep 'em to ourselves," she says. "And we thank the Lord and have a good time."

CHILLED HONEYDEW SOUP

This recipe was inspired by the hot climes of central California and Texas, where melons ripen under the searing summer sun. In those temperatures, the thought of cooking hardly crosses my mind, and all I can think of is the simplest way to get wonderful food to the table.

There aren't many soups simpler than this one, nor are there many that are more refreshing. The keys to its success are obtaining the most flavorful honeydew and mango you can find, and serving the soup chilled but not glacial.

Try this with a German Riesling such as a Spätlese 1988 or a Hunt Country Ravat 1989, and follow it with a light summery salad.

1 tablespoon minced fresh ginger
½ cup boiling water
2 honeydew melons (5⅓ cups flesh)
¼ cup freshly squeezed lime juice
4 teaspoons mild honey
1 medium mango, peeled, seeded, and cut into small (¼-inch) dice
8 small fresh mint leaves, for garnish (optional)

1 Make an infusion of the ginger and water: Place the ginger in a small bowl, pour the boiling water over it, cover, and set aside for 10 minutes. Strain and reserve the liquid.

2 Discard the seeds from the melons and cut the flesh into large chunks; you should have 5⅓ cups. Place the melon in a food processor and process until it is a fine purée. Add the lime juice, the ginger infusion, and the honey, and process until well mixed. Transfer to a large bowl and chill, covered, for at least 1 hour.

3 Divide the diced mango among four chilled soup bowls. Pour the melon soup over the mango, garnish with mint leaves if desired, and serve immediately.

4 servings

HERBFARM'S RICH DUCK STOCK

This recipe comes from Ron Zimmerman, part owner and chef at the Herbfarm in Falls City, Washington (see facing page). Ron is a self-taught cook who loves deep, rich flavors, and duck stock is one of his basic recipes.

It is simple to make and results in a flavorful stock that is nice to have on hand for soups and sauces.

½ teaspoon unsalted butter
2 teaspoons mild vegetable oil, such as safflower
1 duck carcass, cut into large pieces
1 small onion, peeled and finely chopped
1 carrot, peeled and finely chopped
2 sprigs fresh parsley
1 bay leaf
3 sprigs fresh thyme
1 small tomato, coarsely chopped
1 clove garlic, peeled and crushed
2 large button mushrooms, stems trimmed,
*   caps minced*
Salt and freshly ground black pepper
Fresh ginger shavings, for garnish

1 Heat the butter and oil in a large skillet over medium-high heat. Add the duck and brown the pieces, turning often so they don't burn, 8 to 10 minutes.

2 Remove and reserve the duck pieces. Reduce the heat to medium and add the onion, carrot, herbs, tomato, and garlic to the fat in the skillet. Cook until the onions begin to turn translucent, about 5 minutes. Add the mushrooms and cook for an additional 5 minutes.

3 Return the duck pieces to the skillet, add just enough water to cover (about 1 quart), and bring to a boil over high heat. Then reduce the heat to medium and simmer for 45 minutes, skimming off any foam (impurities that rise to the surface of the stock). Add additional water as necessary to keep it at the same level.

4 Strain the stock, discarding the carcass, herbs, and vegetables. Let it cool to room temperature, then refrigerate. Before using, skim any fat from the surface, then bring to a boil in a medium saucepan over high heat and reduce by one third. Season to taste and use as called for or serve as is with shavings of fresh ginger.

1 quart

THE HERBFARM

The Herbfarm is a favorite day trip for Seattleites, who flock there in fine weather for the hundreds of varieties of odd and familiar herbs (all of which are grown without the aid of chemicals or pesticides), a series of cooking and craft classes organized by Ron Zimmerman and his wife, Carrie Van Dyck, and a six-course lunch at the tiny Herbfarm restaurant. Ron, Carrie, and Ron's parents, Lola and Bill, own the farm, and encourage visitors to have a picnic lunch on the lush Herbfarm grounds. They might choose to sit near the thyme garden, a woolly patch in varying hues of blue-green, or in the gazebo that is bordered on one side by fruit trees, or near the vast vegetable garden out behind the restaurant, or in any number of cool, shaded spots. An old apple tree near the garden is loaded come fall, and since Carrie and Ron rarely have time to harvest its full bounty, they encourage guests to pick the apples and add them to their picnic.

LEISURELY ALL-DAY MEALS

Ron does most of the cooking at the restaurant, which has gained a national reputation based on his herb-infused dishes made only with local ingredients. He loves not only to prepare the meals but also to give information about all of the herbs used in their making—either he or Carrie will wander through the dining room between courses, carrying a basket of the herb that stars in the dish that is being served. The meals take the better part of an afternoon and are accompanied by the Herbfarm's homemade switchel—an herbal drink farmworkers used to carry with them to the fields—or a small selection of Northwest wines. If you'd like to visit the Herbfarm and need more information, phone (206) 784-2222.

HERBFARM DELUXE CHICKEN STOCK

This recipe is another staple at the Herbfarm, where chef/owner Ron Zimmerman makes a cornucopia of flavorful soups year-round. He uses vegetables from his kitchen garden, and this flavorful stock is usually the base. It has a rich, meaty flavor, and it's called deluxe because it uses whole chicken pieces. You can make a lighter version when a less hearty stock is needed (see Note).

1 tablespoon unsalted butter
2 medium onions, peeled and sliced
1 tablespoon mild olive or safflower oil
4½ pounds chicken pieces
3 cups water
1 carrot, peeled and thinly sliced
1 rib celery, trimmed and sliced
3 sprigs fresh thyme, or ½ teaspoon dried
1 bay leaf

1 In a large stockpot, melt the butter over medium heat. When it is hot, add the onions and sauté until they are soft and pale golden, about 10 minutes.

2 Remove the onions and set aside. Add the oil to the pot and heat over medium heat. Add the chicken pieces and lightly brown them, 5 to 8 minutes.

3 Add the water, carrot, celery, herbs, and the cooked onions to the chicken. Cover and bring to a boil. Skim any foam

(impurities) that comes to the surface. Reduce the heat to low, and simmer until the chicken has completely fallen from the bone, 2 to 3 hours.

4 Strain the stock, reserving the liquid and discarding the chicken meat, bones and vegetables. Strain again through a very fine sieve.

5 Let the stock cool to room temperature, then refrigerate, covered. Before using or freezing, skim off any fat that has solidified on the surface.

3⅓ to 3½ cup

Note: For a lighter version of this chicken stock, use half the amount of chicken, leaving the other ingredient amounts the same. You can use either version, according to your preference, in any recipe calling for chicken stock.

RICH
BEEF STOCK

A good stock is the foundation of many a good meal, and many farm kitchens I visited had a pot of beef stock, usually called broth, simmering on the stove. Sometimes it was the basis for a soup and by dinnertime was chunky with vegetables and rich and mellow with flavor. Other times it cooked to a slow turn and was put in the freezer where it would rest until needed for a soup, a sauce, a casserole or a restorative hot drink.

This recipe is an amalgam of many—I've added ginger because I love the beguiling depth it gives to the stock. Its flavor is so subtle it doesn't interfere but lends a certain warmth that is welcome in any dish. It's best not to season stock with salt or pepper. That way you can add it to any dish and it will impart its flavor without throwing the seasoning of the dish off balance.

Beef stock will keep for several days in the refrigerator, and for a few months in the freezer. Try freezing the stock in ice cube trays, then popping out the cubes and storing them in a plastic bag. With frozen stock cubes on hand, you can add a touch of flavor just where you want it.

1 tablespoon mild vegetable oil, such as safflower
3 pounds beef stewing bones with marrow
2 slices fresh ginger, about ¼ inch thick
1 large carrot, peeled and cut into 2-inch lengths
1 medium onion, peeled and cut into 8 wedges
2 whole cloves
2 bay leaves
10 peppercorns
7 cups water

1 Heat the oil in a large stockpot over medium-high heat. Add the bones, stir, and brown until they begin to turn golden, about 7 minutes. Add the vegetables, stir, and continue browning until the vegetables turn golden, 7 to 8 minutes more. Add the remaining ingredients, bring to a boil, partially cover, and boil gently, skimming occasionally, until the liquid has been reduced by about half, 2 hours.

2 Remove the pan from the heat and strain the stock, discarding the bones and vegetables. Allow the stock to cool to room temperature, then cover, and refrigerate overnight. Skim the fat from the top of the stock and use immediately or freeze in a covered container. It will keep for 3 to 4 days in the refrigerator or for 3 months in the freezer.

3½ cups

FISH STOCK

F ish stock is quick and easy to make and comes in handy for any number of dishes. I always have some in the freezer, ready to add to a sauce or soup.

2 pounds bones from white fish, such as
   snapper, sole, or rockfish
2 tablespoons unsalted butter
2 medium carrots, peeled and coarsely chopped
1 large onion, peeled
Leaves of 2 celery ribs
10 cups water
1 bay leaf
1 bunch parsley stems
1 sprig fresh thyme
12 peppercorns
2 teaspoons salt

1 Rinse the fish bones well under cold running water until the water runs clear.

2 Melt the butter in a large heavy saucepan over medium heat. Add the vegetables and stir to coat with the butter. Add the water, herbs, spices, and fish bones; bring to a boil. Reduce the heat to low. Simmer the stock for 18 minutes, skimming off any foam (impurities that rise to the surface of stock).

3 Remove the stock from the heat. Strain, discarding the solids. When the stock is cool, either refrigerate or freeze it.

8 cups

FLAVORFUL MEAT DISHES

MEATS:
THE CHOICEST OF THE CHOICE

As you might expect, meat plays a large part in farmhouse cooking. If farmers don't raise their own stock, they buy meat from a neighbor, so the quality is always good and the price economical. Because there is no lack, meat turns up in nearly every meal, including breakfast. In fact, one of the most memorable farm breakfasts we had was fried steak strips, scrambled eggs, fried potatoes, and fresh bread.

I was surprised by the variety of meat on the farm. I expected plenty of beef, but instead I found more lamb and pork. Many farmyard populations included at least one sheep and what I gathered from farmers is that they just plain like having a sheep around.

Hogs are always in good supply, too, particularly in the Midwest, where we found pork on every menu and in every household, in dozens of different ways. There were thick ham sandwiches dripping with juice, roast pork, fried chops, meatballs, and ham steaks. I knew for sure I was in pork country when I was served a huge Iowa pork chop that weighed at least a pound and was expected to eat every bite. I did, of course, and it was tender, moist, and delicious.

I picked up plenty of tricks for cooking meats, and many mouthwatering recipes, and there are some for every mood, every style of living. Some are quickly grilled and roasted. Others reflect the rhythm of farm life, with their slow simmering. Make them when you have time to let them cook and enjoy the resulting luscious flavors.

FARMHOUSE BEEF STEW

There is nothing quite so warming and restorative on a blustery night as a big bowl of rich, flavorful beef stew. It satisfies the senses from the browning of the meat to the simmering of the corn. By the time the steaming bowls are set on the table, spoons are poised to scoop it up.

This stew is based on one served to us by Linda Stoltzfus in Millersburg, Pennsylvania. Linda, her mother, and her sister get together each fall to can their flavorful stew, using the last harvest from the garden, trapping its golden flavors in each jar. Until then I'd viewed beef stew with ho-hum interest, but my attitude changed after that hearty bowlful.

The secret to a good stew is simple. It must be made with well-browned good-quality beef (I like to include shinbones because the marrow adds a depth of flavor), sweet onions and carrots, a dot of marjoram for background flavor, and a good seasoning of paprika, all of which must be cooked together slowly. About half an hour before serving, the vegetables and potatoes are added so they cook through but still retain their fresh, sprightly taste, and so the potatoes hold their shape. Right at the end a sprinkling of fresh corn kernels add their sweetness and soft golden color.

Drink lightly chilled beer or a simple red table wine along with this stew.

2 pounds boneless stewing beef, such as chuck
2 pounds center-cut shinbone
⅓ cup all-purpose flour
Salt and freshly ground black pepper
4 to 5 tablespoons mild vegetable oil, such as safflower
2 small onions, peeled and cut into ¼-inch-thick lengthwise slices
5 medium carrots, peeled and cut diagonally into 1-inch pieces
5 to 6 cups water
2 pounds ripe plum tomatoes or 1 can (28 ounces) plum tomatoes, coarsely chopped
2 bay leaves
2 teaspoons paprika
2 teaspoons fresh marjoram leaves, or ¾ teaspoon dried
10 black peppercorns
12 ounces green beans, trimmed and cut diagonally into 1-inch pieces
1 pound Russet potatoes, peeled and cut into ½-inch chunks
½ cup hearty red wine (optional)
2 cups fresh or frozen corn kernels

1 Cut the stewing beef into 1-inch chunks. Trim the meat from the shinbones and cut it into similar-size pieces.

2 Mix the flour with salt and pepper to taste on a piece of waxed paper. Dredge the beef and the bones in the flour mixture.

3 Heat 2 tablespoons of the oil in a large heavy skillet over medium-high heat. When the oil is hot but not quite smoking, brown the beef and the bones on all sides until the pieces turn an even rich color, 8 to 10 minutes; do this in small batches so the pan isn't crowded, adding more oil as needed. Transfer the meat and the bones to a plate. Add the onions and carrots to the skillet and cook, stirring frequently, until the vegetables are lightly browned, about 4 minutes. Add ¼ cup of the water and stir, scraping up any browned bits. Remove the skillet from the heat.

4 Place the beef, bones, onions, carrots, and their cooking juices in a 12-quart stockpot. Add the tomatoes and enough of the remaining water to cover. Then add the bay leaves, paprika, half the marjoram, and the peppercorns; bring to a boil. Lower the heat to medium, partially cover the pot, and simmer until the meat is tender, 1½ to 2 hours, stirring occasionally to prevent the meat from sticking to the bottom of the pot.

5 Add the green beans, potatoes, and the remaining marjoram, stirring them into the stew. Add the wine if desired. If the stew is very thick, add some more water—the mixture should be liquid enough to cook the beans and potatoes. Continue cooking, partially covered, until the potatoes are tender, about 30 minutes. Add the corn and cook just until it is hot through, about 5 minutes. Season to taste.

8 to 10 servings

KITCHEN-SINK POT ROAST

T his is an amalgamation of pot roast recipes garnered from a variety of farmers and from the source of all good recipes while I was growing up, my mother. It's a kind of kitchen-sink recipe that will take a good cut of meat and just about any seasonal vegetables and bring out the best of their flavors.

Use this recipe as a guide—add other vegetables such as leeks, parsnips, young turnips, or rutabagas if you like. Try to make it the day before you serve it, as it improves and mellows with some age and will be almost twice as good the next day.

This is ideal for winter, of course, but I like to serve it in spring, too, when the choice of young and tender vegetables is legion and the evening air often has an unexpected chill.

⅓ cup all-purpose flour
Salt and freshly ground black pepper
2 cups canned tomato sauce
½ cup robust red wine or water
2 sprigs fresh thyme, or ¼ teaspoon dried
2 bay leaves
1 bunch parsley stems, tied together with
  kitchen string
2 cloves garlic, peeled and thinly sliced
  crosswise
3 allspice berries
3 pounds boneless beef rump roast, trimmed of
  excess fat
1 tablespoon unsalted butter
2 tablespoons olive oil
2 large onions, peeled and thinly sliced
  lengthwise
5 small carrots, peeled and cut into
  ½-inch-thick rounds
4 large ribs celery, trimmed, strings removed,
  and cut into ½-inch-thick crescents
1 large bunch kale (10 ounces), trimmed and
  coarsely chopped
4 medium Russet potatoes, peeled and cut into
  eighths

1 Mix the flour with a generous amount of salt and pepper on a piece of waxed paper.

2 Combine the tomato sauce, wine, herbs, and spices in a medium bowl and mix well.

3 Rinse the roast and pat it dry. Dredge it in the flour, covering all surfaces.

4 Heat the butter and oil in a large heavy saucepan, stockpot, or Dutch oven over medium-high heat until it is hot but not smoking. Brown the meat on all surfaces, watching it and turning it frequently, about 8 minutes. The roast will get quite brown on the outside, which is fine, though it shouldn't burn. Transfer the meat to a plate.

5 Reduce the heat to medium and add the onions, carrots, and celery to the pan. Cook, stirring frequently, until the onions are translucent and the other vegetables have softened, about 10 minutes. Place the roast on top of the vegetables, and pour the tomato sauce mixture over all. Turn the roast and stir the vegetables as much as possible, making sure the liquids are evenly distributed. Season with salt and pepper, cover, and bring to a boil. Reduce the heat to medium-low and simmer, covered, until the meat is almost completely tender, about 2 hours.

6 Add the kale and the potatoes, mixing them into the liquids. Cover the pan, and continue cooking until the meat is cooked through, the potatoes are soft, and the kale is tender, at least 45 minutes. Serve

the pot roast immediately, after adjusting the seasoning and removing the parsley stems, or continue cooking it all day. The longer it cooks, the better it is, as long as the cooking is gentle.

7 If you prepare the pot roast a day ahead, cover and refrigerate it. The next day, skim off any solidified fat, and reheat gently.

8 To serve, remove the pot roast from the pan and cut it into thin slices. Arrange the slices on a warmed serving platter, ladle the vegetables on and around the slices, and pour the juices over all.

8 to 10 servings

BARBECUED STEAKS WITH PEANUT SAUCE

This seems an appropriate recipe for Texas, the land of both peanuts and beef. I love to serve the steaks in the winter, when it's cold outside and the warm flavors in the sauce take me right to the sunny heat of Texas. It's big, robust, and earthy, yet artfully flavorful.

If you're like me, you'll like the peanut sauce so much that you'll want to make a double recipe of it so there's some left over. It will last in the refrigerator for about 10 days, and it comes in handy for impromptu meals that need a little dressing up. It's good with chicken, as a dip for vegetables, or spread on warm tortillas. If you don't like a hot zing in the sauce (something I find essential), use less or altogether omit the jalapeño.

A lightly chilled ale is a good choice to accompany this meal.

2 tablespoons olive oil

1 medium onion, peeled and minced

1 small green bell pepper, cored, seeded,
and diced

½ fresh jalapeño pepper, minced with
seeds

1 cup Herbfarm Deluxe Chicken Stock
(page 86), good-quality canned broth,
or water

½ cup chunky unsalted peanut
butter

2 plum tomatoes, diced

¼ cup freshly squeezed lime juice

Salt

Vegetable oil

6 T-bone or porterhouse steaks (9 to
12 ounces each), trimmed of fat

Freshly ground black pepper

1 Heat the oil in a large heavy skillet over
medium heat. Add the onion, green pepper, and jalapeño pepper, and cook, stirring
frequently, until the onion is nearly transparent, about 8 minutes. Add the broth, and

then stir in the peanut butter until well
mixed. Reduce the heat to low, and simmer
until the sauce has thickened, 7 to 10 minutes. Add the tomatoes and cook until they
are hot through, about 5 minutes. Add 2 tablespoons of the lime juice, stir, and then
season to taste with salt. Keep warm.

2 While the sauce is cooking, prepare the
grill: Preheat the broiler, or light a
medium-size fire in a barbecue and when
the coals are red and dusted with ash,
spread them out in an even layer.

3 Lightly oil the grilling rack with vegetable oil, and grill or broil the steaks to
your liking.

4 Drizzle each steak with 1 teaspoon of
the remaining lime juice, season them
generously with salt and pepper, and top
them with the sauce. Serve immediately.

6 servings

NORTH-OF-THE-BORDER FAJITAS

I arrived at the Schimelpfenings' peanut farm in Pleasanton, Texas, ex-
pecting to head immediately out to the fields with Bob. But Bonnie
Schimelpfening had another idea. "Relax—you can't work all the time.
Let's sit down for lunch," she said.

"Have you ever had *fajitas*?" she asked as she set a platter in the center of the table, which was set with warm fresh tortillas and bowls of guacamole. I hadn't, and so the Schimelpfenings instructed me in *fajita*-making and etiquette.

Fajitas, "little belt" or "sash" in Spanish, are indigenous to south Texas. As local lore has it, they originated with the Hispanic workers on beef ranches there, who often received skirt steaks as partial payment for their work. On slaughtering day the workers would build huge mesquite fires and grill the skirt steak, then eat it wrapped in corn or flour tortillas.

Your favorite beer is what goes best with *fajitas*.

3½ pounds skirt, round, or flank steak
⅔ cup freshly squeezed lime juice
1 recipe Homemade Flour Tortillas (page 155)
1 recipe Piquant Guacamole (page 53)
Picante Sauce (recipe follows)
1½ cups sour cream (optional)

1 Place the steaks on a work surface, cover with waxed paper, and with a meat pounder pound them until they are ¼ inch thick. Place them in a nonreactive shallow dish, add the lime juice, cover, and marinate, turning occasionally, for 6 to 8 hours or overnight in the refrigerator.

2 To cook the steaks, preheat a gas grill or broiler, or build a good-size fire in a barbecue.

3 When the grill or broiler is heated, or when the coals are red and dusted with ash (spread them out), place the meat on the grill about 3 inches from the heat. Grill until the meat is crisp and browned on both sides, about 3 minutes per side for rare, about 4 minutes per side for medium-rare.

4 Slice the steak against the grain, holding your knife at a 45° angle, into ½-inch-thick slices and transfer them to a warmed serving platter, pouring any juices over them. Serve the tortillas, guacamole, picante sauce, and sour cream in separate dishes.

5 To assemble, place several slices of meat on a tortilla; top them with guacamole, picante sauce, and sour cream if desired. Roll up the tortilla, and eat as neatly as possible!

6 servings

PICANTE SAUCE

Y ou haven't had a great picante sauce until you've made your own with fresh-from-the-farm tomatoes bursting with flavor. Cinnamon adds an exotic allure, and jalapeño peppers give it a zing.

1 jalapeño pepper

1 pound plum tomatoes, peeled and chopped

1 clove garlic, peeled and minced

4 scallions (green onions), trimmed and minced

2 tablespoons distilled white vinegar

¼ teaspoon ground cinnamon

Salt

⅛ teaspoon cayenne pepper

1 handful cilantro leaves or to taste

1 Preheat the broiler.

2 Place the jalapeño pepper on a piece of aluminum foil, and roast it under the broiler, turning it frequently, until the skin is darkened evenly, about 8 minutes. Remove it from the broiler and wrap it loosely in the foil; set aside until it is cool enough to handle. Then remove and discard the skin and the stem. If you like your picante sauce very hot, leave the seeds; otherwise discard them, too. Mince the pepper.

3 Place all the ingredients except the cilantro in a medium-size bowl and mix well. Mince the cilantro leaves, add them, and mix again. Cover and set aside to ripen for at least 1 hour. Taste for seasoning and serve.

2½ cups

NATE PENNELL'S BOILED DINNER CUM HASH

Nate Pennell described this to me as we bumped along a road through the blueberry barrens in northern Maine (see page 444). His mother prepared it when he was growing up, and now he prepares it for his family. It's a great winter dish because it fills the plate with warmth and flavor. And it's two meals in one: the dinner and the hash (recipe follows). I can never decide which I like best.

Steamed or boiled beets are a traditional accompaniment to a New England boiled dinner. I like to serve Caryl's Beet Relish (see Index), which is a sweet/tart foil. Whether or not beets are part of your menu, be sure to serve horseradish alongside.

The hash is a simple matter of cooking the leftovers in a substantial amount of unsalted butter. Try it for breakfast as a bed for fried eggs, and be sure to pass a pitcher of white vinegar along with it, to enhance the deep flavors. To make red flannel hash, add cooked beets, which will turn the entire dish a deep red.

Try this with a full-style and buttery California Chardonnay.

5 pounds corned beef, trimmed of fat and
    cut into 2-inch chunks
6 allspice berries
2 bay leaves
Salt and freshly ground black pepper
3 medium onions, peeled and halved
    horizontally
12 medium potatoes, preferably a waxy
    type, scrubbed
5 medium carrots, peeled and cut into
    1-inch pieces
4 small turnips, peeled
1 medium rutabaga, peeled and quartered
    (optional)
1 large green cabbage, cut into 6 wedges

1 Place the corned beef in a large (at least 8-quart) stockpot, cover with cold water, and bring to a boil over high heat. Remove from the heat and drain.

2 Add fresh water to a depth of about 2 inches. Then add the allspice berries and bay leaves, cover, and bring to a boil over medium-high heat. Reduce the heat to low, and simmer the corned beef until it is tender, about 2 hours.

3 Season the corned beef and its liquid with salt and pepper, if desired. Add the onions and potatoes to the corned beef, pushing them under the liquid, and cook until the potatoes begin to soften, about 15 minutes.

4 Add the carrots, turnips, and the rutabaga if you are using it, pushing them under the liquid. Cover and cook until all the vegetables are tender, 30 minutes.

5 Add the cabbage wedges, pushing them under the liquid if possible or just allowing them to sit on top. Cook, covered, until the cabbage is tender but still a vivid green, about 15 minutes.

6 To serve, drain the meat and vegetables and arrange them on a large heated platter, cutting the cabbage wedges and the potatoes into quarters. (Or spoon the meat and vegetables into large shallow soup bowls.)

10 to 12 servings

NEXT DAY HASH

6 tablespoons (¾ stick) unsalted butter
8 cups diced leftover Boiled Dinner (meat
    and vegetables)
¾ cup distilled white vinegar

1 Melt the butter in a large heavy skillet over medium-high heat. When it is hot, press the hash into the skillet. Cook, checking the underside frequently, until it browns on the bottom, 10 to 15 minutes.

2 Turn the hash over in one piece and continue cooking until it has given up all its liquid, is generally browned throughout and is slightly crusty, about 25 minutes.

3 Serve immediately, and pass the vinegar in a pitcher.

6 servings

SHEPHERD'S PIE

Shepherd's pie is a homey, golden, gather-round-the-table dish to be eaten on a cold winter's night. Hardly common in the city, it is still a favorite on farm and country tables, and I collected a handful of recipes for it in my travels.

Originally a British dish, in this country shepherd's pie has a distinct East Coast orientation. My husband, who grew up in Virginia, remembers it fondly from his childhood, and all the farmers who mentioned it lived east of the Mississippi.

Here is my version, which is a cinch to make. The caramelized onions give it a deep flavor; the allspice gives it breadth. It couldn't be simpler, yet when brought piping hot to the table, the dish has a certain dignified presence. Serve a green or root-vegetable salad alongside, and either chilled beer or a red table wine—or, in fine farm tradition, a piping hot cup of coffee!

2 pounds Russet potatoes, peeled
1 pound lean ground beef
¼ teaspoon ground allspice
Salt and freshly ground black pepper
2 medium onions, peeled and thinly sliced
¼ cup water
2 cups fresh or frozen corn kernels
⅔ cup milk
⅓ cup heavy (whipping) cream

1 Steam the potatoes in a steamer basket over boiling water until they are soft, 20 to 25 minutes.

2 Meanwhile, place the ground beef in a small bowl and mix it, using your hands, with the allspice and salt and pepper to taste. Then brown it in a large heavy skillet over medium-high heat, stirring constantly to break up the pieces, until it is almost cooked through but still somewhat pink. Using a slotted spoon, transfer the meat to a medium-size bowl.

3 Add the onions to the fat in the skillet, cover, and cook, stirring frequently, until they are deep golden to dark brown, about 10 minutes. The onions should get quite dark brown and caramelized. Add the water and stir, scraping any browned bits from the bottom of the skillet. Add the onions and the cooking liquid to the ground beef, and stir until combined. If you are using fresh corn kernels, stir them into the mixture. Season to taste and set aside.

4 Preheat the oven to 350°F.

5 Transfer the potatoes from the steamer to a large bowl or to the bowl of an electric mixer. Using a potato ricer, fork, or the whisk attachment, mash the potatoes until they are completely smooth, adding the milk and cream as you mash them.

Season to taste with salt and pepper. The potatoes will have a quite soft consistency.

6 If you are using frozen corn kernels, add them to the meat mixture now. Pile the mixture into a 9-inch glass pie plate, pressing down on it gently. Using a pastry bag fitted with a large star tip, pipe the potatoes evenly over the meat mixture in an attractive pattern, making sure you completely cover the meat. (Alternatively, simply spread the potatoes evenly over the meat mixture.) The potatoes will make quite a thick covering. Avoid piling them in the center of the pie, as they will burn when it is placed under the broiler.

7 Bake the shepherd's pie until it is hot through, about 30 minutes. Remove it from the oven and heat the broiler.

8 Place the shepherd's pie about 2 inches from the heat, and broil just until the potatoes are golden, 3 to 4 minutes. Serve immediately.

4 to 6 servings

COUNTRY MEAT LOAF

I collected numerous meat loaf recipes along the farm trail and have combined elements from each to make one that is an exemplary version of this American favorite.

While I was developing the recipe, I polled many meat loaf lovers, relying particularly upon the taste of my brother, John, who has a good palate for all foods and is a meat loaf fan of uncommon devotion.

"It's got to have just the right onion flavor, and ketchup is essential or you can't really call it meat loaf," he insisted. "The bacon isn't absolutely necessary, but I know a meat loaf will be good when it's got some on top." As for green pepper, well, he was adamantly opposed, and when I mentioned the addition of capers, he cringed. He also insisted that the true test of a meat loaf is the quality it gives to a sandwich the next day (the one meat loaf fact I knew).

With his advice and my sheaf of farm recipes, I came up with this one, and I have served it many times to rave reviews. It satisfies that nostalgia for a dish that nearly every American, it seems, grew up loving.

2 medium onions, diced (to give 2 cups)
1½ pounds ground chuck
½ pound ground pork
2 tablespoons prepared horseradish
1 teaspoon salt, or to taste
1 teaspoon dry mustard
1 teaspoon dried thyme leaves
½ cup minced Italian (flat-leaf) parsley
2 large eggs
¼ cup milk
2 cups fresh white bread crumbs
¼ cup Amish Tomato Ketchup (page 335)
3 slices bacon

1 Preheat the oven to 350°F.

2 Place the onions, meat, horseradish, salt, mustard, and herbs in a large bowl and lightly toss them together, using your hands, until they are thoroughly mixed.

3 Whisk the eggs and the milk together in a small bowl. Add this to the meat mixture, and again mix with your hands, working lightly. Sprinkle the bread crumbs over the mixture, and continue mixing until they are incorporated.

4 To test for seasoning, make a tablespoon-size patty of the mixture and sauté it in a small skillet over medium heat until it is cooked through. Taste, and adjust accordingly.

5 Place the meat loaf in a 10 x 13-inch baking dish or on a jelly roll pan, gently shaping it into a long loaf that is 4½ to 5 inches wide. Slather the top with the ketchup, and then lay the bacon slices diagonally across the width of the loaf.

6 Place the dish in the center of the oven and bake until the meat loaf is cooked through and brown around the edges, about 50 minutes.

7 Remove the meat loaf from the oven, and let it rest for 5 minutes in the pan. Remove it from the pan, cover it loosely with aluminum foil, and let it rest an additional 5 to 10 minutes before slicing.

8 servings

Mom's
Oxtail Ragout

I grew up eating oxtail soup and stew. My mother learned to cook them from her mother, who was raised on a farm and who was familiar with all cuts of meat. I still remember the full, hearty flavor of those oxtail dishes.

I have re-created those memories here. I love to make this dish in the winter, when root vegetables are firm and crisp and the weather demands a warm, hearty meal. The cooking times for this stew are approximate—I often let it simmer for half the day, or make it the night before and reheat it to serve the next day, when it is really at its best. It improves with time, and is an ideal dish to make on the weekend and serve during the week.

One warning about oxtails— they can be very fatty. Trim them carefully, and skim any fat that rises to the surface of the sauce. (The ideal way to do this is to refrigerate the ragout overnight. The fat will solidify, making it easy to skim off.) Try this with a velvety red Côtes du Rhône, such as a Guigal 1985 or 1986.

3½ to 4 pounds oxtails, cut into 2-inch lengths
½ cup all-purpose flour
Salt and freshly ground black pepper
2 tablespoons unsalted butter
2 medium onions, peeled and finely chopped
5 cloves garlic, peeled and crushed
2 tablespoons vegetable oil
4 cups Rich Beef Stock (page 87), good-quality canned broth or water
2 cups dry white wine, such as a Vouvray
Large handful of fresh thyme sprigs, or 1 teaspoon dried
2 bay leaves
2 tablespoons tomato paste
1 strip orange zest, 3 to 4 inches long
2 large Russet potatoes, peeled and quartered
4 carrots, peeled and sliced into ½-inch pieces
3 long ribs celery, trimmed and sliced diagonally into ½-inch pieces
2 medium leeks, trimmed, rinsed, and cut into ½-inch rounds (white and green parts)
2 medium turnips, peeled and sliced into thin rounds
4 medium parsnips, peeled and sliced diagonally into ½-inch pieces

1 Rinse the oxtail pieces and pat dry.

2 Place the flour on a plate or a piece of waxed paper, and season it generously with salt and pepper. Roll the pieces of oxtail in the flour until they are covered. There will be some extra flour.

3 Melt the butter in a large heavy saucepan or stockpot (at least 9-quart size) over medium heat. Add the onions and garlic and cook, stirring constantly, until they soften and begin to turn translucent but aren't brown, about 5 minutes. Transfer them to a bowl and set aside. First making sure that the pan is completely free of any pieces of onion or garlic, add the oil and raise the heat to medium-high. When the oil is hot but not smoking, brown the oxtail in it on all sides, in batches if necessary to avoid overcrowding.

4 Add the stock and the wine and stir, scraping up any browned bits from the bottom of the pan. Stir in the reserved onions and garlic, and then add the thyme, bay leaves, tomato paste, orange zest, and a generous amount of salt and pepper. Stir well, cover, and bring to a boil. Reduce the heat to low, and simmer until the meat is tender, about 2 hours. If you want to make this the night before, stop here, let the oxtails cool, and refrigerate.

5 Add all the vegetables except the parsnips to the oxtails, stirring so they are completely submerged. Cover, and continue cooking until the vegetables are tender, about 30 minutes. Then add the parsnips, and continue cooking until they are tender, another 30 minutes. Taste to check the seasoning, and serve.

8 servings

IOWA HAMBURGERS

After spending the day with Mike and Judy Mohr at their hog farm outside Iowa City, we were asked to stay for a supper of pork burgers, the family favorite.

The Mohrs like ground pork so much that they have most of their yearly pork supply ground, and Judy uses it in everything from burgers to tacos, spaghetti sauce, and casseroles. In fact, she uses it anywhere that ground beef is traditionally used.

Judy serves her burgers with all the traditional fixings—ketchup, mustard, mayonnaise, lettuce, and garden tomatoes. I've expanded on them in this spicy, aromatic recipe, which I like to serve on toasted whole-wheat hamburger buns or on toasted good-quality Italian bread.

Serve beer—I like Tsing Tao, Rolling Rock, or Heineken—with these pork burgers.

1 pound lean ground pork

1 tablespoon minced fresh ginger

2 scallions (green onions), trimmed and sliced into thin rounds

1 serrano or small jalapeño pepper, trimmed (seeds and membranes removed, if desired) and cut into thin rounds

2 teaspoons soy sauce

1 teaspoon red Szechuan peppercorns (available at Asian groceries), ground and sifted (optional)

4 hamburger buns, or 1 loaf Italian bread

6 tablespoons good-quality mayonnaise, or to taste

1 bunch watercress, rinsed and patted dry

1 Preheat the broiler.

2 Place the pork, ginger, scallions, pepper, soy sauce, and ground peppercorns in a medium-size bowl. Using your fingers or a wooden spoon, mix the ingredients until thoroughly combined. Form into four patties.

3 Heat a medium-size heavy skillet over medium-high heat. Add the pork burgers, and cook until they are browned and crisp on the outside, about 5 minutes per side.

4 Meanwhile, quickly toast the hamburger buns under the broiler.

5 To make the sandwiches, spread the mayonnaise on the buns. Place a burger on the bottom half of each bun and top it with a handful of watercress. Add the other half of the bun and serve, with any remaining watercress on the side.

4 pork burgers

TWO CHILES

When choosing chiles, be sure you know which pepper you're getting. Jalapeños are small, stubby, conical, and green ripening to red. Their heat increases with color. Although they are very hot, their heat can be precisely adjusted by removing the interior ribs and seeds, leaving a mild to peppery flesh. Serranos look like miniature jalapeños. They turn red as they ripen, and the heat increases with color. This chile is searingly hot.

MIKE MOHR AND HIS HOGS

Mike Mohr raises hogs on the 100-acre farm his father bought in 1948. He learned to farm alongside his father, and he still raises all the corn, oats, and soybeans used to feed his hogs. "I don't sell feed to anyone else," he said. "I just feed it to my hogs."

Until 1984 Mike was a conventional farmer. He used synthetic fertilizers, pesticides, and herbicides to pump up his crops and to keep the soil productive. Then, one day, several bags of herbicides spilled off a truck driving by his house. The bags broke open, spewing chemicals onto the road, down an embankment, and into a field. All the greenery growing in their path turned yellow and died. "I got to thinking about what that stuff was doing," he said, pointing to the path, which is still bare. "It's been eight years. I was putting that stuff on my land and I just didn't know how strong it was."

Because of that incident Mike began farming organically. "I quit using chemicals and I saw my land come back in three years," he said.

The hogs in Mike's field are Poland Chinas, which are black with a big white stripe like a belt around their bellies, and Durocs, which are a rusty brown. They meander at will, taking shelter from the sun in hog houses, prancing around with the piglets, and generally giving the impression of being fat and happy.

We walked through one of Mike's small barns, looking at the huge, hairy, pale pink sows that had just farrowed, or given birth. They were lying on their sides with a dozen or more tiny bright pink piglets suckling at their massive teats. It smelled sweet and clean inside. "That's *lactobacillus*," Mike said. "I spread it in the barn after I clean it and it keeps it clean." (*Lactobacillus* is a bacterium Mike uses for a variety of purposes, including adding it to his soil and his hog feed.)

Such a scene is in stark contrast to a conventional hog farm, where the animals are confined cheek by jowl in concrete buildings, the odor so strong it permeates the air.

Mike sells a percentage of his hogs to a local natural foods store, which pays a premium. The rest go to the conventional market and get lost in the shuffle. "I get paid what everybody else gets paid," he said. "But we're looking for other specialty markets, and I'm sure it's just a matter of time."

HALUPKI

This is the dish that Aili Takala served for supper when we arrived at her farm in Stockett, Montana. I'd heard about Aili and her halupki for years from her grandson Stuart, and when she set down the fat steaming packets, my senses were tickled. They revealed themselves to be savory little bundles of beef, pork, rice, and onions, all mildly spiced and wrapped in a tender cabbage leaf. They were set off with lightly tart sauerkraut, or what Aili calls simply "kraut."

This dish, Aili told me, is a national treasure in her native Finland, and she and her Finnish neighbors serve it often. It's flavorful and hearty, a revivifying lunch after a morning's work on the farm, an antidote to leaden winter skies that seem filled with nothing but sleet and snow, and in any situation a deliciously flavorful meal. Halupki are lovely to look at, with the flecks of red bell pepper and the delicate green of the cabbage leaves.

Be sure to serve plenty of fresh bread alongside for sopping up the juices—try Aili Takala's Pulla (a Finnish bread; see Index), which is an ideal match. I also like to serve pickled beets, and stewed tomatoes if I've got some from summer's canning or if I find a good commercial brand.

Try a chilled Riesling with this dish.

1 medium green cabbage
Salt
½ cup rice
¾ cup water
8 ounces lean ground beef
8 ounces lean ground pork
1 medium onion, peeled and diced
½ large red bell pepper, cored, seeded, and diced
2 cloves garlic, peeled and minced
¼ teaspoon cayenne pepper
Freshly ground black pepper
½ cup fresh dill, packed
6 cups sauerkraut with liquid (see Note)

1 Carefully remove ten large leaves from the head of the cabbage. To do this, slit the stem end of each leaf and gently peel it from the head.

2 Bring a large pot of salted water (about 1 tablespoon salt per quart) to a boil. Fill a large bowl with ice water. Place several of the cabbage leaves in the boiling water, being careful not to crowd the pot, and boil them until they begin to

soften and turn a vivid green, 4 to 5 minutes. Then transfer the leaves to the ice water. Repeat this process until all the leaves are blanched and cooled. Drain the leaves and pat them dry. Set aside.

3 Place the rice in a small heavy saucepan, and add the water and a generous pinch of salt. Bring to a boil over medium-high heat, and boil until the rice has absorbed most of the water and there are bubble holes on top, about 3 to 5 minutes. Then cover the pan, reduce the heat to low, and cook for 10 minutes. Remove from the heat and leave covered for 5 minutes. The rice will be partially cooked.

4 Preheat the oven to 350°F.

5 In a large bowl combine the rice, ground beef, ground pork, onion, bell pepper, garlic, cayenne, and salt and pepper to taste. Mince ¼ cup of the dill and using your fingers, mix it in thoroughly. To test for seasoning, sauté 1 tablespoon of the mixture in a small pan over medium-high heat until it is golden on both sides and cooked through, 3 to 5 minutes. Taste, and adjust the seasoning as needed.

6 Place one-tenth (about ⅓ cup) of the filling mixture on the bottom third of a cabbage leaf. Roll the bottom up and over the filling, then continue rolling, tucking in the edges of the leaf to enclose the filling. Repeat with all the leaves and filling.

7 Spread 4 cups of the sauerkraut over the bottom of a 9½ x 14-inch enamel or earthenware baking dish. Arrange the cabbage rolls in a single layer on top, and then top with the remaining 2 cups sauerkraut. Pour enough sauerkraut liquid over the rolls to reach just over halfway up the sides of the pan. Cover, and bake in the center of the oven for 1¼ hours. Reduce the heat to 250°F, and continue baking until the filling is cooked through and the cabbage leaves are quite soft, with just the edges retaining their green color, 1 hour.

8 Remove the dish from the oven. Mince the remaining ¼ cup dill, sprinkle it over the cabbage rolls, and serve immediately.

8 to 10 servings

Note: If the sauerkraut you purchase does not come with plenty of juice, add low-salt chicken stock. The result won't be quite so tart, but it will be just as delicious.

Buy sauerkraut fresh from the barrel, or in bags or jars—never in cans. For this recipe you will need two 1-quart jars, which generally hold 1½ cups liquid and 4¼ cups sauerkraut. Use all of the liquid from one jar and half from the second, for a total of 2¼ cups.

JAYNE DEE'S MARINATED PORK CHOPS

T his quick, tasty recipe is a version of one given to me by Jane Dee, wife of pig farmer Eric Dee and a real cheerleader for the pork industry.

Her husband works on the family farm outside State Center, Iowa, but the Dees live in town, in a smart little turn-of-the century home. Jane wanted us to try the pork industry's latest product, "Iowa cut" pork chops, a he-man cut that is at least 1½ inches thick. She grilled them outdoors, just until they were slightly pink in the center and bursting with flavor and juice.

Pork has flavor, texture, and versatility and needs little embellishment. This simple treatment results in a surprisingly elegant main course. I like to serve a sautéed vegetable alongside—pea pods in the spring, any number of vegetables in the summer, and tender sweet root vegetables and greens in the fall—touched with a bit of fresh ginger and soy sauce.

For a wine, I suggest a Pinot Noir.

4 "Iowa cut" pork chops (see Note), trimmed of fat if necessary
2 teaspoons minced fresh ginger
⅓ cup "natural" apple juice
1 tablespoon freshly squeezed lemon juice
2 tablespoons light usukuchi soy sauce (available at Asian groceries)
1 tablespoon mild honey

1 Rinse the pork chops and pat them dry. Rub the ginger into both sides of the chops, and place them in a nonreactive dish.

2 In a small bowl, whisk together the remaining ingredients, and pour the mixture over the chops. Turn the chops to coat them, and marinate, uncovered, at room temperature for 30 to 45 minutes, turning them every 15 minutes.

3 Preheat the broiler, or build a small charcoal fire in a grill.

4 Place the chops under the broiler, about 3 inches from the heat, and broil until they are golden but still moist in the center, about 6 to 7 minutes per side for "Iowa cut" chops; about 4 minutes per side for thinner cut chops.

If you are using an outdoor grill, spread the coals out when they are red and dusted with ash. Lightly oil the grill rack, and place it about 3 inches above the coals. Place the chops on the grill and cook for the same amount of time as the broiled chops.

Remove from the heat and serve immediately.

4 servings

Note: If you can't find "Iowa-cut" pork chops, have your butcher prepare them. Otherwise, use center-cut chops that are at least ½ to ¾ inch thick.

PORK CHOPS WITH MACE AND APPLES

D ave Kobos is a farmer at heart (see page 258) and a constant source of recipes. This is one of my favorites because it takes pork chops into an entirely new dimension. It's also one of those dishes you can make in your sleep—as long as you pay careful attention to the seasonings—and serve it as though you'd spent hours in the kitchen, for that is how it will taste.

Try a chilled 1988 Vouvray Sec from Foreau, or a ripe dry Alsatian Riesling such as the Cuvée Frederic Emile 1985, from Trimbach, with this elegant dish.

6 pork chops (½ inch thick, about
  8 ounces each)
Salt and freshly ground black pepper
¼ teaspoon ground mace

2 tablespoons minced orange zest
1 tablespoon unsalted butter
1 tablespoon mild vegetable
  oil, such as safflower
4 large tart apples, such as
  Gravensteins, Granny Smiths,
  or Winesaps, peeled, cored, and cut
  into eighths
⅓ cup dry white wine

1 Preheat the oven to 350°F. Generously butter a 10 x 14-inch baking dish, and set it aside.

2 Rinse the pork chops and pat them dry. Season them with salt and pepper to taste. Rub each side with the mace, and then with the orange zest.

3 Heat the butter and oil in a large skillet over medium-high heat until hot but not smoking. Brown the pork chops on both sides until they are golden, about 2 minutes per side.

4 Spread the apples over the bottom of the prepared baking dish, and season them lightly with salt and pepper. Arrange the pork chops on top, pour the wine over them, and bake until the apples have softened somewhat and the wine has reduced by about half, about 30 minutes. Turn the chops, and bake until they are tender and thoroughly cooked, another 40 minutes. Serve immediately.

6 servings

PORK LOIN WITH A CORIANDER AND GARLIC CRUST

After visiting several hog farms in the Midwest and eating pork prepared in dozens of ways, I developed a real fondness for this lean white meat and had hours of fun experimenting with it in the kitchen.

This recipe was inspired both by Elizabeth David, who makes a coriander crust for lamb, and by a dish I once sampled at the Heathman Hotel in Portland, Oregon. I love the aromatic flavor that the coriander gives to the pork, heightened by fresh garlic and flavorful olive oil.

Barley with Saffron and Lemon (see Index) goes well with this, as does a full-bodied Alsatian Riesling or Pinot Gris.

¼ cup coriander seeds
1 cup fresh bread crumbs
2 large cloves garlic, peeled
½ teaspoon salt
¼ cup extra virgin olive oil,
   or more if needed
1 boneless pork loin (2¾ pounds)
Freshly ground black pepper
½ cup water

1 Preheat the oven to 400°F.

2 Place the coriander seeds in a food processor and process until they are crushed, which should take about 30 seconds. Add the bread crumbs and the garlic, and process until they are combined. With the processor running, add the salt and ¼ cup olive oil, and process just until the mixture is combined. It should be moist enough to hold lightly together when pressed. If not, add more oil, a tablespoon at a time, until the mixture holds together.

3 Place the pork on a rack in a roasting pan, and season it with pepper. Then press the bread crumb paste over the top and the ends of the pork loin, and as far down the sides as you can. Don't be concerned if the paste falls off when you try to press it on the sides—just do the best you can, and gather any that falls into the pan and press it on top. The paste should be thickest on the top.

4 Cook until it is nearly cooked through but still pink in the center (145° to 150°F on a meat thermometer), about 1 hour and 10 minutes. Let it rest for 10

minutes before slicing, so the juices retreat back into the meat.

5 While the meat is resting, add the water to the roasting pan and bring it to a boil over medium heat, scraping any browned bits from the bottom of the pan. Reduce until the sauce is dark and somewhat thickened, 5 to 8 minutes, and set aside.

6 To serve, cut the strings from the loin, easing them from under the crust. Cut two slices for each person. Place the remaining roast on a heated platter, and arrange the slices attractively around it. Pour the sauce over the slices, and serve. (Or you can place the pork roast on the heated platter and arrange the slices in an attractive overlapping row.)

4 to 6 servings

COOKING PORK

The pork industry assures us that pork is perfectly safe when cooked to 145° to 150°F—as opposed to the old rule of 160° to 180°F. (Any bacteria are killed when the meat reaches 145° to 150°F.) I follow their directions and urge you to do so as well, because cooking it to that temperature results in moist, tender flavorful meat, whereas further cooking can often render it dry and tasteless.

CARYL'S POSOLE

This recipe comes from Caryl Smith, who with her husband, Barney, farms 1,000 acres in southeastern Iowa. They raise beef cattle, all the grains to feed them, and as a sideline, Morgan horses.

Caryl's mother was born and raised in New Mexico, and Caryl's culinary repertoire includes many dishes with a New Mexican accent. In fact, Caryl is known far and wide for her cooking. I first heard about her in Seattle—from her niece, who insisted I visit her just to taste her *posole*. We made the several-thousand-mile trip on this recommendation, and we weren't disappointed.

We became fast friends with Caryl and Barney, and the *posole*—as well as a bushel of other dishes we sampled—has become a favorite. The hearty chunks of pork and the *posole* are deeply seasoned with a bit of lard and the dusky ancho pepper purée, and it makes a warming, satisfying meal. If you don't care for lard, use a mild-flavored vegetable oil.

Caryl has a tough time getting *posole* (corn kernels that have been soaked in lye and dried) in Iowa, so she usually uses hominy. I follow her lead, using golden hominy, which gives a spark of color as well as flavor to the dish.

Caryl doesn't garnish the posole with cilantro, because that's an herb she rarely finds at her local markets, but I like to add it at the last minute for a contrasting flavor. Try the dish with cornbread, along with a big green salad and lightly chilled beer.

1 tablespoon lard or mild vegetable oil, such as safflower
2 large onions, peeled and chopped
2 pounds pork loin or shoulder butt, trimmed of fat and cut into 2-inch chunks
1 cup Ancho Chile Purée (page 315)
1 bay leaf
¼ cup fresh oregano leaves, or 2 tablespoons dried
1 teaspoon salt, or to taste
1 can (1 pound) yellow hominy
2 cups hot water
Cilantro leaves, for garnish (optional)

1 Melt the lard in a large heavy skillet over medium heat. When it is hot but not smoking, add the onions and cook, stirring

frequently, until they are translucent and softened, about 10 minutes.

2 Stir in the pork, and then the chile purée. Add the herbs, salt, and hominy. Then add the hot water and stir.

3 Bring the mixture to a boil, increasing the heat to medium-high if necessary. Then reduce the heat to low and

simmer the *posole*, partially covered, until the pork is tender but not dry and the liquid has reduced by about half, about 3 hours. Check the *posole* every 20 minutes or so, and stir it to be sure it isn't sticking to the pan. Season to taste, and serve immediately with the cilantro leaves sprinkled on top.

6 servings

CARYL SMITH'S BARBECUED PORK SANDWICH

This is a variation on Caryl Smith's Iowa pork barbecue, one of her favorite dishes, and a favorite with her family and neighbors too. The pork cooks for hours in an aromatic tomato sauce lightly spiked with vinegar and lemon, until it literally shreds itself. All that's left to do is to scoop it over fresh hamburger buns or thick slabs of bread, arm yourself with a stack of napkins, and eat away.

I like to use pork shoulder for this recipe; pork butt also works well. Be sure to leave the bone in because it deepens the flavor; it's easy to remove when the meat is cooked.

If you make the barbecued pork a day ahead, you can refrigerate it and then easily skim off the solidified fat before reheating and serving it. I have found, however, that if the pork is well trimmed to begin with, there isn't much fat to skim at the end.

Serve this with a good amber beer like Anchor Steam alongside.

6 pounds pork shoulder, bone in, trimmed
   of fat and skin
3 cloves garlic, peeled and minced
1½ cups tomato juice
1 can (28 ounces) plum tomatoes
1 bay leaf
½ cup distilled white vinegar
¼ cup freshly squeezed lemon juice
1 medium onion, peeled and minced
2 tablespoons dark brown sugar
6 tablespoons Worcestershire sauce
½ teaspoon salt
¼ teaspoon cayenne pepper
½ heaping teaspoon ground cinnamon

1 Rub the pork all over with the minced garlic. Place it in a large heavy stockpot, and add the tomato juice, the tomatoes and their liquid, the bay leaf, and ¼ cup of the vinegar. Bring to a boil over medium-high heat. Reduce the heat to medium-low and break up the tomatoes with a wooden spoon. Cover and cook, turning the meat occasionally, until it is very tender and beginning to fall apart, about 3 hours.

2 Add the remaining ¼ cup vinegar and all the other ingredients to the pork, stirring them into the juices. Cook, uncovered, over medium-low heat until the pork shreds easily and has absorbed most of the liquid, another 3 hours. Stir and turn the pork every hour so it cooks evenly in the juices and doesn't stick to the bottom of the pan. Remove and discard the bone when the meat easily falls off it. Stir frequently during the last 30 minutes to break up any large pieces and to prevent sticking. Serve the pork immediately; or refrigerate it overnight, remove any excess fat, reheat, and serve.

10 to 12 servings

ROBERT BARNUM'S SPARERIBS

R obert Barnum, a farmer of exotic fruits and medicinal plants in Homestead, Florida, is one of those people who offers recipes at every turn. He just can't help it. He loves to cook just about as much as he loves working in his Possum Trot Nursery.

Robert's small, cluttered home is nearly obscured by the Jamaican allspice, miracle plant, lime, avocado, and bayberry that surround it, almost growing in the windows. His enthusiasm is infectious, and if I had to be stranded on a tropical island with a handful of people, I'd make sure he was along, because I know he'd find the tastiest plants and we'd have wonderful things to eat.

I could hardly write fast enough to keep up with all Robert's recipe ideas. This one particularly impressed me. It's perfect for summer because it requires practically no preparation. The spareribs cook quickly, and come from the oven or the grill crisp and brown, with a beguiling exotic aroma.

Accompany these with a potato or fruit salad; fresh rolls or bread, and a light beer such as Heineken or Rolling Rock to drink.

4 to 6 pounds meaty spareribs, cut into
*   individual ribs*
Grated zest of 2 limes
¼ cup freshly squeezed lime juice
1 tablespoon distilled white vinegar
2 cups dry white wine
¼ cup light soy sauce (usukuchi; available
*   at Asian groceries)*
2 cloves garlic, peeled and minced
1 teaspoon freshly grated nutmeg
1 large sprig fresh rosemary, or 2 teaspoons
*   crushed dried*
2 limes, quartered, for garnish

1 Arrange the spareribs in a single layer in a large nonreactive dish. Whisk together all the ingredients through the rosemary in a medium-size bowl, and pour this over the spareribs. Turn the ribs so they are moistened on all sides, cover, and refrigerate for at least 24 hours, turning them several times so they are evenly marinated.

2 Preheat the oven to 400°F, or build a good-size fire in a barbecue.

3 Drain the spareribs, reserving the marinade. Place them in a nonreactive baking pan in one layer (use two baking pans if necessary), and bake in the center of the oven, basting frequently, until they are golden, crisp, and cooked through, 55 minutes to 1 hour. Turn them occasionally to make sure they cook evenly.

If you are using a charcoal grill, spread the coals out when they are red and dusted with ash. Lightly oil the grill rack, and place it about 3 inches above the coals. Cook the ribs, basting and turning them, 55 minutes to 1 hour.

4 To serve the spareribs, drain off the fat and transfer them to a warmed shallow serving bowl or platter. Garnish with the lime wedges, and provide plenty of napkins.

4 to 5 servings

THE KIRSCHENMANN FAMILY FARM

red Kirschenmann, a biodynamic (see page 216) and organic farmer, sits on the lawn outside his parents' farmhouse near Windsor, North Dakota, chewing on a blade of grass and considering the day. The sun is high, the sky completely blue; the air is cool and the wind whips the laundry on the line. It's May and a busy season on the farm, but he's set the morning aside to talk.

Fred grew up on the farm, but left to pursue an academic career. "I got degrees in philosophy and religion, and a Ph.D. in 1964, and I fully intended my career to be in higher education," he says. But in 1976 his father had a heart attack, and Fred came back to help. "My wife and I decided to stay, but only with the understanding that the farm could be converted to organic."

Fred knew he had a receptive audience when he set out his condition. "My father came to this land with a team of horses in

the 1930s," Fred explains. "He was always progressive, looking for new ways to do things. When chemicals came out in the '50s, he was the first to use them, and he was the first farmer to plant sunflowers here, which have proven to be a successful crop."

Theodore Kirschenmann had a condition for his son, as well. He agreed to the transition, but if the farm began to fail, they would return to conventional farming.

The first year was a banner success, but several tough years followed as the land weaned itself from synthetic chemicals. Gradually, however, things turned around, and after nine years the major hurdles were crossed, crops flourished, and Fred had a system in place. Now the farm is on its feet.

FRED'S PLAN

When Fred was beginning the transition from conventional to organic farming, he came up with a five-year plan. "You need to be a student of nature and to understand weed cycles and things. You need to know, for example, that weed-based plants have an affinity for drought resistance and should be planted in low-moisture areas, or that certain grains thrive in poor soil." Drought is a big concern for farmers in the plains of North Dakota, where about 19 inches of precipitation fall each year. "The solution is soil care," Fred says. "If you have good soil structure, it will absorb and hold what moisture there is."

The first year Fred planted crops that did well in poor soil, like buckwheat, oats, and legumes. The second year he concentrated on building up the soil by planting

clover, digging it up when it flowered, and leaving it on top of the soil to decompose and protect the soil at the same time. He weeded the fields mechanically, rather than using a chemical spray, and applied composted cow manure. He points across the field to large mounds of steaming cow manure, gathered from his herd. "I've found the best compost is raw and chunky, so it doesn't take us that long to make it."

The following year he planted a crop that didn't require completely balanced soil, and by the fifth year he was back to planting a legume. He continues this cycle to maintain the health of the soil. "I go from a soil-building year to wheat, rye, sunflower, buckwheat, then a legume," he says. "If we grow food on soil that is only

fertilized with nitrogen, phosphorus, and potash, the way much farming is done, we ignore certain important trace minerals. But if it's grown on soil fed with compost and green manure that contain all the minerals, those are in the food as well."

Fred raises cattle for their valuable compost contribution and for their meat. Of his 3,100 cultivated acres, 900 are devoted to grasses to feed the cattle and about 200 are in alfalfa for their forage. The way he figures it, each cow needs 4 acres of grass for nourishment, so his 200 head have plenty. Once they come off pasture they go to a feedlot, where he feeds them alfalfa and crop residues like baled oat and millet straw.

SURVEYING THE DOMAIN

▪▪▪▪▪

Later in the afternoon I ride with Fred in his 165-horsepower John Deere, a tiny tractor in comparison to many I'd been in. Fred says his soil is loose enough that he has no need for a huge tractor. He is also aware of studies being done on soil compaction caused by heavy machinery. Apparently the weight of the machinery creates layers of hardpan several feet below the soil surface, which can inhibit drainage and eventually the growth of the crops.

The 20-foot seeder makes furrows, drops in seed, and covers it with a light layer of soil. We're seeding millet mixed with clover, which is called intercropping. The

▶▶▶

clover feeds the soil, the millet feeds people. A cloud of seagulls follows the tractor. "They're scavengers," Fred says with a laugh. "I don't know why we have seagulls way out here, but we always did when I was a kid, and then they disappeared. They've returned since we've farmed organically."

Fred turns philosophical in the tractor, which is warm from the sun. Seeding and ploughing are monotonous to some farmers, who have radios and even televisions in their cabs for diversion. But not to Fred. He's so busy most of the time that tractor driving is a respite, a time to think and consider.

He talks about the advantages of his

type of farming. "I can be a good steward of the soil," he says. "That's satisfying, and it's the way I want to do things. But farming is an art, and it's different for every farm manager. I would be arrogant to tell anyone else how to farm, but I do try to let people see that this works."

The economic advantages of Fred's farming style are mixed. "I spend $3,500 on biodynamic preparations each year, instead of the $50,000 a conventional farmer spends on chemicals," he says. But his farming style is labor-intensive, and he had to give up some of the government subsidies on his land because he wanted to grow crops that weren't included in the govern-

ment programs. That cuts down on his income.

There is a distinct advantage in the marketplace, however, where he gets a 15 percent premium on organic crops and slightly more than that for biodynamic. The largest market for biodynamic foods is Europe, where the farming system is more familiar and a substantial demand exists.

Fred is concerned about the public's insistence on low-cost food. "If there weren't government subsidies, which include oil and irrigation, food grown conventionally would cost even more than organic food," he says. "The cost of growing food organically is the real cost of growing food." Though Fred didn't come out and say it, many farmers involved in alternative agriculture feel that government subsidies exert too much control over farming, so that often a farmer is forced to grow a crop that might not be to his advantage or fit in with a crop-rotation plan. But since he, like others, is economically dependent on the government subsidy check at the end of each year, he has got to plant what the government programs stipulate.

Fred maintains that if consumers really understood that healthy food comes from healthy soil, they would insist it all be grown organically, even if they had to pay more. "But right now, people think food that looks good is good for them, and they prefer low prices to good nutrition," he says.

EFFICIENCY IN SMALLNESS

Fred is progressive, but he has some old-fashioned ideas about what should happen in farming. "If people were willing to adopt a policy of locally grown food, things would be different, communities wouldn't be dying, and food would be fresher and better. That would mean the proliferation of small farms, which is efficient. But they aren't perceived as efficient, so the government doesn't encourage them. The political view holds that the fewer and larger farms there are, the more efficient food production is," he says. "That hasn't been proven true."

When Fred's father ploughed with a team of horses, one farmer could feed three people. Currently, one farmer feeds 125 people. The current numbers look efficient: fewer feed more. But there are so many hidden costs, according to Fred, that the numbers don't mean much. Large-scale farming has brought about the demise of the farm town, because the managers of large farms don't go to the hardware store for a part or two, or to the equipment salesman for a new tractor. They buy in bulk from somewhere else. The owner is often absent, or is a corporation, so the farm contributes little to the fabric of the community.

Fred, as well as being a successful organic and biodynamic farmer, is an alternative-farming missionary. He speaks to groups around the country whenever he can get away, and his message is clear, and backed up by success. He has a vibrant personality, and when he gets behind a podium and begins to speak, his blond hair slicked into place, his big frame confined in a turtleneck, town trousers, and a tailored corduroy jacket, his enthusiasm washes through the

room. He's funny, and he makes jokes other farmers understand—sometimes on them, and sometimes on the restrictive farming systems that have overtaken agriculture in the U.S. Invariably, when his talk is finished he is surrounded by an eager knot of farmers who want his advice or have stories to share.

The ruts in the road to the Kirschenmann farm are deep, and visitors are frequent. Fred hires apprentices and gives occasional alternative-farming workshops, and he invites farmers to come walk through his prairie and his fields, feel the loamy soil, see the birds that roost in the grasses, and smell the incomparable perfume of life teeming on the farm.

As we step down from the tractor and look out across the prairie where nothing but his own home disturbs the horizon, he reflects on farming. "The immediacy and the independence are the rewards," he says. "And the economics, of course." I watch him turn the tractor back into the field to finish seeding those long, even rows. I have a suspicion I'm already long forgotten, as he turns his full concentration back to his farm.

SAUSAGES, ONIONS, AND POTATOES WITH APPLE DUMPLINGS

This recipe is an adaptation of one from Pauline Kirschenmann of Windsor, North Dakota. Pauline and her husband, Theodore, are Russian-German—their English still heavily accented—and the food she prepares daily for her husband, son, and the farm crew is laced with Russian-German specialties.

Now in her eighties, Pauline has cooked three meals a day for as many years as she can remember. She says she always loved to cook, but by now, though she turns out delicious food and a cornucopia of baked goods daily, she admits to being a trifle tired.

Fatigue didn't stop her from giving me a taste-bud-expanding tour of her recipes after my husband and I spent the day with her son, Fred, who is one of a handful of bio-dynamic farmers in the country (see page 216). As we ate at Mrs. Kirschenmann's table—steaming beef stew, homemade venison sausage, salad, and a fresh cream tart for dessert—she frequently got up to check on the apple cream sweet rolls in the oven. She set a steaming plateful in front of us and insisted we eat until they were gone.

This apple, potato, and sausage dish is a standby at the Kirschenmanns'. It satisfies a hearty appetite, and its delicate flavors appeal to anyone who has even a touch of hunger. I make it often in the fall and winter because it is a panacea for chilly, drizzly weather. What I particularly like about it is the sweet edge given by the apples—and of course the pillowy apple-studded dumplings.

Try a crisp floral Alsatian Riesling, vintage 1988, with this.

1 pound bratwurst, cut into 1-inch pieces
2 small onions, peeled and thinly sliced
1 pound Russet potatoes, peeled, halved
lengthwise, and cut into ⅛-inch-thick
slices
1 cup dry white wine, such as a Vouvray
2 cups water
1 teaspoon crumbled dried sage leaves
Several sprigs fresh thyme, or ¼ teaspoon dried
1 bay leaf
6 fresh sprigs parsley, coarsely chopped
3 allspice berries
Salt and freshly ground black pepper
2 teaspoons freshly squeezed lemon juice
2 small tart, crisp apples, such as Northern
Spies or Winesaps, or 1 large Granny Smith
¾ cup all-purpose flour
⅓ cup cake flour
2 teaspoons baking powder
¼ teaspoon baking soda
1 large egg, beaten
2 tablespoons unsalted butter, melted
⅓ cup buttermilk
¼ cup minced fresh parsley, for garnish

1 Brown the bratwurst in a large heavy skillet over medium-high heat, turning them frequently about 5 minutes. When they are quite brown, remove them from the pan and add the onions. Reduce the heat to medium and cook, stirring constantly, until the onions just begin to turn translucent, about 3 minutes.

2 Stir in the potatoes, and add the wine, 1 cup of the water, the herbs, and the allspice berries. Bring the mixture back to a slow boil, increasing the heat slightly if necessary, and stir, scraping up all the brown bits from the bottom of the skillet. Return

the sausages to the skillet, and season generously with salt and pepper. Cover, and cook at a slow boil, reducing the heat if necessary, until the potatoes are nearly tender, about 25 minutes. Gradually add the remaining 1 cup water, if necessary, to keep the mixture just submerged in liquid.

3 While the potato mixture is cooking, fill two small bowls with water, and add 1 teaspoon lemon juice to each. Peel and core the apples. Slice half the apples into ¼-inch-thick slices, and place them in one bowl of acidulated water. Dice the remaining half, and place them in the other bowl. Set aside.

4 Make the dumplings: Sift both flours, the baking powder, baking soda, and ½ teaspoon salt into a medium-size bowl. Make a well in the center and add the egg, melted butter, and buttermilk. Mix the wet ingredients together, using a fork or a small whisk. Then, working quickly, incorporate the dry ingredients into the egg mixture, using a fork to make a fairly soft dough. Drain the diced apple, and fold it into the batter so the pieces are well distributed.

5 When the potatoes are nearly cooked, drain the apple slices and add them to the skillet, stirring them in gently. Taste and adjust the seasoning if desired. Drop the dumpling batter in six equal spoonsful on top of the mixture. Cover, and cook until the dumplings have risen to nearly twice their size and are firm when you touch them, no longer than 12 minutes. Serve immediately, garnished with the minced parsley.

6 servings

LAMB WITH YOUNG MUSTARD GREENS

This is a dish that celebrates spring, using tender lamb chops and tiny young mustard greens. The idea came from Mary McPherson, who was the best backyard farmer/gardener I knew. She grew up in the South and moved to Seattle nearly thirty years ago.

At one time, we shared a fence with Mary, whom everyone called Miss Mary. She was the matriarch of the neighborhood, with a personality as feisty as the heat in the young spring greens she cultivated with such care.

Mary gardened for hours every day, hoe in hand, just "workin' the dirt" and making sure her plants had room to grow. When the mustard and turnip greens got to be a couple of inches tall, she'd harvest a mess and often as not see if we wanted to join her for supper. She always cooked them the same way— with a touch of hot pepper and a chunk of bacon. I learned to cook them that way too, but more important, I learned to love the flavor of tender greens.

Try a young Chinon or a ripe California Cabernet Sauvignon with this dish.

2 teaspoons dried rosemary
8 loin lamb chops
2 pounds young mustard greens, rinsed
Salt and freshly ground black pepper
8 tablespoons (1 stick) unsalted butter
1 teaspoon minced lemon zest
4 teaspoons freshly squeezed lemon juice

1 Preheat the broiler and set the rack 3 inches from the heat.

2 Lightly crush the rosemary with a mortar and pestle. Rub it into both sides of each lamb chop, and set them aside.

3 Steam the mustard greens in a vegetable steamer over simmering water until they are limp and tender but still

bright green, 8 to 10 minutes. Remove the greens from the heat and set them aside.

4 Season the lamb chops with salt and pepper, and broil until they are crisp and golden outside but still rosy pink inside, 3 to 4 minutes per side.

5 Meanwhile, melt the butter in a large skillet over medium-high heat, and add the steamed mustard greens, lemon zest, and salt and pepper to taste. Cook, tossing to coat the greens with butter, until all the flavors are thoroughly blended, about 5 minutes.

6 Taste the greens for seasoning, adjust if necessary, and arrange them in the center of four warmed dinner plates. Top each with 2 lamb chops, sprinkle the chops with the lemon juice, and serve immediately.

4 servings

FREDA CENARRUSA'S BRAISED LAMB SHANKS

Freda is the wife of Pete Cenarrusa, the secretary of state for Idaho (and the aunt of Michael, whose special leg of lamb recipe is on page 128). Pete's family came to Idaho, as almost all the Basques there did, to herd sheep. Most Basques, including Pete, have done well and now own many of the sheep ranches. Though Pete's job with the state is full time, he still manages to slip away to his ranch, about a half-hour flight east of Boise.

Freda isn't Basque, but she has learned many recipes from Pete. This dish has Basque overtones, which means it is loaded with flavor. The long, slow cooking makes it so tender it melts in your mouth.

Try a Castello di Rampola 1986 Chianti or a medium-bodied Bordeaux Haut-Médoc, such as Sociando-Mallet 1985, with these lamb shanks.

4 lamb shanks (16 to 18 ounces each),
   trimmed of excess fat
Salt and freshly ground black pepper
1 large onion, peeled and diced
3 cloves garlic, peeled and minced
½ cup hearty red wine
Alices' Mother's Noodles (page 60), or
   1 pound dry egg noodles
1 cup loosely packed fresh parsley leaves,
   for garnish

1 Brown the lamb shanks in a large skillet or a Dutch oven over medium-high heat, 8 minutes. As they brown, generously season them with salt and pepper to taste.

2 When the lamb shanks are browned, reduce the heat to medium. Add the onions and garlic, and work them down so they are on the bottom of the skillet. Cook, stirring as best you can by moving the lamb shanks around in the skillet, until the onion and garlic are golden, about 5 minutes. Then stir in the wine. When it begins to boil, reduce the heat to low, cover, and simmer until the cooking juices have thickened somewhat and the lamb is tender enough to fall from the bone. Depending on the size and quality of the lamb shanks, this will take from 3 to 4 hours (be sure to check them occasionally). If the cooking juices are browning too rapidly, add ½ cup water and continue cooking.

3 When the shanks are done, remove them from the cooking juices. Remove all the meat from the bone, and cut away the gristle. Cut any very large pieces of meat into bite-size pieces. Keep the meat warm. Raise the heat under the skillet to medium and reduce the cooking juices, stirring up any brown bits from the bottom of the pan, until they are thickened, about 5 minutes. Season to taste.

4 While the sauce is reducing, bring a large pot of salted water to a boil. Add the egg noodles, stir, and cook until they are tender but still firm to the bite, 5 minutes for Alice's Mother's, 8 to 10 minutes for dry. Drain.

5 While the noodles are cooking, mince the fresh parsley, if you are using it.

6 To serve, divide the noodles among six warmed dinner plates or shallow soup bowls. Place the lamb atop the noodles, and pour the sauce over all. Garnish with the parsley, and serve immediately.

6 servings

BUYING ONIONS

You probably shop for onions so often, choosing them is almost by rote. But, it shouldn't be. When buying onions, select those that are firm and have papery skins. Avoid any with black discoloration, called soot; it is a mold with a nasty flavor. Green coloration signifies age and it, too, should be avoided. If you buy onions in a bag, check each onion individually for freshness, because one spoiled onion will quickly spoil the others.

LAMB CHOPS IN A HAZELNUT CRUST WITH ROSEMARY CREAM

This recipe comes from Sandy Shea, owner of Chez Shea, a restaurant at Seattle's Pike Place Market. Sandy grew up on a farm in Oregon, and she naturally uses seasonal local ingredients like lamb from eastern Washington and hazelnuts from her home state.

This is a signature dish at Chez Shea, which overlooks the market and Elliott Bay beyond. With it try a rich young Merlot from California, such as Clos du Bois 1987.

3 tablespoons Dijon mustard
8 thick loin lamb chops (4 ounces each), trimmed of fat
Freshly ground black pepper
½ cup toasted hazelnuts (see Note), finely chopped
½ cup fresh bread crumbs
¼ teaspoon salt
3 cups Rich Beef Stock (page 87) or good-quality canned broth
1 sprig fresh rosemary
1 cup heavy (whipping) cream
¼ cup mild vegetable oil, such as safflower
2 tablespoons brandy
2 teaspoons minced fresh rosemary
Salt
Fresh rosemary sprigs, for garnish (optional)

ROSEMARY

Rosemary has a wild, racy aroma and flavor and it is perfect with lamb, poultry, in cured olives, with marinated cheeses, in breads and biscuits, and with meaty seafoods such as swordfish, marlin, tuna, bluefish, and mackerel. Throw rosemary stems on the coals to flavor grilled foods. Dried rosemary maintains much of its character, though it is more pungent than fresh.

1 Brush mustard on all surfaces of the lamb chops, using about 7 teaspoons. Generously pepper the chops on both sides.

2 In a medium-size bowl, mix together the hazelnuts, bread crumbs, and salt. Press an even layer of the mixture onto all surfaces of the lamb chops.

3 Combine the stock and the sprig of rosemary in a medium-size saucepan over high heat, bring to a boil, and reduce to 1 cup, about 10 minutes. Whisk in the cream and the remaining mustard, reduce the heat to medium, and simmer until the mixture is slightly thickened, about 5 minutes. Set aside.

4 Heat the oil in a large heavy skillet over medium-high heat. When it is hot but not smoking, sauté the lamb chops until they are golden on the outside but still pink in the middle, about 4 minutes per side. Do this in batches, if necessary, so you don't crowd the pan. Transfer the chops to a double thickness of paper towels on an oven-proof plate, and keep warm.

5 Remove the skillet from the heat, and pour off any excess oil. Add the brandy, light it with a match, and when the flame has burned down, pour the stock mixture through a strainer and into the skillet. Place the skillet over medium heat and simmer until the mixture is thick enough to coat the back of a spoon, about 4 minutes, stirring with a spatula and scraping any brown bits from the bottom of the pan. Stir in the minced rosemary, and season to taste with salt and pepper.

6 To serve, arrange two lamb chops on each of four warmed dinner plates. Pour the sauce over them, and garnish each plate with a sprig of rosemary. (You could also pour the sauce on the plates first, set the chops on top, and garnish with the rosemary.) Serve immediately.

4 servings

Note: To toast hazelnuts, preheat the oven to 350°F. Place the nuts in a baking pan large enough to hold them in a single layer, and toast, stirring once, until they give off a toasted aroma, about 10 minutes. Wrap the nuts in a kitchen towel and rub them between your hands to remove the skin.

FLAMING DISHES

*F*laming (flambéing) not only provides a touch of drama, it gives a dish a rich, mellow flavor once the alcohol is burned off. When flaming is called for, keep in mind a couple of things. First, never flame something while it is still on the stove burner. Always remove it from the heat before beginning. Second, if flaming a dish makes you a little uncomfortable, buy yourself long kitchen matches. They allow you some distance between the flame and your hand.

MOM'S LAMB AND LENTILS

Simple, fresh, flavorful farm cooking is the basis of my mother's culinary background. Her food creativity always results in lusty dishes and this one is a good example—she was raised on lamb, which came fresh from the farm, and lentils have always been standard fare at her table.

Not surprising, any dish that includes lentils scores high in my book because I love their rich, nutty flavor. When cooked just to a slightly crisp tenderness they have an alluring texture, which teams well with lamb.

The cooking time for the lentils will vary dramatically, from 15 to 35 or 40 minutes, depending on the variety. For reasons no one has really been able to assess, most imported lentils take much longer to cook than those grown in the Northwest, which is where American lentils are cultivated. There isn't any way to tell what you've got unless the container lists a country of origin, which is unlikely. So begin checking them for doneness at 15 minutes. If they are nearly tender, cook them an additional 5 minutes, then continue with the recipe. If they are hard as rocks, continue cooking for another 20 minutes, testing periodically.

Lightly seasoned rice, pasta, or quinoa rounds out the meal, along with Green Beans with Walnuts and Lemon or Root Vegetable Salad with an Anchovy Vinaigrette (see Index).

2 teaspoons olive oil
1 pound boneless lamb (see Note), cut into
  ½-inch chunks
2 cups water
1 cup lentils, rinsed and picked over
1 medium onion, peeled and chopped
2 cloves garlic, peeled
1 teaspoon salt
10 black peppercorns
4 sprigs fresh thyme, or ½ teaspoon dried
4 large fresh sage leaves, or ½ teaspoon
  crumbled dried
2 tablespoons freshly squeezed lemon juice
Grated zest of ½ lemon
2 medium carrots, peeled and cut into ¼-inch
  rounds
2 cups coarsely chopped green cabbage
Salt and freshly ground black pepper

1 Heat the olive oil in a large skillet over medium-high heat. Add the lamb and brown 3 to 4 minutes per side. Add the water, lentils, onion, garlic, salt, peppercorns, and the herbs. Bring to a boil, reduce the heat to medium, and cook until the lentils are tender but still slightly crisp, about 20 minutes.

2 Stir in the lemon juice and zest, and then the carrots and the cabbage. Cover, and cook until the cabbage is wilted and the carrots are just tender, still slightly crisp in the center, about 15 minutes. Season to taste, and serve immediately.

4 servings

Note: Lamb steaks are a good choice here.

FOURTEEN HOUR LEG OF LAMB

No, it's not a typographical error: The long, slow cooking is the key to the success of this recipe. Just give it a try. When you finally pull it from the oven, the meat will be stunningly flavorful, and so tender you can eat it with a spoon.

A heavy, airtight cooking dish is essential for this recipe. I use a glass-lidded cast-iron Dutch oven so that I don't even need to remove the lid to check on the progress. If you must take a peek, do it quickly and replace the lid immediately so you don't let too much steam escape.

For the best results, begin the lamb the night before you plan to serve it. Let it cook overnight, then allow it to cool. Refrigerate the lamb; skim off any solidified fat before reheating and serving it.

Serve a big green salad alongside, and a hearty red wine such as a young California Cabernet Sauvignon, perhaps a Shafer 1987.

If you're lucky enough to have leftovers, cut the meat and vegetables into bite-size pieces, warm them, and add them to a salad of winter greens, and toss with a well-spiced vinaigrette.

CENARRUSA LAMB

▪▪▪▪

Michael Cenarrusa comes from Guernica, in Spain's Basque country. He had never herded sheep there, but when he came to Idaho about fifteen years ago he took it up—as Basques in this country have for decades—when he went to work for his uncle, Pete. Up in the mountain pastures with the flock, he often cooked dishes from home.

Like most of Idaho's Basques, Mike has moved on from sheepherding full time, and he now manages his uncle's ranch. He supervises a crew of Peruvian sheepherders, seasonal workers who return to their native country after bringing the sheep down from the mountains in the fall.

Fourteen Hour Leg of Lamb is Mike's specialty, and he prepares it several times a year, though no longer over a campfire. He makes it for the crew, the family, and especially for Pete when he visits the ranch. According to Pete in fact, this is the reason the Cenarrusa ranch never has trouble attracting and keeping a crew. They come, and stay, for the leg of lamb! (For another Cenarrusa family lamb recipe, see page 123).

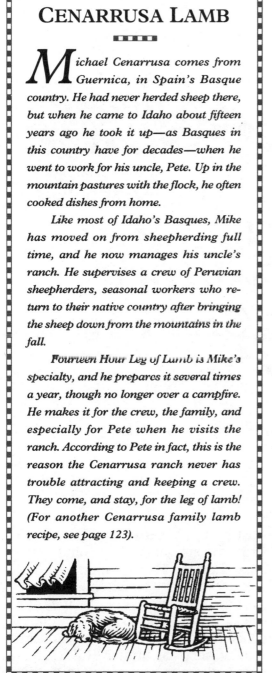

1 leg of lamb (4 to 5 pounds), trimmed of excess fat (see Note)
10 large cloves garlic, peeled
¼ cup olive oil
Salt and freshly ground black pepper
2 pounds Russet potatoes, peeled and quartered
1½ pounds medium-size white onions, peeled and halved
4 medium carrots, peeled and cut into 1-inch pieces
1 small bunch Italian (flat leaf) parsley, for garnish

1 Preheat the oven to 200°F.

2 Brown the leg of lamb on all sides in a large flameproof casserole or Dutch oven over medium high heat, about 7 minutes. Place the garlic cloves on top of the lamb, and drizzle the olive oil over all. Season lightly with salt and pepper. Cover, transfer to the oven, and bake until the lamb is tender and has given up quite a bit of juice, and the garlic cloves are beginning to turn golden, 8 to 10 hours.

3 Increase the oven heat to 300°F. Add the potatoes, onions, and carrots to the lamb. Season with additional salt and pepper, cover, and continue baking until the vegetables are tender, the garlic cloves are golden, and the meat falls from the bone, an additional 4 hours.

4 To serve, mince the parsley and sprinkle it over the lamb, and bring the Dutch oven to the table. Or divide the lamb and

vegetables among eight shallow soup bowls, garnish each with parsley, and serve.

8 servings

Note: Mike recommends always using American lamb; it is more meaty and moist, and less sinewy, than New Zealand lamb. He also says the garlic cloves must not be inserted into the meat because this allows the juices to run out before the meat is cooked, causing it to dry out.

LEG OF LAMB WITH ROASTED ARTICHOKES

T ony Leonardini loves to eat artichokes as much as he loves to grow them, and when he does the cooking–which is often–chances are there'll be an artichoke somewhere in the meal. This recipe is one of his favorites, and it could accurately be called a Castroville regional dish. (For more about Tony and Castroville, see page 132.)

I love to make this for Easter dinner, when lamb and artichokes are at their tender best. It's simple and unusual, and it is almost guaranteed to make you an artichoke devotee. Because I'm an unabashed artichoke-a-holic, I use plenty in this dish–three pounds is about twenty-five. That has never seemed too many to me, but if it is for you, just reduce the amount. Be sure to trim the artichokes carefully, to reveal their tender interiors.

Some say artichokes bring out the tannic quality of wine, but I disagree and like to serve a delicate Washington State Merlot (Columbia Winery) or Shafer Hillside Select Cabernet Sauvignon with this.

1 leg of lamb (4 to 5 pounds), trimmed of
   excess fat
1 tablespoon olive oil
Coarsely ground fresh black pepper
1½ pounds new potatoes, scrubbed
4¼ cups water
1 tablespoon freshly squeezed lemon juice or
   white vinegar
2 to 3 pounds baby artichokes
Salt

1 Preheat the oven to 350°F.

2 Place the lamb on a rack in a roasting
pan, drizzle it with the olive oil, and
season generously with pepper. Roast the
lamb in the center of the oven until it is
golden and crisp, basting it with the cooking juices when it begins to give them up
after about 30 minutes, and every 30 minutes until it is done to your taste. Total
cooking time will be 1 hour for rare, 1 hour
and 15 to 25 minutes for medium.

3 Fifteen minutes before the lamb is
cooked, add the potatoes to the pan,
rolling them so they are covered with cooking juices.

4 While the lamb is roasting, prepare the
artichokes: Combine 4 cups of the
water and the lemon juice in a large bowl;
set it aside. Remove the tough outer leaves
of the artichokes by pulling them back and
letting them snap off naturally at the base.
Continue removing leaves until only the
tender pale yellow leaves of the center remain. Trim any prickly tops off the remaining leaves and any dark green off the stem.

Cut the artichokes in half lengthwise, and
immerse them immediately in the acidulated water.

5 When the lamb is cooked, transfer it to
a warmed serving platter. Cover it
loosely with aluminum foil to keep it·warm,
and let it sit for at least 20 minutes to allow
the juices to retreat back into the meat.

6 While the meat is resting, increase the
oven heat to 400°F. Remove the rack
from the roasting pan and add the artichokes. Roll them around so they are covered with cooking juices. Season with salt
and pepper, and continue cooking the potatoes and artichokes, turning them frequently so they brown evenly, until they are
golden and tender, 20 to 30 minutes.

7 Remove the vegetables from the oven
and transfer them to the serving platter,
arranging them around the lamb. Add the
remaining ¼ cup water to the roasting pan
and place it over medium-high heat. Stir the
cooking juices, scraping up any browned
bits from the bottom of the pan, and cook
just until they are mixed and slightly reduced, 2 to 3 minutes. Adjust the seasoning, and pour the sauce over
the lamb and vegetables or
serve it on the side.

6 to 8 servings

THE ARTICHOKE GROWER OF CASTROVILLE

Castroville, California, calls itself the artichoke capital of the world, and if you consider the world the United States, it's an accurate description. In the global scheme, France, Spain, and Italy grow most of the world's artichokes, but 90 percent of those consumed in the U.S. come from the misty beachside fields of Castroville, near the old whaling station of Moss Landing.

I met Tony Leonardini, whose family has been a major player in the Castroville artichoke industry for generations, at the Giant Artichoke, a restaurant on the outskirts of Castroville whose concrete namesake dwarfs the front door.

Tony farms 2,000 acres in Castroville and owns part of the Cara Mia cannery there, which processes artichoke hearts (really trimmed baby artichokes), artichoke bottoms marinated in soy oil, and blanched artichoke quarters. He started farming right out of high school, working and learning from his father who bought the family's first 65 acres during the Depression. "It might be more accurate to say my mother bought the land," Tony said. "She was a schoolteacher, and she was making the money."

At one time, 90 percent of the Leonardini land produced artichokes. Then, in the late seventies, artichoke prices plunged. "I took a beating in '79 and '81, and I said enough is enough." Tony diversified into iceberg lettuce, broccoli, and cauliflower, and opened a roadside fruit stand that he stocks with seasonal fruit and artichokes.

A few years after that Spain, a major producer of canned artichoke hearts, dumped thousands of cases on the market and prices plummeted again. "We're playing in an international market," Tony said. "And we're just a small part."

BREEDING ARTICHOKES

▪▪▪▪▪

One problem facing the industry is the artichoke plant itself. Though the plant produces nearly year round, the bulk of artichokes ripen in April and flood the market, bringing low prices to growers who often don't get as much as it costs to produce them. Much research has been done to develop an artichoke that would bear consistently throughout the year, but it has yet to be successful.

Part of the difficulty in breeding artichokes originates with its mysterious origins. Artichokes are thought to have come from North Africa, and cuttings were taken to Egypt and parts east more than 2,500 years ago. The plants eventually made their way to France, Spain, and Italy. It's not certain, however, that the artichoke of earlier times isn't really a cardoon, which is a relative of the plant we now know as the artichoke.

The cardoon has a wide, fleshy stem and a tiny bud. The prevailing thought is that years of cultivation and selection of the cardoon in monastery gardens resulted in the large budded artichoke. Originally they cultivated two types, the French artichoke, which was conical and spiny, and one that was round and appears to be the ancestor of the globe artichoke, (*Cynara scolymus*), which is grown commercially today.

Because of the mystery, researchers can't go back to a certain parentage for the plant, and every time a seed is selected and planted it throws off something wild and strange. "There is so much variability that we're just not sure we can develop seed that will give the consistency of size and flavor that we want," said Pat Hopper, director of marketing for the Artichoke Advisory Board in Castroville.

Growers are anxious for a source of artichoke seed because it would reduce their cost of production. Currently, the only way to propagate the globe artichoke is by cuttings, which is labor intensive. The root stock, which is about 6 inches thick, must be sliced in half by hand, then holes must be dug, and the severed portion replanted by hand.

The result of this frustrating lack of breeding success is further cutbacks in artichoke acreage. "Growing artichokes is expensive and the small farmers just can't make it when they're not getting what it costs to grow them," Tony said.

A FIELD OF SILVER

▪▪▪▪▪

What artichoke fields remain are strikingly lovely. Miles of the spiky silvery-green plants grow right to dunes, which separate them from the roiling Pacific surf. Mist boils up and over the dunes and creeps down into the fields, coddling the plants into what is impressive productivity.

Walking through the fields with Tony, who is tall and burly, we were dwarfed by the plants which tower an average height of

▶ ▶ ▶

nine feet, and a breadth of more than a yard. A tall, thick central stalk is crowned with a gorgeous, tight green globe that resembles a lamp on a post. Each plant, called a clump, has about 12 shoots, and the primary growth on those is a hefty artichoke. Secondary and even tertiary shoots produce increasingly smaller artichokes, the smallest of which are referred to as baby artichokes. "They aren't babies," Tony says. "They're fully mature but grown on a lower branch of the plant."

As we ambled through the fields Tony gave me some artichoke education. "Summer artichokes are open, while winter artichokes are tightly shut," he said. "All globe artichokes have tiny thorns on the ends of the leaves which are bigger and more prickly during summer, while in winter they're nearly imperceptible."

Sometimes, a winter artichoke has a brown scale on it from frost, which doesn't affect flavor or texture. "You don't eat the outside of the leaf or the tip, so it doesn't really matter if it's a little brown on the outside," Tony said.

What does matter is withering, blackening, or wrinkling on an artichoke, indications of age and a bitter, grassy flavor.

During the peak of the season, the artichokes are harvested about every seven days. The largest artichokes are sold to the fresh market, as are most of the smallest artichokes. But a large proportion of those in between are sold to processing plants and turned into marinated artichoke hearts, frozen artichoke quarters, or artichoke crowns, or bottoms.

By the end of May most of the plants are nearly spent, and they are cut down to the soil line to concentrate energy in the roots. "Artichokes are 90 percent plant, and we scrape over the root and dig the cuttings in around it so we don't have to fertilize much," Tony said. Four months later, the plant has sent up new shoots and is back in production.

Unlike his father, who left a plant in the ground for 25 years, Tony digs his up every five years and plants broccoli or fennel to give the field a rest. Though as he points out, growing artichokes takes little from the soil, and gives back much. Nonetheless, rotating crops cuts down on pests like rodents and gophers.

A group of artichoke growers put their heads together and came up with a plan to eradicate the destructive rodents by spreading poisoned culls–imperfect artichokes treated with poison—on the fields. "That worked," Tony said.

Tony isn't a fan of poisons, chemicals, or even synthetic fertilizers. The black, claylike adobe soil needs little nitrogen, and he prefers to use a minimum of chemicals for weed and pest control as well. "I want to be sure there is something left for the generation after me," he said.

PIPESTONE LAMB STEW

This recipe comes from Ann Olson, whose husband, Sherman, raises sheep—and the grains they eat—on their farm in Danvers, Minnesota. Anne makes a variety of lamb dishes throughout the year, and this is one of her favorites. ("Pipestone" is the name of a town in southern Minnesota, the home of a school where youngsters learn to raise sheep. This stew, which has evolved over the years, is made there.)

Horseradish is a curious seasoning for lamb, but it adds a pleasant bite, and the herbs give the dish a full, round flavor. There isn't anything much better, or more warming, for a winter night. Serve it with Feather Light Biscuits and Root Vegetable Salad with an Anchovy Vinaigrette (see Index) for a satisfying meal.

Lamb stew meat is often neck meat, which is some of the most flavorful on the animal. If you do use neck meat, consider removing the considerable amount of bone before serving the stew.

Try this with a St. Francis Merlot 1987.

2 bay leaves

Leaves from 1 large bunch fresh thyme sprigs (about 2 tablespoons), or 1 teaspoon dried

4 allspice berries

4 pounds lamb stew meat with bones, trimmed

2 medium onions, peeled, halved, and cut into ¼-inch-thick slices

6 large cloves garlic, peeled and coarsely chopped

1½ cups dry white wine

¼ cup prepared horseradish

¼ cup Worcestershire sauce

1 can (28 ounces) plum tomatoes

3 medium carrots, peeled and cut diagonally into ½-inch-thick slices

8 ounces button mushrooms, stems trimmed, caps coarsely chopped

3 large ribs celery, trimmed and cut diagonally into ½-inch-thick slices

2 medium waxy potatoes, peeled and quartered

2 medium Russet potatoes, peeled and cut into eighths

Salt and freshly ground black pepper

1 small bunch Italian (flat-leaf) parsley, for garnish (optional)

1 Tie the bay leaves, thyme, and allspice berries together in a piece of cheesecloth. Set it aside.

2 Brown the lamb on all sides in a large (at least 8-quart) heavy stockpot over medium-high heat, 8 to 10 minutes. Add the onions and garlic, and cook, stirring frequently, until the onions begin to turn translucent, 3 to 4 minutes.

3 Add the cheesecloth bundle, wine, horseradish, Worcestershire, and all the vegetables to the meat, crushing the tomatoes with your hands or a wooden spoon. Season generously with salt and pepper. Bring to a boil, then cover, reduce the heat to medium, and cook until the potatoes are tender and the lamb is falling from the bone, about 3 hours. (You can also transfer the stew to a preheated 350°F oven and cook it there for the same amount of time.)

4 Remove the cover and continue cooking the stew until it has thickened somewhat but is still soupy, an additional 1 to 1½ hours. Remove the cheesecloth bundle and season to taste, adding more horseradish if you like. Mince the parsley, and sprinkle over the stew. Serve immediately.

8 to 10 servings

Note: This is a good dish to prepare a day ahead. Remove the cheesecloth bundle and refrigerate the stew overnight. The next day, skim any fat that has solidified on the surface, and reheat the stew. Season to taste, adding more horseradish if you like. Garnish with the parsley, and serve.

FOWL AND FISH

POULTRY IN EVERY POT, AND A SMALL KETTLE OF FISH

Poultry is a mainstay on the farm table, and not surprisingly, chickens are the favorite. In large part this is because they are easy to raise. You can be sure when there's a barnyard full of animals, a few chickens scratching around fit right in. They add their clucks to the farm cacophony, their meat to the big hearty meals. Turkeys aren't amiss, either, and I saw plenty of them on farms, strutting around, their wattles wiggling as they walked.

During my travels, I gained much appreciation for the flavor of "real" poultry found in chickens, ducks, turkeys, and geese that had the freedom to run around, were given good feed, and had room to settle in a barn when they liked. Their flavor is true and robust, their texture more satisfying than any I've found in mass-produced birds.

Start your dishes off right, and if possible, buy poultry from a nearby farmer or farmer's market. But the quality of the meat is only part of the secret. Much has to do with the way it is prepared, the little tricks that bring out flavor. Take the Extra Crisp Fried Chicken in this chapter, for instance. Letting the chicken sit after it's dredged in flour–a tip I picked up in the South–makes all the difference between a good dish and a great one.

The Lemony Herbed Chicken Wings, too, might be ordinary if they weren't marinated for so many hours. And there is no doubt that the roasted Wild Turkey is so succulent because of continual basting, and cooking right to the point of doneness and no longer.

It may seem odd to find fish in a book about farming. But it isn't. Fish farming is rapidly becoming a very large and economically important part of agriculture. Fish are planted, harvested, and processed just like any other crop, the result being a continuous and abundant supply. Trout and catfish are two of the most popular farmed fish, and there are recipes in this chapter for both.

ROAST GINGER CHICKEN WITH POTATOES AND ONIONS

Pennsylvania Dutch farmers, most of whom are Amish, prepare myriad chicken dishes, and this is based on one of them. I admire the way the Amish use herbs and spices in unusual, intriguing ways, and here ginger–a popular, early American spice that is an Amish favorite–adds a gentle spark of heat and sweetness to the chicken.

Try a full-bodied Alsatian Gewürztraminer, such as Zind-Humbrecht 1987, with this chicken.

1 chicken (3 to 4 pounds), with giblets
Salt and freshly ground black pepper
1 tablespoon unsalted butter, at room temperature
1 tablespoon minced fresh ginger, or 1 teaspoon dried
½ teaspoon salt
¼ teaspoon freshly ground black pepper
1½ pounds waxy potatoes (about 10), each potato cut into 8 wedges
6 large pearl onions (about 8 ounces total), peeled
3 tablespoons water

1 Preheat the oven to 400°F.

2 Rinse the chicken well inside and out until the water runs clear. Pat it thoroughly dry. Sprinkle the cavity with salt and pepper.

3 In a small bowl mix together the butter, ginger, ½ teaspoon salt, and ¼ teaspoon pepper.

4 Carefully separate the skin from the breast meat and legs of the chicken by running your fingers between the skin and the meat. Using a paper towel, gently pat the meat dry. Spread the butter mixture under the skin of the breast and the legs.

5 Place the chicken in a roasting pan, and roast for 15 minutes. Turn the chicken on its side, basting it if there are any juices, and roast for 10 minutes. Turn it on its other side, baste it, and roast it for an additional 10 minutes.

6 Arrange the potatoes and the onions around the chicken, turning them as best you can so they are covered with cooking juices. Roast the chicken, breast side up, for an additional 20 minutes, until it is golden, the legs move freely in their sockets, and the juices run clear when you hold the chicken up to drain.

7 Transfer the chicken to a warmed platter and let it sit for 15 minutes, propped up slightly at the neck end to allow the juices to retreat back into the meat. Add the giblets to the pan and stir so they are coated with cooking juices. Continue roasting the vegetables, basting and turning them frequently, until the potatoes are golden and crisp and the giblets are cooked through, about 15 minutes.

8 Transfer the vegetables to the platter holding the chicken. Drain all but about 3 tablespoons of the fat from the roasting pan. Add the water, and place it over medium-high heat. Stir the liquid, scraping up any browned bits from the bottom of the pan. Continue cooking until the sauce has reduced and thickened somewhat, 1 to 2 minutes. Season to taste, and pour over the chicken and vegetables. Serve immediately.

4 to 6 servings

Note: If you don't want to carve the chicken at the table, cut it into serving pieces after letting it rest, and pour any juices into the roasting pan. Arrange the chicken pieces on the warmed platter, surrounded by the vegetables. Deglaze the pan and reduce the juices, then pour them over all. Serve immediately.

ROAST CHICKEN WITH TARRAGON

This simple yet elegant recipe was inspired by a visit to the Herbfarm outside Seattle. It serves equally well as the basis for an informal family meal or one for very special guests. The chicken is easy to prepare, and it emerges infused with flavor from the herbs tucked under the skin and the garlicky croutons inside. Be sure to buy the best-quality chicken you can find, and remove as much of the fat from the tail and neck areas as possible.

Try a rich, perfumed Fleurie, such as a Georges Duboeuf 1988 or 1989, with this.

1 chicken (3 to 4 pounds), with giblets
Salt and freshly ground black pepper
6 ounces day-old French bread, cut into
    1½ x 1½ x ½-inch pieces
1 clove garlic, peeled
4 sprigs fresh tarragon
1 cup fresh tarragon leaves
2 tablespoons unsalted butter
2 tablespoons olive oil

1 Preheat the oven to 400°F.

2 Rinse the chicken well inside and out until the water runs clear. Pat it thoroughly dry. Sprinkle the cavity with salt and pepper.

3 Rub the bread on all sides with the garlic, and place two of these croutons, with the tarragon sprigs, inside the chicken.

4 Carefully separate the skin from the breast meat of the chicken by running your fingers between the skin and the meat. Rub the meat with salt and pepper, and place ½ cup of the tarragon leaves under the skin, spreading them out so they cover the entire breast.

5 Heat the butter and olive oil in a roasting pan over medium-high heat. Add the chicken, and brown it well on all sides,

POULTRY PREPARATION TIP

*P*oultry can harbor bacteria, so when preparing it, be sure to clean all surfaces and utensils with a mild solution of bleach and water after you've used them.

about 8 minutes. Set the chicken breast side up, transfer the pan to the oven, and roast for 30 minutes.

6 Add the remaining croutons, the neck, and the giblets to the pan, and continue roasting the chicken until it is evenly golden all over and the juices run clear, 12 to 15 minutes. Turn the croutons occasionally so they brown evenly.

7 Remove the chicken, croutons, and giblets from the roasting pan, and transfer them to a platter. Cover loosely with foil and keep warm in a low (200°F) oven.

8 Place the roasting pan, with the cooking juices in it, over medium-high heat. When the juices are hot and bubbling, scrape the browned bits from the bottom of the pan, add the remaining ½ cup tarragon

leaves, and cook just until they are wilted, about 1 minute. (You need just enough cooking juices to wilt the tarragon. If there is no juice at all—which can happen—add ¼ cup dry white wine to the roasting pan, bring it to a simmer, and deglaze the pan. Add the tarragon, and cook until wilted.) Taste for seasoning.

9 To serve, cut the chicken into serving pieces and arrange them, with the croutons and the giblets, on a warmed serving platter. Pour the sauce over the chicken, and serve immediately.

4 servings

EXTRA CRISP FRIED CHICKEN

W hile visiting farms around the country, we tasted many kinds of fried chicken, each completely different from the other and each delicious in its own way. I couldn't choose a favorite, so instead I came up with my own recipe, which is a combination of those we sampled. It is light and crisp, and the delicately spiced flour highlights the flavor of the chicken.

The spices may sound unconventional, but they are actually quite traditional, particularly in the South. You can vary or expand upon them, as I sometimes do. Now and then I rub the chicken all over with minced garlic, which adds a vibrant layer of flavor, and occasionally I rub it with Tabasco sauce, when I know a spicy foods fan is coming for dinner.

The trick to keeping the flour on the chicken is letting it sit, so don't stint on the time. Otherwise, all the spice will be left in the pan and your chicken won't have its luscious crisp crunch.

I urge you to make this dish often—in summer for a picnic, and in winter to evoke the picnics of summer. It's good, it's quick, and it won't spread grease all over your kitchen or leave you with a heavy, full feeling. In fact, when the fat is at the right temperature—so drops of water sizzle in it—the chicken will emerge crisp and light. Drain it on a brown paper bag (rather than paper towel, which tends to steam the chicken), place it on a warmed platter, and roll up your sleeves for a great finger-licking meal.

For dinner, serve salad and spring vegetables, cornbread or muffins, and a good-quality, lightly chilled ale. I also like to serve Amish Tomato Ketchup or Tomato Horseradish Sauce (see Index) alongside.

1 large chicken (4 pounds), cut into pieces
1 cup all purpose flour
½ cup whole-wheat flour
1 tablespoon salt, or to taste
½ teaspoon cayenne pepper
1 teaspoon freshly grated nutmeg
1 teaspoon ground ginger
¼ cup peanut oil
1 bunch parsley, rinsed and patted dry, for garnish

1 Rinse the chicken well and pat it thoroughly dry.

2 Sift the flours and the spices together into a small paper bag, so they are well mixed. Drop the chicken, two or three pieces at a time, into the bag, hold the bag closed, and shake it so the chicken is thoroughly covered. Transfer the chicken to a

CHICKEN FOR BREAKFAST? WHY NOT?

In many areas, particularly the South, fried chicken is served as often at breakfast as it is at lunch or dinner. Now and then an unconventional breakfast— or brunch—is a treat, so you might think about this for your next early to midday event. Serve Corn Pancakes and Cream Biscuits (see Index) alongside, and plenty of good strong coffee.

wire cake rack and let it sit, refrigerated, for 2 hours, so the flour will adhere. Reserve the remaining flour mixture.

3 Heat the oil in a large skillet over medium-high heat. Dredge the chicken once more in the flour mixture, shaking off the excess.

4 When the oil is hot but not smoking, and a drop of water sprinkled into the pan sizzles, add the chicken, making sure you do not crowd the pan. Cover, and cook until the chicken begins to turn brown, about 8 minutes, reducing the heat slightly if necessary. Turn the chicken, cover, and continue cooking until it is cooked through and the juices from the thigh run clear when pricked with a fork, an additional 10 minutes.

5 Arrange the chicken on a brown paper bag to drain, and leave it for about 5 minutes. Then transfer the chicken to a warmed serving platter, garnish with the parsley, and serve immediately.

4 servings

LEMONY HERBED CHICKEN WINGS

I f you're a chicken wing fan like me, you will love these tart, tender, meaty little morsels. They marinate slowly in a small lake of lemon juice, olive oil, rosemary, and coarsely ground black pepper, then bake in a hot oven to a crispy turn. I love their lemon and rosemary-infused flavor, so I often let them marinate for a day or more.

These are great picnic fare, served along with Marinated Vegetable Salad, Tomato Salad, Country Potato Salad (see Index) and crusty bread or rolls.

Try this with a crisp Vouvray Sec 1988.

4 pounds chicken wings (about 24 pieces)
½ cup freshly squeezed lemon juice (3 large lemons)
½ cup olive oil
⅓ cup fresh rosemary, minced, or 3 teaspoons dried rosemary, crumbled
4 large cloves garlic, peeled and minced
Salt and coarsely ground fresh black pepper

1 Rinse the chicken wings well and pat them thoroughly dry. Tuck the end of each wing under the tiny drumstick, so they keep their shape.

2 In a medium-size bowl, mix together the lemon juice, olive oil, rosemary, garlic, and salt and pepper to taste. Arrange the chicken wings in one or two nonreactive ovenproof dishes, so they aren't crowded. Pour the marinade over them. Turn the wings to coat them with the marinade, cover the dishes, and refrigerate overnight or for at least 8 hours. If possible, turn the wings once or twice as they marinate.

3 Preheat the oven to 400°F.

4 Bake the chicken wings in the marinade, uncovered, until they are golden and crisp, turning them once, 30 minutes.

Remove them from the oven and let them cool. Serve at room temperature or slightly chilled.

4 to 6 servings

BECKY CAMPBELL'S CHICKEN WITH CARAMBOLA

This dish is adapted from one that Becky Campbell (see box, next page) makes often during carambola season. It has become a favorite with the family, not only because of its lively flavor, but also for the stars that dance around in the sauce.

When you buy carambola, also called star fruit, look for ones that are uniformly yellow to orange and have a subtle perfume. If they are green, they aren't ripe and won't yield a great deal of flavor. At their ripest, their flavor is unmistakably tropical, a beguiling combination of apple, banana, and lychee.

This can be prepared up to 2 days in advance. Try a semi-dry German Kabinett, such as Deirhard 1989, and either a green salad or the Pineapple Salad (see Index).

1 chicken (3½ to 4 pounds), cut into pieces
¼ cup olive oil
¼ cup freshly squeezed lime juice
Zest of 2 limes, minced
2 small onions, peeled and thinly sliced
2 tablespoons mild honey
1 tablespoon minced fresh ginger
1 fresh serrano or jalapeño pepper, with seeds, minced
4 carambola (4 ounces each), cut into ¼-inch-thick slices
Salt
½ cup whole raw almonds
1 small bunch cilantro, for garnish (optional)

1 Rinse the chicken well and pat it thoroughly dry.

2 In a large bowl, whisk together the olive oil, lime juice, lime zest, onions, honey, ginger, and minced pepper. Stir in three-fourths of the carambola slices. Then add the chicken, and turn it until it is coated with the marinade. Cover and refrigerate overnight, or up to 2 days, turning the chicken occasionally so it marinates evenly.

3 Preheat the oven to 375°F.

4 Arrange the chicken in a single layer in a 9 x 13-inch baking dish, and season generously with salt. Add the almonds to the marinade, stir, and spoon it over the chicken. Bake in the center of the oven, basting frequently with the pan juices and turning any chicken pieces that get too brown, about 35 minutes. Add the remaining carambola, stir, and continue cooking until the chicken is golden and a thigh yields clear juice when pricked at its thickest part, 15 to 20 minutes.

5 Taste the sauce and adjust the seasoning. Just before serving, mince the cilantro if you are using it. Serve the chicken right from the baking dish, or divide it among four warmed dinner plates. Spoon the sauce over the chicken, garnish with the cilantro, and serve.

4 servings

STAR FRUIT QUEEN

■ ■ ■ ■ ■

*B*ecky Campbell became a tropical fruit aficionado through the career of her husband, Carl, who is an internationally known tropical fruit expert. He researched and taught at the University of Florida, where he is now professor emeritus. She became an expert on cooking with tropical fruits, and lectured and taught cooking classes for years. Together they developed a small tropical fruit orchard in the backyard of their home near Homestead, Florida.

Becky refers to the tropical fruit orchard that surrounds their single-story home as a "mini experiment station." Her husband does the experimenting, and she brings the bounty into the kitchen. Their orchard produces everything from Key limes and carambola to black sapote and mangoes.

Becky and Carl were recently in Uganda, where carambola is as common as green grapes are here. There she picked up valuable tips for using the lovely star-shaped fruit, and she set out samples for us to taste: golden star-shaped slices of dried carambola, carambola leather, and carambola preserves, where the stars were suspended in a thick sweet syrup. They were all delicious. "You know, I'd like to market all this," she said, her eyes lighting up. Then she gave herself a little shake. "I've already got too much to do. Let me rephrase that. I'd like someone else to market all this."

DO-SI-DO AND PROMENADE HOME

"**P**ut your hoe down, buddy. Let's go to a dance," they said on the farm when the work week was over. Hoes went down, and everyone for miles around gathered at the local grange, general store, or barn to allemande left and right.

It might have been a barn raising, a sheep shearing, or a simple family celebration that brought out the fiddler and his tunes. He'd stand on a box, feet tapping and voice popping as he led dancers on, both music maker and master of ceremonies. Sometimes he'd set down his fiddle, jump down on the floor, and grab a partner himself to teach a new dance.

Easy and raucous, hoedowns gave farmers and their families an excuse to see their neighbors and have a rousing good time. They would come for miles and bring a covered dish or two to a huge, hearty supper. When the meal was done they'd pull back the chairs and kick their heels up high.

Casual and energetic, square dancing was the lingua franca of the hoedown, and the two have become synonymous. No one had to learn the steps because the caller provided instruction, so everyone, from grandmothers to little children, joined in. The calls were often improvised, and the liveliness of the dance depended on the quick tongue and music of the fiddler.

Dancing at the hoedown, usually done in lines, sometimes in couples, followed the tradition of European contra dancing. When it was adopted by urban folk and taken back to the city, it became more ritualized, and a highly specific form of dancing called western square dancing developed.

Hoedowns are still a big part of farm life, particularly in the East and Midwest. A farmer still puts down his hoe—today that means parking the air-conditioned tractor in the barn—puts on his Sunday duds, and gets to town. There is nothing quite like the easy fun of swinging round and round, do-si-doing, and the "Grab your honeys and don't let 'em fall, shake your boots and balance all" of a real farm hoedown.

CHICKEN POT PIE WITH THYME CRUST

Chicken pot pie evokes memories of a warm, cozy kitchen filled with happy times and the aromas of hearty meals. It's a dish to treasure because it satisfies on so many levels.

First there is the toasty fragrance of the pastry as it bakes. Then there are the clean herbal aromas that waft throughout the house as the sauce cooks. When the pie is drawn from the oven, it satisfies the eye with its golden crust. Finally, as it's cut, a furl of steam dances out, laden with all the warm, full flavor inside.

All of this is only a prelude to that first bite of flaky pastry and the tender chunks of meat inside.

Make this dish on a cold, blustery day, and it will warm you from the inside out. Serve a Root Vegetable Salad (see Index) or a tossed green salad alongside, along with a glass of Ravenswood Merlot.

1 recipe Thyme Pastry Crust (recipe follows)
1 cup Herbfarm Deluxe Chicken Stock (page 86) or good-quality canned broth
1 bay leaf
6 black peppercorns
3 tablespoons unsalted butter
1 tablespoon all-purpose flour
¼ cup heavy (whipping) cream
Salt and freshly ground black pepper
Pinch of freshly grated nutmeg
6 cups water
4 ounces new potatoes, scrubbed
1 medium onion, peeled and diced
2 ribs celery, trimmed and diced
1 clove garlic, peeled and minced
4 cups cubed cooked chicken
½ cup fresh or frozen (not thawed) green peas
2 hard-cooked eggs, thinly sliced
1 egg mixed with 1 teaspoon water

1 Preheat the oven to 375°F.

2 On a lightly floured surface, roll out half the pastry dough into an 11-inch circle and line a 10-inch removable-bottom tart

pan or a 9-inch pie plate with it. Trim and attractively crimp the edge. Cover the pie crust with a layer of parchment paper, then fill it to the rim with dry beans or pastry weights. Bake until the crust begins to turn golden around the edges, about 15 minutes. Remove the weights and paper, and continue baking until the bottom of the crust is set and light golden, 5 to 10 minutes. Remove the crust from the oven and let it cool. Leave the oven on.

3 Combine the chicken stock, bay leaf, and peppercorns in a small saucepan, and bring to a boil over high heat. Remove the pan from the heat, cover, and set it aside to infuse for 5 minutes.

4 Melt 1 tablespoon of the butter in a small saucepan over medium-high heat. Whisk in the flour, and cook until the mixture bubbles. Continue cooking, whisking constantly, for another 2 minutes. Strain the hot chicken stock into the mixture, whisking constantly, and cook until it has thickened, 3 minutes. Whisk in the cream, and season to taste with plenty of salt and pepper and a touch of nutmeg. Remove the white sauce from the heat, and set aside.

5 Bring the water to a boil in the bottom of a vegetable steamer. Place the potatoes in the steamer basket, cover, and steam until the potatoes are tender, about 15 minutes. Remove the basket from the heat. When the potatoes are cool enough to handle, thinly slice them.

6 Melt the remaining 2 tablespoons butter in a large saucepan, and add the onion.

Cook over medium-high heat until it begins to turn translucent, about 5 minutes. Add the celery and garlic, and cook just until the celery begins to soften, 2 to 3 minutes. Add the chicken, and cook just until it is warm through, about 3 minutes. Stir in the peas, and remove from the heat.

7 On a lightly floured surface, roll out the remaining pastry dough into a 12-inch circle. Add the white sauce to the vegetable and chicken mixture. Adjust the seasoning.

8 Line the baked pastry shell with the sliced potatoes. Top with the vegetable and chicken mixture, then the sliced eggs. Brush the edge of the pastry with some of the egg wash. Fit the top crust over the mixture, and press the edges gently but firmly onto the edges of the bottom crust to seal them. Crimp the edge attractively.

9 Cut several holes in the top crust to allow steam to escape. Brush the crust with the remaining egg wash, and place the pie in the bottom third of the oven. Bake until the pastry is golden, about 30 minutes.

10 Remove the pie from the oven and let it sit for 10 minutes before serving.

6 servings

THYME PASTRY CRUST

■■■■■■■

This pastry is meant for the chicken pot pie, but you may think of other things to do with it. I sometimes roll it out to about ¼ inch thickness, cut it into shapes, and bake it to serve as crackers.

2 cups all-purpose flour
¼ teaspoon salt
4 teaspoons fresh thyme leaves, or
*   1 teaspoon dried*
⅔ cup unsalted butter, chilled, cut into
*   small pieces*
⅔ cup lard, chilled, cut into small
*   pieces*
⅓ to ½ cup ice water

1 Place the flour, salt, and thyme in a food processor, and pulse once, just to mix them together.

2 Add the butter and the lard, and process with short pulses until the shortening ranges in size from peas to coarse cornmeal.

3 Slowly pour in the cold water, and pulse to incorporate it into the flour mixture. (Add just enough water so the mixture is moist enough to hold together if you press it with your fingers; but don't process it to the point that it forms a ball, or it will be tough.)

4 Divide the pastry in half and press each half gently to form a flattened ball. Wrap the balls separately in waxed paper, and chill for at least 1 hour.

Makes two 10-inch pie crusts

ARKANSAS BARBECUE

When I visited the Carpenters' farm in Grady, Arkansas, they were serving a huge barbecue lunch to the crew of twenty-five, and we were asked to join them. Our plates were laden with chicken, pork, and thick slabs of baloney. There were baked beans and potato salad, fruit salad, cake, and ice cream. It was a festive meal enjoyed in great company.

After we'd eaten lunch I got some barbecue tips from Katie and her daughter Bobbie Clark. Later I got some more ideas from quite another source, Jimmy Lee Edwards. I've used them all here.

Try this on a fall or winter evening to bring back the flavor of summer with Bass ale or a chilled Beaujolais-Villages 1989.

1 chicken (3½ to 4 pounds), cut into pieces
1½ pounds pork spareribs or
    country-style ribs
¼ cup olive oil
1 teaspoon dried savory
1 large handful fresh oregano
    leaves, or 1 teaspoon dried
1 large handful fresh thyme
    leaves, or ½ teaspoon dried
3 cloves garlic, peeled and
    minced
½ teaspoon salt
Freshly ground black pepper to taste
1 cup Jimmy Lee Edwards's Barbecue
    Sauce (page 313)

1 The night before you plan to cook the barbecue, marinate the chicken and pork: Rinse the chicken and pork well and pat thoroughly dry. Mix the olive oil, herbs, garlic, salt, and pepper together in a small bowl. Place the chicken and the pork in a nonreactive dish, and pour the marinade over the meat. Turn the meat several times so it is coated with the marinade, cover, and refrigerate for at least 8 hours. (You can marinate the meat for as long as 2 days.) Turn it occasionally so it marinates evenly.

2 Prepare a good-size fire in a barbecue, or preheat the broiler.

3 When the coals are glowing red and dusted with ash, spread them out in an even layer. Lightly oil the grill and place it about 3 inches from the coals. Place the chicken and the pork on the grill, letting the excess marinade drip off before you do so.

If you plan to broil the chicken, line the broiler pan with aluminum foil, place the chicken on it and set it about 3 inches from the heat.

4 Grill or broil the meat, turning it frequently so it doesn't burn and brushing it occasionally with the marinade, for about 30 minutes.

5 Brush a thick layer of barbecue sauce over the meat. (Some of it will drip off into the coals, but don't use so much sauce that great globs run off and into the grill to burn, or it will give a burned taste to the meat.) Turn the meat after about 5 minutes, and brush it on the other side with the barbecue sauce. Continue cooking it this way until the chicken and ribs are done, about 15 minutes more, turning and brushing them repeatedly with the barbecue sauce. To test for doneness, pierce a chicken drumstick at the thickest point with a sharp knife; the juices should run clear (the ribs will be done at this point, too).

6 Transfer the ribs and chicken to a warmed serving platter, and serve immediately.

6 servings

MARY NAVARETTE'S GARLICKY ENCHILADAS

For this recipe I thank Mary Navarette, of the Christopher Ranch in Gilroy, California, the largest garlic farm in what is referred to as the garlic capital of the world.

After a day touring the ranch, owner Donald Christopher introduced me to Mary, who among her other duties cooks lunch once a week for the Christopher Ranch employees. She has a repertoire of favorites that range from roast turkey with all the fixings to her family's enchilada recipe, which the employees regularly beg for.

For the enchiladas, Mary makes everything from scratch, from the tomato sauce to the tortillas—which are so light and tender that it's hard to resist eating them before putting the dish together. She is rightfully proud of them, and when I told her I'd never made tortillas before, she took me by the hand and led me right into the company kitchen for an impromptu cooking lesson.

Within minutes we, the kitchen, my husband, and one of the babies Mary was caring for were dusted with flour. As she rocked the baby back and forth,

she guided me through the recipe, with the satisfying result of a stack of hot tortillas. She handed the baby to its mother, who was drawn in by the aroma of baking tortillas, and began spreading them with butter and handing them out to several other employees who followed. The rest she wrapped in a package and sent with us, to nibble on in the car.

If you have leftover chicken cooking liquid, save it for soup. It is full of good, rich flavors.

A lightly chilled ale or amber beer is the natural choice with Mary's enchiladas.

FOR THE CHICKEN

1 chicken (3 to 4 pounds)
1 whole head garlic, unpeeled
1 tablespoon salt
2 cups pitted black olives, drained
  and coarsely chopped

FOR THE SAUCE

6 medium tomatoes (about 2½ pounds)
6 serrano or 3 jalapeño peppers,
  with seeds, stemmed
1 tablespoon mild vegetable oil, such as
  safflower
1 medium onion, peeled and diced
4 cloves garlic, peeled and minced
2 tablespoons distilled white vinegar
1 cup gently packed fresh cilantro
  leaves

FOR FINISHING

8 Homemade Flour Tortillas
  (recipe follows)
1 pound mild Cheddar cheese, grated
½ cup cilantro leaves, for garnish
  (optional)

1 Preheat the broiler.

2 Rinse the chicken well inside and out. Place the chicken and the head of garlic in a large heavy stockpot. Cover with water, add the salt, and bring to a boil Continue boiling until the chicken is cooked through, about 30 to 45 minutes. Drain the chicken, reserving the garlic and the cooking liquid. When the chicken is cool enough to handle, remove and discard the skin. Remove the meat from the bones, and shred it by hand into a medium-size bowl. Squeeze the soft cooked garlic out of each clove into the bowl. Add the chopped olives, mix well, and set aside.

3 While the chicken is cooking, cook the tomatoes and peppers for the sauce: Arrange the tomatoes and the peppers on a piece of aluminum foil, and place it under the broiler, about 3 inches from the heat. Broil, turning the tomatoes and peppers frequently. When the pepper skins are evenly dark brown and bubbled, which should take about 20 minutes, remove them from the broiler. Wrap them in a paper towel to steam. Continue broiling the tomatoes until their skins are evenly black, which will take a total of 45 minutes to 1 hour, turning them frequently so they broil evenly. Allow them to cool uncovered.

4 When the peppers and tomatoes are cool enough to handle, remove the skin. (You may not be able to remove all of the skin from the tomatoes; just peel off as much as possible and don't worry about what remains.)

5 Preheat the oven to 350°F.

6 Purée the tomatoes and the peppers together in a food processor.

7 Heat the oil in a large heavy skillet over medium-high heat. Add the onion and sauté until it begins to turn translucent but is still somewhat crisp, 5 to 8 minutes. Reduce the heat to medium-low, and stir in the garlic; then stir in the puréed tomatoes and peppers. Add the vinegar, taste for seasoning, and cook until the sauce is hot through and slightly thickened, about 5 minutes. Stir in about ½ cup of the reserved chicken cooking liquid and remove from the heat.

8 Mince the cilantro and add it to the sauce.

9 To assemble the enchiladas, take a tortilla and dip it into the tomato sauce. (If the tomato sauce is too thick, add a little more chicken cooking liquid to thin it out.

It shouldn't be very watery, but it should be liquid enough to dip the tortilla into it.) Place one-eighth of the chicken mixture in the center of the tortilla, then top with a handful of cheese. Roll the tortilla up and place it, seam side down, in an 8½ x 14-inch baking dish. Repeat with the remaining seven tortillas and filling. If all the tortillas don't fit in the dish, use a smaller one to hold the excess.

10 Pour the remaining sauce over the enchiladas, top with the remaining cheese, and cover the dish with aluminum foil. Bake until the cheese has melted and the enchiladas are hot through, about 30 minutes. Remove from the oven and let cool for 5 minutes before serving. Serve garnished with the cilantro, if desired.

8 servings

HOMEMADE FLOUR TORTILLAS

■ ■ ■ ■ ■ ■ ■

This recipe yields 16 flour tortillas. Since you use only 8 in the enchiladas, you can serve the rest on the side. Warm them in a medium (350°F) oven, wrapped tightly in aluminum foil, before serving.

3½ cups unbleached all-purpose flour
1½ teaspoons baking powder
1 teaspoon salt
⅓ cup lard
1 cup plus 1 tablespoon water

1 Combine the flour, baking powder, and salt in a large bowl. Rub in the lard, using your fingertips, until it is well blended and the mixture is somewhat grainy. Add the water gradually, stirring constantly until the mixture cleans the sides of the bowl and forms a ball. Turn the dough out onto a lightly floured surface, and knead until it is elastic and quite smooth, about 5 minutes. The dough will not look like bread dough, because its surface may be somewhat lumpy, but it should be elastic and well mixed. Divide the dough into 16 equal pieces, and shape each one into a smooth ball. Cover with a damp towel and let rest for 15 minutes.

To make the dough in a food processor, combine and process the dry ingredients. Then add the lard and process until it is blended and the mixture is grainy. Add the water, and process until the dough forms a ball in the work bowl. Remove the dough from the work bowl, knead it a few times until it is smooth, and proceed.

2 On a lightly floured surface, flatten out one ball of dough to form a flat round. Roll it out from the center to the edge, turning it a quarter turn each time, until it is thin, even, and 7 to 8 inches in diameter. You may need to pat the tortilla back and forth between your hands to get it to reach the desired size. Dust the excess flour off the tortilla with a pastry brush, and place it between sheets of waxed paper to prevent its drying out. Repeat with the remaining balls of dough.

3 Heat a dry cast-iron skillet over medium-high heat. When it is hot (drops of water dance off the surface), cook a tortilla just until golden brown spots form on the underside, the tortilla looks cooked, and bubbles form, 30 to 40 seconds (press the bubbles down as the tortilla cooks). Flip the tortilla over, and cook it on the other side just long enough to cook it through, about 10 seconds. Transfer the tortilla to a wire cake rack, and cover it with a dry towel to keep it from drying out. Repeat with the other tortillas, and stack them as they cook, making sure to keep them covered. They will stick together somewhat but can easily be separated.

4 If you are making the tortillas in advance, allow them to cool, then wrap them in aluminum foil, and refrigerate until ready to use, but no longer than 24 hours. These freeze well tightly wrapped in freezer paper, and will keep for at least 2 months.

16 tortillas

THE CHRISTOPHER RANCH

Don Christopher, owner of the country's largest garlic farm, loves to get out in his fields, yank a plant out of the ground, and check the growing bulb for skins. "We want four layers of skin on the outside of the garlic cloves, so that we can peel them down to two," he says, waving a big head of garlic around on its green stem so a faint aroma wafts through the air. "We know we're done irrigating when it's got the number of skins we want." The outer skins may be discolored or blemished, but that doesn't matter because they are peeled off to reveal the pure white skins underneath. And garlic with pure white skins is what the consumer wants.

To call Don flamboyant may be overstating the case somewhat, but he is a successful promoter, and there's nothing he loves to promote more than garlic. He's been raising garlic in Gilroy, California, the acknowledged American garlic capital, since 1955. When he moved there, he did what he says he always does: "I looked at what everyone else was doing, and I copied them."

He planted 10 acres of garlic then, along with his major crop, which was strawberries.

The strawberries are long gone, and garlic has become the flagship of the Christopher Ranch. But he also grows bell peppers, sweet corn, broccoli, and basil. He's even planted a field of ginger.

Though garlic has always done well in Gilroy, Don thought it could do better and wanted to promote it more. So 10 years ago he was instrumental in forming the Fresh Garlic Association, which started the Gilroy Garlic Festival, now a landmark annual event complete with garlic dishes, garlic charms, garlic topping and braiding contests, and a garlic queen.

Whether or not it's a result of the garlic festival, the Christopher Ranch has increased

its acreage and production 15 percent each year since the festival started and now includes 1,500 acres of garlic. Forty percent of those are in Gilroy, and the rest are in the San Joaquin Valley, which Don thinks is even more ideal than Gilroy because it's dry, and garlic likes dryness.

FRENCH VS. ITALIAN

Two varieties of garlic are grown at the Christopher Ranch. There's early French, which is mild, and late Italian, which is more pungent. Fall is garlic planting time, and 45 acres are planted a day. The cloves are put in the ground seven to a foot, and they yield about a dozen to one—that is, one clove of garlic gives a head that is made up of a dozen cloves.

Early garlic is ready to harvest in June, and it's the bulk of the crop—about 16 million pounds. It's also the premium variety, with big heads, big cloves, and a good shelf life.

When the garlic plants look dead, they're ready to harvest. "This field," Don says, sweeping his hand in the direction of the neat rows of tall, green, onionlike stems, "will look like a hayfield when it's ready to harvest. The tops dry down, and that's exactly what we want."

A sled equipped with a steel blade goes through the fields and digs up and shakes the garlic. A crisp layer of skins is left on the soil and dug back under for compost.

FROM FATHER TO SON TO SON

Don is the latest in a succession of Christopher family farmers. His grandparents came to San Jose, California, from Denmark and started with hay and prunes; then the family moved to Gilroy to expand. Don managed the farm until his son, Bill, took over, and they have hired Steve Moss as field manager.

Steve is an innovative young farmer, and he started the farm's drip irrigation system about 4 years ago. It's the latest in irrigation technology, an underground system of rubber tape that drips water into the soil when it's needed. At $300 an acre to lay the tape, it's not cheap, and Steve is installing it a bit at a time. It's proving efficient, however, and it's an overall money- and water-conservation measure because there's no evaporation or wind blowing the water away.

Garlic needs a lot of nitrogen to thrive, and it is dripped into the soil right along with the water. "Before we started the drip irrigation, we were just like the neighbors. Now we're a little bit better again, and that's where you have to be," Don says.

Don moves, talks, and walks a beat faster than most people, and is always willing to try

▶ ▶ ▶

something new. He enjoys risk, but he also understands the market and has an unerring sense of how to make a profit. Nonetheless, farming sometimes baffles him. "I'll tell you, here we thought we were farming and we knew what we were doing, and now the whole thing has changed," he says, referring to changes in agriculture, the public's awakened interest in what goes on and into their food, and impending drought in California. "We're supposed to use fewer pesticides, and there's a lot less water."

He adapts with drip irrigation, and by planting 15 acres of organic garlic. He also dreams up projects like developing a line of products, made in the processing plant he started in 1964. They include bottled

pesto, peeled garlic cloves, mashed garlic, and a host of other products under the colorful Christopher Ranch label. Along with garlic braids and little plastic-wrapped packages of garlic heads, these have proved enormously successful.

GARLIC IN, GARLIC OUT

∎∎∎∎∎

Eighty million pounds of garlic are produced in the U.S. each year, and about one third of it is processed by the Christopher Ranch, though not all of it is grown there. "We have growers all over, including Mexico, which allows us to have garlic year-round," Don says. During the peak California season, which lasts 2 months, a crew of 1,500 packs 150,000 pounds of garlic a day.

The ranch exports garlic all over the world, including Puerto Rico, the Middle East, Australia, and France. "Did you know that France consumes 50 million pounds of garlic?" Don asked. "Or that Koreans eat one bulb per capita per day?"

The Gilroy Garlic Festival is held every year in Gilroy, California, on the last weekend in July.

As we were leaving, we walked back through the office, which smelled just faintly of garlic, and out to the car.

"Let me show you the cherry orchard," Don said and spun off around the drive. We followed, and took a walk through part of the 100-acre orchard. The trees wore color-coded ribbons to tell the pickers when to harvest the different varieties, all of which are sold at the Christopher Ranch roadside stand just down the road. Don picked the earliest cherries, popped some in his mouth and handed the rest to us. Then he bid us good-bye. "Stop anytime, and don't hesitate to call," he said and roared off.

NATE PENNELL'S MULLIGAN STEW WITH BLUEBERRY DUMPLINGS

Blueberry dumplings on a stew sounds more like culinary artifice than hearty farm cooking, but this is a bona fide farm recipe from Nate Pennell, who works with Maine's soil conservation service. Nate is a blueberry farmer, and he works all day long, all week long, with other blueberry growers in Aroostook County, the heart of that state's blueberry country.

Nate has a flair in the kitchen, and he does much of the cooking for his family—taking over for his wife, who is an auto mechanic in one of the town's garages.

It didn't take much to get recipes from Nate. In fact, he shared them eagerly as he talked about his large garden—he sells much of its yield at the Machias farmers' market each summer—his blueberries, the blueberries grown by his friends, and the people he works with.

This is one of his favorite recipes, something he's made all his life. He prefers it when he can add a squirrel, a partridge, and a rabbit or two, though he uses chicken in a pinch. Nate freezes blueberries for many uses, one of them being the flavorful dumplings atop this stew.

The beauty of Maine wild blueberries, or lowbush berries as they're also called, is manifold, but not least among their attributes is that they are hearty and don't dissolve in cooking the way so many cultivated, or highbush, berries do.

Make this stew in summer with fresh berries, or use frozen berries in winter, as Nate does. If you can't find wild Maine blueberries, however, don't use the large, soft cultivated varieties, as they completely fall apart in cooking and the effect is not pleasant! When I can't find the blueberries I like, I use golden raisins. They give a slightly different, but equally delicious, effect. Try a full-bodied Pinot Noir along with this.

1 chicken (3½ to 4 pounds), cut into pieces
1 tablespoon unsalted butter
1 tablespoon mild vegetable oil, such as
    safflower
Salt and freshly ground black pepper
2 bay leaves
4 sprigs fresh thyme
4 allspice berries
1 medium rutabaga, peeled and cut
    into ½-inch cubes
1 large potato, peeled and cut into 2-inch cubes
4 small carrots, peeled and cut into ½-inch cubes
2 cups all-purpose flour
1 tablespoon baking powder
½ teaspoon baking soda
¼ teaspoon freshly grated nutmeg
1 egg, beaten
3 tablespoons unsalted butter, melted
⅔ cup buttermilk
½ cup fresh or frozen wild Maine blueberries,
    or ¼ cup coarsely chopped raisins
2 cups fresh or frozen green peas
3 small parsnips, cut into ½-inch cubes

1 Rinse the chicken well and pat it
thoroughly dry.

2 Heat the butter and oil in a large (at
least 8-quart) heavy stockpot or Dutch
oven over medium-high heat. When it is
hot, add the chicken pieces, season them
generously with salt and pepper, and brown
on both sides, seasoning the other side
when you turn the pieces. Brown the
chicken in several batches to avoid crowding
the pan, 8 minutes per batch.

3 Transfer the chicken to a plate or bowl,
drain off half the fat in the pan, and then
return the chicken to the pan. Add enough

water to just cover the chicken. Then add the
herbs and the rutabaga. Cover, and leaving
the heat at medium-high, bring to a boil.
Cook until the rutabaga is nearly soft
through but still somewhat crisp, about 10
minutes. Add the potato and the carrots,
cover, and cook until the carrots are nearly
tender, about 15 minutes.

4 While the stew is cooking, make the
dumpling dough: Sift the flour, baking
powder, 1 teaspoon salt, the baking soda,
and nutmeg together into a medium-size
bowl. Make a well in the middle, and add
the egg, melted butter, and buttermilk; mix
them together in the well with a small
whisk, a fork, or your fingers. Working
quickly, incorporate the dry ingredients to
make a fairly stiff dough. Fold in the blueberries or raisins.

5 Adjust the seasoning of the stew, and
make sure it is boiling merrily; then stir
in the peas and parsnips. Next, one heaping
tablespoon at a time, drop the dumpling
dough on top of the stew so the dumplings
are not touching. Cover, and cook just until
the dumplings are puffed and cooked
through, no longer than 15 minutes. Check
them occasionally to be sure they don't
overcook and become dry.

6 To serve, cut through the dumplings
with a serving spoon, and ladle the
chicken and vegetables into warmed shallow
soup bowls (remove the thyme and bay
leaves). Place the dumplings on top, and
serve immediately.

8 servings

THE DUFNERS DO IT DIFFERENTLY

Don Dufner dropped to his knees and dug his finger into the rich, dark North Dakota soil to reveal a tiny black bean with a sprout just curling out of it. "I'm just checking on them," he said, looking up a little sheepishly when he saw how intently I was watching. "I can't stop myself this time of year. I'm so anxious for them to sprout that I check on them almost every day."

With his three sons, Don organically farms about 1,100 acres of beans—everything from Great Northerns to navys, Swedish brown beans, black beans, pintos, kidneys, and even a chick-pea or two. Don decided long ago not to use chemicals on his land, and he was recently inducted into a small but thriving group of certified organic farmers in North Dakota. "I do it because I have this notion that I'd like the land to be in better condition for my sons than it was for me," he says. The result of his concern for the soil is bounteous crops of top-quality beans.

Don is something of a maverick in his county, which is noted for sugar beet production. He decided to plant beans because he likes what they do for the soil, with their nitrogen-fixing properties, they are more profitable than sugar beets, and he plain likes to eat them.

Don's also considered something of a character because he works with vintage John Deere tractors that have been discarded by other farmers in favor of increasingly large, sophisticated machines. In fact, whenever he has a free evening he's out "Deere hunting," as Sylvia, Don's wife, puts it. The result is an entire acre covered with John Deere tractors.

Watching Don and his sons farm is a bit of a time warp, as they chug along on those old-fashioned tractors, standing up when the going is rough to save their backs, the way farmers always used to. In contrast, their neighbors sit high off the soil, encased in air-conditioned cabs equipped with radios and maybe a tiny television.

The Dufners do it differently and enjoy themselves in the process, whether they're "Deere hunting," planting, or eating a big serving of home-grown beans.

THE DUFNERS' FAVORITE MEAL

This is the dish that Sylvia Dufner makes for her husband, Don, and their four children at holiday time—along with mashed potatoes and homemade cranberry sauce. They love to eat it, and she loves to cook it because, as she puts it, "You can stick it in the oven and completely forget about it. Sometimes I cook it for an hour, sometimes for three hours, and it always tastes just great."

The fact that the chicken takes no supervision means it is ideal for Sylvia's lifestyle. She helps Don and their three grown sons raise 1,100 acres of organic beans, which doesn't give her much time to run into the house and hover over the stove. This dish is one happy result of her busy life, and one I make often in the winter. Serve a rich, intense California Chardonnay, such as Kistler 1988 with it.

1 chicken (3½ pounds), cut into pieces
2 tablespoons unsalted butter
1 tablespoon mild vegetable oil, such as safflower
Salt and freshly ground black pepper
4 sprigs fresh thyme, or ½ teaspoon dried
4 sprigs fresh oregano, or ½ teaspoon dried
2 bay leaves
2 large onions, peeled and thinly sliced
1 tablespoon paprika

1 Rinse the chicken well and pat it thoroughly dry.

2 Preheat the oven to 350°F.

3 Heat the butter and oil in a large heavy skillet or Dutch oven over medium-high heat. When it is hot but not smoking, brown the chicken all over, 8 minutes, seasoning the pieces on both sides with salt. (If your pan is not large enough to hold the chicken in a single layer without crowding, brown it in batches.)

4 Remove the chicken from the pan, and drain off two-thirds of the fat. Then return the chicken to the pan, and season it generously with pepper. Scatter the herbs over the chicken, and then add the onions, which should nearly obscure the chicken. Sprinkle with the paprika. Cover the pan, and place it in the center of the oven. Bake

until the chicken is cooked through, which will take about 1 hour. Then continue baking until the onions turn a deep rich gold, 1 hour more. Remove the herb sprigs and bay leaves and serve.

4 servings

LILLIAN CAHN'S CHICKEN BREASTS

Lillian Cahn and her husband, Miles, own the Coach Farm in Pine Plains, New York, and this is what she served for lunch the day we visited.

The Coach Farm is a goat farm, and Lillian uses many of their cheeses in cooking, as well as serving a selection after a meal, in fine French tradition.

She is very proud of the abundance of good products in the Hudson Valley, and she incorporates them into her cooking. When she made this dish, everything in it (except the prosciutto)—from the free-range chickens to the Coach Farm goat cheese—was produced locally.

The Cahns make exceptionally smooth, rich goat cheese in a variety of shapes. This recipe calls for soft young cheese, which gives the chicken breasts a creamy tang. I like to serve it with the Asian Broccoli Salad (see Index); follow it with a platter of young and aged goat cheeses as Lillian did, and then end the meal with Lillian's Lemon Bread (see Index). These make scrumptious leftovers, if you should be so lucky.

Try a Silverado Chardonnay with this dish, or a Hudson Valley wine, such as a Milbrook Chardonnay.

8 large skinless, boneless chicken breast halves
3 ounces (6 tablespoons) young, soft goat cheese
1 small clove garlic, peeled and minced
Freshly ground black pepper
8 thin slices prosciutto
1½ cups fresh bread crumbs
Salt
2 eggs, beaten
2 tablespoons extra-virgin olive oil
1 tablespoon unsalted butter
10 ounces button mushrooms, stems trimmed,
   caps thinly sliced
¼ cup dry white wine
1 large bunch fresh dill

1 Preheat the oven to 325°F.

2 Rinse the chicken well and pat it thoroughly dry. Place the chicken breasts between two pieces of waxed paper, and pound on them gently with a rolling pin or a heavy weight until they are about ¼ inch thick throughout.

3 In a small bowl, mix together the goat cheese, garlic, and a generous amount of pepper.

4 Stuff the chicken breasts: Lay a slice of prosciutto on top of one piece of chicken (if the prosciutto is larger than the chicken breast, trim it to fit). Place one-eighth of the goat cheese mixture on the top third of the proscuitto, and roll up the chicken breast to enclose the cheese. Set it, seam side down, on a clean counter or plate, and repeat with the remaining chicken breasts. They will stay rolled quite easily without needing anything to secure them.

5 Place the bread crumbs in a shallow bowl or plate, and season lightly with salt and pepper. Whisk the eggs in a large shallow bowl, and set them next to the bread crumbs.

6 Dip each rolled chicken breast in the bread crumbs to coat it well, then in the beaten egg, then again in the bread crumbs. Use one hand for dipping the chicken in the crumbs, and the other for dipping into the eggs, to minimize the amount of crumbs sticking to your fingers.

7 Heat the oil in a large heavy skillet over medium-high heat. When it is hot but not smoking, brown the chicken breasts, turning them frequently, until they are golden on all sides, about 7 minutes total. (Do not crowd the pan. Brown the chicken breasts in two batches if necessary.) Remove them from the pan and arrange them in a single layer in an 8 x 14-inch enamel or ceramic baking dish. Place the dish in the center of the oven, and bake for 20 minutes.

8 While the chicken breasts are cooking, melt the butter in a medium-size heavy skillet over medium heat. Sauté the mushrooms just until they begin to give up their liquid, about 4 minutes. Add the wine, stir, and continue cooking just until the wine is hot. Season with salt and pepper. Mince the dill and add 2 tablespoons to the mushrooms. Remove the mushrooms from the heat, and set aside.

9 After the chicken breasts have baked for 20 minutes, pour the mushrooms over them and continue cooking until much of the liquid has evaporated and the chicken breasts are cooked through, another 10 minutes. To test for doneness, make a small cut in a chicken breast; if the meat is white throughout, it is cooked. If it is still pink, continue cooking for several minutes. Be very careful not to overcook the chicken,

however. In most cases 30 minutes should be sufficient.

10 Garnish the chicken with the remaining dill, and serve immediately.

8 servings

BASQUE CHICKEN WITH SWEET PEAS

Like so many of the Basque dishes I garnered from the farming community in and around Boise, Idaho, this dish is bright with pure, simple flavors.

I love to make this with the very first peas of spring, because they are so tender and sweet. But, if you can't get fresh-picked peas, by all means use frozen peas—certain brands are excellent, sometimes even better than fresh. (They were picked and frozen within hours of harvest, whereas the little plastic containers of fresh peas at the supermarket may have been rattling around for days or even a week.) Frozen peas also allow you to make this during the winter, when a little jot of spring green is often needed.

Make Basque Chicken the day before, right up to the point where you add the peas. Refrigerate it overnight, then skim off any fat that has risen to the surface. Reheat it, add the peas, and serve.

Several styles of wine complement Basque Chicken. Try a full, oaky Spanish wine such as Marques de Murrieta 1988; a soft, silken Spanish wine such as Marques de Grignon 1986; or a light zinfandel (yes, there is such a thing), such as Frog's Leap 1987.

1 chicken (3½ pounds), cut into pieces
3 tablespoons olive oil
Salt and freshly ground black pepper
2 large green bell peppers, cored, seeded, and
  sliced
1 large onion, peeled and thinly sliced
4 ounces lean slab bacon, rind removed, diced
1 leafy sprig Italian (flat-leaf) parsley, coarsely
  chopped
3 cloves garlic, peeled and minced
2½ cups fresh green peas, or 1 package
  (10 ounces) frozen tiny green peas

1 Rinse the chicken well and pat it thoroughly dry.

2 Heat the olive oil in a large skillet over medium-high heat. When it is hot, brown the chicken on both sides, 8 minutes total, seasoning it with salt and pepper.

3 Remove the chicken from the skillet and set it aside. Reduce the heat to medium and add the peppers, onion, bacon, parsley, and garlic to the skillet. Cook, stirring constantly, until the garlic and onion are translucent, about 5 minutes.

4 Return the chicken to the pan, cover, and cook over medium-low heat, stirring occasionally, until the chicken is cooked through and the vegetables are tender, about 30 minutes.

5 Add the peas, stir gently, cover, and cook just until they are heated through, 3 to 5 minutes. (If you are using frozen peas, increase the cooking time slightly.) Season to taste.

6 Serve directly from the skillet, or transfer the chicken and vegetables to a warmed serving platter, pour the cooking juices over all, and serve.

4 servings

EUREKA FARM CHICKEN WITH GARBANZOS

Li Ochs served a big Dutch oven full of this chicken for supper when we visited her and her family at Eureka Farm, in eastern Washington. She serves it often, and though she prefers to use freshly cooked garbanzos (chick-peas), she sometimes uses the canned variety. Li has a way with ingredients, and this dish is beguilingly unusual, full of satisfying flavor.

It looks beautiful too, and fits the image of a generous farmhouse dish.

Li served it with a buttermilk-dressed broccoli salad, a spicy lentil dip, and plenty of fresh crusty bread. I like to add a fresh green salad, too.

Try a fruity Pinot Gris, such as one from Oregon's Adelsheim Vineyards, with this.

2 chickens (3 to 4 pounds each), cut into
  pieces, with giblets if desired
1 tablespoon unsalted butter
3 tablespoons olive oil
Salt
2 small onions, peeled and minced
2 large cloves garlic, peeled and finely
  chopped
½ teaspoon ground ginger
1½ tablespoons ground cumin
1 small dried hot pepper, crumbled, or
  ½ teaspoon dried red pepper flakes
4 cups Herbfarm Deluxe Chicken Stock (page
  86) or good-quality canned broth
5 cups cooked garbanzo beans (chick-peas;
  recipe follows), or 2 cans (15½ ounces each)
  chick-peas, rinsed and drained
1 cup fresh cilantro leaves
1 clove garlic, peeled

1 Rinse the chicken well and pat it thoroughly dry.

2 Heat the butter and oil in a large stock-pot over medium-high heat, and brown the chicken pieces on both sides, 8 minutes total, seasoning them with salt. Do this in batches to avoid crowding the pan.

3 When all the chicken is browned, pour off half the fat. Add the onions, the chopped garlic, and the spices, including the hot pepper, to the stockpot. Cook, stirring constantly, until the onions begin to turn translucent, about 5 minutes. Return the chicken to the pot and pour the chicken stock over it. Add the chick-peas and stir.

4 Bring the stock to a simmer, reduce the heat to medium-low, and simmer, covered, until the chicken is cooked through, about 45 minutes. About 15 minutes before the chicken is done, add the giblets if desired. Season to taste.

5 Mince the cilantro leaves and the garlic clove together. Stir this into the chicken mixture and serve immediately, right from the pot.

8 servings

FLAVORFUL GARBANZO BEANS

The advantage of cooking your own garbanzos, or chick-peas, is the flavorful result. Though the canned version is just fine, they lack the subtle nutlike flavor of those cooked at home. These take some time to cook but require little or no supervision, and once you've got them on hand, you'll find them fitting into your meals in the most unexpected, and unexpectedly tasty, ways.

2 cups dried garbanzo beans (chick-peas)
12 cups water
1 teaspoon salt

1 Pick over the garbanzo beans for any stones or dirt; then rinse them well. Place them in a large heavy saucepan with 6 cups of the water, cover, and bring to a boil. Boil for 2 minutes. Remove the pan from the heat and let it sit, covered, for 1 hour.

2 Drain the garbanzos, and return them to the saucepan. Add the remaining 6 cups water and the salt. Bring to a boil, re-

duce the heat to medium-low, and simmer, covered, until the beans are tender but still slightly crisp, 50 minutes to 1 hour. Check them occasionally to be sure they have plenty of water. If not, add more water.

3 Drain the garbanzos; they are now ready to use. They will keep, refrigerated, for about 3 days. They can also be frozen for later use.

5 cups

POUSSIN WITH WILD RICE

T his is a midwestern harvest-time dish. It relies entirely on native ingredients like small game birds—which farmers hunt in the fall when they trade their ploughs for rifles—wild rice, and hazelnuts, which can be found here and there in the Midwest in old orchards that have been let go. When it comes to the table, the aroma alone will get your mouth watering.

Poussins (very young chickens) are not always available, so I suggest using good-quality Cornish game hens, which are a tasty, if somewhat larger, substitute.

Though the Midwest is widely recognized as the home of wild rice, there's a secret worth knowing, and that is that the best-quality wild rice in the country is grown in St. Maries, Idaho. Its grains are long, black, and shiny, its flavor is rich with the nuttiness that only good wild rice has. And it is available by mail order from St. Maries Wild Rice, Inc., P.O. Box 293, St. Maries, ID 83861.

Try a young red burgundy, such as a Côtes de Beaune, with this.

4 poussins (1 to 1½ pounds each) or Cornish
  game hens
Salt and freshly ground black pepper
1 lemon, halved
1 tablespoon extra-virgin olive oil
1½ cups wild rice
4 cups Herbfarm Deluxe Chicken Stock (light
  version; page 86), good-quality canned
  broth, or water
1 tablespoon goose fat or unsalted butter
1 large shallot, peeled and minced
10 ounces button mushrooms, stems trimmed,
  caps finely chopped
½ teaspoon coriander seeds, crushed
Zest of 1 lemon, minced
1 tablespoon freshly squeezed lemon juice
½ cup hazelnuts, toasted and skinned (see
  Note), and coarsely chopped
2 tablespoons minced fresh Italian (flat-leaf)
  parsley

1 Preheat the oven to 450°F.

2 Rinse the hens well, inside and out, until the water runs clear. Pat them thoroughly dry. Season the cavities of the birds with salt and pepper and a squeeze of lemon juice. Truss the birds. Rub them all over with the olive oil.

3 Place the birds in a roasting pan with plenty of room between them, and roast until they turn pale gold, about 30 minutes. Check them frequently, and when they begin to give up fat and juices, use these to baste them, basting every 10 to 15 minutes.

4 Reduce the heat to 350°F, and continue roasting until the birds are deep golden in color and their juices run clear when the thigh and leg joint are pricked with a sharp knife. This will take 10 minutes for the 1-pound birds, about 20 minutes for larger birds. Remove from the oven and set aside.

5 While the hens are roasting, prepare the rice: Combine the rice, stock, and salt to taste in a large saucepan. Cover, and bring to a boil over high heat. Reduce the heat to medium and continue cooking, covered, at a slow boil until two-thirds of the rice kernels have burst and show their white interior, and they have absorbed most of the water, about 35 to 45 minutes. The rice should still be full of texture and somewhat chewy, though not hard or unpleasant. While it is cooking, check the rice and add more stock if it is drying out; it should stay moist. If you prefer the rice to be more tender, cook it for an additional 5 to 10 min-

WHAT IS A CORNISH GAME HEN ANYWAY?

The Cornish hen isn't Cornish at all, but an American hybrid, a cross between a Plymouth Rock hen and Cornish or bantam rooster. It is often called a Cornish game hen, but because it has no gamey flavor, and *doesn't run wild or even pretend to, it is most commonly and properly referred to simply as a Cornish hen.*

utes. Be sure not to overcook it, however, as it becomes mushy. (The cooking time for wild rice varies dramatically, depending on its age and quality.)

6 While the rice is cooking, melt the goose fat or butter in a large skillet over medium heat. Add the shallot and cook, stirring constantly, until it begins to turn translucent, 3 to 5 minutes. Then add the mushrooms and cook, stirring occasionally, until they've given up all their liquid and it has evaporated, 8 to 10 minutes. Add the coriander, lemon zest, and the lemon juice. Stir in the rice, and season to taste with salt and pepper. Keep the rice warm over low heat, partially covered.

7 Just before serving, stir the hazelnuts into the wild rice. Divide the rice among four warmed dinner plates, and place a bird atop each portion. Sprinkle the rice with the minced parsley, and serve immediately.

4 servings

Note: To toast hazelnuts, preheat the oven to 350°F. Place the nuts in a baking pan large enough to hold them in a single layer, and toast, stirring once, until they give off a toasted aroma, about 10 to 15 minutes. Wrap the nuts in a kitchen towel and rub them between your hands to remove the skin.

ARMADILLO TURKEY

The idea for this recipe comes from Robert Barnum, owner of Possum Trot Nursery near Homestead, Florida (see also page 114). Robert grows all manner of exotic medicinal and edible plants, trees, and herbs, from mangoes to allspice to Key limes. While he doesn't grow pineapples, he has a good source for them and uses them often in cooking. They're in peak season around Thanksgiving, which is why they are used on his holiday turkey.

He calls this Armadillo Turkey because the pineapple skin, with its spiky points, reminds him of a lumbering armadillo. He puts the pineapple skin on the turkey to protect it from drying out and to allow the sweet pineapple juices to penetrate the meat. I went a step further by basting the turkey with pineapple juice, in part because the pineapples most of us get aren't as sweet and juicy as those in Florida. Buy the most fragrant pineapple you can find, but make sure it isn't overly soft. The salad makes use of the pineapple fruit itself.

The cooking juices from the turkey are golden, slightly thickened, and full of rich, good flavor. Try this for your next Thanksgiving dinner—it will add a breath of soft Florida air to your holiday meal.

Serve Armadillo Turkey with a lightly chilled, rich, full California Chardonnay, such as one from Silverado, alongside.

---

1 fresh turkey (12 to 15 pounds)
1 lime, halved
Salt and freshly ground black pepper
1 small onion, peeled and quartered
1 large pineapple
1½ cups canned pineapple juice

1 Preheat the oven to 325°F.

2 Rinse the turkey well, inside and out, until the water runs clear. Pat it thoroughly dry. Squeeze the lime in the cavity of the turkey, to season it. Sprinkle the cavity with salt and pepper, and place the squeezed lime halves and the onion in the cavity.

3 Truss the turkey, and place it in a roasting pan large enough to hold it without crowding.

4 Scrub the pineapple well with a brush under hot water. Slice off the top of the pineapple, and set it aside. Remove the skin from the pineapple in four equal pieces, cutting it from top to bottom with a stainless steel knife. Leave ¼ inch of the pulp on two pieces of the skin. Set aside those two pieces and the fruit (for the Pineapple Salad). Discard the extra skin pieces.

5 Pour ½ cup of the pineapple juice over the turkey, and place the turkey in the center of the oven. Roast until it is a deep golden brown, the thigh is tender when pressed, and the leg joints move easily up and down in their sockets, which should take 3½ to 4 hours. Baste the turkey every 30 minutes, using ½ cup pineapple juice each time until it is gone, then using the accumulated juices and fats in the bottom of the pan. One hour before the turkey is done, place the two pieces of pineapple skin on the breast meat, completely covering it. Secure them in place with small metal skewers. Continue basting the turkey, pouring the basting liquid over the pineapple skin.

6 Remove the turkey from the oven and the roasting pan, and let it rest for at least 30 minutes, or as long as 45 minutes, before serving. While it is resting, turn the turkey over so that it is resting on its breast. Prop the legs so they are slightly higher than the breast, allowing the juices to run back into the breast meat. Reduce the cooking juices slightly over medium-high heat, about 2 minutes, scraping up any brown bits. Season to taste with salt and pepper. Strain and pour into a gravy boat.

7 To carve the turkey, remove and discard the pineapple skins. Place the carved turkey on a heated platter. Arrange

KEEPING LIMES

■■■■■

*P*lace limes in a plastic bag, sprinkle them with a bit of water, and close the bag. The limes will keep that way in the refrigerator for at least a week, often longer. Don't leave them on the shelf out in the air—they'll turn to dry little husks.

the top of the pineapple at the foot of the turkey, for garnish. Serve with the gravy and Pineapple Salad.

10 to 12 servings

PINEAPPLE SALAD

■■■■■■

Fruit from 1 pineapple (see step 4, above)
3 tablespoons extra-virgin olive oil
1 tablespoon freshly squeezed lime juice
1 teaspoon mild honey
1 teaspoon sherry vinegar
¼ teaspoon minced fresh ginger
1 shallot, peeled and minced
Salt and freshly ground black pepper to taste
2 cups diced avocado (about 3 medium)

1 Cut the pineapple into quarters. Then remove and discard the core, and cut the fruit into bite-size pieces.

2 Mix the olive oil, lime juice, honey, vinegar, ginger, and shallot together in a medium-size bowl. Add salt and pepper to taste, and then gently toss in the pineapple. Add the avocado, toss again gently but thoroughly, and refrigerate, covered, until ready to serve.

10 to 12 servings

ROAST TURKEY WITH CHESTNUT STUFFING

W hen chestnuts come into season in the fall, I try to use them in as many dishes as possible because I love their nutty, starchy sweetness. Until the early part of this century, chestnuts were grown commercially in some parts of this country, but their cultivation fell out of favor when a blight attacked the chestnut trees. It is being revived, happily, on a small basis in some regions. In the Northwest, for instance, several growers have resurrected old chestnut trees and brought them back into production, so that for a month or two in the fall fresh chestnuts are available.

Whenever local chestnuts are available, that is what I buy. Otherwise I look for good-quality chestnuts imported from Italy. Ideally they should be stored under refrigeration, because they dry out quickly. Look for full, relatively heavy nuts, which means the meats are in good condition. Avoid those that are light or that rattle when you shake them; the meat inside has dried out.

When I don't feel like going to the trouble of cooking and peeling chestnuts for a special dish, I simply toss some in a hot oven or on top of the wood stove and roast them to nibble in the evenings. They make a snack full of memories of those cities where you can buy a bag from a street vendor and savor them as you stroll along.

Just as frequently, however, I

go ahead and boil, peel, and steam them to add to stuffings, vegetables, tarts, and pastries.

Here chestnuts are combined, in traditional fashion, with a delicately spiced mixture of pork and herbs so their flavor, and texture, comes through.

I like to serve this stuffing with the Thanksgiving turkey, though it is delicious as a stuffing for any poultry, and it can be cooked on its own and served as a side dish to pork roast as well (see Note).

A red Burgundy or a Volnay would be a good choice with this roast turkey.

1 fresh turkey (10 to 12 pounds), with giblets
4 tablespoons (½ stick) unsalted butter, at room temperature
1 pound fresh chestnuts, peeled (see box)
3 cups water
1 pound pork sausage meat
2 shallots, peeled and finely chopped
¼ cup finely chopped fresh parsley
4 sprigs fresh thyme, or ½ teaspoon dried
1 bay leaf
Salt and freshly ground black pepper
2 cloves garlic, peeled and minced
2 eggs, beaten
1 cup dry white wine
2 large onions, peeled and each cut into 8 wedges
4 medium carrots, peeled and cut into 2-inch pieces

1 Remove the giblets and the neck from the turkey, and set aside. Rinse the

PEELING CHESTNUTS

Make a small cut on the flat side of each chestnut, making sure to cut all the way through the outer skin. Place the chestnuts in a medium-size saucepan, cover with water, and bring to a boil over high heat. Then reduce the heat to low. Remove several chestnuts from the water and peel them with a sharp paring knife, being sure to remove both the outer peel and the dark inner skin that is attached to the meat. If the chestnuts cool before you have a chance to peel them, place them back in the water to heat, as it is virtually impossible to remove the inner skin when the chestnut is cool.

turkey well inside and out until the water runs clear. Pat it thoroughly dry. Carefully separate the skin from the breast by running your fingers between the skin and the meat, being careful not to poke any holes in the skin. Spread the butter on the meat.

2 Bring the water to a boil in a vegetable steamer over high heat. Add the chestnuts, cover, and steam until they are tender, about 30 minutes. Remove the steamer basket from the heat.

3 Preheat the oven to 350°F.

4 In a medium-size bowl, gently break the chestnuts into bite-size pieces. Mixing well after each addition, stir in the pork,

shallots, herbs, salt and pepper, garlic, and eggs. Chop the giblets and add them to the mixture, mixing well. To test for seasoning, pinch off a teaspoon of the mixture and cook it in a small skillet over medium heat until it is cooked through. Taste for seasoning, and adjust accordingly.

5 Fill the turkey with as much stuffing as it will hold, but don't pack it tightly, and truss the turkey.

6 Place the turkey in a large roasting pan, and pour the wine around it. Roast until the turkey is golden, basting every 30 minutes with the pan liquids. If the breast is browning too quickly, cover it loosely with aluminum foil. After 2 hours, add the onions and the carrots to the pan, spacing them evenly around the turkey. The turkey is done when the skin is golden, the thigh is tender when pressed, and the leg joints move easily up and down in their sockets, 3 to 3½ hours more.

7 Remove the turkey from the oven, and from the roasting pan and let it rest for at least 30 minutes or as long as 45 minutes before carving. While it is resting, turn the turkey over so it is resting on its breast. Prop the legs so they are slightly higher than the breast, allowing the juices to run back into the breast meat. Reduce the cooking juices slightly over medium-high heat, about 2 minutes, scraping up any brown bits. Season to taste with salt and pepper. Strain and pour into a gravy boat.

8 Scoop out the stuffing into a serving dish and keep warm while you carve the turkey. Serve and pass the gravy boat.

8 to 10 servings

Note: To cook the stuffing separately, bake it in a covered dish at 350°F until it is nearly cooked all the way through, about 30 minutes. Then remove the cover and continue cooking until it has browned slightly on top and is clearly cooked through, an additional 10 to 15 minutes. If you cook the stuffing separately, your turkey may take slightly less time to cook.

ARE TURKEYS REALLY SO DUMB...

...they'll stand out in the rain with their heads upturned and their beaks open until they drown? No, according to turkey farmer David Podoll. He says turkeys have a natural instinct to stand still in the rain and let it run off their feathers, which create a natural barrier and keep them from getting cold and wet. Tame turkeys, however, are larger than wild turkeys and they have more feather follicles and often fewer feathers, so they're vulnerable to rain. Of course it's possible they could get so wet and cold they would, indeed, die in the rain, but definitely not from standing there with their beaks open.

WILD TURKEY

Conventional turkeys are bred with an oversize breast (to satisfy the American penchant for white meat), to the point where they become ▄▄▄ so breast-heavy that they literally tip over when they try to walk. In comparison wild turkeys look long and gangly, though they are wonderfully meaty.

The wild turkeys I've cooked aren't actually wild, but a species called the Appalachian, which are generally raised on small specialized farms. It is closer in flavor and looks to the wild bird than anything raised on large conventional turkey farms.

The best thing about such a bird is the rich, subtle flavor of both the dark and the white meat—a depth of flavor one associates with high-quality game. Despite its rangy appearance, it is moist and succulent too.

To ensure that the meat stays moist, I cover the bird with cheesecloth soaked in olive oil and baste it every 30 minutes. If there isn't enough liquid at first for basting, pour some extra wine or broth around the bird.

These birds cook quickly—2 to 3 hours for a 9- to 11-pound bird, which easily feeds six to eight people. The time will vary greatly because each bird is different, even though their weight may be the same. It is cooked when the thigh is tender and the legs move easily in their sockets. To be sure, remove the turkey from the oven and tip it on end; the juices should run clear yellow. If there are pink juices, return it to the oven; loosely cover the breast and the drumsticks with aluminum foil to keep them from drying out. If you don't stuff the bird, reduce the cooking time by 30 minutes.

1 wild turkey (9 to 11 pounds), with giblets
Salt and freshly ground black pepper
Bread Stuffing (recipe follows)
2 bay leaves
¼ cup olive oil
½ cup dry white wine
½ cup water

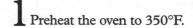

1 Preheat the oven to 350°F.

2 Rinse the turkey well inside and out until the water runs clear. Pat it thoroughly dry. Season liberally with salt and pepper. Fill the turkey with as much stuffing as it will hold, but don't pack it tightly. Truss the turkey, and set it on a work surface, breast side up.

3 Separate the skin from the breast by running your fingers between the skin and the meat. Slip the bay leaves under the skin so that one lies flat on each half of the breast.

4 Soak a doubled piece of cheesecloth—large enough to cover the turkey breast and legs—in the olive oil, and drape it over the bird. Reserve any olive oil that the cheesecloth doesn't absorb to drizzle over the turkey during cooking.

5 Place the turkey in a large roasting pan, and pour the wine around it. Roast the turkey in the center of the oven, basting it every 30 minutes, until it is golden, the thigh is tender when pressed, and the leg joints move easily up and down in their sockets, 2½ to 3½ hours.

6 Remove the turkey from the oven and let it sit, tilted slightly on one end so the juices can run back into the breast meat, for about 20 minutes.

7 While the bird is resting, skim the fat off the cooking juices, if desired, and add the water to the juices. Bring to a boil over medium-high heat, scraping up any browned bits from the bottom of the pan. Simmer until the juices are slightly reduced and have a concentrated flavor, about 2 minutes. Adjust the seasoning and serve alongside the carved turkey.

6 to 8 servings

BREAD STUFFING

▪▪▪▪▪▪

T his is a traditional bread stuffing with a slight difference. It is loaded with lightly sautéed fresh mushrooms, and it has a distinct herbal flavor.

The recipe calls for the uncooked giblets, which give it a wonderful earthiness. I do, however, leave out the gizzard from a domesticated wild turkey because it can be chewier than rubber, and gritty. One from a conventional turkey is fine.

4 tablespoons (½ stick unsalted butter
1 medium onion, peeled and diced
2 long ribs celery, strings removed, cut into small cubes
20 ounces button mushrooms, stems trimmed, caps thinly sliced
1 teaspoon fresh thyme leaves, or ½ teaspoon dried
2 tablespoons fresh sage leaves, or about ½ teaspoon dried
2 tablespoons minced fresh Italian (flat-leaf) parsley
Uncooked giblets from the turkey, coarsely chopped
8 cups bread cubes, freshly toasted
½ cup heavy (whipping) cream
2 eggs
Salt and freshly ground black pepper

1 Preheat the oven to 350°F.

2 Melt the butter in a large skillet over medium-high heat, and when it is foaming, add the onion and celery. Cook, stirring frequently, until the onion softens and turns translucent, about 10 minutes. Using a slotted spoon, remove the onion and celery from the skillet and set aside. Add the mushrooms to the skillet and cook, stirring occasionally, until they turn limp and begin to give up their liquid, about 5 to 8 minutes. Remove them from the heat.

3 Transfer the onion, celery, and mushrooms, with their juices, to a large mixing bowl. Add the herbs and the giblets, and mix well. Then add the bread cubes and mix well again.

4 In a small bowl, whisk together the cream and eggs. Pour this over the stuffing mixture, and mix until thoroughly blended. Season to taste with salt and pepper.

5 Either stuff the cavity of a large turkey with the mixture (without firmly packing it), or transfer it to a 8 x 8 x 2-inch, ovenproof dish and bake until the giblets are cooked through and the stuffing is crisp and golden on top, about 25 minutes.

6 to 8 servings

THE HERBFARM'S DUCK BREASTS WITH HONEY AND THYME SAUCE

W hen Ron Zimmerman, owner of the Herbfarm and chef of its small restaurant, needs inspiration for a recipe, he walks through the Herbfarm's gardens (see page 85). His footsteps on the woolly thyme release a heady peppery scent, and that is where he must have been when he devised this recipe, which makes the most of fresh thyme—not woolly thyme, which is primarily a landscape herb.

Ron brings large armfuls of herbs into the kitchen and turns them into all manner of things, from desserts to drinks. This recipe, which I sampled at the restaurant, demonstrates how herbs can be used in ways other than just sprinkling them on a dish as a garnish.

Try this with a red Burgundy, such as Côtes de Beaume 1988.

2 duck breasts, split, to give 4 pieces
   (about 7 ounces each)
Salt and freshly ground black pepper
2 tablespoons unsalted butter
2 teaspoons good-quality mild honey
2 teaspoons fresh thyme leaves
Caramelized Honey and Thyme Sauce
   (recipe follows)
Glazed Garlic Cloves (page 346)
8 sprigs fresh thyme, for garnish

1 Remove the skin from the duck breasts and trim the breasts neatly. Rinse them well and pat them thoroughly dry. Season lightly on both sides with salt and pepper.

2 Melt the butter in a large skillet over medium heat, add the breasts, and cook until golden, about 2 minutes. Turn and cook on the other side until golden, an additional 2 minutes. With the breasts still over the heat, spread each with ½ teaspoon of the honey, and sprinkle each with ½ teaspoon of the thyme leaves. Continue to cook without turning until the meat is tender and rosy in the center, golden and somewhat firm on the outside, another 2 minutes. Season lightly with salt and pepper, and remove from the heat.

3 Place each breast in the center of a warmed dinner plate, and let it rest for 1 minute. Spoon the caramelized honey and thyme sauce over each, and arrange the glazed garlic cloves alongside. Garnish with the thyme sprigs, and serve immediately.

4 servings

CARAMELIZED HONEY AND THYME SAUCE

¼ cup mild honey
½ teaspoon fresh thyme leaves
¼ cup best-quality red wine vinegar
½ cup Herbfarm's Rich Duck Stock (page 84)
Salt and freshly ground black pepper

1 Place the honey and the thyme leaves in a small heavy saucepan over low heat, and cook until the honey turns a deep golden brown, about 10 minutes. Watch carefully to be sure it doesn't burn.

2 Add the vinegar and mix well. Add the duck stock, stir, and bring to a boil over high heat. Reduce the heat to medium, and cook until the sauce has the consistency of a thick syrup, about 10 minutes. Season to taste with salt and pepper, and serve immediately.

About 1 cup (4 servings)

GRILLED SHRIMP IN CHILE MARINADE WITH THREE MELONS

I saw melons in every hot climate I visited, and I ate my share of sweet, juicy slices. I came to the conclusion that eating them in the field, with their hot sweet juice dripping down my arm, was the way they were intended to be consumed. However, once back home I devised this recipe, combining three cool melons with marinated shrimp, and I think it makes the most of all the ingredients.

Try this with a light Sancerre or California Sauvignon Blanc.

½ cup peanut oil

1 tablespoon minced lime zest

2 tablespoons freshly squeezed lime juice

4 medium cloves garlic, peeled and minced

1 teaspoon Indonesian chile paste (usually called sambel odelek)

¼ teaspoon salt

1 pound medium shrimp (about 24)

1 cup fruitwood chips, for the fire (optional)

½ cup loosely packed fresh cilantro leaves

½ medium honeydew melon (about 1 pound), seeded, peeled, and cut into thin (just under ¼ inch thick) lengthwise slices

1 small cantaloupe (about 1½ pounds), halved, seeded, peeled, and cut into thin (just under ¼ inch thick) lengthwise slices

½ medium casaba melon (about 1 pound), halved, seeded, peeled, and cut into ¼-inch dice (see Note)

1 Soak six 10-inch bamboo skewers in warm water for 15 minutes.

2 In a medium-size nonreactive bowl, whisk together the oil, lime zest, lime juice, garlic, chile paste, and salt.

3 Thread the shrimp on the skewers, brush them with the marinade, cover, and refrigerate for at least 1 hour, or as long as overnight. Set aside the extra marinade.

4 Prepare a medium-size charcoal fire in a barbecue grill. Thoroughly oil the grill rack, using a paper towel dipped in vegetable oil.

5 When the coals are red and dusted with ash, spread them out in an even layer, and sprinkle with the wood chips. Place the rack about 3 inches above the coals, and

lay the skewers on the rack. Cook, turning once, until the shrimp are opaque, have curled on the skewers, and are firm but not hard to the touch, about 3 minutes. Remove the shrimp from the rack and use a long fork to ease them off the skewers. Set the shrimp aside.

6 When the shrimp are cool enough to touch, remove the shells and devein them if desired. (The veins are so small they will not affect the flavor. Deveining now is an aesthetic consideration.)

7 Mince the cilantro, and stir it into the reserved marinade. Add the shrimp,

toss to coat, and marinate, covered in the refrigerator, for at least 1 hour, or overnight.

8 To serve, arrange the melon slices, alternating cantaloupe and honeydew, in a circular pattern on each dinner plate. Arrange the shrimp in the center, sprinkle with the diced casaba, and drizzle the marinade equally over the shrimp and the melon. Serve immediately.

4 servings

Note: If you can't get casaba melon, use another small cantaloupe dicing it as you would the casaba.

TROUT WITH WILD MUSHROOMS

A long with catfish, rainbow trout are the backbone of the American aquaculture industry. Because they are now farmed all around the country, trout are available to the public from coast to coast and everywhere in between. They come from the water glistening and fresh, their flavor mild, their flesh tender.

I like to cook trout whole. The flavor of the meat benefits from being cooked on the bone, and they make a dramatic presentation. Because their meat is so mild, I like to team them with a

full-flavored accompaniment. Here they are garnished with hearty wild mushrooms spiked with garlic and herbs, which highlights their delicate flavor. Morels are a luxury—if you can't find them, use button mushrooms and add 1 tablespoon fresh lemon juice when you sauté them. Try a young Pinot Noir, such as a Saintsbury Garnet along with this.

4 whole trout (7 to 8 ounces each), cleaned
    and gutted, head and tail left on
Salt and freshly ground black pepper
6 tablespoons extra-virgin olive oil
3 cloves garlic, peeled and minced
1 pound waxy potatoes, peeled and cut
    into ½-inch cubes
1 pound wild mushrooms, preferably morels,
    brushed clean, or button mushrooms,
    stems trimmed
1 tablespoon fresh lemon juice, if using
    button mushrooms
¼ cup dry white wine
1 small bunch fresh chives, minced,
    for garnish

1 Rinse the trout and pat them dry. Generously season each cavity with salt and pepper. Place the trout in a nonreactive dish, and pour 4 tablespoons of the olive oil over them. Turn so they are coated on both sides with oil, rub half the garlic onto them, and season again with salt and pepper. Cover and refrigerate for at least 2 hours or up to 24 hours.

2 Heat the remaining 2 tablespoons oil in a large nonstick skillet over medium-high heat. Add the potatoes, stir to coat with oil, season generously with salt and pepper, and cover. Cook, stirring occasionally, until the potatoes are golden and nearly cooked through, 7 minutes. Transfer the potatoes to a warmed dish and keep warm in a low (200°F) oven.

3 Place the mushrooms, the remaining garlic, and 2 tablespoons of the trout marinade in the same skillet, and cook over medium heat, stirring frequently, until the mushrooms are softened and cooked through, 12 to 15 minutes for wild mushrooms, about 8 minutes for button mushrooms. Season generously with salt and pepper. (If you are using button mushrooms, add the lemon juice, then season.) Transfer the mushrooms to the dish holding the potatoes.

4 Place the trout in the same skillet, along with the remaining marinade. Cook, covered, over medium high-heat for 4 minutes. Turn the trout and continue cooking until they are golden on both sides and cooked through, another 4 to 5 minutes.

5 Transfer the trout to a warmed serving platter, and cover loosely with aluminum foil to keep warm. Place the potatoes and the mushrooms back in the skillet over medium-high heat, and sauté until they are thoroughly crisped, which should take about 3 minutes. Arrange the vegetables around the trout. Add the wine to the skillet and stir, scraping up any brown bits from the bottom of the pan. Pour the sauce over the trout, sprinkle with the chives, and serve immediately.

4 generous servings

HALIBUT AND SWEET POTATO STIR-FRY

The idea for this recipe comes from Marie Galyean, who grows sweet potatoes in Mineola, Texas. Marie's recipe calls for pork, but is so flexible, that I could easily substitute fresh sweet halibut. Try a chilled fruity Gewürztraminer with the halibut.

1¼ pounds halibut or swordfish
2 tablespoons peanut oil
3 thin slices fresh ginger, about the size
   and thickness of a quarter, peeled
6 scallions (green onions), trimmed and
   sliced diagonally into 1 inch lengths
2 cloves garlic, peeled and thinly sliced crosswise
2 medium sweet potatoes, peeled and
   cut into thin 1 x 3-inch pieces
½ cup water
¼ cup dry sherry
3 tablespoons light soy sauce
1 teaspoon minced fresh ginger
Zest of 1 lemon, minced

1 Rinse the halibut and pat it dry. Cut it into ½ x 1-inch pieces. Cover and refrigerate until ready to cook.

2 Heat the oil with the ginger slices in a large heavy skillet or a wok until hot but not smoking. When the ginger begins to turn golden, remove it from the oil and discard. Add all but 1 tablespoon of the scallions.

Cook, stirring constantly, until the scallions begin to turn translucent, 3 minutes. Add the garlic, stir, and cook just until it begins to turn translucent, about 2 minutes. Transfer the mixture to a plate and keep it warm.

3 Add the sweet potatoes to the skillet and stir; then add the water. Cover and cook, stirring occasionally, until the sweet potatoes have softened but are still somewhat crisp, about 4 minutes.

4 Add the halibut to the sweet potatoes, along with the sherry and the soy sauce, and cook, stirring gently but constantly, until the fish is nearly opaque through, 5 to 7 minutes. Return the scallions and garlic to the pan, and add the minced ginger and lemon zest. Toss, and cook just until all the ingredients are warmed.

5 Transfer the mixture to a warmed serving platter, and sprinkle the remaining scallions over all, for garnish.

4 to 6 servings

AQUACULTURE

In the past decade, aquaculture—the farming of seafood—has grown into an immense industry. What began with a few trout farms at the turn of the century has blossomed into a booming business that produces everything from softshell crawfish to sturgeon.

Its success is based largely on three things: It produces fish and shellfish that are available year-round, are uniform in size, texture, and flavor, and are consistently priced. And it's a form of agriculture that has pulled many an ailing rural area out of the doldrums and into productivity and prosperity.

CATFISH

There are more catfish farmed in the U.S. than any other species. Most are farmed in the Mississippi delta, which until the 1960s was covered with cotton and soybeans. Those crops were headed in a downward spiral, however, for a variety of reasons. Nearby states were raising catfish with reportedly huge profits, and it didn't take long for Mississippi farmers to get bitten with the catfish-farming bug. Now their farmland is a flat plain dotted with shallow fish ponds that stand out like giant shining mirrors.

Catfish—normally bottom dwellers who snuffle along in lakes and rivers, looking for food—live a fat life on the farm. They are regularly fed a manufactured food that contains all the vitamins and minerals necessary to make them grow, so they can relax and dawdle around.

The feed also controls their flavor. Wild catfish aren't known to be picky eaters, and left on their own they will literally eat anything they see. This freewheeling habit gives their meat a characteristic earthiness, which is prized by catfish aficionados. For the farmed-catfish industry, however, it signals poor sales.

The industry has pitched catfish as a lean, mild, white-meat fish. Any earthiness or "off" flavor is unappealing to the general public. To try to control it, each pond is sampled before harvest. If the fish taste earthy, they stay in the pond. Only those that taste sweet and clean are harvested.

Catfish are actually harvested by tractor. Two move along either side of a pond, with a

net stretched between them. Several men, chest-deep in water, ride the bottom rope of the net to keep it running evenly across the bottom, scooping up all the fish.

The fish are graded and sent to the processing plant. When they emerge, some are spiced with Cajun spices, others with lemon pepper, and others are sold just plain.

Catfish meat is soft, almost flabby. It cooks quickly, and because its meat is watery, it is forgiving—leave it on the heat a minute too long and it will still be moist and tender.

The wateriness is not natural to catfish, but rather the result of its being dipped in a tripolyphosphate solution during processing. Phosphates are used as a preservative, and they cause the meat to absorb a certain amount of liquid. They aren't considered harmful to eat, and they give the fish a long shelf life—up to 2 weeks if they are properly cared for.

TROUT

Although trout has been raised in this country far longer than catfish, at least since before the turn of the century, it ranks number two behind catfish.

Ninety percent of our farm-raised trout comes from south central Idaho, where the dry landscape conceals a mighty aquifer that makes it a trout-farming paradise. There, Clear Springs Trout Co. raises rainbow trout

in raceways along the Snake River.

Aside from their coloring, these trout bear little resemblance to the wild rainbow. They are shorter and stubbier, with thicker sides, smaller heads, and generally smaller frames. Their distinct shape, which fits neatly on a 10-inch dinner plate, is the direct result of genetic manipulation, the province of Clear Springs' research department.

Clear Springs takes very good care of their trout. First they are hatched inside and kept in small raceways until they are about 3 inches long. Then they are transferred out into the larger raceways, where they learn to feed themselves: when they're hungry they jump out of the water and bump an overhanging rod, which releases food into the water. If left on their own they would eat until they pop, so the amount of food is controlled. When it's gone, the refrigerator is bare until the next day.

Clear Springs makes the food their trout eat, an oil and soy combination. Certain trout, however, get a special feed mixed with crawfish shells which turns their meat a pale pink, so they look more like wild trout.

By the time the trout at Clear Springs are 7 to 10 inches long, they are on their way to markets and restaurants around the country.

The beauty of fish farming is that any time anyone wants trout, catfish, salmon, tilapia, or shrimp, all they have to do is ask. There are no seasons, no storms, no uncontrollable occurrences to stop their production. And though the farmed version may be a far cry from what's found in the wild, they *are* a fish in the hand. And that's better than no fish at all.

CURRIED CATFISH

Catfish farming has become a booming industry in the past decade, and much of the Mississippi Delta has been transformed into ponds, which glimmer in the flat landscape like mirrors.

In general, catfish is popular for its mild flavor and soft texture. It cooks quickly—a ½-inch-thick fillet cooks in just 6 to 7 minutes. If overcooked too much, it will become soft and mushy.

This dish offers a nice change from the traditional fried catfish.

4 catfish fillets (7 ounces each)
¼ cup boiling water
¼ cup dried currants
1 tablespoon unsalted butter
2 shallots, peeled and diced
¼ cup dry white wine, such
*   as a Sauvignon Blanc*
Salt and freshly ground black pepper
1 cup heavy (whipping) cream
½ to 1 teaspoon best-quality curry
*   powder*
Minced fresh chives, for garnish

1 Rinse the catfish fillets and pat them dry. Cover and refrigerate until just before cooking.

2 Pour the boiling water over the currants to plump them, and let stand for 15 minutes. Drain and set aside.

3 Melt the butter in a nonstick skillet over medium heat Add the shallots and cook, stirring, until they are nearly transparent, about 2 minutes. Add the catfish fillets in one layer, and pour the wine over and around the fillets. Season with salt and pepper. Cover the skillet and cook until the fillets are nearly opaque through, 6 to 7 minutes.

4 Transfer the fillets to a warmed platter, and keep warm in a low (200°F) oven.

5 Add the cream and the currants to the cooking juices in the skillet, stir, and reduce the heat to low. Simmer until the sauce has thickened and reduced by about one third, about 3 minutes. Stir in the curry powder.

6 Divide the fillets among four warmed dinner plates. Pour the sauce over each one, and garnish with the chives. (Or you can spoon a portion of sauce in the center of each plate, arrange a fillet on top, and garnish with the chives.) Serve immediately.

4 servings

Fresh Vegetables, Beans, and Grains

FARMHOUSE COOKBOOK

FRESH VEGETABLES

A HEAPING BOUNTY OF VEGETABLES AND GRAINS

I've always been partial to vegetables—"vegetable-minded," as my husband puts it. I was a vegetarian for years, not because I didn't like meat, but because with all the vegetables I did like, I hardly found room for anything else.

I was in heaven visiting vegetable farms while researching this book. There was something almost spiritual about being surrounded by soft green artichoke plants in a California field and visiting a small farm in the Ozark mountains, where golden Jerusalem artichokes towered languidly on one side and rows of space-ship-like kohlrabi sprouted on the other, with a small patch of rice in between.

Even better than looking, however, was tasting the vegetables from the farms. Caryl Smith worked simple wonders with the bounty from her garden, and her dish of Barney's favorite vegetables is one of my favorites. Dave Kobos has one of those farms where all grows in profusion, and his Winter Vegetable Medley is a regular addition to our meals, while Helen Pavich's potatoes and

collard greens dish is another I could eat nearly every day.

I learned all manner of regional ways with vegetables, using them in wonderful quirky recipes like Bobbie Clark's King of Naples, which gives eggplant a whole new look, and Turnip Greens and Chard with Salt Pork, which is spicy and gutsy and good.

Such a style of eating always includes grains and legumes, so you'll find some recipes in this chapter that will remind you just how delicious these nutritious foods are. They're hearty and versatile, and perfect for the vegetable- and non-vegetable minded.

STUFFED ARTICHOKES

Tony Leonardini (see page 132), the font of my favorite artichoke recipes, prepares this often for his family. I've adapted it slightly, but it is true to the recipe he gave me.

The best way to eat these artichokes is to pull off the outer leaves and eat their juicy stuffing-flavored meat, then gradually make your way to the center. Try this with a soft Merlot such as a Columbia Milestone 1988.

4 medium artichokes, rinsed

3 cups water

1 small onion, peeled and diced

3 tablespoons pine nuts, toasted

1 serrano pepper, trimmed, seeds left in, and minced

Salt and freshly ground black pepper to taste

2 cloves garlic, minced

1 pound lean ground pork

7 tablespoons fresh bread crumbs

1 cup dry white wine, such as a Macon Villages

2 teaspoons extra-virgin olive oil

1 Using scissors, trim the tips off the artichokes leaves, except for the leaves at the very center. Trim the stem flush with the base, so the artichokes will stand on their own.

2 Bring the water to a boil in the bottom of a vegetable steamer, and place the artichokes in the steamer basket. Steam the artichokes, covered, until they are nearly cooked, about 20 minutes; the flesh should still resist somewhat when you pierce the stem end with a knife.

3 Preheat the oven to 350°F.

4 While the artichokes are steaming, combine the remaining ingredients except for 2 tablespoons of the bread crumbs, the wine, and the olive oil.

5 Remove the basket from the steamer and allow the artichokes to cool. When they are cool enough to handle, pull out the center portion of leaves, leaving several layers of outer leaves still attached to the base. Either eat the center leaves or dis-

card them. Using a small stainless steel spoon, carefully scoop out the choke from the center. You should have a good-size cavity that is completely free of choke to contain the stuffing. Gently press out on the remaining leaves to enlarge the cavity.

6 Divide the stuffing mixture equally among the artichokes, mounding it above the leaves. Place the artichokes in an ovenproof dish, and pour the wine around them. Cover with aluminum foil, and bake in the center of the oven for 30 minutes. Remove the foil and top the artichokes with the remaining 2 tablespoons bread crumbs. Drizzle the olive oil over them, and continue baking until the bread crumbs are browned and the stuffing is cooked through and firm but not dry, about 30 minutes more.

7 Remove the dish from the oven, and serve immediately.

4 servings

BOBBIE CLARK'S BAKED BEANS

I tasted the best baked beans of my life at the Carpenter farm in Grady, Arkansas (see page 81). It was Labor Day, and my husband and I had visited the farm during the morning, spending time out in the fields as the whole family picked and thinned turnip greens, lettuces, and beans.

At noon they all piled into a truck and drove back to the house, singing and joshing each other along—a hard-working, close-knit bunch. Though our itinerary had been planned differently, when an invitation for lunch was issued, I eagerly accepted—I wouldn't have turned down a meal with this cheerful group for love or money. The bonus was just the kind of scrumptious, messy, sticky, delicious food that barbecue dreams are made of. Bobbie Clark and her mother Katie Carpenter had cooked all the food, and they hovered over everyone, keeping plates full while making sure they got some chicken and beans for themselves.

Of all the food on the menu— barbecued meats, potato salad, lemon cake, and ice cream—these beans won my heart. This is my re-creation of their recipe, since the instructions Bobbie gave me were rife with "a little bit o' this and a little bit o' that."

I keep the barbecue sauce on hand to liven up all sorts of dishes, and to make sure a pot of baked beans is never far away. These take some time, but it's time that gives them their flavor and mellow sweetness, so don't skimp on it. And when you eat this warm, sunny dish, imagine the Carpenter family at work, and at play.

1 pound dried pink or navy beans
1 bay leaf
1 tablespoon unsalted butter
1 large onion, peeled and diced
1 large green bell pepper, cored, seeded, and diced
2 cups water
8 ounces salt pork, cut in half
2 cups Jimmy Lee Edwards's Barbecue Sauce (page 313)
¼ teaspoon cayenne pepper, or to taste

1 Place the beans in a large pot, cover them with water, and soak them overnight. (Or for a faster method, cover them with boiling water and let sit for 1 hour.) Drain the beans, discarding the liquid.

2 Return the beans to the pot, cover with fresh water, add the bay leaf, and bring to a boil, covered. Reduce the heat to medium-low and simmer, partially covered, until the beans are tender but not soft,

about 30 minutes. Drain the beans, saving the cooking liquid.

3 While the beans are cooking, prepare the vegetables: Melt the butter in a large heavy skillet over medium heat. Add the onion and pepper, stir, and cook, stirring occasionally, until the onion is translucent and the pepper is softened but still slightly crisp, about 10 minutes. Remove the skillet from the heat and set aside.

4 Preheat the oven to 325°F.

5 Bring the 2 cups of water to a boil in a small saucepan. Add the salt pork, cover, and return to the boil. Then remove from the heat and drain. Score both pieces of salt pork by cutting them in squares just to the rind (don't cut through the rind). Place one piece of the salt pork in a large (3½-quart), heavy ovenproof pan or casserole. Cover it with the beans. Stir the onion and pepper into the beans so they are thoroughly mixed.

6 In a medium bowl, mix together 2 cups of the reserved bean cooking liquid, the barbecue sauce, and the cayenne pepper. Pour this mixture over the beans, stir gently, and place the second piece of salt pork on top, pushing it down into the beans. Cover, and bake until the barbecue sauce has been absorbed by the beans and the beans are tender, 4½ to 5 hours. Check them occasionally, and if they are getting the least bit dry, add some more bean cooking liquid or water. They should be moist, neither dry nor soupy.

7 Reduce the heat to 300°F, remove the lid, and cook the beans for 1 more hour, until they are crisp on top.

8 Taste for seasoning, and serve the beans hot from the oven. (These are also delicious cold the next day, if you're a cold-baked-bean fan. Otherwise they're exquisite reheated, and in fact improve with age. When reheating them, you may need to add some water to keep them from sticking.)

6 to 8 servings

BARLEY WITH SAFFRON AND LEMON

Barley is too often relegated to the unglamorous world of health foods. While it *is* very good for you, it also has a beguiling flavor and a gorgeous texture that resembles arborio rice.

I like barley slightly *al dente*—firm to the bite. If you prefer a softer texture, increase the cooking time slightly. However, don't overcook it. It won't get mushy, but there is a point beyond which it loses its unique texture.

This dish goes very well with roast meat, or with grilled or steamed fish. Try it alongside the Pork Loin with Coriander and Garlic Crust (see Index).

1 tablespoon extra-virgin olive oil
1 large onion, peeled and diced
1 cup hulled barley
3 cups water
¾ teaspoon saffron threads, crushed
4 teaspoons freshly squeezed lemon juice
1 large clove garlic, peeled and minced
Salt and freshly ground black pepper

1 Heat the oil in a medium-size heavy saucepan over medium heat. Add the onion and cook, stirring frequently, until it begins to soften and turn translucent, about 3 to 5 minutes.

2 Add the barley, stir, and then add the water, saffron, and lemon juice. Bring to a boil, cover, and reduce the heat to medium-low so the barley is simmering vigorously. Cook until most of the liquid has been absorbed and the barley is tender but still has texture, about 35 minutes.

3 Remove the cover from the pan, and stir in the garlic. Season to taste with salt and pepper. Cook, stirring constantly, until the flavors have blended, 4 to 5 minutes. The barley should not be dry, nor should it be in a pool of liquid. Serve immediately.

4 servings

AROMATIC BARLEY

During my travels, I met several farmers growing organic barley. It is one of those grains that should be right up with rice in terms of popularity. Barley has a subtle toasty flavor, and its texture alone keeps you asking for more.

I like barley because it is versatile, and its subtlety opens up innumerable possibilities. You can serve it seasoned with salt, pepper, and a drizzle of olive oil, or you can jazz it up—as in this exotic, aromatic mixture. I serve this dish with roast poultry or meats; or if I have leftovers of either on hand, I cut them into chunks and add them to the barley for a one-dish supper.

If you feel virtuous, as well as satisfied, when you eat barley, you are entirely justified. It is rich in protein and fiber, and is a good source of phosphorus, potassium, and vitamin B_6.

¼ *teaspoon ground ginger*

½ *teaspoon ground cinnamon*

½ *teaspoon ground cumin*

½ *teaspoon turmeric*

½ *teaspoon mace*

¼ *teaspoon freshly ground black pepper*

½ *teaspoon finely ground coriander*
    seeds

Pinch of ground cloves

½ *teaspoon yellow mustard seeds*

½ *teaspoon brown mustard seeds*

¼ *teaspoon dried red pepper flakes*

2 *tablespoons extra-virgin olive oil*

1 *cup hulled barley*

1 *large onion, peeled and diced*

3 *small carrots, peeled and diced*

2 *ribs celery, trimmed and diced*

3 *cups Herbfarm Deluxe Chicken Stock*
    (light version; page 86), or good-quality
    canned broth

Salt

1 Combine the spices in a small bowl, and
set aside.

2 Heat the oil in a large heavy skillet over
medium-low heat. Add the barley and
cook, stirring, until it turns golden brown, 4
to 5 minutes. Watch it carefully so it doesn't
get too brown.

3 Add the vegetables, and cook, stirring
constantly, until the onion begins to
turn translucent, 3 to 4 minutes. Stir in the
spice mixture and cook, continuing to stir,
until they send up their perfume, which will
take a minute or two.

4 Add the stock, season with salt, and increase the heat enough to bring the liquid to a boil. Then reduce the heat so the
stock is simmering vigorously, cover, and
cook until the barley has absorbed nearly all
of the stock and is tender but still has texture, 45 to 50 minutes. Adjust the seasoning, transfer to a serving bowl, and serve
immediately.

6 to 8 servings

DILLED BEETS
AND POTATOES

T his dish was inspired by a walk through the Pine Bluff, Arkansas,
farmers' market. Among the riot of vegetables were big, dusty red
beets, good-size new potatoes, and bunches of scallions.

I like to serve this alongside fish or chicken in late spring, when all the vegetables are tender and sweet and asparagus is in its element. The dark red beets stain the potatoes with their color, and the asparagus provides a bright counterpoint.

⅓ cup extra-virgin olive oil
2 teaspoons best-quality red wine vinegar
1 clove garlic, peeled and minced
Salt and freshly ground black pepper
2 pounds beets, tops trimmed off without cutting into the beet, well rinsed
4 small waxy potatoes, peeled and halved
1 pound asparagus, trimmed, stems peeled
4 scallions (green onions), trimmed and cut into ⅛-inch-thick rounds
½ cup loosely packed fresh dill

1 Whisk together the olive oil, vinegar, garlic, and a generous amount of salt and pepper in a large bowl. Set aside.

2 Bring 1 quart of water to a boil in the bottom of a vegetable steamer, and steam the beets until they are tender, about 30 to 45 minutes depending on their size. About 20 minutes before the beets are cooked, add the potatoes to the steamer and steam until they are tender. Remove the vegetables, and add the asparagus to the steamer. Cook just until it is crisp-tender, 4 to 5 minutes. Remove it from the steamer and keep warm.

3 As soon as the beets are cool enough to handle, peel and trim them, and cut them into bite-size chunks. Cut the potatoes

FLUFFY OR WAXY?

▪▪▪▪▪

*P*otatoes are generally divided into two basic categories, fluffy and waxy. As an example, a Russet (commonly referred to as an Idaho since that is where most of them are grown) is a fluffy, starchy potato, its meat light in color and texture. It is best for baking and mashing because it fluffs right up to absorb butter, cream, chicken broth, or whatever you choose to stir into it.

The Red Rose potato, the small red-skinned variety found nearly year-round in the supermarket, is a waxy variety. It is best for boiling and steaming and makes a good salad choice because it holds its shape and has a firm, waxy texture.

Within these categories are dozens of potato varieties. For example, Peruvian purple potatoes are fluffy, while Yellow Finns and Yukon golds are waxy. Urgenta, a relatively "new" potato variety, is a fluffy/waxy mix, and any "new" potato— that is one that has been recently harvested and has thin, papery skin—has a more waxy texture regardless of its variety, and is best treated as such.

into chunks as well, and toss the vegetables in the prepared dressing. Add the scallions and the dill, and toss. Transfer the vegetables to a warmed platter. Arrange the asparagus around the edge of the platter, taste for seasoning, and serve immediately.

4 to 6 servings

SEATTLE'S PIKE PLACE MARKET

The Pike Place Market, established in 1907 so that farmers could sell directly to the public, is Seattle's rowdy, colorful soul. "Meet the Producer" a sign proclaims on the side of the market building, and this has been the market's continuing theme, allowing it to survive Seattle's wild growth to cityhood.

At first glance the market looks like a clip from a 1920s film—the rambling series of newly restored buildings is part of the city's historic district. It has stayed that way because of the efforts of activists and architects who fought the city's plan to tear it down, and the whole market area has retained the flavor and character of its rich history.

Shortly after the market was saved from destruction it underwent a grand remodeling, which was completed in 1986. The ten-year project was so subtly done and so successful that the market has since been used as a model for other market developments around the country.

Unlike other markets, however, Pike Place Market is still true to its original mandate, which is to provide an arena where local farmers can sell their produce directly to the consumer, and where prices and quality remain competitive.

The market is located on 7 winding acres above the shore of Elliott Bay. It descends hills, rounds corners, dribbles south toward Pioneer Square, and stops on the north end at a pair of trendy restaurants and a health club.

Brick-paved Pike Street cuts the market in half. Some produce is sold on the east side of the street, where everything from juicy red raspberries to burnished plantains spill onto the sidewalk and the lively notes of musicians drift overhead. The real heart of the produce market is located across the street, however, in what is called the main arcade and is the site of the original market.

Inside the arcade are permanent "high stalls," so called because the vendors originally stood on raised platforms behind counters. Though the market is dedicated to local farmers, "high stallers" also bring in produce from around the world so that customers can find oranges, lemons, avocados, and pineapples throughout the year.

THE SET-UP

A t 8:30 A.M., JoAnn Laskowski, in preparation of the 9:00 A.M. opening, is rapidly stacking oranges at Manzo Brothers Produce. She examines the arrangement, then drapes it with bunches of tiny deep purple grapes that are so sweet she calls them "caviar on a stem." JoAnn fills more counter space with melons, ruby tomatoes, and Belgian endive, creating a vivid still life that will gradually diminish throughout the day.

Across from her, the well-known and raucous fishmongers at Pure Food Fish Company are already yelling "Get yer fresh salmon here," and down the way other vendors compete with their early morning hawking.

More than 100 local farmers display an astonishing array of produce on the "low stalls," long green tables on either side of the high stalls, that run nearly the length of 2½ city blocks. Market rules require that "low stallers" sell only produce and processed foods—jams, jellies, syrups, cordials—that they grow and make themselves. Most farmers are from Seattle, though some come all the way from eastern Washington, Idaho, and Canada.

The market's original farmers, mostly of Italian and Japanese descent, have been succeeded by a new generation. Some, like Mike and Sue Verdi, who specialize in greens like arugula, basil, escarole, and mâche, are children of the original farmers. Mike's mother, Pasqualina Verdi, has been the market's quintessential Italian *mama* for decades.

Members of Seattle's Indochinese Farm Project, which was established to teach Asian immigrants modern farming techniques (see page 62), produce mounds of bok choy, *tat soi*, radish buds, and flowering kale. And there is another type of farmer too, young, seriously involved with bringing old crops back and growing them organically; they grow chestnuts, figs, and flowers on a neighboring island, and salad greens and edible flowers on an urban farm.

AND THAT'S NOT ALL

T he market wouldn't be the same without DeLaurenti Specialty Food Market, a well-loved mainstay. The DeLaurenti family was selling extra-virgin olive oil, prosciutto, and balsamic vinegar long before the rest of us knew what they were. They still do, but they have grown into a full-service Italian delicatessen with freshly made pasta, sausages, dozens of cheeses, vinegars, capers, and sun-dried tomatoes.

Another more recent Pike Place cornerstone is Sur La Table, across from the main market. The proprietor, Shirley Collins, has one of the most complete kitchen shops in the country and offers everything from cookbooks and pop-up sponges to fish poachers and weighty copper pots.

Sprinkled throughout the market are a generous handful of restaurants. There is Chez Shea, an elegant bistro set above the hurlyburly of the market; Place Pigalle, which overlooks Elliott Bay; Café Sport, which is locally touted as producing the city's finest examples of "Northwest cuisine"; and Campagne, in the courtyard of the Alexis Hotel, which offers a slice of Seattle *à la campagne*.

There's even more to the Pike Place Market, which changes according to the season. It's a living, breathing, entity, and buying the local produce is almost as good as growing your own.

STEAMED BROCCOLI WITH HOT PEPPERS

This recipe comes from Bobbie Clark, who farms with her family in Grady, Arkansas, just outside of Pine Bluff (see page 81). Though Bobbie's parents, Abraham and Katie Carpenter, actively farm along with twenty-three other members of the family, Bobbie takes the helm, cooks the meals with her mother, and gets and keeps everyone organized.

The Carpenters grow broccoli and chile peppers, and this is one of Bobbie's favorite ways to combine them.

You can adjust the heat of the sauce by removing the seeds and membranes from the pepper, but you will find that the heat is mild even if you leave all the seeds in.

1¼ pounds broccoli, stems trimmed
1 cup plus 2 tablespoons milk
1 bay leaf
1½ tablespoons unsalted butter
1 jalapeño or serrano pepper, trimmed, seeds left in, and minced
3 scallions (green onions), trimmed and cut into thin rounds (¼ cup)
1½ tablespoons all-purpose flour
1½ cups grated sharp Cheddar cheese
Salt

1 Separate the broccoli into florets and stems. Peel the stems, and slice them on the diagonal into 1-inch pieces.

2 Prepare the cheese sauce: Scald 1 cup of the milk with the bay leaf in a small heavy saucepan over medium-high heat. (Do not let the milk boil.) Remove the pan from the heat, cover, and set aside for 10 minutes.

3 Meanwhile, melt the butter in a medium-size heavy saucepan over medium heat. Add the pepper and the scallions, and sauté until they begin to wilt, 2 to 3 minutes. Stir in the flour and cook, stirring frequently, until it foams, at least 2 minutes. (It is very important to cook the flour at this point, to avoid a floury-tasting sauce.) Do not let the flour brown. Strain the milk into the pan and cook, stirring frequently, until it comes to a simmer and the sauce thickens. Add the cheese and stir it until it has melted. Taste for salt, and keep warm over low heat.

4 Bring water to a boil in the bottom of a vegetable steamer or in a wok fitted with a steamer rack. Steam the broccoli

stems in the steamer basket, covered, until they begin to turn tender, 1 minute. Then add the florets and steam until they are tender but not soft, 1½ minutes. Transfer the broccoli immediately to a warmed serving bowl or shallow dish. Thin the cheese sauce with the remaining 2 tablespoons milk if desired, and pour the sauce over the broccoli. Serve immediately.

4 servings

GARLICKY BROCCOLI RABE

B roccoli rabe is a favorite in Italian and Chinese cooking, but it is still considered a specialty vegetable in many parts of this country. I think it may well be one of the best aspects of fall and winter.

Broccoli rabe has a deep, pleasantly bitter green flavor with a hint of broccoli's mellow taste. It can be served in a salad—tossed with escarole and curly endive—or prepared this way.

When buying broccoli rabe, look for bunches with tightly closed buds rather than delicate yellow flowers, which are a signal of age.

3 large cloves garlic, peeled
1 cup fresh bread crumbs
3 tablespoons olive oil
1 pound broccoli rabe, rinsed and stems
  trimmed to about 1 inch
Salt and freshly ground black pepper
2 tablespoons freshly squeezed lemon juice

1 Mince 2 of the garlic cloves and mix them with the bread crumbs in a small bowl. Heat 2 tablespoons of the olive oil in a large skillet over medium-high heat. Add the bread crumb mixture and cook, stirring constantly, until the crumbs are toasted and the garlic is beginning to turn golden, which will take 3 to 4 minutes. Remove the skillet from the heat and spread the bread crumbs out on a plate to cool.

2 Bring a large pot of boiling salted water (1 tablespoon salt per gallon of water) to a boil over high heat. Add the broccoli rabe and leave it in the pot just until the water returns to a boil. Then drain it in a colander, and squeeze it gently to remove the excess

water. Coarsely chop the broccoli rabe, leaving any florets whole, and set aside.

3 Heat the remaining 1 tablespoon olive oil over medium heat in the same skillet that you used for toasting the bread crumbs. Coarsely chop the remaining garlic clove, and add it to the oil. Cook, stirring constantly, until it begins to turn translucent, about 5 minutes. Add the broccoli rabe and cook, stirring, until it is hot and the garlic is golden, about 7 minutes. Season generously with salt and pepper, and transfer to a warmed serving bowl or plate. Drizzle with the lemon juice, sprinkle with the bread crumb mixture, and serve immediately.

4 servings

SLIGHTLY TAMED GARLIC

*A*s garlic ages, it develops a green "germ" inside the center of each clove. If the clove were planted, this germ would grow and become the stalk of a new garlic plant.

The germ can be strong-flavored and occasionally bitter. To avoid this, remove it, particularly in dishes where garlic will be eaten raw. Cut the garlic clove in half lengthwise and gently pull out the germ.

AMISH BRUSSELS SPROUTS WITH BROWN BUTTER

T he Amish have a knack for making the most of fresh-from-the-garden flavors. Traditionally, they pour brown butter over cooked vegetables. I like to flavor the butter with garlic and a splash of lemon juice, which add an extra dimension. You will find that this simple preparation works wonderfully with broccoli, cauliflower, leeks, and green beans. You will also find that vegetables prepared this way are a universal favorite.

3 tablespoons unsalted butter
1 clove garlic, peeled and minced
1 tablespoon freshly squeezed lemon juice
1½ pounds Brussels sprouts, trimmed
2 cups water
Salt and freshly ground black pepper

1 Combine the butter and garlic in a small saucepan over medium heat. When the garlic begins to turn dark gold, remove it with a slotted spoon and discard. Stir the lemon juice into the butter, and keep warm over low heat.

2 Cut an X in the stem end of each Brussels sprout (this prevents them from falling apart during cooking). Bring the water to a boil in the bottom of a vegetable steamer, and steam the Brussels sprouts until they are just tender, but not soft or mushy, 8 to 10 minutes.

3 Transfer the Brussels sprouts to a warmed serving bowl. Pour the browned butter over them, and toss so they are coated with it. Season to taste with salt and pepper, and serve.

4 to 6 servings

LEEKS AND CABBAGE ON A BED OF WILD RICE

I first learned the true merits of wild rice when I went to St. Maries, Idaho, to do a story on Alexander Bruner and Jeffrey Baker, who cultivate and harvest a large stand of wild rice in nearby Lake Benewah. While there, I stayed at a bed-and-breakfast and the owner, Vickie Hedlund, served a meal one night that included perfectly cooked and seasoned wild rice. I've loved wild rice since, and am grateful for her instructions.

I prefer St. Maries wild rice because its long, dark kernels are cleaner and more flavorful than others I've tasted. Of course, the experience of riding a harvesting boat into a stand of wild rice in Lake Benewah on a day when the sky was blue, the rice a vivid green, and the air full of birds may add to my preference, though everyone I've served the rice to agrees with me.

At first you may wonder at the flavors combined here, but don't judge this dish until you've tasted it. It is surprisingly sophisticated and delicate, with a lively texture and delicious flavor. A lightly chilled Beaujolais would be perfect alongside.

1 cup wild rice
3 cups Herbfarm Deluxe Chicken Stock
   (page 86) or good-quality canned broth
Grated zest of 1 lemon
1 tablespoon freshly squeezed lemon juice
1½ teaspoons loosely packed saffron threads
Salt and freshly ground black pepper
2 tablespoons olive oil
4 medium leeks, trimmed and well rinsed, white
   and green parts cut into ¼-inch-thick rounds
1 medium green cabbage, cored and cut into
   ⅛-inch-thick slices
4 thin slices (about 3 ounces) prosciutto, cut
   into ¼-inch-wide ribbons

1 Combine the wild rice and the chicken stock in a medium-size heavy saucepan over medium-high heat, cover, and bring to a boil. Add the lemon zest, lemon juice, and saffron threads. Reduce the heat to

HOW TO COOK WILL RICE

There are two tricks to perfectly cooked wild rice. The first is to buy the best quality you can find. The kernels should be whole and long, of an even dark brown almost black color, and clean. The aroma should be nutty with no hint of sourness. The second is to remove the rice from the heat before it overcooks and becomes mushy. If you prefer rice slightly chewy, then you want half the kernels cracked and showing white. If you like it a bit softer, let it cook until two thirds are cracked. Check it occasionally as it is cooking—it doesn't hurt to lift the lid once in a while—so you can catch the rice at its best.

medium, cover, and cook until half the rice kernels have split, 45 to 50 minutes. Season to taste with salt and pepper, if desired. Most likely there will still be some cooking liquid left. Remove from the heat and keep warm.

2 While the rice is cooking, heat the oil in a large skillet over medium-high heat. Add the leeks, and toss so they are coated with the oil. Cover, reduce the heat to medium, and cook until they are slightly softened, about 5 minutes.

3 Add the cabbage to the leeks, toss so they are well mixed, season with salt and pepper, and cook until the cabbage is

slightly softened and has turned bright green, about 8 minutes. Taste and adjust the seasoning.

4 Mound the rice in the center of a warmed serving platter, pouring any remaining rice cooking liquid over it.

Arrange the cabbage and leek mixture around the rice. Sprinkle the prosciutto over the cabbage mixture, and serve immediately.

6 servings

SWEET CARROTS AND PEARLS

I was inspired to make this one day after visiting Purepak Farms in Lompoc, California, and watching the field workers unload bushel after bushel of gorgeous carrots from a truck. Their hands were caked with soil and so were the carrots, but not for long. One of the workers unleashed a powerful blast of water from a hose and the carrots came clean. I munched on one and found it to be the sweetest carrot I'd ever eaten.

This recipe accentuates the sweetness of carrots and makes a beautiful side dish.

1½ tablespoons unsalted butter
1 pound carrots, peeled and cut diagonally
  into 1-inch pieces
25 pearl onions, peeled
1½ tablespoons light brown sugar
Salt and freshly ground black pepper

1 Melt the butter in a large saucepan or skillet over medium-high heat. Add the

carrots and the onions, sprinkle with the brown sugar, and stir until the vegetables are coated with the sugar.

2 Reduce the heat to medium, cover, and cook until the vegetables are nearly tender, about 12 minutes. Season to taste with salt and pepper, and continue cooking, covered, until they are lightly caramelized and soft, 6 to 7 minutes. Serve immediately.

4 servings

THE WORLD'S SWEETEST CARROTS

Purepak is a farm worthy of note, and not just because they grow the world's sweetest carrots. Until about six years ago, Dean Walsh, part owner of Purepak, grew vegetables conventionally and sold them through traditional channels. Then one day, as he walked through the supermarket and watched consumers reading labels like crazy, he had an epiphany. "The market looked like a bookstore," he explains. "People were reading labels to find out just what was in the food they were buying."

Dean got to thinking, and he developed a strategic plan. He decided, against the advice of most of his peers, friends, and family, to start growing some of his vegetables organically.

"It paid off immediately because organic produce commands a higher price at market than produce grown conventionally," he says. "It wasn't easy. I had to become an environmentalist. I had to find out what a bug likes, then find an environment it likes, so I don't have to buy bugs and bring them in," he says, referring to the beneficial insects that live in his fields and keep harmful insects at bay.

"Organic farming is incredibly labor-intensive too. We pay as much to have our fields weeded as we did just to grow a crop conventionally. And we've seen a drop in yield in our organic fields, but that doesn't matter. A drop in yield means a market that sustains a price that actually pays the farmer."

Paul Carpenter is the farm manager at Purepak, and he's livid about what's happening to the land in California. "I see good land go bad awful fast with chemicals. As an organic farmer, you have to have a five-year plan for the land. You can't just do what the conventional farmers do and call up the chemical company and tell them to spray your fields.

Both Dean and Paul are committed to organic farming. It isn't easy, they say, and it takes more time. But the workers don't get sick, they don't lose crops to overfertilization or toxic chemicals, and they supply a burgeoning organic market with top-quality vegetables.

"We sell 50 percent of our crops through organic channels, the rest into the conventional market," Dean says. "It's paying off, and we're watching the land come back too. Who would complain about that?"

CORN ON THE COB WITH PEPPER BUTTER

This recipe was inspired by visits to a number of farms in the Midwest during the fall corn harvest. Little stands were set up at the edge of cornfields, offering mounds of ears fresh from the fields, and we stopped every day to pick up a bag. We'd boil up some water, throw in the ears and eat just that for supper. Nothing compares with corn straight from the field.

From having such a wealth of corn I turned to serving it with seasoned butters. I keep the seasoning subtle and mellow because the flavor of the corn itself is so intoxicatingly sweet and fresh. But every now and then, during corn season when ears can be had for a song, it's nice to add some variety, and this pepper butter does the trick. I pass it separately so guests can use as much as they like. (This butter is also good atop cooked frozen corn in winter, when a shot of summer is in order.)

6 tablespoons (¾ stick) unsalted butter, at room temperature
1 red bell pepper, roasted (page 322), peeled, and seeded
1 tablespoon freshly squeezed lemon juice
¼ teaspoon salt, or to taste
Pinch of cayenne pepper (optional)
6 to 8 ears fresh corn

1 Place the butter in a food processor, and process until smooth. Add the pepper, lemon juice, salt, and cayenne, and process until thoroughly combined. Taste for seasoning.

2 Transfer the butter to an attractive crock or dish, cover, and refrigerate until hardened, at least 1½ hours.

CORNY CUSTOM

Once upon a time in the Midwest, after corn was grown, harvested, and dried, husking bees were held in each family barn. Whoever shucked an ear of predominantly red kernels won the privilege of kissing any member of the opposite sex.

3 Bring a large pot of water to a boil. Add the corn and cook, pushing the ears

down into the water so they cook evenly, just until the kernels have softened slightly and are hot through, no more than 4 to 5 minutes. Drain the ears and place them in a warmed serving dish. Pass the butter alongside.

6 to 8 servings

BRAISED CELERY

O n the day I visited Purepak Growers (see page 204), there was celery being harvested as well as carrots. I'd never thought much about celery, but the pungent aroma that filled the air as it was being cut filled me with creativity.

Wait until you try this recipe. The celery cooks gently to a tender flavorful crunch, and as it softens it turns a delicate green. This is a wonderful winter vegetable dish, delicious with meats, fish, or poultry.

7 large ribs celery, trimmed
1 tablespoon freshly squeezed lemon juice
1 clove garlic, peeled
1 small onion, peeled and halved
1½ cups water
Salt and freshly ground black pepper

1 Using a vegetable peeler, remove the strings from the celery. Cut the ribs diag-

onally into 4-inch lengths. Place them, along with the remaining ingredients, in a deep skillet over medium-high heat. Bring to a boil, reduce the heat to low, and cook until the celery is tender but still somewhat crisp, about 20 minutes.

2 Using a slotted spoon, remove the celery from the cooking liquid and place it in a warmed serving bowl. Serve immediately.

4 servings

AMISH CORN PUDDING

This delicate pudding is full of sweet corn, lightly seasoned with scallions and nutmeg, and so tasty that you'll need to make a double batch to keep up with the demand.

I start making this pudding toward the end of the local sweet corn season, when my appetite craves corn in ways other than boiled on the cob, and I continue making it right through Thanksgiving. In fact, it has become a traditional part of our Thanksgiving meal, because it really is something special.

2 tablespoons unsalted butter, melted
3 small scallions (green onions), trimmed and
  cut into thin rounds (¼ cup)
2 tablespoons all-purpose flour
2 cups milk
4 large eggs
1 teaspoon salt, or to taste
Freshly ground black pepper
½ teaspoon ground nutmeg
4 cups corn kernels, fresh or frozen (see Note)

1 Preheat the oven to 375°F. Lightly oil a 6-cup soufflé or baking dish.

2 Melt 1 tablespoon of the butter in a small heavy skillet over medium heat.

When the butter is hot, add the scallions and cook, stirring, just until they begin to turn translucent, 3 to 4 minutes. Remove from the heat.

3 In a small bowl, whisk together the flour and ½ cup of the milk until smooth. Set aside.

4 In a large bowl, whisk together the eggs, the remaining 1½ cups milk, and the seasonings. Add the milk and flour mixture and the remaining 1 tablespoon melted butter; whisk until combined. Quickly stir in the corn and the sautéed scallions, and pour the mixture into the prepared soufflé or baking dish.

5 Bake until the corn pudding is cooked through, 50 minutes to 1 hour. It will jiggle when you move it, but it should not be liquid in the center. Remove from the oven and serve within 10 minutes.

6 to 8 servings

Note: If you make this pudding when only frozen corn is available, check that the corn rattles in its bag or box; this tells you it hasn't thawed and refrozen. Process the frozen corn in a food processor to chop it (it won't really chop, but it will break it up slightly and so release more of its juice during cooking).

Caryl Smith's Tamale Pie

C aryl Smith's cooking has a New Mexican flair inherited from her mother (see her *posole* on page 112). However Iowa, where Caryl and her husband, Barney, raise beef cattle, isn't exactly a hotbed of exotic ingredients, so she makes the best of her regular visits to New Mexico. "Most people bring back turquoise and silver," she says with a laugh. "I bring back chiles and *posole*."

When I asked Caryl for her favorite Thanksgiving dish, she didn't miss a beat. "Oh, my mother's tamale pie," she said. "My sister and I just can't wait for Thanksgiving each year so we can make it."

This is unusual for a tamale pie because the only meat it contains is a bit of bacon for flavoring. It is, instead, like a spicy version of corn pudding. You'll find it a welcome addition to a traditional meal, but don't wait for Thanksgiving. It is a terrific one-dish supper, along with a green salad, a dish of steamed fresh vegetables, or a bowlful of ripe tomatoes in a vinaigrette dressing.

Be sure to use the best, freshest chili powder you can find, as it is a vital element in the dish. The chili powder from the supermarket can be weary with age. Color is a good indicator: If the chili powder is a faded orange, pass it by. It should be a deep brick red, and loaded with aroma.

8 ounces slab bacon, cut into 1½ x ¼ x ¼-inch
  pieces
1 large onion, peeled and diced
2 cloves garlic, peeled and minced
1 large can (28 ounces) plum tomatoes
1 can (6 ounces) pitted black olives, drained
  (halved crosswise if large)
1¼ cups milk
3 tablespoons top-quality chili powder
2 cups fresh corn kernels, or 1 package
  (10 ounces) good-quality frozen corn kernels
3 eggs, beaten
2 cups yellow cornmeal
2 tablespoons olive oil

1 Preheat the oven to 375°F.

2 Place the bacon in a large heavy
  saucepan over medium heat, and cook,
stirring occasionally, until the fatty parts
are translucent, about 5 minutes. Add the
onion and garlic, and cook over medium-
low heat, stirring occasionally, until the
onion is soft and translucent, about 10
minutes.

3 Add the tomatoes and their liquid, and
  the olives, bring to a boil, and cook
until the mixture has reduced and thickened slightly, about 5 minutes. Add the
milk, chili powder, and corn, and return to
a boil. Remove the pan from the heat and
whisk in the eggs. Then gradually add in
the cornmeal, whisking fast to avoid lumps.

4 Pour the oil into a 9 x 12-inch baking
  dish. Spoon the mixture into the dish
and smooth the top. Bake in the center of
the oven until the pie is cooked through and
has cracked slightly on top, 30 minutes.
Serve immediately.

8 to 10 servings

EGGPLANT PARMESAN

This recipe comes from Helen Pavich, whose sons Stephen Paul and
Tom own and manage the largest organic vineyard in the country, in
California's San Joaquin Valley (see page 448). Mrs. Pavich lives at the
home farm, and her ranch-style house and garden are carved right out of
one of the vineyards, so she has grapes at her fingertips—as well as oranges
and a cornucopia of vegetables from her sizable vegetable garden. She's always been an organic gardener, and likes to think her example helped in-
spire her eldest son, Steven, to begin farming organically nearly 20 years ago.

Mrs. Pavich often cooks for her sons and their families, and this is a version of one of her favorite dishes. It's a simple preparation, without the traditional tomato sauce, which makes it a celebration of the flavor and texture of firm summer eggplant. I added the peppers, because when we were visiting the Pavichs, peppers were bursting off the vines and they seemed a natural partner for flavor and color.

Though this dish tastes rich and lush, it is lighter than the usual version of eggplant Parmesan because the eggplant isn't fried and the amount of oil is minimal. Fresh mozzarella cheese makes it silken and smooth, but if you can't find it, use the harder processed variety.

Serve this with a big green or chilled cucumber salad, plenty of bread for sopping up the juices of the eggplant Parmesan, and a bottle of young Chianti or a Zinfandel.

3 large eggplants, rinsed and patted dry

3 tablespoons salt

4 medium green bell peppers, rinsed and patted dry

2 to 3 tablespoons olive oil

⅔ cup finely grated Parmesan cheese

2 cloves garlic, peeled

12 ounces fresh mozzarella cheese, cut into thin (⅛-inch) slices

1 Preheat the broiler. Line two large baking sheets with aluminum foil.

2 Trim the eggplants, and slice them lengthwise into ¼-inch-thick slices. Salt the slices generously on both sides, and then stand them upright in a large colander to drain for 30 minutes.

3 Meanwhile, place the peppers on a large piece of aluminum foil 3 inches from the broiler, and roast until their skins have darkened and bubbled, rotating them frequently so they are evenly browned, which should take about 15 minutes. When the peppers are roasted, remove them, still on the foil, from the oven. Gather and crimp together the edges of the foil around them, sealing it well so they steam inside, 10 to 15 minutes. When the peppers are cool enough to handle, peel off the skin, remove the seeds and membranes, and cut the flesh into lengthwise slices 1½ inches wide.

4 Reduce the oven heat to 500°F.

5 Rinse the eggplant slices under cold running water, and firmly pat them dry with a paper or cotton towel. Lightly brush them on each side with olive oil, place them on the prepared baking sheets, and bake in the center of the oven until they are slightly golden and have softened, 15 to 20 minutes. Remove the eggplants from the oven, slip the slices off the baking sheets, and cool on wire racks.

6 Reduce the oven temperature to 350°F.

7 To assemble the eggplant Parmesan, generously brush an 8½ x 12½-inch

baking dish with olive oil, and line the bottom of the dish with a layer of eggplant slices. Sprinkle generously with Parmesan cheese, then arrange half the pepper slices on top of the eggplant. Sprinkle half the garlic over the peppers, then top with half the mozzarella slices. Repeat with the remaining ingredients, ending with mozzarella.

8 Bake until the cheese has melted and the eggplant is thoroughly soft, about 30 minutes. Remove from the oven and let cool for 5 minutes before serving.

6 to 8 servings

KING OF NAPLES

This homey dish is one of Bobbie Clark's specialties. She isn't sure where the name comes from, but says she makes it often for the family on their Arkansas farm (see page 81). I've adapted it slightly by adding herbs and homemade instead of canned tomato sauce. The eggplant becomes tender but retains a toothsome texture that might be described as *al dente*. Try this with a full-bodied red wine.

1½ pounds Italian plum tomatoes, quartered, or 4½ cups canned plum tomatoes
2 tablespoons olive oil
1 small onion, peeled and minced
3 cloves garlic, peeled and coarsely chopped
Salt and freshly ground black pepper to taste
6 ounces spaghetti
1 eggplant, peeled and sliced into ¼-inch-thick rounds
1 cup fresh basil leaves, loosely packed, or 1 tablespoon dried
⅓ cup fresh mixed herb leaves, such as oregano, thyme, winter savory, or marjoram, or 2 teaspoons mixed dried herbs

1½ cups shredded sharp Cheddar cheese
1 cup heavy (whipping) cream
¼ cup minced fresh parsley, for garnish

1 Preheat the oven to 325°F.

2 Prepare the tomato sauce: Purée the tomatoes in a food processor or blender. Set aside. Heat the oil in a medium-size saucepan over medium heat. When the oil is hot, add the onion and sauté until it begins to turn translucent, about 5 minutes. Add the garlic, stir, and

continue cooking, stirring frequently, until the onion is translucent, another 5 minutes. Add the tomatoes and bring to a boil. Reduce the heat to medium-low and cook just until the tomatoes don't taste raw anymore, about 10 minutes. Season to taste with salt and pepper.

3 While the sauce is cooking, cook the spaghetti in a large pot of boiling salted water until *al dente*. Drain thoroughly.

4 To assemble the dish, place a layer of eggplant slices on the bottom of a 10 x 14-inch oval enamel or glass baking dish. Season generously with salt and pepper. Mince half the basil leaves and half the mixed herbs, and sprinkle over the eggplant. Top with a layer of half the spaghetti,

then one-third of the cheese. Pour half the tomato sauce over, and repeat, using up the remaining ingredients and ending with the remaining one-third of cheese.

5 Pour the cream over all, and press lightly on the layers so the eggplant slices are covered with liquid, or have at least been well moistened. Bake, covered, for 40 minutes. Remove the cover and continue baking until the eggplant slices are softened—they will be somewhat firm but cooked through—and the cheese is bubbling, an additional 20 minutes.

6 Garnish with the parsley, and serve immediately.

8 to 10 servings

EGGPLANT, MOZZARELLA, AND BASIL PIZZA

H ow could you lose with the ingredients in this pizza? You can't, particularly when the mozzarella is freshly made, the eggplants small, gorgeous, and firm, and the basil right out of the garden.

The inspiration here comes from the southern states. In Texas I visited the basil-scented greenhouses of Golden Circle Farms outside Dallas and when in the city, sampled fresh mozzarella from the Mozzarella Cheese

Company there. I saw eggplant growing throughout the South, their large star-shaped flowers giving the fields a purplish hue.

This pizza is quick to make—the dough rises in less than an hour, and it cooks in less than 30 minutes. You can even make the dough in the morning, refrigerate it, and roll it out when you get home from work.

Though fresh mozzarella is best here because of its rich milk flavor, packaged mozzarella is a reasonable substitute.

Try the pizza with a California Merlot.

FOR THE PIZZA DOUGH

1 package active dry yeast
1¼ cups lukewarm water
3½ cups unbleached all-purpose flour
1 teaspoon salt

FOR THE PIZZA

1 pound small eggplants (about 4 inches long) or thin Japanese eggplants, rinsed and patted dry
3 tablespoons olive oil
2 cloves garlic, peeled and thinly sliced crosswise
12 ounces fresh mozzarella, cut into ⅛-inch-thick slices

FOR THE PESTO

2 cups gently packed fresh basil leaves
5 tablespoons olive oil
2 tablespoons pine nuts, toasted (see Note)
2 cloves garlic, peeled
⅓ cup grated Parmesan cheese
¼ to ½ teaspoon salt

1. To make the dough, dissolve the yeast in the lukewarm water in a large bowl or in the bowl of a heavy-duty electric mixer. Stir in 1 cup of the flour. Then add the salt and 2 more cups of flour, 1 cup at a time, mixing well after each addition. If you are using an electric mixer, set the speed at medium and gradually add the remaining ½ cup flour until the dough is no longer sticky. Increase the speed to high, and mix the dough until it is smooth and glossy, about 4 minutes. If you are making the dough by hand, turn it out onto a heavily floured work surface and gradually knead in the remaining ½ cup flour until the dough is smooth and glossy, which will take about 8 minutes.

Return the dough to the bowl, cover with a damp towel, and let it rise in a warm spot (68° to 70°F) until doubled in bulk, about 1 hour. (To refrigerate the dough after it has risen, place it in a bowl, cover tightly, and leave for up to 10 hours.)

2. Preheat the oven to 450°F. Brush a baking sheet lightly with olive oil.

3. Slice the eggplants lengthwise into thin (¼-inch) slices leaving the stem end intact. Place the eggplants on the prepared baking sheet, fanning them out gently. Brush them lightly and thoroughly with oil, and bake them in the center of the oven until they begin to soften and turn golden, about 10 minutes. Remove from the oven, and gently press them so they fan out slightly

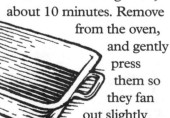

more. When the eggplants have cooled enough to handle, remove them from the baking sheet and set aside.

4 Reduce the oven temperature to 425°F.

5 Punch down the dough and roll it out on a lightly floured surface to fit the same baking sheet. Sprinkle the dough with the garlic slices, and then cover it with the mozzarella. Arrange the eggplants attractively on top of the cheese, drizzle with any remaining olive oil, and bake in the center of the oven until the dough is golden, the cheese is melted and bubbling, and the eggplants are cooked through, about 25 minutes.

6 While the pizza is baking, make the pesto: Place the basil, olive oil, pine nuts, and garlic in the bowl of a food processor. Process to a fine purée. Remove the blade from the processor, and stir in the cheese by hand. Season with salt and set aside.

7 Remove the pizza from the oven. Drizzle the pesto evenly over the pizza, and let it sit for about 5 minutes, to warm the pesto and to let the pizza cool slightly so it isn't molten when you serve it. Cut into pieces, and serve.

6 to 8 servings

Note: To toast pine nuts, preheat the oven to 350°F. Place the nuts in a baking pan large enough to hold them in a single layer, and toast, stirring once, until they are golden and give off a toasted aroma, 10 to 12 minutes.

GRILLED JAPANESE EGGPLANT WITH CILANTRO SAUCE

I love eggplant just about any way I can get it, and I envy the farmers who grow it and have as much as they want during the long, hot summer season. Fresh farm eggplant, what a luxury!

There are dozens of varieties of eggplant, from white to yellow to the familiar purple, and this dish can be made with one and all. The flavors of the different eggplants vary, but all are good prepared this way.

I serve this summer dish most often to start a meal. I slice the eggplants but leave them intact at the stem end, so that I can fan them out, and arrange them atop the pesto on a large platter. This makes for a dramatic, unusual presentation.

This dish is also good alongside roast meats or with full-flavored seafood. Serve it hot from the oven or at room temperature.

¼ cup extra-virgin olive oil
8 to 10 thin purple Japanese eggplants,
  rinsed and patted dry
1 recipe Cilantro Sauce (page 325)
Salt and freshly ground black pepper
Small handful cilantro leaves,
  for garnish

1 Preheat the oven to 450°F. Oil a baking sheet with 1 tablespoon of the olive oil.

2 Cut the eggplants into ½-inch-wide lengthwise slices, leaving the stem intact. Place the eggplants on the prepared baking sheet, and fan them out as much as possible, so a good bit of the surface of each slice shows. Brush the eggplants with 1 tablespoon of the oil, and bake until they begin to soften and turn golden, about 10 minutes.

3 Fan the eggplant slices out a bit farther, working quickly so you don't burn your hands, and brush them with another tablespoon of oil. Bake until the eggplants are golden and soft through, 10 to 15 minutes.

4 To serve, pour the cilantro sauce in the center of a serving platter. Using a wide metal spatula, transfer the eggplants from the baking sheet to the platter, arranging them over the sauce in an attractive fashion. Season lightly with salt and pepper. Garnish with the cilantro leaves, and serve immediately. (Or, if you prefer to serve the eggplants at room temperature, let them cool on the baking sheet, then transfer to the platter and garnish with the cilantro leaves.)

6 to 8 servings

EGGPLANT

The most familiar eggplant in the U.S. is large, bulbous, and purple, but in recent years other varieties have appeared. White eggplant and long, slender Asian varieties tend to be sweeter and have firmer flesh than their larger purple cousins. Miniature Italian eggplants are small versions of the familiar variety, with a similar taste.

Regardless of color, choose eggplants that are very firm and have tight, shiny skin. They should be entirely without soft spots, or bruises, and their stems should be evenly green, not mushy or moldy.

BIODYNAMIC FARMING

The biodynamic principles of agriculture have been gaining increasing attention in the United States as interest is focused on farming methods that produce nutritionally balanced crops from healthy soil.

The principles of biodynamic farming were outlined in a series of lectures given in 1924 by Rudolf Steiner, a German scientist and reputed clairvoyant, who was also founder of the Waldorf Schools, where his educational method is still used today. The term *biodynamic* (from the Greek *bios*, which means "life," and *dynamis*, which means "energy") was coined by the first group of farmers who decided to apply Steiner's principles.

Steiner believed in a "farm organism," a farm as an entity in itself. He felt that everything a farm needed—in the form of fertilizers and soil nutrients—should be generated on the farm rather than purchased or collected elsewhere. Translated into farming methods, his philosophy involves bringing together the earth's energies and biological systems in a spiritual and practical manner. ("Spiritual" in having to do with life forces and energies rather than religion.) It was, and still is, viewed as

unorthodox by many because of its spiritual emphasis, and because it encompasses an astrological approach to the earth, soil, and plants.

The biodynamic system focuses on creating and maintaining a fertile, healthy soil. It divides the forces that constitute a plant's environment into the earthly and the cosmic. The earthly forces are the life of the soil, the abundance of soil nutrients, the water supply, and the average atmospheric moisture. The cosmic forces involve light, warmth, other climatic conditions, and their daily and yearly rhythms.

Biodynamic farmers rely on crop rotation, on building up the soil with green manure, and on fertilizing with livestock manure and an assortment of mixtures which, according to Steiner's theory, return to the soil any nutrients and minerals that are used up by a crop, as well as enzymes and natural growth hormones.

The biodynamic preparations and methods must be used together to achieve a balanced soil that can resist or at least cope successfully with extreme forces of nature, such as drought or pests. Healthy soil can also produce high crop yields, nutritious crops, and great crop diversity.

COACH FARM'S EASY HERBED FARFEL

It was hard to choose the recipes I loved best from the meal we had at the Coach Farm in New York's Hudson Valley, so I asked Lillian Cahn, farm owner and resident cook, for all of them.

This one is as easy as can be, and it's the simplicity of flavors and the pleasing texture of the farfel—tiny pasta squares—that make it so good. It goes well with everything from the chicken breasts stuffed with Coach Farm goat cheese (see Index) to roast meats, fish, stews, and salads. In short, it can go anywhere.

1 tablespoon unsalted butter

8 ounces farfel (about 1¼ cups)

2 shallots, peeled and minced

1 small onion, peeled and diced

3 cups Herbfarm Deluxe Chicken Stock (page 86), or good-quality chicken broth

1 bay leaf

3 sprigs fresh thyme, or ½ teaspoon dried

Salt and freshly ground black pepper

1 Melt the butter in a large heavy saucepan over medium-high heat. Add the farfel and cook, stirring frequently, until it is light golden brown. Add the shallots, and cook, stirring frequently, just until they begin to turn translucent, about 2 minutes. Then add the onion and cook just until it begins to turn translucent, about 4 minutes.

2 Add the chicken stock and the herbs, stir, and bring to a boil. Cover, reduce the heat to medium-low, and simmer until the liquid has been absorbed and the farfel is tender, about 15 minutes. Season to taste with salt and pepper, transfer to a warmed serving bowl, and serve immediately.

4 to 6 servings

GRANDMOTHER'S GREEN BEANS

I am sure this is a universal grandmother dish. My grandmother prepared beans this way; my mother, who is now a grandmother, prepares them this way; and my recipe-sharing friends all seem to have had grandmothers who prepared flavorful green beans this way. Despite being recently held captive by the "crisp-vegetable-only" school of cooking, I have always loved beans cooked to a flavorful tenderness.

Beans are perhaps the most notable victim of the undercooking movement. Not to say they don't have merit when cooked so they're still crisp—many like their somewhat pungent grassy taste and texture. But when they're slow-cooked they yield a rich, round flavor and tenderness that is so enticing and delicious it almost seems like a whole new vegetable.

Traditionally, a square of salt pork or slab bacon is added to the beans, but sometimes I use smoked pork, or goose fat if I have it, for a change. Even if all you add is a touch of butter and a seasoning of salt and pepper, you'll find your perception of beans changed forever by this simple old-fashioned recipe.

Serve these alongside Meat Loaf (see Index).

1 pound fresh green beans, stem ends removed, cut into 2-inch pieces
⅔ cup water
1 ounce salt pork or slab bacon (1¼-inch chunk), or 1 tablespoon goose fat
Salt and freshly ground black pepper

1 Place the beans, water, and pork or fat in a medium-size saucepan over medium-high heat. Cover and bring to a boil. Reduce the heat to low and cook, stirring occasionally, until the beans have turned an olive color and are tender, about 45 minutes. Remove the cover and continue cooking until most of the liquid has evaporated, 20 minutes.

2 Season to taste with salt and pepper, and serve immediately.

4 to 6 servings

GREEN BEANS WITH WALNUTS AND LEMON

I've eaten and enjoyed green beans in every form—uncooked, fresh from the garden; steamed until they are bright green and still crisp; or cooked in the old-fashioned way—long and slowly with a piece of ham, bacon, or salt pork. Though they remain lovely and bright green, the beans in this recipe are cooked enough to remove their raw grassy taste.

I like to serve this dish throughout the summer and into the fall, when green beans are at their best. It also perks up a traditional Thanksgiving meal, offering an alternative to the usual vegetable dishes.

Once the beans are mixed with the butter and lemon juice, they should be served immediately, as the acid of the lemon juice will cause their bright green color to fade. Try tossing other vegetables—such as small leeks, broccoli, or cauliflower—in the same garnish.

2 cups water
1 pound green beans, ends trimmed, cut
   diagonally into 2-inch pieces
Grated zest of 1 lemon
3 tablespoons unsalted butter
1 to 2 tablespoons freshly squeezed lemon juice
Salt and freshly ground black pepper
⅓ cup walnuts, toasted (see Note) and coarsely
   chopped

1 Bring the water to a boil in the bottom of a vegetable steamer or in a wok. Place the beans in the steamer basket, cover, and steam until they are tender but still bright green, about 8 minutes.

2 When the beans are cooked, transfer them to a medium-size bowl and toss with the lemon zest, butter, and lemon juice. Season with salt if desired, and generously with pepper.

3 Transfer the beans to a warmed serving dish, sprinkle with the toasted walnuts, and serve immediately.

4 servings

Note: To toast walnuts, preheat the oven to 350°F. Spread the nuts out in a baking pan large enough to hold them in a single layer, and toast, stirring once, until they give off a toasted aroma, 10 to 15 minutes.

TURNIP GREENS AND CHARD WITH SALT PORK

This is a direct contribution from Mary McPherson, my former neighbor in Seattle. I never have known quite such an efficient farmer—Miss Mary never bought any vegetables at the store, instead she grew whatever she wanted in a patch of her backyard. She gave me this recipe one day while she was leaning on the fence, checking to see what we were up to in our garden. That same afternoon she made the dish and brought us a heaping plateful. She also gave me a recipe for Lamb with Young Mustard Greens (see Index).

I love this—it's simple and full of goodness and flavor. I like to serve it alongside roast or grilled meat, poultry, or fish.

6 ounces salt pork

2 cups water

8 ounces turnip greens, rinsed, stems removed

8 ounces Swiss chard, rinsed

1 teaspoon sugar

2 fresh hot chile peppers (Fresno, jalapeño, or chimaya), trimmed, seeds removed if desired, finely chopped

Salt and freshly ground black pepper

1 Cut the salt pork into bite-size pieces. Bring a small pot of water to a boil, and blanch the salt pork for 5 minutes. Drain and pat dry.

2 In a large skillet without any oil, cook the salt pork over medium-high heat until golden, about 5 minutes. Add the 2 cups water, turnip greens, chard, sugar, and chile peppers, and stir. Reduce the heat to medium-low, cover, and cook until the greens are tender, about 20 minutes. Season to taste, and serve immediately.

4 servings

THOSE LUSTROUS WINTER GREENS

L et's face it. With names like collard, kale, turnip, and mustard, winter greens lack cachet. But what they lack in image they make up for with distinctive, unforgettable flavors. They are a boon to the winter table, valuable not only for the texture, color, and vitality that they lend to everything from soups to savory tarts, but also for their ample amounts of vitamins A and C, as well as minerals such as potassium and iron and trace elements such as folic acid.

The world of winter greens seems to expand each year, as does the length of time they are in season. Newcomers include *mizuna*, a Japanese relative of mustard; small, tender turnip greens, usually attached to tiny purple-tinged turnips; bok choy, also called *pak choi*, with its creamy white stalks and deep, often silvery, green leaves; and red Russian kale, a hybrid that

closely resembles regular kale except for a hint of purple at the edges of its flatter jagged leaves.

Though not entirely green, rhubarb chard—its large leaves crinkled, its stalks a vivid garnet—is another winter favorite, as is broccoli rabe. Flowering kale is also available in winter, though it appears more often as an ornamental garden plant than as a comestible. It has less flavor than regular kale, but its bright purplish leaves add lovely color to salads and make a good edible garnish.

SOUTHERN FAVORITES

K ale, collard, mustard, and turnip greens have always been staples in the South, and just a generation or two ago they were familiar on tables around the country. My grandmother, who originally came from Michigan but spent most of her life in Oregon, cooked greens often. Her standard preparation was to cook them long and slowly, with a chunk of salt pork

▶ ▶ ▶

and a pinch of sugar. Between her generation and mine, however, greens fell out of favor, replaced by milder vegetables. But the tide has turned, and what my grandmother considered a delicacy is popular once again.

The jagged-edged leaves of turnip and mustard greens, slow-cooked with smoked pork neck bones or ham hocks and hot peppers, are often referred to as a "mess of greens" in the South. Popular for their flavor, they are also known for their restorative properties. Mustard greens, along with mustard seeds, are thought to stimulate circulation. A dose of "pot likker"—cooking juices from turnip greens—is said to cure everything from depression to the worst hangover.

Kale, with its tightly ruffled leaves, and collards, with their smooth large leaves, are highly underrated members of the cabbage family. Again southern specialties, they are similar in flavor, mellower than turnip or mustard greens, and can be substituted for each other in most recipes. They both grow year-round, but like most winter greens are best after the first frost, when their leaves become snappy, crisp, and sweet. In early spring, the new young leaves are so tender they can be added raw to salads. But taste them in the heat of summer, and they will be leathery and rather acrid.

All these greens benefit from both slow

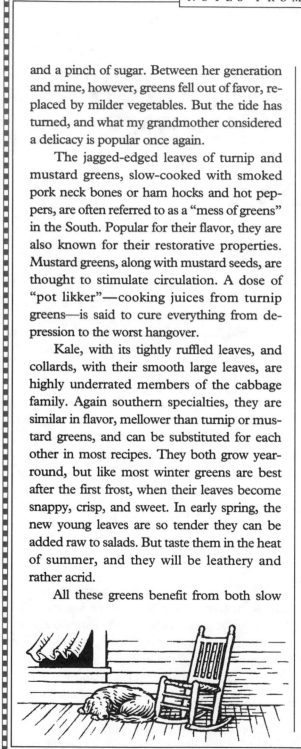

and quick cooking, though the results are completely different. They become deep-flavored when slow-cooked and retain their peppery vigor when quick-cooked. To gentle that pepperiness and their rather substantial texture—which aren't to everyone's taste—yet still get the fresh green flavor of quick-cooked greens, blanch them first in boiling salted water.

Kale and collards are ideal for wrapping around stuffing mixtures or for lining molds. They stand up well to herbs and spices, yet are delectable when cooked plain and simply tossed in butter.

MIZUNA, CHARD, AND BROCCOLI RABE

Mizuna is one of the loveliest winter greens; its narrow feathery leaves have a slim white center. As befits its lacy appearance, it is mild with a slightly mustard-like flavor. It makes a beautiful edible garnish, and when the leaves are small and tender, usually in spring and fall, they make a wonderful addition to a salad. Larger leaves are best cooked quickly, in a sauté or stir-fry, when they take on a soft green flavor.

Chard, the lush greens of a variety of sugar beets that are bred for their greens and not their roots, is often referred to as Swiss chard because the leaves reputedly withstood harsh Swiss winters while its root shriveled in the cold. It is similar to rhubarb chard, though Swiss chard's leaves are larger, its stalks a brilliant white instead of red. Milder than other winter greens, the stalks can be

eaten raw, and they add a welcome crunch to winter salads. Chard is best when cooked quickly, preferably just until the raw crunch disappears. Rhubarb chard is slightly tangier than Swiss chard, and it adds a bright touch of color to the winter table.

Broccoli rabe is a close relative of the turnip, which becomes evident with the first taste of this peppery green. Its flower buds resemble broccoli, to which it is also related, but where broccoli is mild and becoming, broccoli rabe shouts for garlic, hot peppers, and plenty of olive oil. Popular in Italian and Chinese cuisine, it is best either steamed or blanched, which calms its flavor down a bit, before sautéing.

CHOOSING GREENS

When buying winter greens, shop with care. Those on display in 24-hour supermarkets may be sad-looking, waterlogged, and wilted from overexposure to hot lights and frequent sprinklings. Avoid those, as well as any extremely yellowed leaves. Look instead for fresh, lively, vigorous leaves. Find out when produce is delivered to your market, so you can obtain the freshest possible greens.

As for all produce, wash greens thoroughly. Fill a sink with cold water, plunge them in, and swirl them around vigorously. Repeat this process, using several changes of water, until there is no silt at the bottom of the sink. Don't scrimp on washing; there is nothing more unpleasant than a mouthful of gritty greens. If you can't use the greens immediately, wrap them, unwashed, in paper towels and refrigerate them in perforated plastic bags.

Although most greens come in huge bunches that look like enough to feed the neighborhood, they cook down considerably; 1 pound raw will yield four moderate portions cooked.

Winter greens may take getting used to, because they all have distinct, assertive personalities. For new initiates, collards and mustard greens softened with Swiss chard is a good mixture. Steam them briefly—about 8 minutes if you like your greens still colorful and lively—then sauté them quickly in butter, or olive or walnut oil, and season with salt and pepper. Or to retain their pungency, simply stir-fry them in a touch of peanut oil. Whether you choose greens that are best cooked quickly or simmered for hours, you'll find them ample compensation for the privations of winter.

KALE CUSTARD WITH SAUTEED RADISHES

This dish takes the best of tender spring kale and hot new radishes and combines them in an unusual way. Its robust flavor belies its elegant look and makes it a surprising, and very popular, first course. Serve it immediately after the radishes have been sautéed, so they don't lose their bright red color. (You can jump seasons, if you have a source of winter radishes and sweet winter kale, and serve it at Christmas. It's a natural.)

Try this with a full-flavored, earthy Pinot Noir such as a Saintsbury Pinot Noir Carneros 1988.

1½ pounds kale, rinsed, stems removed
1 cup milk
½ cup heavy (whipping) cream
2 cloves garlic, peeled and crushed
2 sprigs fresh summer savory, or ½ teaspoon crushed dried
½ cup fresh white bread crumbs
4 tablespoons (½ stick) unsalted butter
3 large eggs
1 egg yolk
Salt and freshly ground black pepper
1 shallot, peeled and minced
2 cups radishes, trimmed and thinly sliced

1 Preheat the oven to 350°F. Butter six small ramekins, and set aside.

2 Cook the kale in a large pot of boiling salted water (1 tablespoon salt to 1 quart water) until tender, about 8 minutes.

Drain, and rinse under cold water. Squeeze the kale to remove as much water as possible, chop finely, and set aside.

3 In a small saucepan, scald the milk and cream with the garlic and savory. (Do not let the milk boil.) Remove the pan from the heat, cover, and set aside for 5 minutes. Discard the garlic cloves and savory sprigs. Add the bread crumbs to the milk and cream, stir, and set aside.

4 In a large skillet, melt 2 tablespoons of the butter over medium-high heat. Add the chopped kale and cook until any liquid has evaporated, about 5 minutes. Remove from the heat and set aside.

5 In a large bowl, whisk together the eggs, egg yolk, and the milk mixture. Stir in the kale, and season to taste with salt and pepper. Pour the mixture into the prepared ramekins. Place the ramekins in a baking

dish or roasting pan, and add enough boiling water to reach halfway up their sides. Bake in the oven until the custards are firm in the center, 25 to 30 minutes. Let sit for 5 minutes, then unmold onto the center of six warmed plates. Cover loosely with aluminum foil, and keep warm in a low (200°) oven.

6 Melt the remaining 2 tablespoons butter in a large skillet over medium-high heat. Add the shallot and cook until it be-

gins to turn transparent, 4 minutes. Then add the radishes and sauté just until they are hot through, about 2 minutes. Remove from the heat and season with salt and pepper. Arrange the radish slices around the kale custards, and serve immediately.

6 servings

HERBED LENTIL PUREE

This purée is exquisite alongside grilled salmon or bluefish in summer, with roast poultry in winter. It has a robust texture, yet the fresh herbs give it a surprising delicacy.

2 cups lentils, rinsed and picked over
6 cups cold water
3 small sprigs fresh oregano, or ½ teaspoon dried
1 handful fresh basil leaves (to give about 1 tablespoon minced)
2 tablespoons minced fresh oregano, or 1½ to 2 teaspoons dried
1 small shallot, peeled and minced
1 clove garlic, peeled and minced
1 teaspoon minced fresh thyme, or ¼ teaspoon dried

¼ cup minced fresh parsley
4 to 6 tablespoons extra-virgin olive oil
Salt and freshly ground black pepper
2 tablespoons minced fresh parsley, for garnish (optional)

1 Place the lentils, water, and oregano sprigs in a medium-size saucepan over medium-high heat. Bring to a boil, then lower the heat to medium, and cook until the lentils have softened but are still firm to

the bite, about 15 minutes. Check the lentils frequently to be sure they don't overcook.

2 Drain the lentils, reserving about ½ cup of the cooking liquid, and transfer them to a food processor. Mince the basil, and add it to the lentils, along with the minced oregano, shallot, garlic, thyme, parsley, and 4 tablespoons of the olive oil. Process, using short pulses, until the mixture is smooth. (You may have to process the lentils and herbs in two batches.) Add salt and pepper to taste, and check the consistency. If it is too dry, add either the remaining olive oil or enough of the reserved cooking liquid to moisten it. The purée should be quite stiff but pleasantly moist.

3 To serve, transfer the purée to a pastry tube fitted with a large star-shaped tip, and pipe it into a dish or around the seafood or meat it will accompany. Or transfer the purée to a serving bowl, sprinkle it with the parsley, and serve immediately.

6 to 8 servings

CREAMED LIMA BEANS

T he Amish and the Mennonites are renowned farmers. Both groups have a tradition of stewardship of the soil and good farming practices. They know what many farmers have forgotten—that without healthy soil not even the most sophisticated society can survive.

I came across many Amish restaurants in Pennsylvania, where it's common to see farmers ploughing their fields with teams of sturdy horses. The menus were filled with the foods of the farm—hearty, hefty fare with few spices but lots of good clean flavor. There were huge platters of vegetables in brown butter, stews sending off mouthwatering aromas, creamed vegetables, and plenty of cakes, cookies, and pies.

We were lucky enough to be invited to eat in Amish homes, where we also sampled their simple, unadorned preparation of vegetables. This is an Amish recipe, and one that I am particularly fond of. You will be surprised at how people swoop down on it at the table.

Lima beans are one of my favorite vegetables, particularly when they are fresh from the garden, tender and sweet. They also freeze well, and are one of few vegetables I pull from the frozen food section at the supermarket.

This goes well alongside fish and chicken.

2 tablespoons unsalted butter
1 small onion, peeled and diced
1½ tablespoons all-purpose flour
1¼ cups half-and-half
2½ cups fresh lima beans or 1 package
    (10 ounces) frozen
⅓ cup milk (optional)
Salt and freshly ground black pepper

1 Melt the butter in a large heavy skillet over medium heat. Add the onion and cook, stirring occasionally, until it turns translucent, about 5 minutes. Sprinkle the flour into the skillet, stirring until it absorbs the butter. Continue cooking until the mixture bubbles, at least 2 minutes, so the raw taste cooks out of the flour.

2 Slowly add the half-and-half, stirring constantly, and cook until the sauce has thickened to the consistency of heavy cream. Add the lima beans and cook, stirring, 8 to 10 minutes for fresh, 10 to 12 for frozen. If necessary, add enough milk to thin the sauce to the consistency of thin cream. Season to taste with salt and pepper, and serve immediately.

6 servings

BEANS

*N*ative to the New World, beans are part of a large and varied group of vegetables also known as the pulses (which includes peas and lentils as well). Native Americans taught early settlers to grow them, along with corn and squash. For a long time fresh and dried shell beans played a low-key role at the dinner table. Finally they are regaining favor, not only for their rich flavors and varied uses, but also because they are a good source of protein and fiber.

Fresh shell beans can be eaten raw in salads, cooked as a side dish or as part of a stew, and also pickled. The pods should be fresh-looking and not withered, the seeds plump and full. Two favorites are lima and fava beans.

Fresh lima beans are a bright, vivid green and have a nutty flavor; they are tender and sweet when cooked.

Fava beans, or broad beans, can be eaten uncooked in the spring. Toss them raw in olive oil and salt or added them to salads with early ripening tomatoes and onions. They are also delicious cooked in vegetable mixtures, soups and stews, or sautéed with garlic and herbs in butter or olive oil.

TOM SPICER'S SAUTEED OKRA ON PASTA

Tom Spicer, manager of Golden Circle Farms outside Dallas, supervises the growing and marketing of a cornucopia of specialty herbs and vegetables, from entire greenhouses full of headily fragrant basil to rows of red okra, green okra, melons, and salad greens.

This is one of his favorite recipes, and to make it he prefers small—about 2-inch-long—red okra, which looks like green okra with a deep red dress on. If you can't find red okra—and most of us can't because it's grown in small amounts primarily in Texas, where it tends to stay—go ahead and use green; it has the same flavor. Just try to find the smallest buds you can. The flavors here are simple and pure, and the lemon juice gives it all a bright tang.

When trimming okra, don't cut into the pod; just slice off the stem end.

4 tablespoons extra-virgin olive oil

3 cloves garlic, peeled

1 pound small red or green okra, trimmed

8 ounces ripe plum tomatoes, cored and coarsely chopped

Salt and coarsely ground fresh black pepper

1 pound corkscrew pasta (tortiglioni)

1 tablespoon freshly squeezed lemon juice

1 Heat 3 tablespoons of the olive oil in a large skillet over medium heat until hot but not smoking. Add the garlic and cook, stirring constantly, just until it begins to turn golden, 3 to 4 minutes. Add the okra and cook, stirring, until it begins to soften slightly and turn a very bright red or green, depending on the type you use, about 5 minutes. Add the tomatoes, season with salt if desired and with pepper, cover, and continue cooking, stirring occasionally, until the okra is tender but still has some body, about 10 minutes.

2 While the okra is cooking, bring a pot of salted water to a boil. Cook the pasta until it is tender but still firm to the bite, 8 to 10 minutes. Drain, and toss with the remaining 1 tablespoon olive oil.

3 To serve, drizzle the lemon juice over the okra, stir, adjust the seasoning, and toss with the pasta.

4 servings

ANNE FRIAR THOMAS'S BUTTERED OKRA

I love okra in just about any form. But this preparation, suggested to me by Anne Friar Thomas of the J. Carter Thomas ranch in Cuero, Texas, is my favorite. It is simple, and the gentle cooking brings out the flavor and incomparable texture of the okra.

When buying okra, look for small buds, 3 to 4 inches long, that are an even green color. The tiny amount of vinegar in this recipe was suggested to keep the okra from developing its characteristic slippery texture, although I've found there isn't any danger of slipperiness as long as you don't cut into the bud (so trim the ends carefully). I still use the vinegar, because it adds a subtle tang. Serve this with just about any roast meat or fish.

1 pound okra, ends trimmed
½ teaspoon apple cider vinegar
½ cup water
1 to 2 tablespoons unsalted butter, or to taste
Salt and freshly ground black pepper

P lace the okra, vinegar, and water in a medium-size saucepan. Cover, and bring to a boil over medium-high heat. Reduce the heat to medium, add the butter and salt and pepper to taste, and partially cover. Cook, stirring occasionally, until the okra is tender and has turned from bright to olive green, about 12 minutes. Adjust the seasoning and serve immediately, pouring any cooking juices over the okra.

4 to 6 servings

Microwave variation: Place the okra, water, and vinegar in a microwave-proof bowl. Cover tightly, and cook at high power until the okra has softened but is still green, 6 minutes. Remove the dish from the oven and let it rest, covered, until the okra has softened somewhat more but still is slightly crisp, about 3 minutes. Season with the butter, salt, and pepper, and serve immediately.

ONION PIE WITH BACON

This is an Amish-influenced recipe, one I make often because it is simple, hearty, and satisfying. There are two variations and I enjoy them both: When the onions are piled in the pastry uncooked, the resulting pie is crisp and full of fresh onion flavor. When they are cooked briefly first, the result is richer and more elegant. Try a chilled Sauvignon Blanc, a Fumé Blanc, or a Sancerre with this vegetable pie.

1 prebaked 9-inch pie pastry (page 431)
2 large (10 ounces each) onions, peeled
  and very thinly sliced
Salt and freshly ground black pepper
¼ cup heavy (whipping) cream
4 ounces slab bacon, rind removed, cut into
  ⅛-inch-thick slices

1 Preheat the oven to 350°F.

2 Place half the onions in the prebaked pastry, and season with salt and pepper. Repeat with the remaining onions. Pour the cream over the onions, and arrange the bacon slices on top, overlapping them slightly if necessary.

3 Bake until the onions are softened and the bacon is crisp, about 55 minutes. Cool for 5 minutes, then serve.

Makes 1 pie (6 to 8 servings)

Variation: Melt 1 tablespoon butter in a large heavy skillet over medium-high heat. When the butter has melted, reduce the heat to medium. Add the onions, and stir so they are mixed with the butter. Cover and cook, stirring occasionally so they don't brown, until they are translucent and softened, about 8 minutes. Remove from the heat, and season to taste with salt and pepper.

Pile the onions into the prebaked pastry. Pour the cream over them, and top with the bacon slices, overlapping them slightly if necessary. Bake until the bacon is cooked and crisp, about 40 minutes. Remove from the oven and cool for about 5 minutes, then serve.

SWEET PEAS AND NEW POTATOES

This is LaRene Reed's favorite spring dish. Her husband, LeRoy Reed, farmed 350 acres of potatoes in central Idaho until recently when he sold the farm to his son, Brian. LeRoy still enjoys working on the farm as much as when he owned it. Indeed, he can keep close watch over the acreage from just about any window in their ranch-style home.

Having fields so close is very handy for the Reeds, who are potato lovers. In early spring, when tiny new potatoes are forming, Mr. Reed heads into the field and "robs" just enough to make this special dish. ("Rob," by the way, is a near-technical term which means pulling the small new potatoes from the perimeter of the plant without touching the roots closer to the center.)

With sweet green peas from the garden, this dish is a rare springtime feast. It is meant to be served alongside a roast leg of lamb or grilled pork chops, but we sometimes enjoy it as a main dish.

1 pound small new potatoes, scrubbed
8 cups water
1 tablespoon coarse (kosher) salt
½ cup heavy (whipping) cream
1 cup small fresh green peas
Salt and freshly ground black pepper

1 Combine the potatoes, water, and coarse salt in a medium-size saucepan over medium-high heat. Bring to a boil, and cook until the potatoes are tender but still slightly hard in the center, about 15 minutes.

2 Drain the potatoes and return them to the saucepan along with the cream. Place the pan over medium heat, and swirl the potatoes around so they are coated with the cream. Cover, and bring just to a boil. Reduce the heat to low, add the peas, and stir. Cook until the peas are hot through and have softened slightly, no longer than 2 to 3 minutes. Remove from the heat, season to taste with salt and pepper, and serve immediately.

4 side-dish or 2 main-course servings

POLISH UP THOSE FRUITS AND VEGETABLES

You may have wondered why certain fruits in the market are unnaturally shiny, or what that thick layer of wax is doing on that fat rutabaga, or why the skin of a cucumber sometimes feels gummy. Well, it has to do with the wacky distribution system that most of the food in this country is subjected to. Fruits and vegetables often travel far from where they were harvested, then sit in cold storage or on a grocery shelf much longer than nature ever intended. Travel and sitting time can cause wear and tear on freshness, necessitating some kind of assistance to keep the produce alluring enough to make it into the consumer's shopping basket.

Waxes are applied to many fruits and vegetables to slow down spoilage and preserve cosmetic appearance. Called "post-harvest treatments," they all too often either contain or seal in chemical fungicides and growth and sprout inhibitors, and many pose potential health risks. The FDA requires labeling on shipping crates for produce that has been subjected to such treatments, but this regulation is frequently ignored.

Peeling the produce takes care of the problem. For produce that can't be peeled, washing in hot soapy water for 3 minutes has been suggested for removing post-harvest residues whether or not they are in wax, though a study shows that at best it will remove only 50 percent.

Maine is the first state to require that supermarkets alert consumers to the presence of post-harvest treatment. If you want to know the score, ask the produce manager where you shop; he or she should be able to tell you. Otherwise, shop at markets where you are assured that produce is free of post-harvest treatment.

According to information released by the Maine Organic Farmers and Gardeners Association, produce subject to dips and waxes includes apples, cherries, pears, potatoes, apricots, carrots, kiwis, nectarines, peaches, plums, sweet potatoes, grapefruit, lemons, oranges, bananas, almonds (in the shell), grapes, grains, and seeds.

PAPA A LA HUANCAINA

This deliciously different potato dish was imported from Peru by Chuck Brown, a research geneticist for the USDA who works with potatoes. He finds the tastiest, hardiest strains of wild potatoes and uses them to develop new potato varieties that have better color, flavor, and disease resistance. The goal is to cut down on pesticide use in potato farming, but an important side benefit is tastier, better-quality potatoes.

Chuck, who is an avid fan of potatoes and very interested in enhancing their flavor through his work, likes to make this dish with a potato called Urgenta, a combination waxy and fluffy potato that has come on the market within the past couple of years and is currently cultivated in Washington. A good substitute is a waxy Yellow Finn potato, a Yukon gold, a Cobbler, or a Red Rose potato.

This dish can be served at room temperature, or you can time it so the potatoes are still hot when you pour the cheese sauce over them. Don't be concerned about there being too much peppery heat in this sauce from the jalapeño and its seeds. The pepper gives it a mild, pleasant bite.

2 pounds potatoes, such as Urgenta, Red Rose, or Yellow Finn
1 tablespoon salt
2 slices white bread, crusts removed
1 cup half-and-half
¼ cup mild vegetable oil, such as safflower
1 large red bell pepper, cored, seeded, and coarsely chopped
1 jalapeño pepper, trimmed, seeds left in, finely chopped
1 cup skim milk ricotta cheese
Salt
2 hard-cooked eggs, coarsely chopped

1 Place the potatoes in a large heavy saucepan, cover them with water, add the 1 tablespoon salt, and bring to a boil over high heat. Reduce the heat to medium-high and cook until the potatoes are tender, about 20 minutes.

2 Drain the potatoes, and when they are cool enough to handle, peel and cut

them into ½-inch-thick slices.

3 Soak the bread in the half-and-half in a small bowl until soft, 15 minutes. Set aside.

4 Heat the oil in a large skillet, and when it is hot but not smoking, add both peppers and cook until they are softened, about 15 minutes. Don't be concerned if the peppers brown slightly. Transfer the peppers

and oil to a food processor, and purée until smooth.

5 Add the soaked bread and the ricotta to the peppers, and purée until smooth. Season to taste with salt, and pour over the potatoes. Garnish with the hard-cooked eggs, and serve.

4 servings

SCALLOPED POTATOES WITH BACON AND CHEESE

This recipe comes from Barbara Fischer, who works on the farm with her husband, Gideon, and cooks three meals a day for her household of nine. An Amish family, they live on a lovely old dairy farm near Millersburg, Pennsylvania. They used to keep cows for milking, but it wasn't paying the bills, so Gideon transformed the dairy barn into a gorgeous carpentry shop and planted horseradish, which they process and sell through local markets.

Barbara prepares traditional Amish dishes, such as this light variation on scalloped potatoes. It gives the potato star status, its flavor heightened by the bacon and the touch of celery seed. Use top-quality potatoes—Russets give a

fluffy result, but also try Urgenta or Maine potatoes, both of which fall somewhere between a fluffy and a waxy potato.

Barbara sometimes turns her scalloped potatoes into a main

course by adding cooked beef, ham, corn, or peas—but when I serve it as a main course, I simply serve a big salad alongside. Enjoy a full, fruity Pinot Noir, such as one from Oregon's Adelsheim Vineyards, with this dish.

1 garlic clove, peeled and halved lengthwise
4 pounds Russet potatoes, peeled and quartered
6 ounces slab bacon, cut into 1 x ¼ x ¼-inch pieces
Salt and freshly ground black pepper
2 cups milk
½ cup heavy (whipping) cream
Heaping ¼ teaspoon celery seeds
2 ounces Swiss-type cheese, such as Gruyère
2 ounces sharp Cheddar cheese

1 Preheat the oven to 350°F. Rub the garlic over the sides and bottom of an 8½ x 12½-inch earthenware or enamel baking dish.

2 Steam the potatoes in a steamer basket over boiling water until they are nearly cooked through but still slightly firm in the center, about 15 minutes. Remove from the heat and allow to cool.

3 Sauté the bacon in a medium-size heavy skillet over medium-high heat just until it turns translucent and is beginning to turn golden—don't let it get crisp—about 8 minutes. Remove the bacon from the fat, reserving both.

4 Grate half the potatoes into the prepared baking dish, using the large holes of a standard grater. Season with salt and pepper, sprinkle with half the bacon and 2 teaspoons of the bacon fat, and repeat with the remaining potatoes, bacon, and another 2 teaspoons bacon fat.

5 Combine the milk and the cream, and pour over the potatoes (see Note). Sprinkle with the celery seeds, then with the cheeses. Cover the dish with aluminum foil, and bake in the center of the oven for 25 minutes. Remove the foil and continue baking until the cheese has melted and the potatoes are beginning to turn golden at the edges, 20 minutes. Remove from the oven, and let cool for 5 minutes before serving.

6 to 8 servings

Note: Depending on the age and quality of the potatoes, they may not absorb all of the milk and cream. You may want to add just the 2 cups of milk, and then check the potatoes halfway through the baking. If they have absorbed all the milk, pour the cream over them and continue baking.

HEARTLESS POTATOES

▪▪▪▪▪

*I*f you cut into a potato and find a brown spot at the center, don't be concerned—just cut it out. Called "hollow heart" in the potato industry it was caused by high temperatures and accelerated growth of the potato. The cells in the center ruptured and never filled out again, causing that little brown spot.

BASQUE POTATOES

E very time I eat these potatoes—which is as often as possible—I think of Juanita Hormachea. When I drove up to her tidy white house in Boise, Idaho, she was waiting at the door and waving. "Hi there honey, glad you're here, come on in." I'd talked with Juanita several times on the phone, but I'd never met her. She took me in and made me feel I'd known her all my life.

Juanita, though well into her eighties, has a lively, youthful spirit, and as she flitted around the house she regaled me with stories of Boise's Basque community—most of whom came to Idaho to herd sheep—and their rich culinary heritage. She keeps an unofficial history of the Basque people and has stacks of scrapbooks. She also has mountains of recipes in her collection, and this is one she passed my way.

It is good enough to eat as a meal all by itself, though it also complements meat, fish, or fowl.

4 medium Russet potatoes, peeled

½ cup olive oil

4 cloves garlic, peeled and mashed

1 teaspoon paprika

Cayenne pepper

1 tablespoon fresh rosemary, or 1 teaspoon crumbled dried, minced

1 tablespoon fresh thyme leaves, or 1 teaspoon dried, minced

¼ cup coarsely chopped fresh parsley

Salt and freshly ground black pepper

1 Preheat the oven to 375°F.

2 Scrub the potatoes well. Cut them in half if they are large, but leave whole if they are medium to small.

3 Heat the olive oil in a large ovenproof skillet over medium heat. When it is hot, add the garlic, paprika, and cayenne to taste; stir. Stir in the rosemary and thyme, and then sprinkle in the parsley. Add the potatoes to the skillet, turn once to coat, and season generously with salt and pepper.

4 Cover the skillet, transfer it to the oven, and bake until the potatoes begin to soften, 15 minutes. Uncover, stir, and continue cooking until the potatoes are golden and tender, 25 to 35 minutes; turn them occasionally so they brown evenly. Remove from the oven and serve immediately.

4 to 6 servings

THERE'S GOLD IN THE HILLS

Not all the best Cheddar comes from Wisconsin, Vermont, or New York. There is a small creamery in the eastern Washington town of Pullman that produces a Cheddar so popular that they have a hard time keeping up with the demand. Called Cougar Gold, the ivory creamy-sharp cheese is sold through exclusive gift catalogs and at gourmet food markets throughout the state.

As surprising as the quality of the cheese is the creamery's location—in the basement of a stately brick building on the campus of Washington State University (WSU).

Like many land-grant colleges, the assets of Washington State University include a herd of dairy cattle. Milk from the herd has been processed on campus since 1922, when an enterprising group of professors leased a creamery that eventually supplied all the university dining halls. It also served as a laboratory where students gained practical experience. There was one problem: a constant surplus of milk during school vacations. The logical solution was cheese.

During the 1940s Dr. N. S. Golding, a WSU food scientist, began working on a recipe for cheese. At the time, canning processes were being developed for wartime food supplies, and he wanted to perfect a cheese that could be canned. His experiments weren't without hazard. The canned cheese continually exploded until he came up with a recipe that didn't produce explosive gases. Not only did the cheese stay in the cans but it aged to a delectable richness, the sort of cheese that gives Cheddar a good name. It was named Cougar Gold after the university's mascot, a cougar, and Dr. Golding.

Until 1979 the cheese—which is still aged and marketed in enamel-lined cans decorated with the university's logo—was made only in summer, aged one year, and then sold. Since then, however, cheese has become the creamery's emphasis. In addi-

►►►

tion to Cougar Gold, which is its signature and best cheese, the creamery produces several other varieties.

SAY CHEESE

The WSU creamery has become a self-sustaining business, part of the university's food sciences and nutrition program. A staff of twenty-five, all but four of them students, produce 650 to 700 pounds of cheese five days a week, year-round.

Though the creamery no longer supplies milk to the university, it still produces a small quantity so student workers can learn milk processing. It also makes ice cream, which is sold at Ferdinand's, a tiny upstairs bar at the creamery.

Aging is expensive, and it is rare to find cheese aged as long as the Cheddars at the WSU creamery. Operating under the auspices of WSU affords the creamery that luxury. All of the cheeses are a cut above most commercial cheeses in flavor, texture, and creaminess. "It's the good milk," according to Marc Bates, creamery manager. It may also be because every batch is tested, and because the creamery benefits from research by the food sciences department, which allows for continual improvement.

According to Marc, the Cheddars are best when they are about five years old. "I tasted a twenty-one-year-old Cougar Gold someone had found stashed away on a shelf, and now that I've tasted one past its prime, I'm not interested in anything older than four or five years," he said.

The oldest cheese available from the creamery is eighteen to twenty-four months old, when they are already extremely flavorful and sharp. If an older cheese is preferred, Marc suggests buying a supply and storing it, in the can, on the bottom shelf of a refrigerator so it is kept at a constant temperature. Once opened, refrigeration is necessary.

The best time to order the cheese is well before Christmas, the creamery's busiest season, when they often have to start dipping into their younger stocks.

To order WSU creamery cheeses, write: WSU Creamery, Troy Hall 101, Pullman, WA 99164-4410; or call (509) 335-4014. The current price for a 30-ounce tin is $9.50 plus shipping.

NORTHWEST POTATO GRATIN

The Northwest has more than delectable seafood to offer the world of gastronomy. Both Idaho and Washington contribute fluffy Russet potatoes, and Oregon adds a variety of cheeses and the nation's largest hazelnut crop.

These ingredients are combined here in a harmonious marriage of flavors. The blue cheese is unconventional, but it adds a surprising depth of mellow flavor and should not be left out. The hazelnuts top it all off not only with their sweet nuttiness but with a tender, pleasant crispness as well.

Keep in mind that the potatoes will cook more quickly in an earthenware dish than in one that is enamel, and adjust the cooking time accordingly.

1 clove garlic, peeled and halved
2 pounds Russet potatoes, peeled and cut into
   1/16-inch-thick slices
8 ounces sharp Cheddar cheese, grated
2 ounces blue cheese, crumbled
1½ cups milk
1 cup heavy (whipping) cream
¼ teaspoon salt
Freshly ground black pepper
½ cup hazelnuts, toasted and skinned (see
   Note), then coarsely chopped

1 Preheat the oven to 375°F.

2 Rub the inside of a 9 x 14 x 2-inch oval earthenware or enamel baking dish with the garlic.

3 In a large mixing bowl, combine the potatoes, cheeses, milk, cream, salt, and a generous amount of pepper. Mix well, then pour the mixture into the prepared baking dish, spreading the potatoes out evenly.

4 Bake the potatoes in the center of the oven for 10 minutes. Then reduce the heat to 350°F and continue baking until they are nearly cooked through and are turning golden, 35 minutes. Sprinkle the hazelnuts over the potatoes, and continue cooking until the potatoes are tender through and the gratin is covered with a lovely golden crust, 15 minutes. If the potatoes are browning too much, loosely cover them with a sheet of aluminum foil.

5 Remove from the oven, and serve immediately.

6 to 8 servings

Note: To toast hazelnuts, preheat the oven to 350°F. Spread the nuts out in a baking pan large enough to hold them in a single layer, and toast, stirring once, until they give off a toasted aroma, 10 to 15 minutes. Wrap the nuts in a kitchen towel and rub them between your hands to remove the skins.

THE FATHER OF THE POTATO DID MORE

*L**uther Burbank, widely acclaimed to be the "father of the American potato," developed the Russet, a superior potato variety before he was twenty-two. Then, in 1875 he moved from Massachusetts to California and during the next fifty years created the Shasta daisy, the nectarine, and new varieties of tomatoes, asparagus, corn, squash, and peas, among other things.*

HERBED QUINOA

I've always loved grains, and the first time I tasted quinoa (pronounced KEEN-wa), I was hooked. It is mild yet nutty, and it has such an appealing texture that it is almost impossible to stop eating it. While it is versatile and will highlight soups and salads, I like it relatively unadorned, and this is my favorite way to serve it.

Quinoa is a new old grain, reputedly one that sustained the ancient Incan population. Native to South America, it is now grown in this country and is rapidly gaining a following for both its flavor and the substantial amount of protein and minerals it contains. Many farmers, aware of an increasing demand for healthy protein-rich foods, are planting quinoa.

Quinoa is high in linoleic acid, fiber, minerals, and vitamins, and it has an amino acid content similar to milk. All that aside, it's a delicious grain and one that is worthy of being incorporated into your repertoire.

It makes a wonderful accompaniment to grilled or steamed fish, or to roasted meats or poultry. I like it so much that when I'm in the mood for a simple meal, I serve it as a main course along with a variety of vegetables and salads.

If you can't get the suggested fresh herbs, try an equal amount of parsley, or 1 teaspoon dried thyme, basil, or oregano.

1 cup quinoa, thoroughly rinsed
2 cups water
1 teaspoon salt
¼ cup extra-virgin olive oil
1 medium clove garlic, peeled and
   minced
Freshly ground black pepper
½ cup packed fresh basil leaves, or
   ¼ cup fresh tarragon leaves and
   2 tablespoons fresh thyme leaves

1 Place the quinoa, water, and salt in a medium-size saucepan, cover, and bring to a boil over medium-high heat. Reduce the heat to medium, cover partially so the steam can escape, and cook at a slow boil until the grains have doubled in size, become translucent, and cracked open, so that the spiral germ of the grain is visible, about 12 minutes. If necessary, continue cooking, uncovered, until all the liquid has been absorbed or has evaporated, which may take 1 more minute.

2 While the quinoa is cooking, combine the olive oil, garlic, and a generous amount of pepper in a warmed medium-size bowl. Just before the quinoa is cooked, coarsely but neatly chop the basil leaves, and mix them into the olive oil mixture. When the quinoa is ready, add it to the olive oil, tossing until it is thoroughly combined. Check the seasoning and serve immediately.

4 servings

RURAL ELECTRIFICATION

■■■■

Although the common incandescent bulb was invented in 1879, electric power companies did not extend their service to rural areas and by 1935 only one-tenth of the nation's farms and ranches had electricity. To rectify this, the government created the Rural Electrification Administration, which approved low-interest federal loans to farmer cooperatives to construct dams, generating plants, and power lines. The Tennessee Valley Authority, Grand Coulee Dam, and many other projects were undertaken under this program, but it was still not until the early 1970s that nearly all farms and ranches had electricity.

HERBED WEHANI

This dish was inspired by a walk through the rice fields with Eldon Lundberg, owner with his three brothers of Lundberg Family Farms in Richvale, California (see facing page). Wehani rice is full of the toasty goodness of the warm days and nights in the Sacramento Valley. It has a wonderful, slightly chewy texture that falls somewhere between sticky rice and wild rice, and a flavor that gladly welcomes the accent of fresh herbs.

I always like the combination of hot and room-temperature foods. Here the sauce is a fresh summer combination of ripe-from-the-vine cherry tomatoes—whose distinctive sweet flavor goes perfectly with the rice—and pungent fresh thyme. I go easy on the thyme because I don't want it to interfere with the flavor of the rice, but rather to complement it. (Sometimes I use tarragon instead, for a subtle flavor difference.)

Serve this as a side dish with roast chicken, beef, or lamb. It is also good the next day as a salad.

1½ cups Wehani rice
3¼ cups water
¾ teaspooon salt, or to taste
1 tablespoon olive oil
1 teaspoon freshly squeezed lemon juice
3 scallions (green onions), trimmed and cut
    into thin rounds
2 teaspoons fresh thyme leaves
10 ripe cherry tomatoes, halved
Freshly ground black pepper

1 Combine the rice, water, and salt in a medium-size saucepan over medium-high heat, and bring to a rolling boil. Cover, reduce the heat to low, and cook until the rice has absorbed the water and has little wells in it, 35 to 40 minutes. The rice should be soft but still somewhat chewy. Remove from the heat and let rest, covered, for 10 minutes.

2 While the rice is cooking, mix together the olive oil, lemon juice, scallions, thyme, and tomatoes in a large bowl. When the rice has rested, add it to the dressing and toss gently until it is coated and the tomatoes are mixed in. Season with pepper to taste, and serve immediately.

4 to 6 servings

LUNDBERG RICE

Eldon Lundberg, straw hat jammed on his head, wiry body leaning slightly forward, steadily climbed the metal ladder to a catwalk spanning his silver silos. As I followed I dared not look down, nor to the right or left. I knew that if I did, I'd see the earth swimming around, and what I'd climbed all this way to see was the rice inside a silo.

Eldon cranked open a hatch on the silo's conical roof, throwing a window of sunlight onto a golden mountain of short-grain brown rice inside. An auger slowly turned through the rice, releasing tiny chips that floated in a cloud out the hatch. I inhaled the warm, toasty aroma.

I've eaten Lundberg rice for years and have been intrigued by its quality and deep, rich flavors. Now here I stood, precariously balanced high above the ground, learning what makes it so. The height made me dizzy, but it was balanced by the view beyond the silo: miles of flat land soon to be planted with rice.

The Lundberg's—four brothers and their families—farm about 3,000 acres in the lush Sacramento Valley, where Eldon's parents migrated in the 1930s.

"My grandparents came from Sweden to the Midwest, and were farmers there," he said. "When the family moved here, I remember my dad saying he thought they'd hit the Garden of Eden."

The soil in this "garden" is heavy adobe with a layer of hardpan under it, perfect for cultivating rice. "With the proper cultural practices it's workable soil, and the hardpan holds the water," Eldon explained.

For the Lundbergs, proper cultural practices include minimal use of chemical fertilizers, pesticides, or herbicides; rotating rice with nitrogen-rich crops like purple vetch; and digging in the rice straw after harvest.

"We don't burn the fields like most people do, because who wants to fill a beautiful day with smoke?" Eldon said. "And we also think the rice straw gives humus to the soil."

KEEPING IT IN THE FAMILY

The Lundbergs learned to farm from their father. "He taught us what he

▶ ▶ ▶

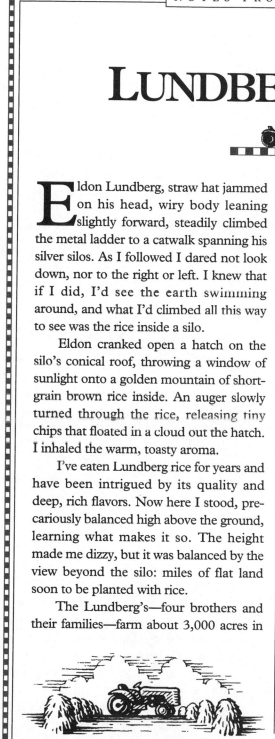

knew, and when he retired we took over," Eldon, who is in his sixties, said with undisguised pride.

Despite the Lundbergs' dramatic success with the rice—they produce enough to keep a city of 24,000 people alive for a year, eating one pound of rice a day—they are constantly trying new cultivation practices. "In farming you get one chance a year to try your plan, and if it doesn't work, you have a year to sit it out and see what happens."

Organic rice is just one thing that makes the Lundbergs stand out in the rice industry. Another is their skill at selecting new rice varieties. "We even selected a variety that outgrows the weeds," Eldon said. "It happens to have a marvelous taste, too."

They grow six varieties, including basmati types, colored types, and long- and short-grain types. Perhaps the best known among them is Wehani, a long, flat, burnished brown rice originally from India, with a toasty flavor and marvelously chewy texture. "We've trademarked that one, and have had nothing but success with it," Eldon said.

He was running his hands lovingly through the rice in the silo as he talked. "Once our rice is harvested, we let it sit out in the sun to develop fissures and get brown and beautiful. Most of the rice industry is concerned with white rice, which is the same as brown, only with seven layers of bran and germ removed. White rice has to be harvested when it's more full of moisture so it won't break during grinding. Rice left to dry in the sun reaches a different peak of flavor."

HULLED TO ORDER

▪▪▪▪▪

After harvest and before the rice is put in the silos, 2 to 5 percent of the moisture must be removed. "We put it in bins and blow in ambient air, which removes the moisture," Eldon explained. "We test it daily, and we don't leave it alone until it's ready to store."

Once it's storable, the temperature must be kept below 70°F or weevils (small insects) will come to eat their fill. Many companies use a fungicide to prevent such infestations, but that is contrary to the Lundberg philosophy. They pump harmless carbon dioxide into bins to prevent insects, though their best hedge against them is time.

"We like to sell our rice as soon as possible. As orders come in, we take rice to the mill and remove the fibrous hull," Eldon said. That turns it into edible brown rice.

The Lundbergs start working the soil after the winter rains, in April and May. Then they determine whether or not they'll flood first and plant, or plant and flood. The deci-

sion is based on the quality of the soil, and to a certain extent on avoiding risk. "We can't plant everything organic because we can't take that big a risk, in case there should be a failure," Eldon said. "We plant at least a third of our land organic, leaving certain fields fallow to encourage and build up the soil."

Getting land to a stage where the rice can be raised organically is a tricky, time-consuming process. It must be so rich and self-sustaining that it doesn't require disking and ploughing, and not all of their acreage is up to it. On land that does require working, the Lundbergs farm conventionally—that is they flood it and plant by air, sowing the rice from a plane. Because this method encourages weeds, they later have to apply a herbicide. They can't sell that rice as organic, so they label it "premium."

For the organic rice they wait until the rice plant, or "thread," is 4 inches high before flooding the field to a depth of 6 inches. As the plants grow they emerge above the water, creating a velvety green blanket over the fields, which are kept flooded for 100 days. Then the fields are drained, the rice left to dry on the stalk. When the soil can accommodate a combine, which is usually in October, harvest begins.

A COUPLE OF TIPS

Once we were back on the ground, Eldon continued talking about rice. "I'll tell you a couple of secrets," he said, leaning close

as though someone might walk by us in the middle of the field and hear what he was about to say. "Short-grain rice has more flavor than long-grain. And the longer you chew brown rice, the more flavor you'll get out of it," he said. "Try it next time and you'll get a whole variety of flavors."

Back near the office we walked by a squat building where Lundberg rice cakes are made. Eldon stopped. "We don't want anyone to know exactly how our rice cakes are made," he said, "so I can't take you into the plant. But you just have to come in the door and take a whiff."

My nose was flooded with a warm popcorn-like aroma, and I caught a glimpse of machines popping out the disks, which bumped along on a conveyor belt.

Eldon walked in, grabbed a couple, and handed me one. "I love rice just about any way," he said. "I'm around these all the time but I never get tired of 'em."

PUREED RUTABAGA

Rutabagas are one of the best-kept secrets of the vegetable world. They're sweet and full of distinctive flavor, yet mild enough to appeal to the most varied tastes, and their delicate apricot color makes them a lovely addition to any meal. I love their flavor, and this is one of my favorite ways to prepare them. Although I call this a purée, you can make it as coarse or as smooth as you like. Serve the dish alongside baked, broiled, or poached fish, or with roasted meat.

1½ pounds rutabagas, peeled and quartered
3 tablespoons unsalted butter
2 small shallots, peeled and very thinly
   sliced
Salt and freshly ground black pepper

1 Bring water to a boil in a vegetable steamer. Place the rutabagas in the basket, cover, and steam until they are tender, about 40 minutes.

2 Melt 1 tablespoon of the butter in a small skillet. Add the shallots and cook, stirring constantly, until they are translucent, 3 to 5 minutes. Set aside.

3 Transfer the cooked rutabagas to a food processor. Add the shallots and their cooking butter, and the remaining 2 tablespoons butter. Using short pulses, process the mixture until it is puréed. Season to taste with salt and pepper, and serve immediately.

4 servings

RUTABAGAS

Rutabagas and turnips suffer from identity confusion. Although both developed from the field cabbage, their differences are dramatic. The turnip can be eaten raw when young and small, and its flavor is similar to a radish. When larger it benefits from cooking, which mellows its hot flavor. The rutabaga has a sweet, almost caramel, flavor when cooked, with none of the turnip's heat.

Look for artichoke-size rutabagas with their stem and root ends attached. Most are coated with a very thick wax, which may contain fungicides. It is imperative that the skin be peeled before cooking.

STUFFED TURNIPS IN CIDER

This dish is a symphony of Pacific Northwest ingredients. Tender lamb is raised in eastern Washington and Idaho, turnips crown the loamy maritime soil on the western side of the Cascade mountains, and hard apple cider is made from the crisp, flavorful apples that are part of a burgeoning apple industry, also on the west side of the mountains.

The turnips are tender-crisp, the lamb enriched with herbs and spices, and the dry cider adds a touch of acidity to balance them both. If you can't find good dry cider, use a crisp dry white wine instead. If you can't find ground lamb, buy lean lamb and grind it either in a meat grinder or in a food processor.

If you want to serve these turnips over rice, increase the amount of cream to 1 cup, so there will be plenty of sauce to moisten the rice.

Try this with a Caymus Cabernet Sauvignon 1987.

4 medium turnips
1 medium red bell pepper
Salt and freshly ground black pepper
2 tablespoons fresh tarragon, or
   ¼ teaspoon dried
½ teaspoon packed fresh thyme leaves,
   or scant ¼ teaspoon dried
8 ounces lean ground lamb
2 tablespoons dried currants
1 small onion, peeled and minced
½ teaspoon ground cinnamon
1 large egg, lightly beaten
1 slice good-quality white bread, crumbled
1 tablespoon unsalted butter
2 cups extra-dry apple cider
1 bay leaf
½ cup heavy (whipping) cream

1 Preheat the broiler.

2 Peel the turnips. Using a melon baller or a stiff vegetable peeler, hollow them out, leaving the sides and bottom approxi-

mately ⅜ inch thick. Reserve the turnip pulp for another use, such as adding to a soup or salad.

3 Blanch the turnip shells in boiling salted water to cover until they have softened slightly, 2 to 3 minutes. Drain and set aside.

4 Place the red pepper on a piece of aluminum foil under the broiler, and roast it, turning it as the skin blisters and turns black, which will take 15 minutes. Remove the pepper from the broiler, wrap it in the foil, and set it aside to steam, 10 to 15 minutes. When it is cool enough to handle, peel it and remove the membranes and the seeds. Cut the pepper into ½-inch-wide strips.

5 Line each hollowed-out turnip with three strips of red pepper, then season with salt and pepper. Dice any remaining pepper strips.

6 Mince the tarragon and thyme. In a medium-size bowl, combine the lamb, currants, onion, herbs, cinnamon, and salt and pepper to taste. Add the egg, bread, and diced pepper, and mix well. To check the seasoning, sauté a teaspoonful of the filling in a small pan over medium-high heat. Adjust the seasoning to taste.

7 Fill the turnips with the stuffing, mounding it slightly at the top.

8 Melt the butter in a medium-size saucepan over medium-high heat. When it is foaming but not smoking, brown the turnips on all sides. (This is a bit tricky because the turnips tend to roll around, but it is possible and does make a big difference to the dish.)

9 When the turnips have browned, set them upright in the pan and pour the cider around them. Add the bay leaf and bring the cider to a boil. Reduce the heat to low, cover the pan, and let simmer until the stuffing is cooked through, 25 to 30 minutes. Remove the turnips from the pan and arrange them on a serving dish. Cover with aluminum foil and keep warm in a low (200°F) oven.

10 Reduce the cooking liquid by one third over medium-high heat, 5 minutes. Then whisk in the cream and continue to cook until the sauce has thickened slightly, 2 to 3 minutes. Season to taste with salt and pepper, and pour around the turnips. Serve immediately.

4 servings

TARRAGON

◼ ◼ ◼ ◼ ◼

*T*arragon has an elegant aniselike flavor that enhances mild seafood such as sole, cod, scallops, and snapper. It goes well with chicken, with carrots, and in cream sauces, egg and cheese dishes, salads, and fresh vegetable mixtures, and can be used as a flavoring for white or red vinegar. Dried tarragon can be used in a pinch.

DON PATTERSON'S SWEET POTATO SHAM

Don Patterson is the resident sweet potato expert of east central Texas. His primary interest in the bulbous reddish tubers is scientific—what soil they prefer, what pests prefer them—but he's a fan of their culinary attributes as well. When asked for his favorite way to eat them, he didn't miss a beat and recited this recipe from memory.

Though sham is sweet and spiced like a pie, in Texas sweet potato country it is eaten as a vegetable. I love it that way, along with a good dish of okra and onions, and grilled beef ribs, roast turkey, or chicken. Consider it for a Thanksgiving dish as well, though you may then want to omit the pumpkin pie, which it resembles.

The cooking time for the potatoes depends on their age. At the beginning of the season, which is generally early fall, they will cook more quickly because they are still quite full of moisture. As the year progresses they lose moisture and take longer to cook.

If you have a source for good sweet potatoes, buy them up, store them in a cool place, and you'll have them the year through.

6 good-size sweet potatoes
1 tablespoon salt
4 tablespoons (½ stick) unsalted butter, at room temperature
½ cup granulated sugar
½ cup (firmly packed) light brown sugar
1 large egg
½ cup milk
½ teaspoon freshly grated nutmeg, or to taste
½ teaspoon ground cinnamon, or to taste
Salt

1 Place the sweet potatoes in a large kettle, cover with water, and add the 1 tablespoon salt. Bring to a boil over high heat, and cook until the potatoes are soft through, 30 to 50 minutes.

2 Preheat the oven to 350°F.

3 Drain the potatoes, and as soon as they are cool enough to handle, peel them and place them in a large bowl. Using a fork or a potato masher, mash the potatoes until the texture is even.

4 In a medium-size bowl, whisk together the butter and the sugars. Add the egg, whisk until mixed, and then add the milk and mix well. Stir this mixture into the potatoes, and mix until they are thoroughly incorporated. Season to taste with the spices and salt. Transfer to an ovenproof baking dish, smooth out the surface, and bake until the potatoes are lightly golden on top, about 1 hour.

8 to 10 servings

YAMS AND APPLES

W e had this delicious purée at the Yaegers' home, near Gettysburg, Pennsylvania. Larry Yaeger is the area marketing agent for seven counties in Pennsylvania, meaning he works with farmers to help them market their crops. Larry grew up on a farm, and he's a farmer at heart. He just can't stay out of the soil, and his expansive backyard, which might better be described as a small farm, is bursting with fruits, vegetables, herbs, hot peppers—just about anything that grows, it seems.

This is one of the dishes Betty Yaeger made when we were there, with tart apples picked from trees in the backyard. She served the dish as a vegetable, though it was sweet enough for dessert, and it was one of the best things I'd ever tasted.

The amounts of cream and butter are suggestions—use or don't use them according to your taste. The walnuts, too, are optional, but they add a wonderful flavor.

6 cups water

4 large yams, peeled, rinsed, and cut into eighths

3 large tart apples, such as Granny Smith, Winesap, or Newton, peeled, quartered, and cored

⅓ cup heavy (whipping) cream

2 to 4 tablespoons unsalted butter, cut into small pieces

½ teaspoon vanilla extract

Salt and freshly ground black pepper

¼ cup walnuts, toasted (see Note) and finely chopped, for garnish

1 Bring the water to a boil in a vegetable steamer over high heat. Place the yams in the basket, cover, and steam until they are almost soft all the way through, about 15 minutes. Add the apples, and steam until the apples and yams are entirely soft, 10 minutes.

2 Transfer the yams and apples to a food processor and purée. (This purée will be very smooth. If you prefer a coarser mixture, mash the yams and apples together in a large bowl, using a fork or a potato masher.) Add the cream, the butter, and the vanilla, and process (or mash) briefly again

until combined. Then season to taste with salt and pepper.

3 Transfer the mixture to a warmed serving dish, sprinkle with the toasted walnuts, and serve immediately.

6 to 8 servings

Note: To toast walnuts, preheat the oven to 350°F. Place the nuts in a baking pan large enough to hold them in a single layer, and toast, stirring once, until they give off a toasted aroma, 10 to 15 minutes.

BARNEY'S VEGETABLE FAVORITES

This bright vegetable dish is as vividly colored as it is filled with full summer flavor. Caryl Smith, who farms grains and cattle with her husband in Iowa, prepares it often in summer, when tomatoes are warm and ripe from the garden and zucchini comes in by the bushel from friends and neighbors, along with corn and onions. Its fresh flavors satisfy the heartiest appetite, and when Caryl serves this to Barney, who is a meat lover from start to finish, he doesn't care if there is any meat alongside or not.

Serve this in a bowl, as it is quite soupy, and be sure to have plenty of fresh bread to accompany it. Serve any leftovers the following day at room temperature.

2 tablespoons unsalted butter

2 medium white onions, peeled and coarsely chopped

1 pound small zucchini, trimmed and cut into ¾-inch-thick rounds

1½ pounds ripe tomatoes, preferably plum type, cut into 1-inch chunks

⅓ cup very loosely packed fresh oregano leaves, or ½ to 1 teaspoon dried

Salt and freshly ground black pepper

4 cups corn kernels, preferably just cut off the cob

1 Melt the butter in a large skillet over medium-high heat. When the butter is foaming, add the onions and sauté until they have begun to soften and turn translucent, about 8 minutes.

2 Stir in the zucchini, tomatoes, and oregano. Season with salt and pepper, cover, and cook until the tomatoes have softened and given up much of their juice, about 15 minutes.

3 Stir the corn into the vegetables, cover, and continue cooking until it is tender, 5 to 8 minutes. Adjust the seasoning if necessary, and serve.

6 servings.

HERBED SUMMER VEGETABLES

This dish is a bit of summer on a plate, and it can be made with any number or combination of vegetables. Tomatoes are essential, as their tartness and color add a necessary balance, but beyond that you can try anything: asparagus, fava beans, baby turnips, baby bok choy, scallions, or garlic shoots—whatever you find at the farm or market.

It's ideal for even the hottest day, as the cooking time is minimal and it can be eaten hot or at room temperature, almost like a salad. The only trick is to use the freshest possible vegetables—cooking them right to the edge of doneness, so they are still a bit crisp—and a good fruity olive oil. And make sure you have a loaf of crusty bread for sopping up the juice.

¼ cup loosely packed mixed fresh herbs,
    such as oregano, basil, chives
8 ounces feta cheese
3 tablespoons extra-virgin olive oil
1 pound yellow patty-pan squash, trimmed
    and cut vertically into ¼-inch-thick
    slices
8 ounces green beans, trimmed and cut
    diagonally into ½-inch pieces
1 pound ripe tomatoes, cored and coarsely
    chopped
Salt and freshly ground black pepper
¼ cup loosely packed fresh dill

1 Mince the mixed herbs. Crumble the
feta cheese into a small bowl, drizzle it
with 2 tablespoons of the olive oil, and stir
in the minced herbs until thoroughly incorporated. Set aside.

2 Heat the remaining 1 tablespoon olive
oil in a wok or a large heavy skillet over
medium-high heat. When the oil is hot but
not smoking, add the squash and cook, stirring constantly, until it begins to soften, 3 to
4 minutes. Add the beans and toss to mix.
Cook, stirring constantly, until they begin
to turn a vivid green, 3 to 5 minutes. Add
the tomatoes and cook, stirring constantly,
until the squash is translucent, the beans are
bright green and crisp-tender, and the
tomatoes have softened, 4 to 5 minutes.
Season judiciously with salt and generously
with pepper. Remove from the heat.

3 Mince the dill and add it to the vegetables, mixing well so it is evenly distributed. Transfer the vegetables to a warmed
serving platter, distribute
the seasoned feta
cheese on top, and
serve immediately.

4 to 6 servings

CROSSROADS FARM'S
STEAMED VEGETABLES

After visiting Crossroads Farm (see following page), I could hardly
wait to get home and sample my vegetables. I decided to apply the
gentlest, simplest cooking method so the flavors would fully emerge.
I steamed them in stages, beginning with the cauliflower and the tender new
garlic, and ending with the more delicate summer squash. After I'd tossed

WELCOME TO CROSSROADS FARM

The Crossroads Farm near Jonesport, Maine, is a lush organic farm that Arnold and Bonnie Pearlman have developed over the past seventeen years. Arnold and Bonnie and their two children, Delia and Jody, work together to produce some of the largest, healthiest, and loveliest vegetables I've seen.

Located in a pocket of land that is sheltered by the surrounding hills, Crossroads Farm is well off the beaten track, up a long, newly paved road that seems to lead nowhere. Suddenly it curves nearly into their yard, which is almost always full of cars. Over the years, through selling at farmer's markets and local supermarkets, they've developed a loyal clientele, particularly among the large

summer population. "These people come from cities and they've never tasted vegetables like ours," Arnold said. "Some of them come here every day."

The Pearlmans, who now sell most of their produce right from the farm, have never used chemicals on the land, and it shows in the rich, deep soil and the quality and verve of their produce. They are able to grow such a variety of vegetables in a relatively hostile climate in large part because of the health of the soil, and also because of the care they take with the crops. All four of them are out there from dawn to dusk, working hard, interrupted only by the customers who come their way.

them in the oil and herbs and set them on the table, we enjoyed the most flavorful mix of vegetables I've ever tasted.

You can make this dish just about any time of the year. Just remember, when you're shopping or harvesting, to think of color as well as texture. And steam the vegetables carefully, so that each retains its texture.

If you can't find fava beans, substitute tiny turnips that are about the size of a big radish; if they're slightly larger, cut them in half or quarters.

4 cups water
8 ounces new potatoes, red-skinned if available, scrubbed
1 large head cauliflower, rinsed, florets and stems separated
1 large head fresh garlic, cloves separated and peeled
1 cup fresh fava beans or 6 radish-size turnips with greens
2 green zucchini, cut into 1-inch rounds
2 yellow zucchini, cut into 1-inch rounds
½ cup loosely packed mixed (2 or 3) fresh herb leaves, such as basil, thyme, marjoram, oregano, and tarragon
6 tablespoons olive oil

1 Bring the water to a boil in the bottom of a vegetable steamer over high heat. Place the potatoes in the steamer basket, cover, and cook until they begin to soften, about 10 minutes. Add the cauliflower stems, garlic cloves, and fava beans; cover, and steam until the stems begin to soften, about 5 minutes. Add the cauliflower florets and steam until they begin to soften, about 5 minutes. Then add the zucchini, and the turnips if you are using them. Cover, and steam until the zucchini has softened and begun to turn translucent, about 8 minutes.

2 While the vegetables are steaming, coarsely chop the herbs, then whisk them together with the olive oil in a large serving bowl.

3 Transfer the steamed vegetables to the bowl, toss gently, and serve immediately.

4 to 6 servings

STEAMING TIME FOR VEGETABLES

Potatoes—15 minutes
Cauliflower florets—8 minutes
Cauliflower stems—12 to 18 minutes
Fava beans—12 to 18 minutes
Small turnips—8 to 10 minutes
Yellow squash—8 to 10 minutes
Zucchini—8 to 10 minutes

PAVICH VEGETABLES

This lusty dish comes directly from the kitchen of Helen Pavich, who always has a patch of greens growing in the organic garden outside her house. Helen learned to garden in Yugoslavia, where she was born, and has always gardened organically. "If I see an unwanted insect in the garden, I go out and smash it myself," she says.

Helen's gardening success helped transform the family farm to an organic system, and now Pavich and Sons is known nationwide for its organically grown table grapes (see page 448 for more about the Paviches).

She always has potatoes on hand, too, so she makes this dish often for her sons and their families, who are regular visitors at her dining table. It is quick, simple, and so satisfying that I like to make a meal of it, with some crusty bread and a simple salad or a plate of ripe tomatoes dressed in vinaigrette alongside. Helen drizzles the vegetables simply with olive oil, salt, and pepper, which is wonderful. I also like to add garlic and hot pepper for a change.

4 large Russet potatoes, peeled and cut into
  eighths
2 teaspoons salt
1 large bunch collard greens or kale,
  stems removed (about 15 ounces
  leaves), rinsed and coarsely
  chopped
6 tablespoons extra-virgin olive oil
4 cloves garlic, peeled and thinly sliced
  crosswise
½ teaspoon dried red pepper flakes

1 Place the potatoes in a large saucepan or stockpot, and just cover with water. Add the salt, stir, and bring to a boil over high heat. Reduce the heat to medium and boil the potatoes gently, partially covered, until they are nearly tender but still firm in the center, about 12 minutes. Add the greens, cover the pot, and cook, stirring occasionally, until they have cooked down and turned dark green, about 15 minutes. The potatoes will be thoroughly cooked and a bit soft at the edges.

2 While the potatoes and greens are cooking, place the oil and the garlic in a

FRESH GARLIC

*F*resh garlic means exactly what it says—the freshest and newest you can possibly get. Depending on where you live, this will be available beginning in mid to late August. The ideal is to get garlic that isn't quite mature, when the cloves are almost pure white and the peel isn't quite as hard. However, any very good quality garlic will do, as long as the green germ inside the cloves hasn't formed. (If it has, cut the clove in half, remove the germ, and reduce the cooking time slightly.)

small heavy saucepan over medium-low heat, and cook until the garlic turns a very pale gold, 10 to 15 minutes. Remove from the heat, stir in the hot pepper flakes, and set aside.

3 When the potatoes and greens are cooked, transfer them to a warmed serving bowl, with any remaining cooking liquid, and either pour the garlic mixture over all, or serve it on the side.

6 servings

AN EARLY SUMMER VEGETABLE HARVEST

This recipe was inspired by an early summer walk through Manhattan's Union Square Greenmarket. I had a different dish in mind, but when I saw the bounty, I changed my dinner plans.

There were mounds of peas in the pod, baskets of mushrooms, bunches of big red radishes with their lush tops, bright spring onions, and the first herbs of summer. I got some of everything and put them all together.

Cooked radishes lose their color if they sit, so add them at the last minute, mix well, and serve immediately.

2 tablespoons unsalted butter
1 pound good-quality button mushrooms,
   stems trimmed, caps quartered
3 scallions (green onions), trimmed and
   sliced diagonally into ¼-inch-thick
   pieces
1 large shallot, peeled and minced
1 pound edible-pod peas (sugar snaps),
   trimmed and left whole (or substitute
   8 ounces fresh peas and 8 ounces
   snow peas)
Salt and freshly ground black pepper
1 bunch radishes (about 8 or 9), trimmed
   and cut lengthwise into ¼-inch-thick slices
¼ cup fresh peppermint leaves

1 Melt the butter in a large heavy skillet or wok over medium-high heat. When the butter foams, add the mushrooms and cook, stirring frequently, until they begin to give up liquid. (They will go through a very dry period, but don't be concerned; just stir them frequently.)

2 Add the scallions and the shallot, stir, and cook until the scallions turn deep green, about 2 minutes. Then add the peas and cook, stirring, until they soften and turn a vivid green, about 5 minutes. Season with salt and pepper to taste.

3 While the peas are cooking, cut the mint leaves into thin strips with a pair of scissors.

4 Add the radishes to the vegetables, stir, and then transfer the mixture to a warmed serving platter. Sprinkle with the mint and serve immediately.

6 servings

A FARMER AT HEART

ave Kobos has his business in the city, but his heart's definitely on the farm.

Dave has owned a coffee, tea, spice, and kitchenware store in Portland, Oregon, for sixteen years. Eleven years ago he and his wife, Susan, moved to a 3-acre farm in Molalla, about 40 miles from Portland, where they live with their three children, a passel of sheep, a variety of chickens, and a vegetable garden that's big enough to feed half the county. Dave commutes to his six-day-a-week job and still manages to have a full life at home, where he usually can be found in either garden or kitchen.

Dave is the kind of person who infects all he knows with his passions, which are far-ranging. He orders seeds for his garden from around the planet, it seems, and is always exulting about something new. "These potatoes are blue, I mean blue all through," he'll say.

Or, "These raspberries have two crops, can you believe it?"

He's turning his garden into a year-round affair, which is entirely possible in the temperate Pacific Northwest. He now grows more than thirty kinds of vegetables and a cornucopia of fruits as well, and what doesn't go onto the Kobos table or into the freezer is liberally shared with friends, employees, and neighbors.

Last year, Dave sent me a sample from his potato patch, a box full of the knobbiest, weirdest little tubers I'd ever seen. There were Peruvian Purples, Ruby Crescents, German Fingerlings, and Yellow Finns—all waxy potatoes—and a snowy Russet called a Butte. Several of each kind were in carefully labeled bags, and each had its own special flavor. I steamed them immediately, without waiting for supper, and savored them slowly with butter, salt, and pepper. They transported me right to the Kobos's fruitful Northwest farm.

DAVE KOBOS'S WINTER VEGETABLE MEDLEY

Dave Kobos (see facing page) makes this dish year-round, with fresh vegetables in various combinations or in winter with those from his freezer. I make this often, too, and I find it a particularly effective antidote to winter's leaden skies.

It's a simple dish to make, yet it invariably elicits a question usually reserved for much more complicated ones: "How on earth did you do this? The vegetables taste so fresh!" When that comes up at Dave's table, he winks and never says a word. He knows it's all in the gardening, and leaving well enough alone after that.

1½ pounds small new potatoes, scrubbed

2 quarts water

2 tablespoons salt

8 ounces small, thin carrots, peeled and cut diagonally into 2-inch pieces

2 medium yellow squash, cut diagonally into 2-inch-thick slices

2 cups fresh or frozen peas

3 tablespoons unsalted butter, melted

Freshly ground black pepper

2 scallions (green onions), trimmed and cut into thin rounds

¼ cup minced fresh parsley

1 Place the potatoes in a large pot, cover them with the water, and add the salt. Bring to a boil and cook until the potatoes are nearly soft, about 13 minutes. Add the carrots and cook until they are tender, about 5 minutes. Add the squash and cook until it is tender but not mushy, about 2 minutes. Then add the peas and cook until they are bright green, about 2 minutes. Drain the vegetables and transfer to a large warmed shallow serving dish.

2 Pour the melted butter over the vegetables and toss gently. Season generously with pepper, and sprinkle with the scallions and parsley. Toss again, and serve the medley immediately.

4 side-dish servings

THE GREENMARKETS OF NEW YORK CITY

In 1976, as Barry Benepe was driving through upstate New York, he noticed several small farms that had gone out of business. The reasons for their demise were all too familiar: Land development was pushing prices higher, and that, combined with the cost of shipping produce to market was making farming too expensive for many small farms.

While farms were going out of business, consumers in New York City were searching in vain for farm-fresh produce. It took Benepe's ingenuity to help the farmer and the consumer come to each other's rescue.

That same year, Benepe signed an agreement with the Council on the Environment (a privately funded organization affiliated with the mayor's office), which agreed to sponsor the Greenmarket Project. Benepe was appointed project director and received permission from the city to transform a vacant lot on the corner of 59th Street and Second Avenue into a farmer's market, the first to be held in the city for several decades.

The Greenmarket program has since expanded throughout the boroughs of New York City to include more than twenty-five farmer's markets. The number of farmers participating has grown from the first seven to more than 140. Consumers can choose from an array of seasonal produce, locally produced wines, dairy products, meats, poultry, seafood, preserves, baked goods, and flowering and leafy plants.

An Early Morning Tradition

▪▪▪▪▪

Most of these eager shoppers seem to be at the Union Square Greenmarket, the city's largest, on Saturday mornings. What is primarily a parking lot four days of the week is transformed into a lush and fragrant market the other three. There, farmers, their skin weathered from working in the fields, get a taste of the city as they sell their wares.

Trading is brisk by 9 A.M. Home cooks vie with professional chefs to choose the best of the fresh produce, and it's easy to decipher their weekend plans as they pile the makings for a dinner party or a terrace garden in their bulging shopping bags.

The aroma of freshly baked goods wafts out in little puffs as people sample the wares, too impatient to wait until they get home. Those who have planned ahead come with a container of coffee and take it along with their fresh doughnuts or bread to a bench in Union Square Park, where they can sit overlooking the market and plan their shopping strategy or exult in their finds.

Benefits Both City and Farm

▪▪▪▪▪

The Greenmarkets, located in eighteen of the city's neighborhoods, have added immeasurable quality to life throughout New York City. They've also been a vital force in keeping small farms alive. More than 75 percent of the farmers who participate say they owe the success of their farms to the Greenmarket. They avoid the price of a middleman while still selling their produce for twice what they could get from a wholesaler. The price to the consumer is often the same as what they would find at the supermarket, or less.

As important to the consumer as price is the fresh quality produce, and an added benefit is the connection they make with the farmer. They can ask questions, obtain cooking tips and recipes, and get a hint about what it takes to farm. In turn, the farmer learns what the consumer wants, and can plan crops accordingly. The result is increased satisfaction on both sides, better food for the consumer, and a continuity of life for the farmer.

SIX-LAYER DINNER

This is a dish that Montana organic grain farmer Alice Berner makes to take out to her husband, Bud, and the others when they're working in the fields. As simple to make as slicing the vegetables, it's a stay-at-home dish, the kind you can put in the oven and forget about while you occupy yourself elsewhere. Sometimes, when I want a bit of a change, I add the herbs; but at other times I just cook the vegetables plain, to enjoy their simple, full sweetness.

You may want to serve this alongside roast chicken or grilled fish; or for an all-vegetable meal, serve a green salad alongside. And don't forget a hearty bread and perhaps a lightly chilled Rosé de Provence.

6 small Russet potatoes, peeled and thinly sliced

3 small onions, peeled and thinly sliced

4 small carrots, peeled and thinly sliced

2 large green bell peppers, cored, seeded, and thinly sliced

Salt and freshly ground pepper

2 large cloves garlic, peeled and thinly sliced

1 sprig fresh rosemary, or 1 teaspoon dried (optional)

Several sprigs fresh thyme, or ½ teaspoon dried (optional)

1 teaspoon honey

1 can (28 ounces) Italian plum tomatoes, with liquid, coarsely chopped, or 4 cups cooked fresh tomatoes

Handful of herbs, such as parsley and chives, minced, for garnish (optional)

1 Preheat the oven to 350°F. Lightly oil a 10 x 12-inch oval baking dish.

2 Layer the vegetables in the baking dish, beginning with a layer of potatoes, then following with onions, carrots, and green peppers, sprinkling the layers evenly with salt and pepper, the garlic, and herbs. Repeat until all the vegetables and herbs are used, ending with the peppers.

3 Mix the honey with the tomatoes, and pour over the vegetables. Cover the dish, and bake in the center of the oven until the vegetables are tender and have blended together, about 2½ hours. Remove from the oven, sprinkle with the garnish if desired, and serve.

8 to 10 servings

VEGETABLE CHILI WITH MILLET

This meatless chili is perfect for a stay-at-home day when the air is cold, the sun is shining, and you want something lively and warming to serve for dinner. The recipe comes from Linnea Jepsen, who gives cooking demonstrations at Walnut Acres, an organic farm in Pennsylvania. Linnea uses only organic produce from the farm, including their organically raised grains, in dishes that are lively and full of flavor and variety.

She added millet to this chili, which gives it a nice texture and adds a certain sparkle, because the little round grains keep their bright yellow color and shape. It also adds considerable nutrition: Millet contains niacin and a significant amount of iron and calcium. Combined with the beans, which are high in vitamin A, have traces of iron and sodium, and contain even more calcium than millet, this chili is a nutritional gold mine.

The nutrition might be considered a bonus, because the real strength of this dish is its flavor, which is rich, deep, and hearty. It's easy to assemble, too, and it can cook in stages when you have the time, or it can just sit there simmering on the stove all day, with an occasional check. You can even start it one night, refrigerate it, and continue cooking it the following day. Time allows the flavors to mellow, so there should be no rush getting this to the table.

Once you've added the millet and the water, check the chili regularly because millet can quickly absorb a great deal of liquid, and it may become dry. Add extra water if necessary, but judiciously. There is a fine line between watery chili and chili that is luscious and full of good flavors. This is the latter kind, and it should be good and thick.

The garnishes are my own addition. Try them—you'll see they give the chili an extra flavor and color dimension.

As with most types of chili, a frosty ale makes the perfect accompaniment.

1 pound dried kidney beans, picked over
  and rinsed
2 tablespoons olive oil
2 medium onions, peeled and diced
4 cloves garlic, peeled and minced
1 large green bell pepper, cored, seeded,
  and cut into ¼-inch dice
1 fresh jalapeño pepper, trimmed and
  minced
4 cups water
1 large can (35 ounces) plum tomatoes,
  coarsely chopped, or 3 pounds ripe plum
  tomatoes, cored and coarsely chopped
¼ to ½ cup Rosella's Lusty Tomato Sauce
  (page 316), or good-quality jarred
3 tablespoons good-quality chili powder
1 tablespoon ground cumin
1 teaspoon turmeric
Several sprigs fresh oregano, or 1 teaspoon dried
1 cup millet, rinsed and drained
Salt

FOR THE GARNISH
2 cups plain yogurt
1 small bunch scallions (green onions), trimmed
  and cut into thin rounds
2 oranges, peeled, sectioned, and cut
  into small pieces

1 Place the beans in a large heavy nonreactive saucepan. Add boiling water just to
cover, and let sit for 1 hour.

2 Drain the beans, cover them with fresh
water, and bring to a boil over high
heat. Reduce the heat to medium, and
cook, partially covered, until the beans are
tender but not soft, 50 minutes to 1 hour.
They should still have body and be not
quite cooked through. Drain and set aside.

3 Heat the oil a in large heavy nonreactive
saucepan over medium-high heat.
When it is hot but not smoking, add the
onions, garlic, and bell and jalapeño peppers. Reduce the heat to medium and cook,
stirring frequently, until the onions turn
translucent, about 9 minutes. Add the reserved beans, 2 cups of the water, the tomatoes and tomato sauce, the spices, and the
oregano. Mix well and bring to a boil. Reduce the heat to medium-low and cook,
partially covered, for 1½ hours.

4 Add the millet and the remaining 2
cups water, stir, and continue cooking
until the millet and the beans are cooked
through but not mushy, the flavors have
mellowed, and the chili is rich and aromatic, at least 2 hours. Once you have
added the millet, you will need to stir the
chili occasionally, to be sure it doesn't stick
to the bottom of the pan and burn. Taste
for salt.

5 To serve, ladle the chili into warmed
bowls, and either top with the yogurt,
scallions, and oranges or pass them separately.

8 to 10 servings

GARDEN SALADS

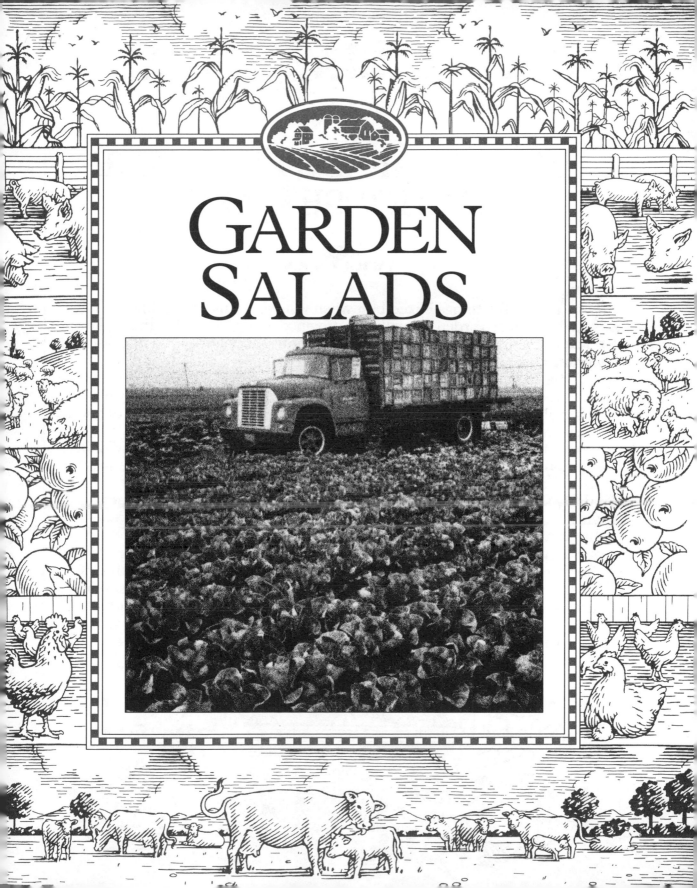

FRESH SALADS FROM THE FARMHOUSE GARDEN

O ne of the things I liked best when visiting farms was seeing the farmer's garden. Usually the province of the farm wife, these plots of land tucked away near the farmhouse are patchworks of color and vibrancy, like miniature farms themselves.

Farm salads are usually simple and extraordinarily inviting, rather like the farm garden itself. They are full of crisp and crunch, vivid colors, and true flavors: a celebration of tiny, tender leaves; marble-size new potatoes; warm, ripe, thickly sliced tomatoes dressed with vinegar, oil, and onions. And they are always made with the best-quality vegetables because, whereas cooking may perk up an aging squash, an overripe tomato, or a rusty-skinned potato, a salad reveals all.

You will enjoy the salads in this chapter for that very reason.

They're not only lively, they're hearty and substantial, full of good flavor, easy to make.

But before you begin, I'd like to make a plea: Grow some salad ingredients, if you can. Start with lettuces. They are very friendly plants to grow, and there is endless variety. They're quick to mature, tolerant of peculiar situations like window boxes and shade, and there are several for every season. You'll find that a fresh leaf of lettuce will make the difference between a ho-hum salad and a gastronomic treat.

AVOCADO AND POTATO SALAD WITH HORSERADISH

Bill Schaefer is director of public relations for J. R. Brooks, the largest exotic-produce wholesaler in the country, and he has a two-avocado a day habit. Bill's favorite way of eating an avocado is simply with lime juice and salt and pepper. He did, however, suggest this salad as an alternative, and it's one I've come to like very well.

You can use any good, ripe avocado. The many Florida varieties have smooth green skin and can weigh as much as 20 ounces. The California Haas avocados are medium-size (about 8 ounces) with dark green to black nubby skin, and are creamier—and higher in fat content—than the Florida ones. Whichever type you choose should be firm with just a slight give. If the avocado is soft enough to hold an indentation, it's overripe and won't have the rich nutty flavor you want.

If you're using only half an avocado, leave the pit in the remaining half, rub the flesh with lemon juice, and wrap it well. Don't refrigerate an avocado—it ruins the flavor and texture.

Like an avocado, this salad has a brief shelf life, so plan to eat it shortly after it is made. Any left-overs won't be very tasty, so try to finish it all up. That shouldn't be hard—of all the potato salads I've made, this has proved to be one of the most popular.

2 pounds new potatoes, scrubbed
¼ cup extra-virgin olive oil
1½ tablespoons best-quality red wine
    vinegar
Salt
½ cup sour cream
½ cup plain yogurt
2 tablespoons prepared horseradish
¼ cup loosely packed fresh dill sprigs
    (thick stems removed)
3 ribs celery, strings removed, cut into
    ¼-inch-thick crescents (1 cup)
2 medium or 1 large avocado
1 tablespoon freshly squeezed lime
    juice
Freshly ground black pepper

1 Bring water to a boil in the bottom of a vegetable steamer. Cut the potatoes in half, and place them in the steamer basket. Cover, and steam until they are cooked through, about 20 minutes. Remove the potatoes from the heat and allow them to cool slightly.

2 While the potatoes are cooking, whisk the oil and vinegar together in a large bowl. Season to taste with salt, and set aside.

3 When the potatoes are cool enough to handle without burning your fingers, cut them into 1-inch cubes. Toss them in the oil and vinegar so they are coated well, and set them aside to cool to room temperature, tossing occasionally.

4 In a small bowl, whisk together the sour cream, yogurt, and horseradish. Mince the dill, and add it to the sour cream mixture, mixing well.

5 When the potatoes have cooled to room temperature, add the celery and toss to combine. Then add the sour cream mixture, and toss again.

6 Halve, pit, and peel the avocados. Cut them into 1-inch cubes, and place in a small bowl with the lime juice. Toss so the cubes are moistened with the juice. Then add the avocados, with all of the lime juice, to the potatoes, and toss gently until they are well distributed and coated with the dressing. Add pepper and additional salt to taste, and either serve immediately or chill for 30 minutes and then serve.

6 to 8 servings

FLORIDA SALAD

This salad was inspired by visits to two Florida farms. On one the avocado trees shaded the ground with their lush canopies thick with hard green fruit. At the other, grapefruits and oranges hung heavy on trees whose branches reached right to the ground, so the trees looked like huge bushes hung with orange and yellow ornaments. The sweet tartness of the grapefruit plays off the creamy richness of the avocado, and the lime juice and olive oil balance them perfectly.

This is a refreshing summery salad, and one I like to serve at the start of a meal or as part of a big picnic lunch in the sun.

2 avocados (preferably a small Florida variety), halved, pitted, peeled, and cut into ¼-inch-thick lengthwise slices
3 medium grapefruit, rind and white pith removed, cut in sections
4 teaspoons freshly squeezed lime juice
8 teaspoons extra-virgin olive oil
Salt and freshly ground black pepper
1 small bunch fresh chives, for garnish

1 Arrange the avocado slices and grapefruit sections on four salad plates, alternating them in a fan pattern.

2 Drizzle each plate with 1 teaspoon of the lime juice and 2 teaspoons of the olive oil. Season each with salt and pepper to taste.

3 Mince the chives, and sprinkle them over the salad. Serve immediately.

4 servings

ARUGULA SALAD

This is an old-fashioned country recipe—arugula was a common salad green in pioneer gardens. The peppery leaves stand up well to the cooked dressing, which is rich and custardlike, and the salad makes a showpiece to start a meal. Try a crisp white wine, such as a Sancerre, with this salad.

5 ounces slab bacon, rind removed, cut into bite-size pieces
2 large eggs, lightly beaten
¼ cup cider vinegar
1½ teaspoons honey
Dash of paprika
Salt and freshly ground black pepper
½ cup milk
4 tablespoons (½ stick) unsalted butter
10 ounces arugula (about 7½ cups), rinsed, patted dry, and torn into bite-size pieces

1 Cook the bacon in a small skillet over medium-high heat until crisp and browned, 5 minutes. Remove the skillet from the heat and set it aside.

2 In a small bowl, whisk together the eggs, vinegar, honey, paprika, and salt and pepper to taste.

3 Warm the milk in a large saucepan over medium heat. Remove the pan from

the heat and add the butter. When the butter has melted, slowly add half the milk mixture to the egg mixture, whisking constantly; then return this to the remaining milk mixture in the pan. Cook over medium-low heat, stirring constantly, until just thickened, about 3 minutes. Do not overheat or the eggs will curdle.

4 Remove the pan from the heat and add the arugula, the bacon, and the bacon fat, tossing until well mixed. Transfer to a room-temperature platter and serve immediately.

4 servings

FRESH BEET SALAD WITH TURNIPS

This is a vibrant, refreshing salad that is best made with small sweet turnips and beets. Beets are sweet and full of flavor, and when finely grated they have a satisfying crunch as well. The turnips are softened slightly by blanching, but they too still have texture. This is an unconventional way to serve both of them, but one that may convert you forever to fresh uncooked beets and the subtle flavor of turnips.

FOR THE TURNIPS
4 small turnips, peeled and trimmed
¼ cup extra-virgin olive oil
2 tablespoons white wine vinegar
Salt and freshly ground black pepper to taste
¼ teaspoon cumin seeds

FOR THE BEETS
3 tablespoons good-quality red wine vinegar
3 tablespoons extra-virgin olive oil
Salt and freshly ground black pepper to taste
1 clove garlic, peeled and finely minced

2 large shallots, peeled
1½ pounds beets, peeled and finely grated
1 hard-cooked egg yolk
2 teaspoons fresh tarragon or Italian (flat-leaf) parsley leaves, minced

1 To prepare the turnips, slice them very thin (about ⅛ inch thick). Blanch them in boiling salted water (1 tablespoon salt to 1 quart of water) until they begin to soften but are still crisp, 1 minute. Drain, and

rinse well with cold water. Drain again and pat dry.

2 In a large bowl whisk together the olive oil, white wine vinegar, salt and pepper, and cumin seeds. Toss the turnip slices in the vinaigrette, and refrigerate for 15 minutes.

3 To prepare the beet salad, whisk together the red wine vinegar, olive oil, salt and pepper, and garlic in a small bowl. Finely slice the shallots, and toss them with

the beets in a large bowl. Pour the vinaigrette over the beets, and toss until they are thoroughly coated with the dressing.

4 Place a mound of the beet salad in the middle of a serving platter. Surround it with the turnip slices, closely overlapping them. For garnish, push the egg yolk through a fine-mesh sieve over the beets, and then sprinkle the beets with the tarragon. Serve immediately.

6 servings

COACH FARM BROCCOLI SALAD

A salad I had at the Coach Farm in upstate New York inspired this one. I was there visiting Miles and Lillian Cahn and their 900 goats, who give tangy sweet milk that the Cahns turn into cheese and yogurt.

When I arrived at the Cahns' home, which is built on a hill in the Hudson Valley and overlooks the working part of the farm, it was lunchtime. Lillian had prepared a lunch that centered on Hudson Valley specialties. It included chicken breast stuffed with Coach Farm goat cheese, this salad, and chilled Hudson Valley white wine.

I've made this broccoli salad often since, and I've found it to be universally appealing. You can vary it by using half broccoli and half cauliflower, as Lillian does. One thing to remember is to serve it within about 45 minutes, as the broccoli will gradually lose its bright green color. Also, rice vinegars vary in their acidity, and you may need to add lemon juice to give this salad the extra sprightliness it needs.

2 tablespoons sesame oil (*Japanese is best; available at Asian or natural foods groceries*)

1 tablespoon mild vegetable oil

2 tablespoons rice vinegar

2 teaspoons light soy sauce (*usukuchi*), or to taste

1 tablespoon freshly squeezed lemon juice (*optional*)

1 teaspoon minced fresh ginger

1 clove garlic, peeled and minced

¼ teaspoon dried red pepper flakes

1 large bunch (*about 1½ pounds*) broccoli, stems peeled and cut into 1-inch lengths, florets separated into bite-size pieces

1 red bell pepper, cored, seeded, and diced

3 scallions (*green onions*), trimmed and diced

1 In a medium-size serving bowl, whisk together the oils, rice vinegar, soy sauce, and lemon juice (if using). Whisk in the ginger, garlic, and pepper flakes, and set aside.

2 Bring water to a boil in the bottom of a vegetable steamer. Place the broccoli stems in the basket and steam until they are nearly soft, 6 to 8 minutes. Add the florets, and steam until they are nearly tender but still bright green, about 3 minutes (no longer than 4 minutes).

3 Transfer the broccoli to the serving bowl and toss thoroughly with the dressing. Adjust the seasoning as needed, adding more lemon juice or soy sauce. Let the broccoli cool slightly; then add the bell peppers and the scallions, and toss. Serve immediately.

4 to 6 servings

SWEET AND TART CARROT SALAD

L innea Jepsen, the proprietor of the Great Grains cooking school in Pennsylvania, gave me the recipe for this salad. She is also a cooking instructor at Walnut Acres, an organic farm that produces everything from stone-ground flour to sugary sweet carrots.

Linnea's message to her students is very much in tune with the philosophy of Walnut Acres, which is simplicity, health, and flavorful organically grown produce. This salad embodies all of those ideals, and most important, it is so refreshing that you'll turn to it again and again.

The chilling isn't necessary, but it adds to the refreshing nature of the salad.

7 medium carrots, finely grated
½ cup raisins
1 tablespoon freshly squeezed lemon juice
1 teaspoon minced orange zest
½ cup freshly squeezed orange juice
1 teaspoon minced lemon zest
Salt (optional)
¼ cup walnuts, toasted (see Note) and
  coarsely chopped

1 Combine all the ingredients except the walnuts in a medium-size serving bowl, and toss well. Taste for seasoning. Chill for 30 minutes if desired.

2 Sprinkle with the walnuts, and serve.

4 servings

Note: To toast walnuts, preheat the oven to 350°F. Place the nuts in a baking pan large enough to hold them in a single layer and toast, stirring once, until they give off a toasted aroma, 10 to 15 minutes.

MONTANA CHICKEN SALAD

This old-fashioned recipe with a twist comes from Alice Berner, who lives in Montana and who keeps it among her collection of favorites. I've modernized it slightly and serve it as a refreshingly light main course for lunch or a summery dinner. Try a soft, lively light red, such as a chilled Gamay de Touraine 1988, with this dish.

FOR THE DRESSING

4 hard-cooked egg yolks
1 teaspoon sugar
2 teaspoons Dijon mustard
½ cup olive oil
⅛ teaspoon celery seeds
¼ teaspoon paprika
Salt and freshly ground black pepper

FOR THE SALAD

Meat from one 3½- to 4-pound cooked
  chicken (about 4 cups)
2 scallions (green onions), trimmed and cut
  into thin rounds
1 cup finely chopped celery
4 hard-cooked egg whites, coarsely chopped
1 small, tart, firm apple, peeled, cored,
  and cut into ½-inch cubes
2 cups thinly sliced Napa cabbage

1 Make the dressing: Mash the egg yolks
with a fork or put them through a sieve.

Mix in the sugar and mustard until smooth. Then add the olive oil in a thin stream, whisking until the dressing is emulsified. Whisk in the celery seeds and the paprika, and season to taste with salt and pepper.

2 In a large bowl, mix together the chicken, scallions, celery, egg whites, and apple cubes. Pour the dressing over the salad, and toss gently but thoroughly, until all the salad ingredients are coated with the dressing. Cover, and refrigerate for about 2 hours. Let the salad come to room temperature before serving.

3 Divide the cabbage among four plates. Top with the chicken salad, and serve immediately.

4 to 6 servings

CRANBERRY SALAD WITH PECANS

V elma Williams, who raises pecans and cattle in Texas with her husband, Walter, created this dessert-like salad. Velma and Walter took me under their wing, showed me around their farm, taught me more than I thought possible about pecans and cattle, and fed me to my heart's content. Though I didn't taste this salad while I was with the Williamses, Velma insisted I take the recipe because it is a favorite with her family.

I'm not usually attracted to bright pink foods, but I make an exception for this, which is sweet, tart, and savory all at once. It's almost tonic, particularly during the fall when cranberries are in season, and it looks wonderful on a long picnic table laden with harvest foods. I like the addition of lime and lemon zest—they give the salad an extra little zing.

1 package (12 ounces; about 3½ cups) fresh or
  frozen cranberries
1½ cups sugar
2 to 3 large ribs celery, strings removed, cut into
  ⅛-inch dice (about 1⅓ cups)
½ cup toasted pecans (see Note), coarsely
  chopped
1 cup heavy (whipping) cream
Grated zest of 1 lemon (optional)
Grated zest of 1 lime (optional)

1 Place the cranberries and sugar in a food processor, and process until the cranberries are finely chopped. There may be some unevenness to the texture, which is fine. (If you are using frozen berries, do not thaw them before chopping them in the processor.)

2 Place the berry mixture in a large bowl and let it sit at room temperature, loosely covered with a towel, for at least 8 hours or overnight.

3 Add the celery and pecans to the cranberries, and mix well. Whip the cream in a chilled bowl until it forms stiff peaks. Fold the zests into the cream, then fold the cream into the cranberry mixture. Chill, covered, for at least 30 minutes, and serve.

6 servings

Note: To toast pecans, preheat the oven to 350°F. Place the pecans in a baking pan large enough to hold them in a single layer and toast, stirring once, until they give off a toasted aroma, 10 to 15 minutes.

IRON HORSE CUCUMBER SALAD

F orrest Tanser, the winemaker at Iron Horse Vineyards in Sebastopol, California, about an hour and a half north of San Francisco, gave me one of the most interesting and informative winery and vineyard tours

I have ever had. He speaks about grapes and their cultivation with an enthusiastic clarity that has even the most uninitiated saying, "For the first time, I really understand about grapes and wines."

My tour included the large organic vegetable gardens on the winery grounds, lush and abundant with a tremendous variety of produce that enjoys the warmth of the Sebastopol spring and summer. Then Forrest gave me a lively collection of recipes used at the vineyard, and among them was this refreshing salad. It is ideal during the dog days of summer, when the air is hot and the appetite craves something cool, full-flavored, and refreshing.

The key to this salad, which is as lovely to look at as it is delicious to eat, is to use the freshest, crispest vegetables you can find. It should be served chilled to get the best effect, but you can avoid a time lag between preparation and serving by refrigerating the vegetables for several hours before beginning, so they go chilled right into the bowl.

The amount of onion you use depends on whether or not you're a real onion fan. I love a sweet onion in this salad, but if you're onion-shy, use half the amount called for. The recipe did not originally call for salt and pepper, and it does not need it, but you should adjust the seasoning to your taste.

2 large cucumbers, peeled, seeded, and diced
1 large onion, peeled and sliced paper thin
1 large bunch radishes, trimmed and sliced in thin rounds
1 green bell pepper, cored, seeded, and cut into thin strips
1 small bunch fresh cilantro, rinsed, dried, stems removed (about 1½ cups loosely packed leaves)
¾ cup rice wine vinegar
1 tablespoon minced fresh ginger
Salt and freshly ground black pepper (optional)

1 Place the cucumbers, onion, radishes, and bell pepper in a large bowl, and toss well. If they are not prechilled, cover and refrigerate for 1 hour.

2 Mince the cilantro leaves.

3 Drizzle the rice wine vinegar over the vegetables, sprinkle the cilantro and the ginger over them, and toss thoroughly to combine. Season to taste, and serve immediately.

6 servings

THE SEED SAVER'S EXCHANGE

Heritage Farm sits just off a country road near Decorah, in northeastern Iowa. Behind the old white farmhouse the land falls into a hollow of sorts, where a gorgeous round-topped brick-red barn draws the eye, its graceful form standing tall and sturdy against the green.

Behind the barn is a pond, and more farmland that gives way gradually to brush and woods. To the right of the shaded farmhouse a 4-acre garden is profuse with hundreds of varieties of vegetables. This early summer day, a small crew is crouching in the garden, thinning plants, tying them up, or bundling seed pods so that when they open, the seeds won't drift away.

Heritage Farm, the barn-cum-meeting center, and the lush Preservation Garden are the home of Kent and Diane Whealy and the Seed Saver's Exchange, headquarters for a nationwide

network of farmers and gardeners dedicated to the reintroduction and cultivation of heirloom vegetables.

HEIRLOOM VEGETABLES

The Seed Saver's Exchange was founded after Kent and Diane received seeds as a wedding gift from Diane's grandfather. The seeds were part of her heritage, brought over from Bavaria by pioneering relatives. The Whealys were struck by their genetic value, and got to wondering if others might have similar heirloom seeds. Like many others, they believed that old, established varieties often have stronger, better flavor than the newer ones. The older varieties also serve as valuable stock for new varieties. Kent started poking around to find out.

He found that many immigrants had brought favorite seeds to America, and that they were still being planted by

▶▶▶

succeeding generations. The Amish and Mennonites preserved the seeds of their traditional plants, as did native Americans. But as the state of farming deteriorated, forcing younger generations to leave the farm, no one was left to continue harvesting the seeds, and the old-fashioned varieties were disappearing. And while the USDA and land-grant colleges were entrusted with establishing a national seed bank to preserve vegetable and flower varieties and maintain genetic diversity, cuts in federal funding had left it sadly neglected.

The Whealys became deeply concerned about the potential loss of genetic diversity. Kent began a letter-writing campaign to farming and gardening magazines in order to locate gardeners with rare seeds, and others willing to sow them. The result was the nucleus of the Seed Saver's Exchange.

Since 1975 the Seed Saver's Exchange has grown from 6 members offering just a few seed varieties to more than 700 members offering their collections of 4 to 5,000. Each year the Exchange publishes a catalog listing members, the seeds they have to offer, and those they are looking for. All who order seeds do so with the understanding that they will grow enough of a surplus to offer seeds in succeeding years.

A collection of 6,000 rare and endangered heirloom seeds is stored at Heritage Farm as an unofficial seed bank, and up to 1,500 of them are planted in the Preservation Garden each year. As garden manager David Cavagnaro puts it, "The only way to ensure genetic preservation is when these varieties are out in people's gardens." Eventually seeds that are "proven" in the Preservation Garden will be available through the Seed Saver's Exchange.

MAINTAINING PURITY

The Preservation Garden is more a laboratory than an ordinary kitchen garden. In attempting to maintain the purity of the varieties planted there each year, much hand labor is involved. The squash, watermelons, muskmelons, cucumbers, and corn must be hand-pollinated, and peppers must be caged to prevent cross-breeding. Other plants are wrapped, bagged, and segregated in careful order. All seeds are then collected, processed, and stored. The dried bean collection alone takes up almost an entire wall of tiny drawers in one of the garden sheds.

Members of the Seed Saver's Exchange go through a similar process to ensure that they will have pure seed to share. Certain members have gone further and taken on the responsibility of curating specific vegetables. Suzanne Ashworth is the eggplant curator; she grows dozens of varieties in her Sacramento garden. Others curate tomatoes, potatoes, or corn. Yet other members, like David Podoll of Fargo, North Dakota, might take on just a single heirloom vegetable at a

time. When I visited him he proudly pointed out his heirloom potatoes, which he grows and makes available each year.

The Whealys continue their search for old seed varieties with a sense of urgency, because they feel there is no time to lose. When they realized that commercial seed catalogs are dropping about 5 percent of their seed offerings each year, representing the potential loss of favorite old varieties, Kent began buying up the discontinued seeds. They now constitute part of the farm's seed bank and will eventually find their way into the Preservation Garden soil.

OTHER ENDANGERED FOODS

■ ■ ■ ■ ■

The Whealys' interest in genetic preservation has stretched to fruits, nuts, berries, and farm animals. They have an orchard of several hundred pre-1900 apple varieties, a small herd of rare beef cattle, and clutches of endangered species of chickens and waterfowl. They want to offer a permanent display of endangered food crops, an expanded educational center, and ever-expanding gardens where seed savers can come look, work, and learn.

The Whealys and the staff of the Seed Saver's Exchange work quietly and without fanfare, relying on grants and donations. The importance of their work is obvious not only in the increasing numbers who join the Exchange, but in the growing collection of heirloom seeds that will now be preserved for future generations.

Interest in preserving heirloom seeds and expanding the number of available crop plants has spread far afield, no doubt due in part to the Seed Saver's Exchange. Some agricultural universities are beginning to preserve seeds, and even large seed companies are looking with interest at collections of plant germ plasm, the hereditary material in seeds, with the possibility of moving genes from one species to another in order to preserve the qualities of heirloom seeds.

If you are interested in becoming a member of the Seed Saver's Exchange, contact Kent Whealy, Director, R.R. 3, Box 239, Decorah, IA 52101.

Other organizations and companies that make heirloom seeds available:

Seeds Blum, Idaho City Stage, Boise, ID 83706

Peace Seeds, 2385 S.E. Thompson St., Corvallis, OR 97333

The Redwood City Seed Company, P.O. Box 361, Redwood City, CA 94064

Southern Exposure Seed Exchange, P.O. Box 158, Northern Garden, VA 22959

Abundant Life Seed Foundation, P.O. Box 772, Port Townsend, WA 98368

The Cook's Garden, Box 65, Londonderry, VT 05148

Johnny's Selected Seeds, 305 Foss Hill Rd., Albion, ME 04910

Native Seeds/Search, 3950 W. New York Dr., Tucson, AZ 85745

Shepard's Garden Seeds, 6116 Hwy. 9, Felton, CA 95018

Shumway Seeds, P.O. Box 1, Graniteville, SC 29829

CORN, ESCAROLE, AND ARUGULA SALAD

Jo Hatton, whose husband grows corn in Florida, suggested this salad, saying that most people are stuck on boiled or roasted corn, but that it is good raw, right off the cob. She was right—it is. And the sweet, mild corn flavor is complemented by the full-flavored greens.

When choosing an ear of corn, look at the stem end, which will be whitened from being cut but shouldn't be brown. Also look at the corn silk, which should be golden and dry, not brown and gummy. Peel back the husk and prick one of the kernels with a fingernail. A jet of juice will shoot out if the corn is tender and sweet. If there isn't any juice, pass it by. This may sound like corn abuse, but it isn't. It's insurance against starchy, flavorless corn.

Try a ripe, full-style Sancerre with this robust salad.

3 teaspoons balsamic vinegar
Salt and freshly ground black pepper
3 tablespoons extra-virgin olive oil
1 small clove garlic, peeled and minced
1 large ear fresh corn
6 cups trimmed escarole or curly endive leaves,
  carefully rinsed and spun dry, torn in pieces
2 cups trimmed arugula leaves, rinsed
  and spun dry

1 In a large salad bowl, whisk the vinegar with salt and pepper to taste. Then add the olive oil in a thin stream, whisking constantly to form an emulsion. Whisk in the garlic, and taste for seasoning.

2 Using a very sharp knife, cut the corn kernels from the cob, right at the base. Separate those that cling together, and stir them into the vinaigrette. Add the two greens and toss until the leaves are well coated with the dressing and the corn is fairly well distributed throughout the salad.

3 To serve, divide the salad among four dinner plates, then spoon any corn remaining in the bottom of the bowl atop each serving.

6 servings

ROOT VEGETABLE SALAD WITH AN ANCHOVY VINAIGRETTE

This salad comes from Karen Malody, who grew up on a farm in north central Washington. She believes that something in her childhood led her to a food career, with a detour for a masters in sociology. Karen now lives in Seattle, where she's done everything from owning and operating a cooking school and catering business to consulting for many of the city's food businesses and restaurants.

Karen's parents grew root vegetables, and she serves them in a more creative fashion than anyone I know. This salad is a perfect example. Karen recommends serving it alongside lamb shanks.

2 large red bell peppers, cored, seeded, and
   quartered
2 fennel bulbs, with fronds
8 ounces rutabaga, peeled
8 ounces small turnips, peeled

FOR THE VINAIGRETTE
7 tablespoons extra-virgin olive oil
3 tablespoons sherry vinegar
1 tablespoon balsamic vinegar
1 teaspoon whole-grain mustard
½ teaspoon sugar
2 cans (2 ounces each) anchovy fillets in oil,
   drained and minced
Salt and freshly ground black pepper to taste

1 Trim any membrane from the inside of the bell peppers, then cut across the quarters to form ⅛-inch-wide strips. Set aside 1½ cups of the pepper strips.

2 Quarter the fennel bulbs lengthwise, then cut the quarters crosswise into ¼-inch-wide strips. Finely chop enough of the fennel fronds to make a heaping ¼ cup.

3 Cut the rutabaga and turnips into ¼-inch-thick slices, then cut the slices into ¼-inch-wide strips.

4 Make the vinaigrette: In a large non-aluminum bowl, whisk together all the vinaigrette ingredients until thoroughly combined.

5 Combine the reserved pepper strips and the finely chopped fennel fronds in a small bowl, and toss with 1 tablespoon of the vinaigrette. Set aside.

6 Add the rutabaga, turnips, and remaining pepper strips to the remaining vinaigrette, tossing until they are thoroughly

coated. Then transfer the vegetables to a large platter, mounding them high in the center. Surround the salad with the reserved pepper and fennel garnish, and serve immediately.

6 to 8 servings

DANDELION SALAD

I love wild dandelion greens. They're at their best in the spring, when the little plants have leaves that are small and spiky, with a touch of tender fuzz, and their flavor is deep, good, and green.

If you have dandelions growing in a patch of grass that you know hasn't been treated with pesticides, get a paring knife or one of those fork-tongued weeders, and go out and get yourself a basketful. Wash and trim them carefully, leaving the tiny plants whole (they should be small enough to fit in the palm of your hand), and toss them with this salad dressing.

You can also buy dandelion greens at the market, of course. They'll be larger, separate leaves—not whole plants—and they too will be crisp and pleasantly bitter. No matter where you find your greens, follow this recipe for an uncommonly delicious treat.

3 scant tablespoons walnut oil
1 tablespoon good-quality red wine vinegar
1 clove garlic, peeled and minced
Salt and coarsely ground fresh black pepper
3 ounces (5 to 6 cups) dandelion greens
¼ cup walnuts, chopped

1 In a large bowl, whisk together the oil, vinegar, garlic, and salt and pepper to taste.

2 Add the dandelion greens, tossing well to coat each leaf with the dressing. Divide the greens among four salad plates, and top each serving with walnuts. Serve immediately.

4 servings

ARKANSAS KALE AND BACON SALAD

The idea for this salad—which I call "renegade salad" because it's wild and colorful—cropped up during the annual summer barbecue at the University of Arkansas, near Pine Bluff. I'd been visiting farms all day with Thomas Vaughn, who worked for the university and is now a VISTA volunteer working with low-income farmers. He has a standing invitation to the picnic, and had offered to take me along.

When we drove up to the university farm, where test plots of scuppernong grapes wound around fence posts near rows of sun-parched corn and ponds stocked with catfish, farm manager Ambus Handcock was tending sauce-slathered turkey and pork ribs in an old oil drum that served as a barbecue grill. Guests arrived carrying covered dishes and drinks, and party talk turned to favorite foods.

Out of that lively conversation came this recipe, which uses a very typical southern food—greens—in an atypical way. Usually greens are cooked long and slowly so they become mellow. Here they have punch, offset by the slightly sweet pickled beets, the smoky bacon, and the eye-catching garnish of hard-cooked egg. It is a lovely and delectable surprise.

When buying the kale, choose it carefully. Look for vigorous bunches that are an even green, with no yellow or spotted leaves, which indicate age. You can save the stalks for soup, or to steam and serve with butter, if you like.

This is a full meal for four, and a satisfying first course for six. Try a rich but balanced Sancerre, lightly chilled, alongside.

2 large bunches kale (about 12 ounces total), stalks removed (about 12 cups leaves)
6 ounces slab bacon, rind removed, cut into 1½ inch x ¼-inch strips
¼ to ½ cup beet pickling juice from Aili's Pickled Beets (see page 331)
3 cloves garlic, peeled and minced
Salt and freshly ground black pepper
1 cup Aili's Pickled Beets, cut into ¼-inch cubes
6 paper-thin slices white onion
3 hard-cooked eggs, thinly sliced

1 Rinse the kale leaves several times, and dry them thoroughly. Tear them into bite-size pieces.

2 Sauté the bacon in a large heavy skillet over medium heat until it is golden and crisp, about 5 minutes. Slowly pour in ¼ cup of the beet pickling juice, and stir. (There will be a lot of steam, but don't be concerned; just stand back. If you have a fan above your stove, turn it on.) Depending on the heat of the skillet, the beet juice may evaporate quickly, so add more if necessary—you want about ¼ cup in the pan.

3 Add the garlic, stir, and then season with salt and pepper. Add the kale leaves and stir to coat them with the dressing. Cook, stirring constantly, just until they wilt and turn a darker shade of green, 3 to 5 minutes. You don't want them soft, just slightly calmed down.

4 Transfer the kale to a large warmed platter, or divide it among six warmed plates. Sprinkle the beets over the salad, garnish with the onion slices, and arrange the eggs around the edges. Serve immediately.

4 main-course or 6 salad servings

WARM LAMB AND POTATO SALAD

This is a salad that began as an entirely different, less exciting meal. The lamb and the potatoes were sitting on the cutting board when I spied the cherry tomatoes I'd found that morning at the farmer's market, and realized something special could be in store. With a drizzle of this, a sprinkling of that, and slivers of red onion for color and flavor, this happy salad evolved.

It must be served warm, so the flavors are mellow and the lamb still succulent and tender.

Try this with an Etude Pinot Noir 1988 or a Carneros Pinot Noir.

6 tablespoons olive oil

¼ cup balsamic vinegar

2 teaspoons Dijon mustard

1 large bunch Italian (flat-leaf) parsley

2 teaspoons dried herbes de Provence, or
¾ teaspoon dried thyme, ½ teaspoon dried
oregano, ½ teaspoon dried marjoram, and
¼ teaspoon dried summer savory

Salt and freshly ground black pepper

1½ pounds red-skinned new potatoes, such as
Red Bliss

½ large red onion, thinly sliced lengthwise

2 tablespoons freshly squeezed lemon juice

2 pounds shoulder lamb chops

24 cherry tomatoes, trimmed and halved
lengthwise

1 Whisk together the oil, vinegar, and
mustard in a large bowl. Mince the parsley, and add ¼ cup to the dressing. Add the
herbes de Provence, mix well, and season to
taste with salt and pepper.

2 Preheat the oven to 450°F.

3 Scrub the new potatoes and place them
in a saucepan. Cover them with at least
2 inches of water, add 1 tablespoon salt,
and bring to a boil over high heat. Cook
until the potatoes are tender, about 18 minutes. Drain, and cut in halves or quarters,
depending on the size of the potato (the
pieces should be slightly larger than bite-
size). Add the potatoes to the vinaigrette,
along with the sliced onions. Toss so they
are coated with the dressing and set aside.

4 Place the lamb chops in a baking dish
and drizzle them with the lemon juice.
Bake the chops in the center of the oven
until they are golden outside and still quite
pink in the middle, 15 to 18 minutes (or to
your taste). When they are cool enough to
handle, trim off all the fat. Cut the meat
into thin strips, and add it to the potatoes
and onions. Add the cherry tomatoes, toss
thoroughly, and sprinkle with the remaining
parsley. Serve immediately.

4 servings

LENTIL SALAD WITH SMOKED TURKEY

This recipe is another treasure from Li Ochs of Eureka Farm in eastern Washington (her Hummus is on page 49). It's a big, hearty
salad, full of fresh herbs. And with its yogurt-based dressing it man-

ages to be light and sprightly, too.

If you can't get smoked turkey, this is delicious with just about any meat—try ham, roast beef, or pork, or even leftover roast lamb.

Lentils are imported into this country from a variety of places including Canada and Spain, and the imports take as much as twice as long to cook as those grown in the Palouse region, where the Ochs farm and where virtually all the lentils in this country are grown. You may not be able to tell where your lentils came from, so be sure to check them periodically while they're cooking; they should still be slightly crisp. The cooking time indicated in this recipe is for Palouse-grown lentils.

Serve this with a chilled Beaujolais Nouveau or a young fruity red such as an Italian Barbera.

1 cup lentils, rinsed and picked over
2 cups Herbfarm Deluxe Chicken Stock (light version; page 86), good-quality canned broth, or water
¼ cup fresh tarragon leaves, or 1 teaspoon dried
About 11 ounces smoked turkey breast, cut into
   ½-inch cubes (2 cups)
¼ cup minced red onion
½ cup minced celery
2 tablespoons minced fresh parsley
¼ cup good-quality mayonnaise
¼ cup plain yogurt
2 teaspoons Dijon mustard
1 tablespoon freshly squeezed lemon juice
1 clove garlic, peeled and minced
Salt and freshly ground black pepper to taste

1 Place the lentils and the chicken stock in a medium saucepan over medium-high heat, and bring to a boil. Reduce the heat and cook at a slow boil until the lentils are softened but still firm to the bite, 15 to 20 minutes. Drain the lentils, transfer to a large bowl, and cool to room temperature.

2 Mince the tarragon leaves and add them, with the turkey breast, red onion, celery, and parsley, to the cooked lentils. Mix gently.

3 Whisk the remaining ingredients together in a small bowl, and add to the lentil mixture. Mix gently but thoroughly. If desired, chill before serving.

6 servings

A SWEET HARVEST

Celery is native to the wetlands of Europe and northeastern Africa, as well as from western Asia to the Himalayas. It was first cultivated in France in the 1600s. A member of the same family as the carrot, celery's flavor ranges from mellow to pungent and almost bitter.

Look for celery that is evenly green with a pale yellow core. The leaves should be vibrant, the stalks crisp and unmarked. Avoid limp stalks with dried leaf ends, dark core ends, or blemishes.

Store celery in the produce drawer of the refrigerator, wrapped in a paper towel and placed in a loosely closed plastic bag.

"OLD FARMER" MICHAELS

Mike Michaels, who is now in his seventies, refers to himself, with glee, as "Old Farmer" Michaels. He always wanted to be a farmer, but he didn't get around to it until after he'd retired from a successful career as a publisher and writer.

Mike's been farming at his Ladybug Farms in Spring Grove, Illinois, for about ten years. Perhaps because he's an innate—and as he puts it, lucky—businessman, he has garnered an impressive clientele who regard him as both an excellent farmer and a maverick.

He uses no synthetic fertilizers or chemicals of any kind, and he labels his produce "organic." The name of the farm is a clue to his farming practices.

"I anointed the fields with about 75,000 ladybugs this year," he said. "Only about ten percent stay, but they do a good job taking care of the aphids." What they don't get is picked up by the crew, one of whose jobs is to hand-pick any insects off the crops.

Each year in January Mike visits the chefs and markets he supplies in Chicago to find out what they'd like him to grow, and that is what he plants. He doesn't presell his crops, but he knows he has a good, consistent market for his prewashed salad greens, hand-polished tomatoes, and peppers and herbs.

When we arrived at Ladybug Farms it was 6:30 A.M., just before the workday was to begin. We drove right by the Michaels' house at first. Built into the ground on the north side for insulation, it is open to the sun on the south, and has an interior courtyard to admit light and sun into the rooms. Set several feet below the roadway, its expansive shake roof sort of melts into the landscape.

Mike took us on a tour of the farm, with a special stop at his 10-acre plot of more than fifty varieties of tomatoes. The real specialty at Ladybug Farms, they sport names like Angora, Grapefruit (yellow outside and rich pink inside), Gray-Husked tomatoes, or Ground Cherries, New Zealand plum tomatoes, and White Beauties (these have pure white skin).

When they are harvested, Mike will sell the tomatoes to markets and well-known Chicago restaurants for a premium price. "I know it's a lot, but my customers know they'll get the best."

Geneva's Wilted Lettuce Salad

Geneva Michaels says this salad is one of her favorites. It's a variation on the wilted-salad theme, but what makes it different and delicious is the choice of greens, which should be full of character. The hot dressing will tenderize them a bit and bring out their full range of flavors.

The key to this salad, as to any other, is using the freshest greens you can buy. Wash them tenderly but thoroughly to remove any grit. Try to include broccoli rabe as part of the greens—the tender buds are delicious with this dressing.

If you can't get slab bacon, use a slightly smaller quantity of good-quality packaged bacon.

8 cups mixed greens, such as escarole, curly endive, broccoli rabe, and curly kale, rinsed, dried, and torn into bite-size pieces

2 scallions (green onions), trimmed and cut into thin rounds

4 ounces slab bacon, rind removed, cut in 1 x ¼-inch pieces

1 large clove garlic, peeled and minced

2 tablespoons good-quality red wine vinegar

2 tablespoons water

1 teaspoon (lightly packed) light brown sugar

Salt and freshly ground pepper

1 Place the greens and the scallions in a large heatproof salad bowl. Toss well, and set aside.

2 Fry the bacon in a medium-size skillet over medium-high heat until crisp, 5 minutes. Stir in the garlic, then deglaze the pan with the vinegar and water, stirring constantly. There will be a lot of smoke, but don't be concerned. Add the brown sugar, stir, and season to taste with salt and pepper.

3 Pour the dressing over the salad greens, and toss until they are thoroughly coated. Serve immediately.

4 servings

WILD MUSHROOM SALAD ON A BED OF STEAMED LETTUCE

This recipe is meant to be used with the first lettuce and morels of spring. Its soft, tender flavors and textures are evocative of warm spring days still tinged at night with the chill of winter.

It works well in all seasons, however. Curly lettuce is available nearly year-round, and you can use dried morels or fresh button mushrooms if fresh morels aren't available. Button mushrooms won't give this salad the delicate woodsy flavor that morels do, but they are a delicious substitute.

6 ounces small morels or button mushrooms,
    or 2 ounces dried morels
4 tablespoons plus 2 teaspoons olive oil
2 teaspoons good-quality red wine vinegar
1 small shallot, peeled and finely chopped
3 sprigs fresh parsley, finely chopped
Salt and freshly ground black pepper
20 large curly leaf lettuce leaves, rinsed
    and dried

1 Carefully wash the morels under running water until all the sand is removed. (If you are using dried morels, soak them in water to cover for 1 hour, then rinse under running water.) Drain on paper towels. (If you are using button mushrooms, simply trim the stems and brush off any dirt from the caps with a damp paper towel.)

2 Pour 2 tablespoons of the olive oil into a medium-size bowl and whisk in the vinegar, adding it in a thin drizzle, until it blends. Then add the shallot, parsley, and salt and pepper. Set aside.

3 Heat 2 teaspoons of the olive oil in a medium-size skillet over medium-high heat. Add the morels and cook, stirring constantly, until they are coated with olive oil and hot through, 3 to 5 minutes. Remove the morels from the skillet, add them to the salad dressing, toss, and set aside. (If you are using button mushrooms, cut them in chunks and sauté in the olive oil until they begin to soften and give up their liquid, about 5 minutes. Add to the salad dressing.)

4 Place the remaining 2 tablespoons olive oil in a medium-size bowl, and season

with salt and pepper to taste. Place the lettuce leaves in a vegetable steamer over briskly boiling water, and cook until they are limp but still bright green, 1 to 2 minutes. Watch so they don't overcook. Transfer the lettuce leaves, shaking any liquid from them, to the olive oil in the bowl, and toss gently. The lettuce may give up some liquid in the bowl, which is fine.

5 To serve, remove the lettuce leaves from the bowl and arrange them on four plates. Divide the mushrooms among the plates, placing them on the lettuce. Serve immediately.

4 servings

RED AND ORANGE SALAD

W hen my grandmother was growing up in Michigan and Oregon, oranges—which appeared around Christmastime—were an unparalleled treat, and her mother sometimes served a salad of thinly sliced oranges and onions. My grandmother, in turn, often served it to us. This is an updated version, with its bed of dark green watercress, but my grandmother would have loved it.

This old-fashioned salad actually makes a very elegant first course, presented on individual chilled plates. It whets the appetite and cleanses the palate at the same time, leaving a feeling of anticipation for what follows. Serve it as a prelude to Pipestone Lamb Stew, Mom's Oxtail Ragout, or Roast Ginger Chicken with Potatoes and Onions (see Index).

3 bunches watercress, trimmed (6 to 7 cups)
3 large navel oranges
½ large red onion, sliced paper-thin
1 tablespoon freshly squeezed orange juice
1 teaspoon freshly squeezed lemon juice
3 tablespoons extra-virgin olive oil
Salt and freshly ground black pepper
1 tablespoon minced parsley

1 Rinse and dry the watercress. Working over a bowl so you catch the juice, cut

the peel from the oranges, making sure you remove all the white pith as well. Slice the oranges crosswise into ¼-inch-thick rounds. Remove all the seeds.

2 Arrange the watercress on four salad plates, and arrange alternating slices of orange and onion on top. Cover loosely, and refrigerate for at least 1 hour.

3 To make the dressing, whisk together the orange juice, lemon juice, and olive oil in a small bowl. Season to taste with salt and pepper.

4 Just before serving, drizzle the dressing over the oranges and onions, and garnish with the parsley. Serve immediately.

4 servings

COUNTRY POTATO SALAD

P otato salad can be a controversial dish. There are those who like it moist and creamy, those who prefer it dry, those who like it dressed in oil and vinegar, and those who prefer egg-rich mayonnaise. Some like it sweet; some like it sour with pickles and green olives.

I tasted every kind while visiting farms around the country, and this one is a hybrid of my favorites. It belongs to the mayonnaise-dressed tart family, and it is bound to satisfy members of that camp. I am normally partial to oil-and-vinegar-based potato salads, yet I love this one.

The real trick to a good potato salad is marinating the potatoes in an olive oil and vinegar mixture right after they are cooked. It seasons the potatoes nicely, keeps them moist, and adds a lovely underlying flavor to the salad.

This salad gets better after it has had a chance to mellow a bit, so try to make it in the morning if you're going to serve it that evening.

1 tablespoon coarse (kosher) salt
2 pounds Yellow Finn potatoes or new potatoes
¼ cup extra-virgin olive oil
1½ tablespoons white wine vinegar
½ teaspoon salt
¼ teaspoon finely ground fresh black pepper
1 cup diced celery
½ cup diced red onion
¾ cup diced dill pickles
¼ cup diced black olives
1 cup good-quality mayonnaise
¼ teaspoon cayenne pepper
3 hard-cooked eggs
Fresh watercress or parsley sprigs, for garnish

1 Bring a large kettle of water to a boil over high heat. Add the coarse salt and the potatoes, and cook until the potatoes are nearly tender but still firm in the center, about 15 minutes.

2 Whisk the olive oil, vinegar, salt, and pepper together in a large bowl.

3 Drain the potatoes, and when they are cool enough to handle, cut them into 1-inch cubes. Place them in the bowl with the vinaigrette, toss until they are coated with the mixture, and then let them cool.

4 When the potatoes are cool, add the diced vegetables, pickles, and olives, and toss until they are thoroughly incorporated.

5 Mix the mayonnaise with the cayenne pepper in a small bowl, and add it to the potato mixture. Toss until all the vegetables are coated with the mayonnaise.

6 Cut the hard-cooked eggs into ½-inch cubes, add them to the salad, and toss gently. Chill for 1 to 2 hours before serving.

About 12 servings

PURSLANE, POTATO, AND TOMATO SALAD

Purslane, also known as rabbit grass, is considered a weed on most farms in this country. Once established, it can cover a field overnight, it seems. It is easy to pull up, and most farmers consider it a nuisance rather than a threat. What most of them don't know is that purslane makes a crisp, juicy, flavorful salad green. I like it so much that I actually planted a domesticated version in our garden—which meant we always had an abundant supply. In fact it was impossible to control. But I love it, and I make salads with it throughout summer.

½ cup extra-virgin olive oil
3 tablespoons balsamic vinegar
1 small clove garlic, peeled and minced
Salt and freshly ground black pepper
8 small new potatoes, scrubbed
6 cups purslane, rinsed, patted dry, and torn
  into bite-size pieces, or 6 cups steamed green
  beans (about 1 pound), cut into 2-inch
  lengths
4 ripe plum tomatoes, quartered

1 Make the vinaigrette: Whisk the olive oil, vinegar, and garlic together in a large bowl. Season to taste with salt and pepper, and set aside.

2 Place the potatoes in a vegetable steamer over boiling water, cover, and steam until the potatoes are tender, about 20 minutes. Remove the potatoes from the steamer basket, and when they are cool enough to handle, cut them in half. Add them to the vinaigrette, toss, and set aside. (This can be done the night before you plan to serve the salad.)

3 Add the purslane and the tomatoes to the potatoes, and toss so all of the ingredients are coated with the dressing. Season to taste, and serve at room temperature.

4 servings

ASIAN SALAD WITH SEA VEGETABLES

A fter I went "harvesting" sea vegetables with Larch Hanson (see page 298) in northern Maine, I was inspired to try a variety of dishes that incorporate these strange, nutritious plants. I enjoyed their flavors and textures and found that *kizami nori*, or sheets of nori cut into thin shiny strips, was one of my favorite garnishes. It adds a subtle, clean sea flavor to salads, and its deep green translucence makes a gorgeous addition to the vegetables.

¼ cup rice vinegar

2 tablespoons sesame oil, preferably Japanese

1 tablespoon soy sauce, or to taste

1 clove garlic, peeled and diced

2 small carrots, peeled and cut diagonally into
¼-inch-thick slices

8 ounces slim green beans (about 3 cups),
trimmed and cut diagonally into ¾-inch
lengths

3 small Kirby (pickling) cucumbers, peeled and
cut into ¼-inch dice

½ large fennel bulb, trimmed and cut into
¼-inch dice

1 cup kizami nori (available at natural foods
stores, usually in the macrobiotic section)

1 Whisk the vinegar and sesame oil together in a medium-size bowl. Add the
soy sauce, adjusting the amount to your
taste; then add the garlic and mix well. Set
aside.

2 Bring a large pot of salted water to a
boil over high heat. Have a large bowl of
ice water ready.

3 Blanch the carrots in the boiling water
just until they begin to turn tender,
about 3 minutes. Using a slotted spoon or
strainer, remove them from the boiling
water and place them in the ice water to
cool. When they are cool, remove them
from the water and place them on a dish
towel or paper towels to drain. Repeat this
process with the green beans, blanching
them for 2 to 3 minutes.

4 When the carrots and the beans are
cool, quickly stir the dressing again, and
add all of the vegetables except the nori.
Toss until they are thoroughly coated with
the dressing, cover, and refrigerate until the
salad is chilled, no longer than 1 hour.

5 Just before serving, toss the vegetables
again and add the nori, continuing to
toss until it is incorporated. Taste for seasoning, and serve immediately.

4 servings

GRILLED TOMATOES WITH PARSLEY SAUCE

W hen tomatoes come into season they make the world a better place
to live. Grilled tomatoes are an appetite-stimulating starter or a
good side dish for grilled seafood, poultry, or meat. Make sure that
you serve plenty of good bread alongside for sopping up the sauce.

2 cups (packed) fresh Italian (flat-leaf) parsley
   leaves
½ cup plus 1 tablespoon olive oil
3 cloves garlic, peeled
Salt
1 fresh serrano or jalapeño pepper, trimmed
½ cup freshly grated Parmesan cheese
Freshly ground black pepper
4 large ripe tomatoes, halved crosswise

1 Prepare a small charcoal fire in a barbecue, or preheat the broiler.

2 Place the parsley, ½ cup olive oil, garlic, ¼ teaspoon salt, and the pepper in a food processor. Process until the ingredients form a fine purée. Transfer the mixture to a medium-size bowl and stir in the Parmesan cheese by hand. Season with salt and pepper to taste and set aside.

3 When the coals are glowing red and dusted with ash, spread them out in an even layer. Lightly oil a grill and place it about 3 inches from the coals. Brush the tomatoes generously all over with the remaining tablespoon of olive oil (but don't use so much that it will drip onto the coals). Grill the tomatoes, cut side down, just until the cut side is golden, 1 to 2 minutes. Turn them carefully, and grill until they are nicely golden all over and the tops are bubbling, about 10 minutes.

If you are broiling the tomatoes, line the broiler pan with aluminum foil, and place the tomatoes on it, cut side down. Set the pan about 3 inches from the heat and broil until the skins are golden, 10 minutes. Turn the tomatoes and broil until the tops are nicely golden, 1 to 2 minutes.

4 Remove the tomatoes from the grill and arrange them cut side up on a large platter. Sprinkle with salt and pepper, and pour the parsley sauce over them. Serve immediately.

4 servings

MULTI-COLORED TOMATO SALAD

O nce you've eaten this salad, you may never want to serve fresh tomatoes any other way. The light vinaigrette, tiny shards of onion, and liberal sprinkling of Italian parsley bring out the tomatoes' sweetness. To make this a success, however, the tomatoes must *be* garden-fresh—or at least purchased from a farmers' market so you know they grew in fertile soil, were picked in recent history, didn't travel too far, and have good, rich flavor.

I recommend using slightly underripe tomatoes in this salad. They have a sharper tang than when they're fully ripe, and a bit more texture. If you can't find a color variety, then use only red tomatoes, but do try to vary the sizes, because they have such pleasing and complementary flavors and textures.

Fresh tomatoes give up so much juice that little dressing is needed, and oil and vinegar are used as a subtle seasoning. If you find there isn't enough liquid, increase the oil by about 1 tablespoon and the vinegar by the same, or simply adjust it to your taste.

Serve this at room temperature soon after you've made it, rather than letting the tomatoes sit.

2 tablespoons extra-virgin olive oil

1 tablespoon best-quality red wine vinegar

1 small onion, peeled and diced

Salt and freshly ground black pepper

1 cup loosely packed Italian (flat-leaf) parsley leaves

5 medium-size red tomatoes, cored and cut in eighths

12 ounces (about 3 cups) yellow or orange cherry tomatoes, stemmed and halved lengthwise

1 In a large bowl, whisk together the olive oil and vinegar. Add the onion, stir, and then season to taste with salt and pepper.

2 Mince the parsley, add it to the vinaigrette, and mix well.

3 Add the tomatoes, and toss until they are thoroughly coated with the dressing. Adjust the seasoning, and serve.

4 to 6 servings

PARSLEY

*C*urly *parsley and Italian parsley both have an assertive, some say strong, healthy green flavor. Italian parsley has a more aromatic dimension and is best for cooking, while curly leaf is best for garnish. However, the difference is subtle. Both lend themselves to meat dishes, stews, soups, fresh tomatoes, omelets, and potato dishes. Use parsley judiciously in salads, and finely minced atop fresh steamed or sautéed vegetables. Parsley does not need much sun, nor top-quality soil, to grow. Dried parsley is not worth bothering with.*

MARINATED SUMMER SALAD

S ummer root vegetables may sound like an oxymoron, but there is a cornucopia of young, tender roots that find their way to market before the heat of the season has really flowered. Turnips and kohlrabi are my favorites, because they're crisp, juicy, and full of hot flavor. I snap them up whenever I see them so that I can make this salad, which I like to serve chilled with a summery picnic meal. It's a little bit different because it takes advantage of unconventional vegetables, using them in an unusual way. Be sure to follow the cutting instructions—the varied shapes are visually exciting, and they add texture too.

2 tablespoons olive oil
2 teaspoons balsamic vinegar
1 teaspoon Dijon mustard
1 large clove garlic, peeled and minced
Salt and freshly ground black pepper
2 tablespoons minced fresh dill
2 small kohlrabi, trimmed and peeled
2 medium yellow patty-pan squash
6 small (radish-size) turnips, trimmed
   and peeled (see Note)

1 In a medium-size bowl, whisk together the olive oil, vinegar, mustard, and garlic. Season to taste with salt and pepper, and whisk in the dill.

2 Cut the kohlrabi and the squash into ⅛-inch-thick slices; then cut the slices into matchsticks about ⅛ inch thick. Thinly slice the turnips crosswise.

3 Add the vegetables to the vinaigrette, and toss until they are thoroughly coated. Cover, and refrigerate until the salad is chilled, at least 30 minutes but not longer than 2 hours before serving.

4 to 6 servings

Note: If you can't find these miniature turnips, buy the smallest you can find, cut them in half, then cut the halves into thin slices.

A SLIPPERY HARVEST

It's still inky black at 5 A.M. when Larch Hanson emerges from his home in the coastal woods of Maine, strides across a dirt road and out onto a rocky beach. Long and lean, he wears a black wetsuit and cap.

At the beach he splashes into the water and vaults into one of two snub-nosed garveys anchored there. He brings the outboard motor to life with a roar, then heads away from shore. His day as a harvester of sea vegetables has begun.

When Hanson returns, his boat will be filled to the gunwales with kelp or with bushel baskets of alaria, nori, or dulse. He will hardly be able to get them dried and packaged before a thriving mail-order business claims nearly everything he has harvested.

Though Hanson harvests a product growing wild, he considers himself a farmer managing a resource. "I've learned how much to take, and when to take it," he says. "I cultivate the resource and don't over-harvest any of it."

Whole dried sea vegetables, which are used primarily in Japanese and macrobiotic cooking, lend subtle, intriguing flavors to foods, have unusual and often appealing textures, and come in a range of translucent colors. Commonly eaten in Asia and in many European countries, sea vegetables are relatively obscure fare in this country, though anyone who has eaten sushi has set his or her teeth into a species of seaweed. The thin, dark wrapping around sushi rolls is made of nori, one of the most commonly eaten sea vegetables.

DULSE AND KELP

Hanson heads his boat towards an outcropping of golden rock called Sheep Island, which he has climbed and slithered over since he began harvesting sea vegetables 15 years ago. He walks gingerly over the rocks, which host a slippery, richly hued

tapestry of sea plants ranging from bright green sea lettuce, to coal-gray nori, to deep burgundy dulse. Most of the plants are edible, but today Hanson concentrates on dulse.

To harvest dulse, which grows in shady crevices and looks like thick, wavy hair, he spreads his fingers wide, runs them up into the dulse, grabs on, and pulls down and away from the rock, his fists full. "You have to harvest it like this to avoid getting your hands torn up by the rocks," he says. He harvests selectively, leaving plenty growing.

Hanson works intensely and quickly fills three bushel baskets, then hops into the boat and rows over to a spot where a thick stand of kelp waves about under the surface of the water. Using a stubby curved knife, he grabs a long, translucent brown frond. "The kelp is usually best from March through May, though this looks pretty good," he says as he whacks it off on this mid-August morning.

PREPARING SEA VEGETABLES

Hanson heads back toward shore where he spreads white nylon mesh over a huge outcropping of rock, which is blistering hot from the sun. He spreads the dulse on the mesh to dry for the rest of the day. Later he packs it in burlap bags and lugs it home.

Kelp is dried in a different manner. "We call this hanging up the laundry," Hanson says as he drapes a frond of kelp, which can grow to more than 10 feet, over a line strung between posts. "The kelp wind-dries in an af-

ternoon; then we bring it in." Once dry, the sea vegetables will keep for months, even years.

Hanson generally harvests about a ton of vegetables a day, which dries down to about 200 pounds. His harvest season (which he refers to as "haying") begins in very early spring, when the water is still cold and the plants are achieving most of their growth, and continues with less frequency through summer and into fall.

What Hanson doesn't sell through mail-order will go to Maine Coast Sea Vegetables, a company that markets nationwide and into Canada. The company began in the early 1970s when owner Shepard Erhardt began harvesting sea vegetables for his own use. Interest spread, the company grew, and it now markets about 13 tons of dried sea vegetables each year.

"The demand grew as the natural and macrobiotic movements grew," says Carl Karusch, business manager. "And it just hasn't stopped growing."

If you'd like to order sea vegetables from Larch, contact him at the Maine Seaweed Company, P.O. Box 57, Steuben, Maine 04680.

CAFÉ SPORT'S WILD GREENS WITH GOAT CHEESE AND WALNUTS

T his salad takes the fresh and sprightly flavors of the garden and brings them right to the table. If you live in a mild climate, or if salad greens and tiny blossoms are available year-round in your area, make this salad in winter (when goat cheese is best) and it will chase away the cold-weather blues. But don't reserve it for that season. Indulge yourself whenever you have a main-course salad in mind, because this not only satisfies but also creates a lovely picture on the plate.

It is an adaptation of a salad served at Seattle's Café Sport restaurant, which is right downtown at the Pike Place Market. There the salad greens come, year-round, from several small farms just outside the city. Looking out at the waters of Elliott Bay and tasting this garden-on-a-plate is an incomparable pleasure.

The salad is enough for four very generous servings—ideal for a luncheon or a summer supper if served with plenty of fresh bread. Or you can reduce the portions and serve it as a first course. (If you are using flower blossoms, be sure you know their source so there isn't any danger they've been sprayed with noxious substances.) For a wine, try a chilled Sancerre.

8 ounces soft goat cheese
½ cup walnuts or pecans, coarsely chopped
¼ cup gently packed fresh herbs, such as basil, tarragon, or herbes de Provence
2 tablespoons good-quality red wine vinegar
⅛ teaspoon Dijon mustard
5 tablespoons extra-virgin olive oil
1 tablespoon minced shallot
Grated zest of ½ large orange
Salt and freshly ground black pepper
12 cups seasonal salad greens, rinsed, dried, and torn into bite-size pieces
Handful of fresh tiny flower blossoms, such as pea, bean, or pansy (optional)

1 Preheat the oven to 400°F.

2 Roll the goat cheese in the chopped nuts until it is thoroughly coated. Place

the cheese in a pie plate or a small baking dish, and bake in the center of the oven until it is soft and the nuts are beginning to turn golden, no longer than 5 minutes.

3 While the cheese is baking, mince the herbs. Combine the vinegar and mustard in a large bowl, and whisk in the oil until the mixture is emulsified. Whisk in the shallot, orange zest, and the herbs, and season to taste with salt and pepper.

4 Add the greens to the bowl, and mix gently but thoroughly until they are well coated with dressing. Divide the greens evenly among four (or six) plates, mounding them in the center of each plate.

5 Slice the goat cheese into four (or six) pieces, and place a piece on top of each salad. Scatter the flowers over the salads, and serve immediately.

4 main-course servings;
6 first-course servings

SALAD OF WINTER GREENS

T his salad will fight off winter's chill like nothing else. It is made with the season's lively greens, each of which has its own cheering and distinct character and which are really not as good at other times of the year. They are generally not as crisp and sweet, with a meaty texture that is particularly satisfying when good fresh vegetables are rare.

2 tablespoons balsamic vinegar
1 clove garlic, peeled and minced
Salt and freshly ground black pepper
⅓ cup olive oil
4 ounces fennel, trimmed and diced
7 cups loosely packed mixed winter greens, such as curly endive (frisée), escarole, and broccoli rabe
2 cups radicchio leaves

1 Combine the vinegar, garlic, and salt and pepper to taste in a large serving bowl, and whisk together. Whisk in the olive oil in a thin, steady stream so the dressing thickens and emulsifies. Add the fennel, toss so it is coated with the dressing, and set aside for at least 15 minutes or up to 1 hour.

2 Meanwhile, carefully rinse and pat (or spin) dry the winter greens and the radicchio. Tear them into bite-size pieces. Add the greens to the bowl and toss, making sure all the leaves are coated with the dressing. Serve immediately.

6 to 8 servings

WARREN WEBER'S FAVORITE SALAD

Warren Weber's favorite salad, which he delivered with a smile, demands *fresh* greens (see box, facing page). Otherwise it's open to interpretation—except that slightly bitter greens are necessary, as a foil for the other ingredients. Delicate greens won't hold up as well.

2 Belgian endives, rinsed
3 cups small frisée (curly endive) leaves or
 green leaf lettuce, rinsed well and dried
2 cups radicchio leaves, rinsed well and dried
1 cup escarole leaves, rinsed well and dried
6 tablespoons extra-virgin olive oil
2 tablespoons fruit vinegar, such as blueberry
 or raspberry
Salt and freshly ground black pepper
½ cup walnuts, coarsely chopped
2 tablespoons diced sun-dried tomatoes

1 Trim the Belgian endives by pulling off any outer leaves that are less than perfectly fresh and trimming off the stem end. Separate the leaves, leaving them whole. Tear the remaining greens into bite-size pieces.

2 Place the olive oil in a large serving bowl. Whisk in the vinegar, and salt and pepper to taste. Add the walnuts and sun-dried tomatoes, tossing them quickly. Then add the greens, and toss until they are coated with the dressing. Serve immediately.

4 to 5 servings

STAR ROUTE GREENS

Warren Weber's Star Route Farms is in Bolinas, California, about an hour north of San Francisco on a hook of land that juts out into the ocean. The fields are washed by a close, damp fog most mornings of the year, which has a lot to do with the lush quality of his salad greens, sold to some of the best restaurants in the country.

The farm's fields are just across a field and through a thicket from his lovely old, recently restored, farmhouse, that lies in a sort of hollow at the base of gently sloping hills. They are protected from any harsh weather, which, along with the gentle fog, allows him to maintain a year-round crop.

Warren has been growing greens organically for some 17 years, patiently building up the soil from near-infertility to a rich, almost black loam. It's a stunning background for the multi-hued greens, which look like little fluffed jewels in their straight, tidy rows.

Off along the edge of a field one of the farm's crew was using a blowtorch to burn off a stand of weedy-looking plants that are planted as a host for pests. "It's our form of pest and weed control," Warren said. "Really, though, the best insecticide is a healthy plant." In addition to constantly building up the soil on his farm, he feeds the plants nutrients through their leaves, by spraying them with kelp and bloodmeal solutions. This technique is called foliar feeding.

The crew at Star Route Farms picks salads selectively, cutting them at the root, washing them, and packing them artfully in boxes to deliver to restaurants, ready for the salad bowl. Small leaves are trimmed from other growing plants and added to the salad mixture.

Warren is always experimenting with greens and herbs, and when I was there the fields were full of red and green oak-leaf lettuce, frisée, romaine, mâche, and a whole variety of herbs and flowers. He's forever on the lookout for new greens to grow, and he rolled his eyes when I asked how many he'd tried. "There are too many to mention," he said. "I don't even think I could remember them all."

SUNBURST LENTIL SALAD

T his salad surprises nearly everyone I serve it to because no one can believe that lentils come so tiny and in such a flaming orange color, and have such a delicate yet satisfying flavor. It further surprises because it is absolutely gorgeous to look at, and while it makes a full meal on its own, it is light to the palate and on the stomach.

I do like it by itself for lunch or a light supper, but it also makes a fine accompaniment to grilled meats—lamb, chicken, or pork—or for meaty fish, such as swordfish or tuna. If you serve it alone, arrange it on a bed of salad greens, such as escarole or mixed romaine and arugula, and make those part of the meal as well—or serve a green salad alongside.

Red lentils, which are bright orange when raw and turn golden when cooked, are available at most stores that sell grains in bulk. Follow the cooking directions strictly, as they will quickly overcook and turn to mush.

Serve this salad immediately after it is made. If you have leftovers, heat them up gently in the oven or in the microwave. Serve a full-bodied tropical California Sauvignon Blanc or Ferrari-Carano 1988 alongside.

2 cups red (small orange) lentils, rinsed and picked over
6 cups cold water
2 tablespoons freshly squeezed lemon juice
2 tablespoons freshly squeezed lime juice
¼ cup freshly squeezed orange juice
½ teaspoon cayenne pepper, or to taste
1 pound slab bacon, rind removed
½ cup diced onion
¼ cup diced red bell pepper
¼ cup diced green bell pepper
½ fresh jalapeño pepper, with seeds, minced
1 large clove garlic, peeled and minced
1 heaping tablespoon finely minced ginger
Salt (optional)
¼ cup minced fresh parsley
8 thin lime slices, halved

1 Place the lentils and the water in a medium-size saucepan over medium heat. **Bring** to a simmer (the water will have white foam on top of it), and simmer until the lentils are just barely tender and have lost their raw taste. This should take no more than 5 minutes after the water has begun to simmer. Test the lentils frequently to be sure they do not overcook. Drain the lentils, and transfer them to a heatproof bowl.

2 Whisk together the citrus juices and the cayenne pepper in a small bowl, and set aside.

3 Slice the bacon into ¼-inch-thick strips, and then cut the strips into ½-inch-long pieces. Place the bacon in a skillet or saucepan over medium-high heat, and cook until golden, stirring frequently, 7 to 8 minutes. Using a slotted spoon, transfer the bacon to the bowl with the lentils. Reduce the heat under the pan to medium, and add the onion, bell peppers, jalapeño pepper, garlic, and ginger to the bacon fat. Cook, stirring frequently, until the onion is transparent and the other vegetables have softened, about 15 minutes. Transfer the vegetables, with the bacon fat, to the bowl and toss gently with the lentils and bacon.

4 Quickly whisk the citrus juices again to make sure they are blended, and add the mixture to the lentil salad, tossing gently until it is incorporated into the salad. Taste for seasoning. Garnish with the minced parsley and the lime slices, and serve immediately.

4 servings

EUREKA FARM SALAD

T his salad is the house specialty at Eureka Farm, where Jon and Li Ochs and their five children raise organic lentils, garbanzo beans, and wheat. From his travels to India Jon brought back a number of different types of garbanzo beans, and they have experimented with growing one in particular, called *desi*, which comes in three colors—green, black, and brown. Desis have a much nuttier flavor than the familiar large garbanzos, and a crisper texture, and they give this salad a lively appearance and flavor.

Desis are usually available at Middle Eastern markets. If you can't find them, substitute all lentils. The salad will be very similar, and equally delicious and healthy.

Try this with an earthy red wine, such as Saintsbury Pinot Noir Carneros 1988 or a Côtes du Rhône.

FOR THE SALAD

½ cup brown garbanzo beans
½ cup green garbanzo beans
½ cup white basmati rice
1 cup water
¼ teaspoon salt
½ cup lentils
3 medium tomatoes, diced
¼ cup minced Italian (flat-leaf) parsley
4 scallions (green onions), trimmed and cut
   into thin rounds

FOR THE DRESSING

2 cloves garlic, peeled and minced
¼ cup freshly squeezed lemon juice
⅓ cup olive oil
3 tablespoons capers, drained
8 anchovy fillets

1 Cook the brown and green garbanzo beans separately: Place the beans in a small saucepan, cover with 1½ inches of water, and bring to a boil. Boil for 2 minutes. Then remove the pan from the heat, cover, and let it sit for 1 hour. Drain, and test. They may be cooked enough, although they will likely need additional cooking. To cook further, cover again with 1½ inches of water, bring to a boil, and cook, partially covered, until the beans are tender but still have texture, about 10 minutes. Drain and let cool.

2 Place the rice, water, and salt in a small saucepan. Bring to a boil and cook, uncovered, until most of the water has been absorbed and there are bubble holes in the rice, about 10 minutes. Cover the pan, reduce the heat to low, and cook for an additional 10 minutes. Remove the pan from the heat and let the rice rest, still covered, for 10 minutes. Uncover the rice and let it cool slightly; then transfer it to a large bowl.

3 Place the lentils in a small saucepan and cover with 1½ inches of water. Bring to a boil and cook, partially covered, until the lentils are tender but still have plenty of texture, 9 or 10 minutes. Drain if necessary, let cool slightly, and then transfer to the bowl containing the rice. Toss to combine the rice and the lentils. Add the garbanzos and toss again. Let cool completely. Then add the tomatoes, parsley, and scallions, and toss until thoroughly combined.

4 Prepare the dressing: Combine the garlic, lemon juice, olive oil, 2 tablespoons of the capers, and the anchovies in a food processor and purée. Add the dressing to the salad along with the remaining capers, and toss well, so all the ingredients are moistened with the dressing. Cover, and let sit at room temperature for at least 2 hours before serving.

8 to 10 servings

SOLVIVA GREEN SALAD AND DRESSING

Anna Edey, who is the owner of Solviva, a small farm outside Vineyard Haven on Martha's Vineyard, Massachusetts (see following page), devised this salad dressing—which is really more of a dip—to complement the salad greens she raises year round.

When I serve it as a dressing, I spread an even layer in the center of a large plate and mound the greens on top. More often, however, I serve it in a bowl as a dip for raw vegetables.

1½ cups cooked garbanzos (see page 167), or
1 can (15 ounces), rinsed and drained
1 small onion, peeled and coarsely chopped
2 medium carrots, peeled and coarsely chopped
1 tablespoon tahini (sesame paste; available at most health foods stores)
1 cup safflower oil
3 tablespoons good-quality red wine vinegar
1 tablespoon freshly squeezed lemon juice
Salt
Small pinch cayenne pepper to taste

FOR THE SALAD
6 cups sturdy winter greens, such as escarole or frisée, rinsed, dried, and torn into bite-size pieces
1 cup arugula leaves, torn into bite-size pieces
1 Belgian endive, trimmed and cut into thin rounds

1 Place the garbanzos, onion, and carrots in a food processor and purée. With the processor running, add the tahini and ½ cup of the oil, and process until smooth. Then add the remaining ½ cup oil, the vinegar, and the lemon juice, and process until the ingredients are thoroughly combined. Season to taste with additional lemon juice if desired, and with salt and cayenne pepper.

2 To serve, spread ¼ cup of the salad dressing in an even layer in the center of each of six large dinner plates. Place the greens and the arugula in a large bowl, and toss until combined. Divide them among the plates, placing them on top of the dressing. Scatter the endive over the greens, and serve.

6 servings salad; 3½ cups dressing or dip

Note: You will have plenty of this dressing leftover. It will keep, covered, in the refrigerator for 2 to 3 days and in the freezer for 1 to 2 months.

SOLVIVA ON MARTHA'S VINEYARD

Solviva, a small farm on Martha's Vineyard in Massachusetts whose name means "sun and life," is an inspiring model of efficiency and year-round abundant productivity. Anna Edey is the proprietor, and a less likely looking farmer would be hard to find. Soft spoken, refined, and elegant, she is a weaver by profession, a farmer by avocation.

Ten years ago Anna decided to live an energy efficient life. To that end she researched many different systems of construction and indoor gardening. The results are the home she built, which is entirely solar heated, and the A-frame greenhouse that sits at the entrance to her property.

In summer, Anna grows greens and other produce outside, on land that is fertilized primarily through the assistance of a herd of sheep, which also provides Anna with meat, and wool for weaving. In winter, the garden moves inside to the greenhouse, which is heated to a toasty warmth by the sun, the body heat from about 25 rabbits who live in a room at one end, and from a clutch of chickens who have a coop adjacent to the greenhouse. When temperatures outside are brittle and cold, lettuces, herbs, and vivid edible flowers in the greenhouse thrive.

The greenhouse allows Anna to supply herself, and restaurants on the Vineyard, and in Boston, with succulent, hand-washed salad greens and edible flowers twelve months a year.

SEASONAL GREENS WITH FRANK MORTON'S HONEY SALAD DRESSING

This dressing recipe comes from Frank Morton, who, along with his partner, Catherine Jacobs, farms salad greens at Entheos Gardens on Washington's Kitsap Peninsula. Though many refer to their greens as wild edibles, Frank says that if they dealt in truly wild edibles, they could harvest for only about two weeks a year. As it is, their season extends from March through October. They grow a cornucopia of extraordinary greens, such as vetch, dandelions, Russian red kale, and arugula, and ship them to restaurants in the Northwest and the Northeast.

They eat a fair amount of greens as well, and this is Frank's favorite dressing. It is mild, with a subtle, appealing sweetness, and it brings out the varied flavors of the greens.

2 tablespoons balsamic vinegar
1 large clove garlic, peeled and finely minced
½ teaspoon mild honey
1 teaspoon fresh rosemary, or scant ½ teaspoon dried, crushed or finely minced
Salt and freshly ground black pepper
6 tablespoons extra-virgin olive oil
12 cups greens, such as arugula or escarole, rinsed, dried, and torn into bite-size pieces

1 In a large bowl combine the vinegar, garlic, honey, rosemary, and salt and pepper to taste. Whisk together. Add the oil, and whisk until the ingredients are combined.

2 Add the greens and toss thoroughly, so all the leaves are coated with dressing. Serve immediately.

6 servings

FRESH GREENS WITH FRAN LOZANO'S ZEST BLUE CHEESE DRESSING

When I visited Maytag Dairy Farms in Newton, Iowa (see page 43), president Donn Campbell called my attention to this blue cheese dressing, one of several recipes printed in a small book put out by Maytag. "You've got to try this. A good friend of ours gave it to us, and it's one of our favorites," he said.

I like it too, because it makes the most of blue cheese flavor and is really zesty with lemon. Its use isn't limited to a salad dressing, either. This makes a good dip for fresh vegetables, crackers, or toast. Try it first with just one clove of garlic, then add the other if you really want a garlicky zing.

2 ounces blue cheese, crumbled (⅔ cup)
¼ cup mild vegetable oil, such as canola or safflower
1 teaspoon grated lemon zest
1 tablespoon freshly squeezed lemon juice
1 cup sour cream
½ teaspoon salt
1 to 2 cloves garlic, peeled and minced
4 quarts mixed hearty salad greens, such as escarole, romaine, and spinach

1 Place all the ingredients except the greens in a food processor. Process, using short pulses, until the ingredients are thoroughly mixed but there are still some lumps of blue cheese. Refrigerate for at least 1 hour to mellow the flavors before serving.

2 Remove the dressing from the refrigerator 30 minutes before you plan to serve the salad. Add the salad greens, and toss until the leaves are thoroughly coated with the dressing. Serve immediately.

8 to 12 servings

Note: This recipe makes 1½ cups dressing, which is enough to dress 6 generous servings or 8 light salad servings. If you are serving fewer people, simply adjust the greens accordingly, figuring between 1½ and 2 cups per person. The leftover dressing will keep, covered, for 3 to 4 days in the refrigerator.

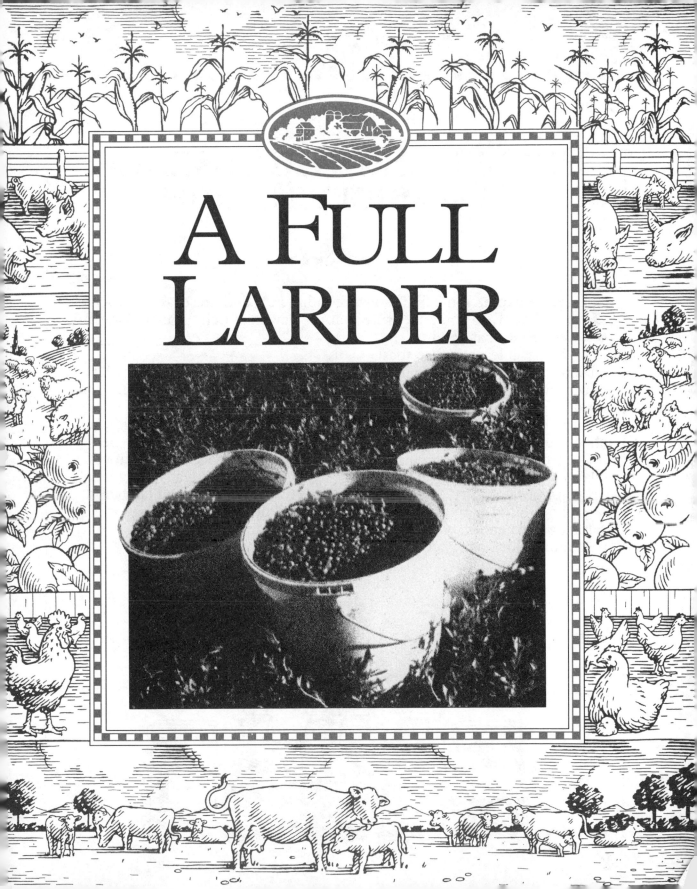

A FULL LARDER

PRESERVING THE ESSENCE:
A FARMHOUSE LARDER

In this chapter you'll find sauces, condiments, and preserves to stock your larder, so you can ensure that the flavors of rich farm cooking are always close at hand.

You will learn how to toast hazelnuts so they're golden and sweet, how to trap the essence of tomatoes in a sweet spicy ketchup, the secret of a dusky red ancho chile sauce, and how easy it is to make a pungent sauce from simple cilantro, to drape on anything from bread to potatoes.

You'll find herb sauces and salsas, glazed garlic, pickled peppers and onions, spicy chutneys, and a barbecue sauce that will make you the toast of the neighborhood.

These recipes are basics, but they might more accurately be termed essentials. Because if you have them at the ready, they'll enliven your cooking and allow for quick meals with all the savor of foods from the farm.

JIMMY LEE EDWARDS'S BARBECUE SAUCE

Jimmy Lee Edwards, the home improvement specialist for the county extension service in Pastoria County, outside Pine Bluff, Arkansas, considers herself a barbecue expert. This is really her recipe, with a bit of Katie Carpenter's and Bobbie Clark's opinions thrown in for good measure.

"Just keep lickin' your fingers till you like it, and don't mop the meat until it's almost done, or it will burn." Jimmy Lee said. That tip, along with her trick of marinating the meat, is the secret to great barbecue.

2 cups good-quality (preferably Heinz)
   ketchup
2 tablespoons tomato paste
¼ cup firmly packed dark brown sugar
3 tablespoons molasses
Several drops Tabasco sauce, or to
   taste
½ cup cider vinegar
1 tablespoon dry mustard, mixed to a
   paste with 2 teaspoons cold water
¼ cup Worcestershire sauce
1 fresh jalapeño pepper, trimmed and
   minced (optional)
¾ cup minced fresh pineapple, or rinsed
   and drained canned pineapple

Mix all the ingredients except the pineapple in a medium-size bowl,

A SWEET HARVEST

When I met Jimmy Lee Edwards, she was ankle deep in dusty soil, pulling up sweet potatoes with some members of the 4-H group she heads. It was her, and their, first sweet potato harvest, and she was as excited as if she'd just won the lottery. "Why, look at these—and how many we got," she said, pointing to the trunk of her car full of grocery sacks nearly toppling over with sweet potatoes.

Jimmy Lee had found a market for all the potatoes, and she was thrilled at the prospect of dividing up the earnings among the group of children, all of whom came from homes where extra money might make the difference between not enough and plenty of food on the table. "We're going to do this again next year. It's been real, real good," she said.

making sure they are thoroughly combined. Then stir in the pineapple, and adjust the seasoning to taste. Use immediately or ladle into hot sterilized canning jars and seal according to the lid manufacturer's instructions.

1½ pints

TOMATO-HORSERADISH SAUCE

This sauce, which Geneva Michaels makes from her husband's abundant tomato crop (see page 287), is one of those things that should always be in your refrigerator because it can be the basis, or the garnish, for a surprising number of meals.

I like Tomato-Horseradish Sauce served warm or at room temperature with grilled meats; poached, grilled, or broiled seafood; fried chicken; or roasts of any kind. I also like to spread it on toasted bread to serve as an appetizer, or on baked pizza dough that has been brushed with olive oil. And then there is always the sandwich that cries for a zesty sauce. My latest discovery is to lightly cook okra and corn kernels, add the sauce, and continue cooking just until it is warm. You will swoon with delight.

A warning about bottled horseradish: It loses its potency with drastic speed once it is opened, so if you have a jar that's been sitting for a while, sniff to be sure it still has flavor.

You may want to omit the final step of puréeing the sauce—it is equally nice left chunky.

1 tablespoon unsalted butter
1 medium onion, peeled and thinly sliced
1 large clove garlic, peeled and minced (about 1½ teaspoons)
1½ pounds ripe tomatoes, cut into ½-inch cubes
1 bay leaf
¼ cup prepared horseradish
Salt to taste
¼ to ½ teaspoon cayenne pepper, or to taste
½ teaspoon fresh thyme leaves, or ¼ teaspoon dried

1 Melt the butter in a large skillet over medium-high heat. When it foams, add the onion and cook, stirring, until it begins to soften, 2 to 3 minutes. Add the garlic, and cook until it begins to turn golden and the onion is turning translucent, about 3 minutes.

2 Add the tomatoes, bay leaf, and horseradish. Stir, reduce the heat to medium-low, and cook, stirring occasionally, until the tomatoes are tender, about 20 minutes.

3 Add the salt, cayenne, and thyme. Mix well, and either serve as is or transfer the mixture to a food processor or blender. Blend, using short pulses, until the mixture is combined but still coarse. Serve hot or at room temperature. The sauce will keep well for several days in the refrigerator. Alternatively, ladle it into hot sterilized canning jars and seal according to the lid manufacturer's instructions.

1 pint

ANCHO CHILE PEPPER PUREE

T his purée gives a wonderfully, dusky, mildly hot flavor to dishes. It is very versatile, too: Mix it to taste with softened butter and serve as an appetizer on fresh-baked bread or tortillas; mix a bit in with a vinaigrette for a salad dressing; rub it on pork or beef loin before roasting. The possibilities are manifold. It is simple to make, and it freezes well.

9 ounces (three 3-ounce packages) dried ancho chiles

1 Place the chiles in a large heatproof bowl. Cover them with boiling water, and soak until they have begun to soften and the water has cooled to room temperature, about 40 minutes. Drain the peppers and set aside any that are very soft and limp.

Repeat the process with the remaining peppers, until they are all soft and limp. (There may be a couple of peppers that need extralong soaking, or that don't ever get very soft. They will not detract from the purée.)

2 Remove the stems and seeds from the peppers. Push the peppers through a

sieve, using the back of a large wooden spoon, to separate the flesh from the skin. Do this in batches, discarding the skin between batches.

3 Allow the purée to cool, then ladle it into jars. Cover and refrigerate for up to 3 months. Alternatively, ladle the warm

purée into a hot sterilized canning jar and seal according to the lid manufacturer's instructions. Or place the purée in a freezer container, allow to cool to room temperature, and freeze. The purée will keep in the freezer for up to 6 months.

1 pint

ROSELLA'S LUSTY TOMATO SAUCE

Erin Rosella learned to make this sauce from her grandfather Michael. The most authentic way to serve it is over polenta, a type of Italian corn pudding, which Ron Rosella's grandmother used to make fresh each week and deliver to all of her seven children! It is also delicious over fettuccine. (See page 318 for the Rosella family's story.)

⅓ cup dried porcini mushrooms
1 cup warm water
⅓ cup unsalted butter
2 tablespoons olive oil
½ small onion, peeled and diced
2 small carrots, peeled and diced
1 rib celery, trimmed and diced
4 large button mushrooms, stems trimmed,
  caps diced
4 cups Fresh Tomato Sauce (recipe follows)
½ teaspoon dried red pepper flakes, crushed
Salt and freshly ground black pepper
1 teaspoon sugar (optional)

1 Soak the porcini mushrooms in the warm water for 1 hour.

2 Heat the butter and the oil in a large skillet over medium heat. When it is hot, add the onion, carrots, and celery. Cook until the onion begins to turn translucent, about 5 minutes.

3 Drain the porcini mushrooms, reserving the liquid and the mushrooms separately. Add the porcini, the button mushrooms, and ½ cup of the porcini soaking liquid to the skillet. Bring to a boil and reduce for about 1 minute. Then add the tomato sauce and the red pepper flakes, and cook until the sauce has thickened somewhat, about 15 minutes. Season to taste with salt and pepper, and sugar if desired.

4 Serve immediately or store, covered, in the refrigerator for 1 to 2 days. Alternatively, ladle the sauce into hot sterilized jars and seal according to the lid manufacturer's instructions.

1 quart

FRESH TOMATO SAUCE

■ ■ ■ ■ ■ ■ ■

This is about the best fresh tomato sauce in the universe, and I am eternally grateful to Erin Rosella for sharing it with me. It came to her from her grandfather Michael, the real cook of the family.

If you've always made a slow-cooked tomato sauce, you'll be excited by the difference in taste of this one. With its sweet, slightly tart flavor, this sauce tastes like sun-kissed tomatoes straight from the garden, and it is a cinch to make. I like to make a lot of it in the summer, and either freeze or can it to have on hand to pour over pasta, add to a soup, or to make Rosella's sauce for pasta or polenta. The one condition is that you must use the ripest, most flavorful tomatoes possible (as often as not they'll be Italian plum tomatoes).

1½ pounds fresh, ripe, flavorful tomatoes,
*   quartered*
½ cup olive oil
½ small onion, peeled and diced

1 Purée the tomatoes in a food processor. Strain, and set aside.

2 Heat the oil in a medium-size saucepan over medium-high heat. Add the onion and sauté until it is translucent, about 5 minutes. Add the strained tomatoes and bring to a boil. Reduce the heat to medium, and cook just until the tomatoes don't taste raw anymore, about 10 minutes.

3 Use immediately, or ladle the sauce into a hot sterilized canning jar and seal according to the lid manufacturer's instructions. Or ladle the sauce into a freezer container, let cool to room temperature, and freeze. It will keep in the freezer for up to 6 months.

1½ cups

ROSEY'S THE NAME, PRODUCE IS THE GAME

Ron Rosella walks into Italian class at the Language School in downtown Seattle carrying two crates of radicchio—a bitter, crisp, red-leafed Italian lettuce—and a crate of pale brown, lightly furred crimini mushrooms. He sets them down on a table at the front of the room, looks at the class, and says, "These were in the ground in Italy two days ago. They just came in."

Ron goes on to explain what to do with them. He tries first in Italian; then with a laugh and a shake of his head he slides into English. "Slice the radicchio real thin and sauté it with garlic in olive oil, then add the mushrooms. Don't cook it too long. Then serve it with pasta." He brought his fingers to his lips and kissed them, Italian style.

Ron and his father, Michael Rosella, are the owners of Rosella's Produce, one of Seattle's largest wholesale produce companies. He is second-generation American and well aware of the irony that has him enrolled in a beginning Italian class.

Ron's grandfather came to Seattle from a tiny village near Naples, and he never spoke a word of English. Ron's father grew up in Seattle speaking the Italian dialect of his father's native village. Ron grew up awash in the culture, but not in the language.

Michael Rosella, 78, explains why his son is learning Italian at age 51: "My parents wanted us to speak Italian when we were young, but when we got older they wanted us to speak English." By the time Ron was growing up, English was the lingua franca of the household.

Ron's mother was Irish, which had something to do with it. "I broke the Italian barrier by marrying an Irish girl," his father says.

SEATTLE'S LITTLE ITALY

Rosella's is an integral part of Seattle's Italian produce culture, which goes back to the turn of the century. Many of the produce buyers then were Italian, and dozens of farmers, most of them Italian, worked the fertile ground of South Park, where the Boeing

aerospace plant now sprawls, and in Wood-inville and Bellevue, areas to the east of Seattle that have also succumbed to development.

The elder Rosella, or "Rosey" as most people call him, worked as a driver and salesman for several produce companies before he started his wholesale business in 1945. He distinguished himself early on. "I started out right away paying the farmers once a week, instead of once a month or two, the way other people did," he says. "I didn't pay them much, but I always paid."

Ron started working for his father when he was 10 years old. Then, produce row was on Western Avenue, where fancy furniture stores and restaurants now stand. "There were Greeks, Italians, Japanese, and Jews," Ron says. "We all used hand trucks to load the produce, and the railroad was here to move it. That was when the business was really colorful." About 30 years ago, produce row moved out to the south part of the city, near where the hamburger-shaped Kingdome is now.

Rosey reminisces about that time as he sits in a small café in Seattle and sips iced tea. "I went to work every day at 3:30 A.M. and stayed till 7 P.M.," he says. "I used to cook down at the business. I'd make ravioli, or spaghetti, or cook steaks or chicken, and feed everybody." He would go home for supper in the evening, but then return to work. "My wife used to say I'd rather sleep with the radishes than with her."

The Italian influence in the produce business has dwindled since the 1940s and '50s. The younger generation has been lured away from the business as small family operations have gradually been bought out by the large grocery chains. "As the chains become more powerful they take the color out of the business, because they want huge lots of a few varieties of things," Ron says. "At the same time that leaves room for specialty wholesalers like me, and for smaller farmers who grow things like baby dill or champagne grapes."

UPSCALE EXPANSION

Though he's kept the old place on Occidental Street, Ron now runs Rosella's from a sleek new 21,000-square-foot warehouse on First Avenue South that services 250 supermarkets in the Seattle area and an occasional national account. He continues his father's tradition of handling specialty produce. "These are all organic vegetables," he says, pointing to a wall of shelves stacked with everything from corn to tomatoes. "I brought in organic corn last year and it had a few bugs in it, but people loved it so much I got all I could this year."

The old 12,000-square-foot warehouse is reserved exclusively for Rosella's 175 restaurant accounts, and the cool air there is redolent with the fragrance of fresh herbs and just-ripe fruit. "We've got baby vegetables," Ron says, pointing to bunches of pinky-size carrots and baby dumpling squash. "Fresh herbs and lemon grass—whatever a restaurant

▶▶▶

needs, I'll try to get. I don't make a lot off the organics or the specialty things," Ron says. "But I want to respond to my customers' needs, and we're small enough to do that."

He has also continued his father's tradition of practically living at the business. The office is a small two-story building built right inside the huge high- ceilinged produce warehouse, like a small house within a house.

AN EARLY START

R on starts work at 5 A.M. by touring the warehouse to see what he's got. By 6 A.M. he's in his second-floor office, whose windows look out onto the warehouse floor. The phones ring ceaselessly as farmers and shippers call in to see what he needs. "I'll hit ya on some leaf lettuce action," he says into the phone. He hangs up and picks it up again to say, "Hey Pete, very good sir, I'm in good shape there but I'll need some broccoli, cauli, and cabbage," and bangs down the phone.

On the flat "roof" of the two-story office is a gym, complete with stationary bicycle and a pair of punching bags. "That's where I go to work out my frustrations,"

Ron explains. "Or I shut the door, lie down, and go to sleep." He points out to me a single bed in a tiny room off of his office.

"The whole game is communication," he continues, retrieving a list of California produce prices from the fax machine before answering the phone again.

A shipper from California calls, and they argue in a fierce and friendly way. They strike a deal, then Ron listens silently. "Now there's a typical transaction," Ron says, hanging up the phone. "He cries, whines, and deals in guilt, then he tells me how his kids are doing in school. We're good friends—when he comes up here he stays with me." The phone rings again, and he picks it up and barks, "Bring me 50 beans and I need 100 next week."

The pressure mounts throughout the morning. "I'm here six days a week, gambling on tens of thousands of dollars a day," Ron says. "Everything we buy is on instinct and feel." The produce business isn't for everyone, but Ron loves it. "You're either made for this business or you aren't. Some people would have a nervous breakdown, but to me it's fun. I couldn't quit if someone offered me $10 million. This is my handball, my golf."

ROASTED RED BELL PEPPER SAUCE

I can never resist red bell peppers when they're piled high at the market. Usually this happens toward the end of summer, when farmers let their green peppers hang on the plants to bake red in the sun. They bring them to market when they are firm, crisp, and slightly sweetened with the sun's heat. I like them uncooked in salads and pasta dishes, but my favorite way to eat them is when they've been roasted. They take on an added flavor dimension that is sweet and smoky, and that goes well with a surprising range of foods.

I make this sauce often and usually serve it as a dip for blanched vegetables. It is also delicious poured over steamed fish, or served with shellfish or chicken. (I make large quantities to have on hand in the freezer.)

Use the recipe as a guide. The sweetness of peppers varies greatly, and the amounts of vinegar and salt may need adjusting.

2 large red bell peppers, roasted (see page 322)
½ cup heavy (whipping) cream
1 tablespoon balsamic vinegar
½ teaspoon salt, or to taste
Pinch of cayenne pepper (optional)

P eel and seed the roasted peppers, and purée them in a food processor. With the processor running, add the cream and vinegar. Season to taste with salt, and cayenne if desired. Serve immediately at room temperature or cover and refrigerate for up to 24 hours. Alternatively, ladle the sauce into a hot sterilized canning jar and seal according to the lid manufacturer's instructions. Or place the peppers in a freezer container and freeze. The peppers will keep in the freezer for up to 3 months.

1 cup

HOW TO ROAST PEPPERS

1 Choose peppers that are firm and that have a smooth skin.

2 Preheat the broiler.

3 Place the peppers on a piece of aluminum foil that is at least 3 inches below the broiler element. Turn the peppers often as they broil until the skin is charred on all sides and it bubbles loose from the meat of the pepper, about 15 minutes. Be careful not to let the skin get too black or it may be difficult to remove.

4 Remove the foil with the peppers still on it. Wrap the foil loosely around the pep-

pers to steam and loosen the skin, 10 to 15 minutes.

5 When the peppers are cool enough to handle, remove the stem end (most of the seeds will come with it) and discard. Peel the skin off the meat of the pepper using your fingers. If it sticks, use the blade of a sharp knife to gently scrape off the skin.

6 Gently scrape all the seeds and the ribs from the inside of the pepper with the blade of a sharp knife. Store, covered, in the refrigerator until ready to proceed with any recipe calling for roasted peppers. These will keep for up to 1 week.

ELIZABETH HUGHES'S BASIL-GARLIC VINEGAR

Elizabeth Hughes has a huge garden every year, out back of her sprawling house at Broken Arrow Ranch, the largest game farm in the U.S., right in the heart of Texas hill country.

The garden is a riot of tomatoes and squash, tomatillos and peppers, and an array of herbs, which take to the dry climate. Elizabeth makes good use of it all in her cooking, and one of her specialties is herbed vinegars. She keeps an extensive collection on the wide, low window sills of the ranch house kitchen. When you look out over the rolling fields—which are usually populated with antelope or axis deer—you can't help but notice their brilliance.

This is one of her favorites, made with basil and hot peppers from the garden. It wakes up a salad, complements grilled chicken, meat, or poultry, and even goes well in a chicken or tuna salad, or on a cheese sandwich.

I like to follow Elizabeth's lead and make a variety of vinegars in bottles of different sizes and shapes—they not only look pretty on the shelf, they are a great addition to the pantry.

3½ cups good-quality red wine vinegar

4 cloves garlic, peeled

2 fresh whole serrano peppers, or ¾ teaspoon dried red pepper flakes

⅔ cup gently packed fresh basil leaves

1 Bring the vinegar to a boil in a medium-size saucepan over medium-high heat.

2 While the vinegar is boiling, put the garlic cloves in a sterilized wine bottle, or in the bottle that contained the vinegar. Add the peppers and the basil, gently pushing each leaf of basil, stem end first, into the bottle so the leaves aren't damaged.

3 Pour the hot vinegar through a funnel over the herbs, seal the bottle with a cork, and let stand at least 2 weeks before using. This will keep 4 to 6 months.

3½ cups

TO STORE FRESHLY CUT HERBS

*P*lace the bunch of herbs in a glass of water, like a bouquet of flowers, and cover the leaves loosely with a plastic bag; or wrap the bunch in a moist paper towel, and then in a plastic bag. Refrigerate; the herbs will keep 4 to 5 days if carefully stored.

MIKE CRAIN'S PESTO

U sually when one thinks of pesto, it is that heady mixture of basil, pine nuts, olive oil, and garlic. This pesto, which is similar but deeper in flavor, came about because Mike Crain, part owner of Dripping Springs Garden in the Ozark mountains, couldn't get a reliable supply of pine nuts but always had sunflower seeds on hand. He toasted some and added them, and this is the tasty result.

Mike served the pesto to me on a cheese sandwich, with some fresh tomato salsa alongside, and it was bright and refreshing on a searing summer day.

Besides as a sandwich spread, I like to serve it as a dip for fresh vegetables, good crackers, or freshly made bread cut in fingers.

1 cup sunflower seeds
2 cups packed fresh basil leaves
2 cloves garlic, peeled
¾ cup olive oil
⅓ cup freshly grated Parmesan cheese

1 Preheat the oven to 350°F.

2 Spread the sunflower seeds out in a single layer on a baking sheet, and toast them in the oven until they are light golden, 10 to 12 minutes. Remove from the oven and allow to cool.

3 Mince the sunflower seeds in a food processor, using short pulses. You do not want them to turn into a paste, but they should be very finely minced. Transfer the minced sunflower seeds to a medium-size bowl and set aside.

4 Place the basil and the garlic in the food processor, and turn it on. With the processor running, slowly add the oil and process until the ingredients are finely minced and thoroughly combined. You may need to stop the food processor once to scrape down the sides of the bowl. The mixture will be somewhat runny.

5 Transfer the basil mixture to the bowl with the sunflower seeds, and mix well. Add the cheese, mix well, and mound in a serving dish. Serve immediately or refrigerate for up to 6 hours.

1½ cups

CILANTRO SAUCE

Cilantro is becoming one of the most popular herbs in this country. It's sprouting up in fields from the Northwest to the Southeast, so much has the demand grown in the past several years.

Also called Chinese parsley and fresh coriander, cilantro has a dusky flavor that does not win the approval of every palate. But for those who love it, cilantro can do no wrong.

I sprinkle cilantro in many different and varied dishes, and I love what it does to their flavor. It is slightly piquant when added to a cool salad, and it becomes soft and aromatic when added to hot dishes at the last minute.

This sauce is one of my favorite ways to use cilantro, and I make it often in the summer—especially for drizzling on grilled eggplant. I also love it on steamed fish—particularly mild white-meat fish such as rockfish, cod, or halibut—and on thick slices of ripe garden-fresh tomatoes.

Its uses are many, however. Add it to mayonnaise for a sandwich spread, to yogurt for a vegetable dip. And if you really want its full, unadulterated effect, then use it as a dip for sourdough bread.

The sauce is best used soon after it is made, though it will keep in the refrigerator for a day or two, with a slight loss of flavor as time progresses.

2 cups packed cilantro leaves
½ cup extra-virgin olive oil
2 cloves garlic, peeled and minced
1 teaspoon minced fresh ginger
Salt
Grated zest of 1 lime
1 tablespoon freshly squeezed lime juice
Freshly ground black pepper

Process the cilantro, olive oil, garlic, ginger, and ¼ teaspoon of salt in a food processor, pulsing until the mixture is a fine purée. Add the lime zest and the lime juice, and process until mixed. Season with salt and pepper to taste. Serve immediately, or cover tightly and refrigerate for up to 2 days.

¾ cup

PEPPERY TOMATILLO SALSA

Come July and August, when the weather in central Texas is hot and still and the cicadas in the live oaks on Broken Arrow Ranch hum like a musical motor, produce from Elizabeth Hughes's gardens practically spills out the kitchen door.

Elizabeth and her husband, Mike, own Broken Arrow Ranch and a company called Texas Wild Game Cooperative, which supplies game for many of the country's leading restaurants, and individuals through mail order. The Hugheses—including their teenage sons—love to eat, and during summer their meals are based on garden-fresh produce.

When I was there, there were tomatillos to spare, which Mike popped into his mouth after removing their husks. Elizabeth had plans to turn them into this salsa, to serve with either grilled chicken or grilled fish. It is tart, and zingy with hot peppers. "I prefer serranos because they have some sweet flavor," she says, but she uses whatever peppers are ripe in her garden, which might just as easily be a jalapeño or a banana pepper.

If you do use serrano or jalapeño peppers, you can adjust the heat by the amount of seeds and ribs you use. More equals more heat. If you want to still feel your tongue discard about half the seeds and ribs.

1 pound tomatillos
1 tablespoon mild vegetable oil, such as safflower
1 large onion, peeled and diced
1 small bunch cilantro (about 1 cup lightly packed leaves)
1 fresh serrano chile, trimmed and halved lengthwise
Salt and freshly ground black pepper

1 Remove the husks from the tomatillos, and rinse them well under cool water. Cut them into quarters if they are small, into eighths if they are large.

2 Heat the oil in a large skillet over medium-high heat. Add the onion and cook, stirring, until it begins to turn translucent, about 5 minutes. While the onion is cooking, coarsely chop half the cilantro.

3 Finely chop the chile pepper, and add it to the skillet along with the tomatillos and the chopped cilantro. Cook, stirring oc-

casionally, until the tomatillos soften but don't lose their shape, about 15 minutes. Season to taste with salt and pepper, if desired. This will keep, covered, in the refrigerator for 1 to 2 days. Or ladle the salsa into hot sterilized canning jars and seal according to the lid manufacturer's instructions.

4 to 6 servings

PICKLED BABY ARTICHOKES

Tony Leonardini, an artichoke grower in California (see page 132), is a pickled-artichoke aficionado. And well he should be—his family started the Cara Mia brand company in Castroville. This is Tony's personal recipe, one he whips up at home with the small artichokes from his fields. I will be forever grateful to him for giving it to me, because the resulting tidbits are lively and fresh, and since they keep virtually indefinitely in their olive oil bath, it is easy to have them on hand. I slip them into sandwiches, put them on pizza, toss them with pasta, and sometimes sneak a few to eat plain, out of the jar. They make a good appetizer with other vegetables, and there are dozens of other ways to put them to use as well.

Baby artichokes, which are really small, fully mature, secondary-growth artichokes and not babies at all, are abundant in spring, though along the West Coast they are available nearly year-round. If you can get them only once a year, make up a big batch of these and keep them in a cool place or on the bottom shelf of the refrigerator.

The marinade here is just a guideline—adjust it to your taste, making it as spicy or mild as you like; or make several different kinds to have on hand. You don't need to seal the jars through processing, but if you don't, make sure the artichoke hearts are completely immersed in oil and refrigerated.

2 cups distilled white vinegar

2 cups water

2½ pounds small artichokes (about 24)

4 cloves garlic, peeled, halved lengthwise, green germ removed

2 tablespoons minced Italian (flat-leaf) parsley

1 bay leaf

1½ cups extra-virgin olive oil, or as needed

1 Mix the vinegar and water in a nonreactive saucepan.

2 Trim the artichokes: Remove the tough outer leaves by pulling back on them and letting them snap off naturally at the base. Continue removing leaves until only the tender, pale yellow leaves of the artichoke heart remain. Trim any dark green off the stem, and the prickly tops off the leaves.

Then cut the artichokes in half lengthwise, and put them immediately in the vinegar mixture to prevent their browning.

3 When all of the artichokes are trimmed, bring the vinegar mixture to a boil over medium-high heat. Reduce the heat so the vinegar is simmering vigorously, partially cover, and cook until the artichokes are tender but not soft, about 13 minutes; they should still have a bit of resistance in the center when pierced with a knife or a metal skewer. Drain the artichokes.

4 While the artichokes are still warm, arrange a layer of them in a large jar. Add the garlic, parsley, and the bay leaf, then the remaining artichokes. Pour the olive oil over all (the artichokes should be completely covered), and let sit, uncovered, until the artichokes cool completely. Refrigerate, covered, for up to 3 months. Or ladle into hot sterilized canning jars and seal according to the lid manufacturer's instructions.

2 pints

PICKLED PEPPERS

This recipe comes from Krueger Pepper Gardens in Wapato, Washington, where more than fifty varieties of peppers flourish from early summer through autumn's first frost. People drive from miles away to buy peppers from bushel baskets that are bursting with colors of every

hue, or to pick their own. The Krueger family couldn't be friendlier—they staff the farmstand, dispensing recipes, family lore, and picking and storing tips for their peppers and the myriad other vegetables they grow. Shopping or picking at Kruegers' is a friendly, fragrantly delicious affair.

Through the years the Kruegers have collected recipes from customers, family members, and neighbors, and this is one that I particularly like. It captures the flavor of peppers in a tangy brine softened with olive oil.

These can be served as an hors d'oeuvre, diced and strewn on pizza, put in an omelette, or minced and folded into cream cheese or fresh goat cheese. The brine makes a wonderful pepper-infused salad dressing. So when peppers are abundant, try putting up several pints this way. You'll be glad when winter rolls around and you can break out a hit of summer.

1 pound green bell peppers, cored and seeded
2 cloves garlic, peeled
¼ teaspoon salt
¾ cup distilled white vinegar
¾ cup extra-virgin olive oil

1 Prepare a large bowl of ice water.

2 Cut the peppers lengthwise into ½-inch-wide strips. Bring a large pot of water to a boil, and add the peppers. As soon as the water returns to a boil, remove the pot from the heat, and let the peppers stand in the hot water until they soften somewhat, about 2 minutes. Then drain, and plunge the peppers into the ice water until they are cool.

3 Drain the cooled peppers and pat dry. Pack them into two hot sterilized pint jars, dropping the strips in vertically. Drop a garlic clove in each jar, and sprinkle each with half the salt.

4 Bring the vinegar to a boil in a medium-size saucepan. Add the olive oil, stir, and bring to a boil again. Pour the mixture over the peppers, and seal the jars according to the lid manufacturer's instructions. Let the peppers sit for at least 24 hours before serving.

2 pints

BUYING PEPPERS

C hoosing good fresh bell or chile peppers is not a difficult task. Just make sure their skin is tight and smooth, not wrinkled, which is a sign of age, and without bruises or indentations, black spots or any soft spots. They should be crisp, not flabby, and have a pepper odor. This is important—there are some peppers that are big, fleshy, and beautiful but have little fragrance and no flavor.

SPICED TRICOLOR PEPPERS AND ONIONS

The inspiration for this recipe came from a visit to Krueger Pepper Farms in eastern Washington. I knew there were dozens of types of peppers, but the incredible variety didn't hit me until I was at their farmstand and saw peppers of every shape, color, size, and flavor.

I use vividly colored bell peppers in this recipe, which is bright with pickling spice and a subtle touch of vinegar, but you can use any combination of peppers you like (keeping in mind that hot ones will get hotter as they sit). I combine them with onions so that, when I open the jar on a drizzly winter day, the aroma of summer will fill the air.

1¾ cups water

1¾ cups distilled white vinegar

¼ cup coarse (kosher) salt

2 tablespoons sugar

2 tablespoons good-quality pickling spice

4 medium yellow onions, peeled and cut into eighths

4 large bell peppers of varying colors, cored, seeded, and cut into ½-inch-wide strips

1 fresh jalapeño pepper, trimmed and quartered vertically, with seeds

1 Combine the water, vinegar, coarse salt, sugar, and pickling spices in a large non-reactive saucepan, and bring to a boil over medium-high heat. Reduce the heat to low, and keep warm.

2 Divide the onions among four hot sterilized canning jars, packing them in the bottom. Then divide the pepper strips among the jars, standing them upright on the onions, making sure to mix the colors. Place one piece of jalapeño pepper in each jar.

3 Pour the vinegar mixture over the vegetables, making sure they are covered (you may have more than enough liquid). Run the blade of a stainless steel knife down the side of each jar, to release any air bubbles that may be trapped among the vegetables.

4 Seal the jars according to the lid manufacturer's instructions. Or ladle into jars, cover, and refrigerate. The peppers will keep in the refrigerator for 2 to 3 weeks.

4 pints

AILI'S PICKLED BEETS

This recipe is an adaptation of one given me by Aili Takala, of Stockett, Montana (see page 106 for a little more about her and another of her recipes). Aili served pickled beets with dinner the first night I arrived, and I loved their fresh flavor. Her directions, when she told me the recipe, began: "First you get the beet seeds...."

She was serious—and when I can raise my own beets, I do. Regardless, I follow Aili's lead in this simple recipe, which produces beets with the same silken flavor I remember from her table. They are mildly spiced and have an extra jot of vinegar, which balances their natural sweetness.

1 large bunch beets (about 1½ pounds)
¾ cup distilled white vinegar
2 tablespoons sugar
6 allspice berries
4 whole cloves
1 bay leaf

1 Trim the beet stems, leaving ½ inch of stem intact. Do not trim the roots.

2 Bring water to a boil in the bottom of a vegetable steamer. Add the beets, cover, and steam until they are nearly tender but still offer resistance when you test them with a sharp knife, 15 to 20 minutes. Remove the steamer basket from the heat.

3 While the beets are steaming, combine the vinegar, water, sugar, and spices and herbs in a medium-size saucepan. Cover, and bring to a boil over medium-high heat. Then reduce the heat to low, and keep warm.

4 When the beets are cool enough to handle, carefully scrape off the skin, and trim the stem and root ends. Slice the beets into ⅛-inch-thick slices, and place them in a medium-size glass bowl or jar. Cover them with the warm vinegar mixture, and set aside until cool. When the beets are cool, cover, and refrigerate them for at least 24 hours before using. Refrigerated they will keep for 3 weeks. Or ladle the beets into hot sterilized canning jars and seal according to the lid manufacturer's instructions.

2 cups

CARYL'S BEET RELISH

One day I received a little package in the mail, and when I opened it up, I found a set of tiny paper boxes, each one a perfect fit inside the next. My reward for opening them all was this recipe and a tiny handwritten note with a bright red heart on it. All were the handiwork of Caryl Smith of Brighton, Iowa, one of my favorite sources for farm recipes (and her husband Barney supplied the Switchel recipe on page 347).

I cooked up the recipe and it was as delicious as Caryl said it would be, with its spices and its gorgeous red color. I keep this relish on hand to serve with stews—it makes a pungent counterpoint to many meat dishes—and to serve atop sandwiches or burgers for a change of pace.

3 pounds beets, leaves trimmed, stem and root ends intact
2 medium onions, peeled and diced
2 cups packed dark brown sugar
2 tablespoons pickling spices, tied in cheesecloth
3 cups distilled white vinegar
1 teaspoon salt
3 tablespoons prepared horseradish

1 Bring water to a boil in the bottom of a vegetable steamer, and steam the beets until they are tender, 25 to 30 minutes. Remove the steamer basket from the heat.

2 When the beets are cool enough to handle, trim off the stems and the roots, and peel them. Then grate the beets, using a hand grater or the standard grating blade of a food processor. You should have about 6 cups. (If you prefer, you may use a fine grater, which will yield slightly more grated beets.)

3 Place the beets in a large heavy nonreactive saucepan, and add the remaining ingredients. Mix well, cover, and bring to a boil over medium-high heat. Then remove the cover and boil the mixture until it has thickened slightly and the onions have softened, about 15 minutes. Allow the relish to cool, then ladle into jars. Cover and refrigerate for up to 3 weeks. Or ladle the boiling-hotbeets into hot sterilized canning jars. Seal according to the lid manufacturer's instructions.

4 pints

MILLION-DOLLAR RELISH

I first tasted this relish when Nancy Lord, a friend of mine, brought a jar she'd made with vegetables from her huge Maine garden. I spread it on a cheese sandwich and understood immediately where it got its name. Its sweet, sour, spicy flavor is worth at least a million dollars.

4 pounds sliced pickling cucumbers (about
   3 quarts)
1 large red bell pepper, cored, seeded, and
   cut into strips
¼ cup coarse (kosher) salt
6 medium carrots, peeled and cut into
   2-inch pieces
6 green bell peppers, cored, seeded, and cut
   into strips
2 large onions, peeled and quartered
4 cups sugar
3 cups cider vinegar
1 teaspoon dry mustard
1 teaspoon ground turmeric

1 Finely grind the cucumbers and the red pepper, separately, in a food processor. Transfer the vegetables to a large bowl, and mix well. Sprinkle with the coarse salt, and toss to mix. Then cover the bowl and set aside at room temperature for 4 hours to macerate.

2 Fifteen minutes before the cucumbers and peppers are ready, finely grind the carrots, green peppers, and onions, separately, in a food processor. Place them in a large heavy stockpot.

3 Drain the peppers and cucumbers. Add them with all the remaining ingredients to the stockpot, stir well, and bring to a boil over high heat. Reduce the heat to medium, and simmer until the vegetables have softened, about 25 minutes.

4 Ladle the boiling-hot relish into hot sterilized canning jars. Run the blade of a stainless steel knife down the side of each jar to release any air bubbles. Seal according to the lid manufacturer's instructions.

About 9 pints

AN AUCTION IN AMISH COUNTRY

arm sunlight sparkled off wagon wheels and horse bridles at the Linebach Produce Auction in Shippensburg, Pennsylvania. It was late September, and with the glory of summer produce now just a memory, the farmers were bringing in their fall harvest. There were still some tomatoes, a few totes of corn, plenty of cabbages and cauliflower, and every imaginable kind of squash. The jewels in the crown were the cantaloupes, latecomers looked over closely by eager buyers wanting to stretch the summer season just a bit longer.

Paul Linebach, a Mennonite, dressed all in black with a black hat balanced on his head, was dashing about organizing farmers, shaking hands with the buyers as they assembled, making sure that all was in order. His wife, Mary who keeps the auction's books, and a handful of the fifteen Linebach children were there too, minding the store next to the auction barn.

Though the auction isn't specifically for the Amish and Mennonite communities in the area, they make up a large percentage of the dozens of farmers who bring their produce. Buyers come from a three-state region to purchase in quantity, taking the farm-fresh produce back to their markets or produce stands.

The growers arrange their wagons (or their cars if they are Mennonite or "black bumper Amish," who are allowed to use them) in a double line leading up to the auction house, a huge open structure with a raised platform at one end where Mr. Linebach and the auctioneer stand. They drive by the auction block, and the crowd of buyers peer at their produce, shake a melon, or taste a proffered slice before the auctioneer begins his yelping and yelling. Loads are bought and sold in the blink of an eye.

When the drive-by part of the auction is finished, the buyers stroll by to review the bins of produce on the auction house floor. In midsummer the auction can take up to four hours, as load after beautiful load of freshly harvested produce is sold. Now it lasts about half that, winding down to a long table filled with bits and bobs—a box of plums, a gallon of honey, a pile of jack-be-little squash, a painted pumpkin. This smaller auction is the province of the housewife, who, if she signals fast enough, can get some down-to-earth bargains.

AMISH TOMATO KETCHUP

This sweet ketchup comes from Mary Linebach, who owns and runs a produce auction with her husband, Paul, in Shippensburg, Pennsylvania (described on the facing page).

I got Mary to pause for a while one day in September, when things were slow (by her standards). We talked about her family's favorite foods, and this ketchup was the first thing she thought of.

"The children love it on pancakes in the morning," she said. "It's sweeter than store-bought and not as tangy, but that's what they like. When I serve store-bought, they don't eat much, but when I serve my own there isn't any left."

It *is* sweet and spicy, and the perfect thing to do with the end-of-summer abundance of tomatoes. The ketchup is as good on morning hotcakes (an Amish custom) as it is on Cheddar cheese sandwiches, as a dip for fresh vegetables or freshly baked bread, and as a condiment with roast or fried meat or poultry. And it has one distinct advantage over the most popular store-bought brand: You won't have any trouble getting it out of the bottle, because it's not thick.

6 ribs celery, trimmed and cut into
  ¼-inch-thick slices
2 medium onions, peeled and diced
  (about 2 cups)
¼ cup water
3 pounds tomatoes, quartered
5 tablespoons vinegar
1 cup (packed) dark brown sugar
½ tablespoon allspice berries
½ tablespoon whole cloves
½ tablespoon celery seeds
1 teaspoon ground mace
½ teaspoon salt

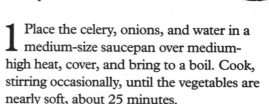

1 Place the celery, onions, and water in a medium-size saucepan over medium-high heat, cover, and bring to a boil. Cook, stirring occasionally, until the vegetables are nearly soft, about 25 minutes.

2 Meanwhile, cook the tomatoes in a large heavy nonreactive saucepan over medium heat, partially covered, until they are very soft and almost a purée, about 25 minutes. Add the cooked celery and onions, and continue cooking until the vegetables

are completely softened, 15 minutes.

3 Strain the tomato mixture in small batches through a sieve into another nonreactive saucepan, pressing down firmly to extract all the liquid. Stir in the vinegar, brown sugar, and the spices. Place the pan over medium-high heat and bring to a boil. Continue boiling, stirring often to be sure the ketchup isn't sticking to the bottom of the pan, until the mixture thickens somewhat, 15 to 20 minutes. Allow the ketchup to cool, then ladle into jars. Cover and refrigerate for up to 2 months. Or ladle the boiling-hot ketchup into hot sterilized canning jars. Seal according to the lid manufacturer's instructions.

1½ pints

ONION MARMALADE

T his marmalade is the creation of Karen Malody, who grew up on a farm in north central Washington, where her mother cooked meals that would feed the world, just in case the world stopped by for supper, Karen says.

Karen is a restaurant consultant with an insatiable desire to cook and entertain. One of the secrets to her meals—which are always composed of many little dishes that go together to make a flavorful whole— is to have a variety of condiments and dishes on hand for unexpected guests, or to round out a meal.

This onion marmalade is just such a creation. Karen makes it regularly and always has some in the refrigerator to serve over mascarpone, cream cheese, or yogurt cheese. I like to spread it on dough for pizza, and to use it in a Cheddar cheese sandwich. The possibilities are without limit, and it keeps indefinitely in the refrigerator.

8 tablespoons (1 stick) unsalted butter
2 pounds onions, peeled, halved lengthwise,
  and cut crosswise into ½-inch-thick slices
1 teaspoon salt
½ teaspoon freshly ground black pepper
½ cup sugar
2 tablespoons dry sherry, such as a Fino
¼ cup good-quality red wine vinegar
1 cup rich red wine, such as a zinfandel
¼ cup mild honey
½ cup chopped dried pitted prunes

1 Melt the butter in a large skillet over medium heat. When it foams, add the onions and stir until they are thoroughly coated with butter. Sprinkle them with the salt and pepper, reduce the heat to low, and cook, stirring occasionally, until they have turned golden, about 20 minutes.

2 Add the remaining ingredients and cook, uncovered, until the mixture is quite thick and very dark, about 1¼ to 1½ hours. Stir the mixture occasionally, and watch it to be sure it doesn't burn. Season to taste, remove from the heat, and cool to room temperature. Either serve immediately or cover and refrigerate. Onion marmalade keeps well for an indefinite amount of time in the refrigerator.

2 pints

CRANBERRY CHUTNEY

A fter visiting the cranberry bogs on the Long Beach peninsula in Washington, I couldn't wait to get home and use the berries in the kitchen. In the American tradition cranberries are used as a condiment, and I followed it in this recipe for chutney. It is simple to make and the flavors are clear and clean.

Cranberries are so full of natural pectin that they are ideal for conserves, and this sweet, tart spread is wonderful. It can be canned or frozen, or kept in the refrigerator for weeks. I like to use it on sharp Cheddar cheese sandwiches, as a condiment with curry, and alongside roast chicken.

1 pound (4 cups) fresh or frozen whole
  cranberries
1 small tart apple, peeled, cored, and diced
2 cups packed light brown sugar
¾ cup cider vinegar
½ cup dried currants
½ teaspoon salt
½ teaspoon ground ginger
½ teaspoon ground cinnamon
¼ teaspoon ground cloves
1 teaspoon yellow mustard seeds
¼ to ½ teaspoon dried red pepper flakes

1 Place all the ingredients in a large heavy saucepan (using only ¼ teaspoon of the

pepper flakes), and bring to a boil over medium-high heat. Reduce the heat and simmer until the mixture thickens slightly, 25 minutes. The cranberries will pop as they cook. Taste and adjust the amount of pepper flakes.

2 Allow the chutney to cool, then ladle into jars. Cover and refrigerate for up to 3 months. Alternatively, ladle the boiling-hot chutney into hot sterilized canning jars, and seal according to the lid manufacturer's instructions. Or place the chutney in freezer containers, allow it to cool to room temperature, and freeze. The chutney will keep for up to 1 year in the freezer.

2 pints

RHUBARB CHUTNEY

I n the Pacific Northwest, where most of the country's commercial rhubarb is grown, the fields begin sprouting huge, leafy plants just as soon as the weather starts to warm, usually in March. By May they have produced a crop of fat tart red stalks and are beginning a second. When the season is finished the plants send up tall, dramatic white seed stalks that look a bit like pampas grass. It's a sad moment for rhubarb lovers, because it means another year will go by before there is any more.

Fresh rhubarb's moment of glory is brief, and those who love its astringent flavor capitalize on it by turning it into jams and chutneys, using it in cakes, pies, and cobblers. Every farm I visited had rhubarb growing somewhere—and had a stash of preserved rhubarb in the cupboard.

Rhubarb is a natural for chutney because of its tart flavor. Here it is combined with a few spices, a dousing of vinegar, and enough brown sugar to soften and mellow it. Though this is delicious the day it is made it improves with age and is even better a month later.

2 pounds fresh rhubarb, diced
2 cups gently packed light brown sugar
1 small onion, diced
1 tablespoon coarse (kosher) salt
Zest of 1 lemon, minced (about 2 teaspoons)
1 cup raisins
2 tablespoons minced fresh ginger
¼ teaspoon ground cloves
½ teaspoon ground cinnamon
2 teaspoons yellow mustard seeds
1½ cups cider vinegar

1 Place all the ingredients except the vinegar in a large heavy saucepan and bring to a boil over medium heat. Cook, stirring occasionally, until the mixture softens, the onion becomes translucent, and the rhubarb begins to lose its shape, about 30 minutes.

2 Stir in the vinegar, and continue cooking until the rhubarb is thoroughly soft and shapeless, another 30 minutes.

3 Allow the chutney to cool, then ladle into jars. Cover and refrigerate for up to 3 weeks. Alternatively, ladle the boiling-hot chutney into hot sterilized canning jars and seal according to the lid manufacturer's instructions, or place the chutney in freezer containers, cool to room temperature, and freeze. The chutney will keep up to 3 months in the freezer.

About 3 pints

RHUBARB PRESERVES

These preserves are sweet, tart, and softened with a touch of orange. I love preparing rhubarb this way because it preserves the flavor so well that when you slather it on a piece of hot toast one winter day, your taste buds tell you that spring is right around the corner.

2½ pounds fresh rhubarb, diced
2 cups sugar
Zest of 2 oranges, minced (about 2 teaspoons)
Juice of 2 oranges (about ⅓ cup)
½ cup water

1 Place all the ingredients in a large heavy saucepan and bring to a boil over medium heat. Cook, stirring occasionally, until the mixture has thickened and the rhubarb has softened, 30 to 45 minutes.

2 Allow the preserves to cool, then ladle into jars. Cover and refrigerate up to 1

month. Alternatively, ladle the boiling-hot preserves into hot sterilized canning jars. Seal the jars according to the lid manufacturer's instructions. Or place the preserves in freezer containers, allow to cool to room temperature, and freeze. The preserves will keep in the freezer for up to 3 months.

2 pints

JIM WALSTON'S NECTARINE PRESERVES

"You know, I got to thinking that apples have a lot of pectin in them, and so I figured why wouldn't some fresh-squeezed apples make this get solid. So I threw some nectarines in a pot, added a cup of apple juice, cooked it down until it thickened. It's great, and the pits give it kind of an almond flavor." So Jim Walston, Texas peach farmer, described how he devised his delicious nectarine preserves.

This is Jim's recipe, and nothing could be simpler, nor more evocative of the juicy nectarines of late summer. When you spread it on toast and take your first bite, you'll be amazed at how much nectarine flavor is contained in each sweet-tart mouthful.

I've added a touch of sugar and a tiny drizzle of almond extract (don't add more than the prescribed amount of extract because all you are doing is accentuating the natural almond flavor of the nectarines). If you would like to have enough preserves on hand to last through the winter, just double or triple the recipe.

7 pounds nectarines, rinsed and patted dry
1 cup unfiltered, unpasteurized apple juice
 (available at natural foods stores)
1 cup sugar
¼ teaspoon almond extract

1 Place the nectarines (whole) and the apple juice in a large stockpot or kettle. Cover and cook over medium-high heat, stirring often to break up the nectarines and to be sure they don't burn, until they soften and begin to give up their juice, 30 minutes.

2 Stir in the sugar and continue cooking for an additional 15 minutes. Then remove the cover and cook, stirring frequently and continuing to break up the nectarines, until they have thickened and turned a deeper shade of orange, 30 minutes more.

3 Remove the pits from the preserves and stir in the almond extract. Allow the preserves to cool, then ladle into jars. Cover and refrigerate for up to 3 weeks. Or ladle the boiling-hot preserves into hot sterilized canning jars and seal according to the lid manufacturer's instructions.

3 pints

PEAR GINGER CONSERVE

My grandmother made this conserve every fall, and I always loved it. It is peppery with ginger, perfumed with pears, and balanced with the tartness of lemon. It looks gorgeous both in the jar and spread on a piece of freshly toasted bread, though I don't confine its use to breakfast. I serve it over vanilla ice cream, atop pear pie, or even over fresh pears when I'm lacking time to make a more elaborate dessert.

This recipe makes a small quantity. I've never made more—neither did my grandmother. I think that part of its charm for me was having a limited amount once a year during pear season, savoring it with every mouthful, and then waiting until the next year to taste it again. However, there is nothing to keep *you* from making a large batch to savor often throughout the year!

1 small lemon, scrubbed and cut into 1/16-inch-thick slices, and seeded (1/4 cup)

2 pounds Bosc or Anjou pears, cored, peeled, halved lengthwise, and thinly sliced (4 cups; see Note)

3 cups sugar

1 1/4 cups preserved ginger, drained, cut into 1/16-inch-thick slices

1 Place all the ingredients (making sure *not* to add the syrup from the preserved ginger) in a large stainless steel or ceramic bowl, and mix well. Cover, and let sit overnight to macerate. It is not necessary to refrigerate the mixture.

2 The next day, transfer the pear ginger mixture to a large heavy saucepan and bring to a boil over medium-high heat. Reduce the heat to low, and simmer until the mixture has thickened and reached a temperature of about 175°F on a candy thermometer, about 35 minutes.

3 Allow the conserve to cool, then ladle into jars. Cover and refrigerate for up to 2 months. Or ladle the boiling-hot conserve into hot sterilized canning jars and seal according to the lid manufacturer's directions.

2 pints

Note: The 1-mm slicing disc of a food processor works well for this.

SPICY APPLE BUTTER

After visiting Elizabeth Ryan at Breezy Hill Orchards, her farm in Dutchess County, New York (see page 482), I could hardly wait to get home and make apple butter. I had a dozen of her apple varieties in the back seat, and they filled the car with their heady fragrance.

I use a combination of apples in apple butter, to give it an extra depth of flavor, and I like it thick, smooth, and relatively tart, so I don't add any sugar.

Though I love apple butter on toast in the morning, it is versatile enough to serve at any time of the day. Sometimes I stir in a teaspoon of brandy to dress it up or use it in tarts and pastries. I also stir in cider vinegar to taste and use it as a condiment with meats or cheese.

12 to 14 pounds mixed apples, such as Jonagolds, Spies, Gravensteins, Golden Russets, Mutsus, and Criterions, peeled, cored, and quartered
Grated zest of 2 lemons
2 tablespoons freshly squeezed lemon juice, or more to taste
3 heaping teaspoons ground cinnamon
1½ teaspoons ground cloves
1 teaspoon ground ginger
½ teaspoon ground allspice
Pinch of salt

1 Place the apples in a large stockpot or kettle, and add about 2 cups of water, to reach about 1 inch up the side of the pot. Bring the water to a boil over medium-high heat. Reduce the heat to medium-low, cover, and cook until the apples are soft, about 45 minutes.

2 Preheat the oven to 300°F.

3 Strain the apples, or purée them in a food processor, and stir in the lemon zest, 2 tablespoons lemon juice, and the spices. Spoon as much of the purée as you can into a 12½ x 8½ x 2½-inch glass or enameled baking dish, leaving enough room to stir it. Transfer the dish to the center rack of the oven.

4 As the purée cooks down, add the remaining uncooked purée in batches until you have used it all. Stir it every 15 minutes or so, so it cooks evenly and doesn't stick to the dish. The apple butter

is done when it is thickened and a uniform reddish brown color, which will take about 4 hours. (The total cooking time will depend on how thick and concentrated you like your apple butter; cook it to your taste.)

5 Taste the apple butter for tartness, and add more lemon juice if necessary. Allow the apple butter to cool, then ladle into jars. Cover and refrigerate for 2 to 3

months. Or ladle the boiling-hot apple butter into hot sterilized canning jars and seal according to the lid manufacturer's instructions.

About 4 pints

BLUEBERRY SYRUP

Every fall, Nate Pennell makes pints of this syrup from the wild blueberries that grow all around his home in Machias, Maine (see page 444). Nate tries to keep himself on a strict low-sugar diet, but as he puts it, there's always room for a little blueberry syrup.

Serve this over pancakes, waffles, or biscuits for breakfast. For dessert, try it over ice cream or Old-Fashioned Indiana Cream Pie (see Index).

5 cups fresh wild or cultivated blueberries
1 cup plus 2 tablespoons sugar
½ cup plus 2 tablespoons water
1 teaspoon freshly squeezed lemon juice

1 Combine the berries, sugar, and water in a medium-size heavy saucepan over medium-high heat and bring to a boil, stirring. Adjust the heat so the mixture is boiling gently, and continue cooking, stirring occasionally, until the berries pop and look

somewhat shriveled, about 10 minutes. Stir in the lemon juice, and remove from the heat.

2 Allow the syrup to cool, then ladle into jars. Cover and refrigerate for 2 to 3 weeks. Or ladle the hot syrup into hot sterilized canning jars, and seal according to the lid manufacturer's instructions.

3 pints

HAZELNUTS BY ANY OTHER NAME

Tiny spiky red flowers and long fluffy golden catkins have been on the trees since midwinter in Benson Mitchell's Newberg, Oregon, hazelnut orchard, about an hour southwest of Portland. Benson, in his forties, ambles through the orchard, pointing at tender new growth on branches and the few husks still clinging to the tree from last year's crop. His dog, Squeak, throws last year's nuts up in the air, catches and cracks them in his teeth, then delicately removes the meats from the shell and eats them. Not the usual canine fare, but then most dogs don't have access to all-you-can-eat hazelnuts.

If left to grow wild, the hazelnut trees would be bushes. Benson prunes them each year so he can get his harvesting equipment through the orchard, and now they rise up to 30 feet above a smooth soil floor. "The floor has to be smooth because the nuts fall from the trees and mechanical harvesters sweep

them up," he said. He is proud of the almost complete lack of grass in this orchard, which is one of his oldest. "The aim is to get the orchard with a full canopy so the trees are using all the sunlight," he said. That keeps the ground dark and cool, and prevents vegetation from growing.

I SAY HAZELNUT, YOU SAY FILBERT

If you asked most of the 1,100 hazelnut orchardists in Oregon what they grow, it is unlikely any of them would say "hazelnuts." To an Oregonian, a hazelnut is a filbert, and though the term "hazelnut" is used for marketing purposes, it is done so grudgingly. "I call 'em filberts," Benson said emphatically. And Robert Gelhar, executive secretary of the Oregon Filbert Commission, pointed out that the names for all the major diseases affecting the nuts begin with "filbert." "There's the Eastern filbert blight, the filbert leaf roller, and the filbert worm," he said. "You don't hear anyone talking about a hazelnut worm."

Filbert or hazelnut, they're both the same

nut, and they've been around for centuries. According to scientific studies, the filbert bush was the dominant vegetation in northern Europe from 8000 to 5500 B.C. In 2830 B.C., it was listed as one of the five sacred nourishments in China, and in ancient Greece the nut was used to cure ills. The bush was associated with early European myth and

witchcraft, and its wood was often, and still is, the douser's stick in a search for water.

Hazelnut orchards cover about 25,000 acres of Oregon's mild, bucolic Willamette Valley, and they produce 98 percent of the domestic hazelnut crop, or about 15,000 tons a year. The other 2 percent comes from north of the border, in Clark County, Washington. Oregon ranks fourth in world production behind Turkey, Italy, and Spain.

The first hazelnut tree was planted in Oregon in 1858, but the industry dates to about the turn of the century, when the first commercial orchard was planted. Some of those early trees are still producing. "The trees will produce for over a hundred years, though the average production is fifty to seventy-five years," Benson said.

Though Benson Mitchell grew up around hazelnuts, he doesn't eat them often. His wife, Kayda, puts them in baked goods at Christmas, and takes toasted hazelnuts along when the couple get together with friends to play bridge. "Once I start eating them, I can't stop," she said, laughing.

A HAZELNUT BONANZA

In contrast, Marlyce Tolvstad, a neighbor of the Mitchells' in the nearby town of Dundee, Oregon, does everything she can think of with hazelnuts, and has ever since she and her ex-husband, Paul Tolvstad, bought 20 acres, including 3 of hazelnuts, 16 years ago.

"I used to grind the nuts by hand to use them for cookies," she said. "Then I got a food processor and started making nut butter. My son would look at me, roll his eyes, and tell his friends, 'Oh, that's my mom, she makes this hazelnut butter.' He still won't eat it."

Marlyce went to Europe in 1980, saw all the things hazelnuts were used in, and came home with a resolve to market her nut butters. She perfected several recipes, leased a nut grinder, and set up shop with a friend—first in her kitchen, then in a small garage at the side of her home. Having bought out her partner, Marlyce now has a thriving business and sells nut butters all over the country under the Dundee Orchards label.

"We came out in the fall of 1984 with creamy and crunchy hazelnut butter," she said. Then came a walnut and hazelnut mix, a chocolate hazelnut butter, and now she's working on a peanut hazelnut butter.

"I just love the nuts, and I use them in any way I can," she said.

HAZELNUT BUTTER

Peanuts aren't the only nuts that can be transformed into a luscious butter. Toasted hazelnuts take on a rich amber flavor, and a butter made with them is nothing short of elegant. Use this for the Dundee Orchards French Toast (see Index), add it to cookies, spread it on crackers, or mix it with a chocolate icing for a real flavor treat.

2 cups skinned toasted hazelnuts (see Note)

Place the hazelnuts in a food processor, and process until they are puréed, stopping to scrape the sides of the bowl occasionally. Transfer the butter to an airtight container, and refrigerate. Hazelnut Butter will keep, tightly covered and refrigerated, for several weeks; frozen, for several months.

1 cup

Note: To toast hazelnuts; preheat the oven to 350° F. Place the nuts in a baking pan large enough to hold them in a single layer and toast, stirring once, until they give off a toasted aroma, 10 to 15 minutes. Wrap the nuts in a kitchen towel and rub them between your hands to remove the skin.

GLAZED GARLIC CLOVES

Ron Zimmerman, owner and chef of the Herbfarm and the Herbfarm Restaurant in Falls City, Washington, serves these garlic cloves with roast breast of duck (see page 178). They are absolutely incredible, not just because of their unexpected natural sweetness, but because they enhance the slight liver flavor of the duck breast. Even those who think they are not garlic fans will love these golden cloves, because the heat of garlic melts away in the cooking.

Serve Garlic Glazed Cloves with any roast meat, poultry, or seafood, or in combination with just about any vegetable.

48 large cloves garlic, peeled
1½ cups milk
3 tablespoons unsalted butter
1 tablespoon sugar
¼ teaspoon salt
Freshly ground black pepper

1 Place the garlic cloves and the milk in a small saucepan over medium heat, and bring to a boil. Reduce the heat to low, and simmer for 5 minutes. Drain the garlic, dis-carding the milk (do not rinse the garlic)

2 Melt the butter in a medium-size saucepan over medium heat. Stir in the sugar and salt, and then add the garlic cloves. Stir so they are coated with the but-ter mixture. Reduce the heat to low, and cook until the garlic cloves are caramelized on the outside and very soft on the inside, shaking the pan often so they caramelize evenly, 20 to 25 minutes. Season to taste with pepper, remove from the heat, and set aside until ready to use. The glazed garlic cloves can be cooked up to 1 week in ad-vance if stored, covered, in the refrigerator. Reheat in a small saucepan, covered, over low heat.

4 to 6 servings

BARNEY'S SWITCHEL

B arney Smith, who raises longhorn cattle, wheat, and Morgan horses in Iowa, maintains that this switchel—an old-fashioned recipe— quenches his thirst better than anything else, and he always has a bottle of it in the refrigerator for those hot hardworking days.

I agree with him, and I make this frequently during the summer. Try it over ice; you'll find it deli-cious, and tonic as well. Be sure to shake the bottle before pouring, as the ginger settles to the bottom.

This switchel will last almost indefinitely in the refrigerator— though you may never have it that long, as it is a tempting, beguilingly refreshing drink.

1 cup sugar

7 tablespoons cider vinegar

1 tablespoon grated fresh ginger, or 1 teaspoon
   ground ginger

¼ cup freshly squeezed lemon juice

8 cups cold water

Mix all the ingredients together in a large bottle or jar, and shake thoroughly. Refrigerate before drinking.

2 quarts

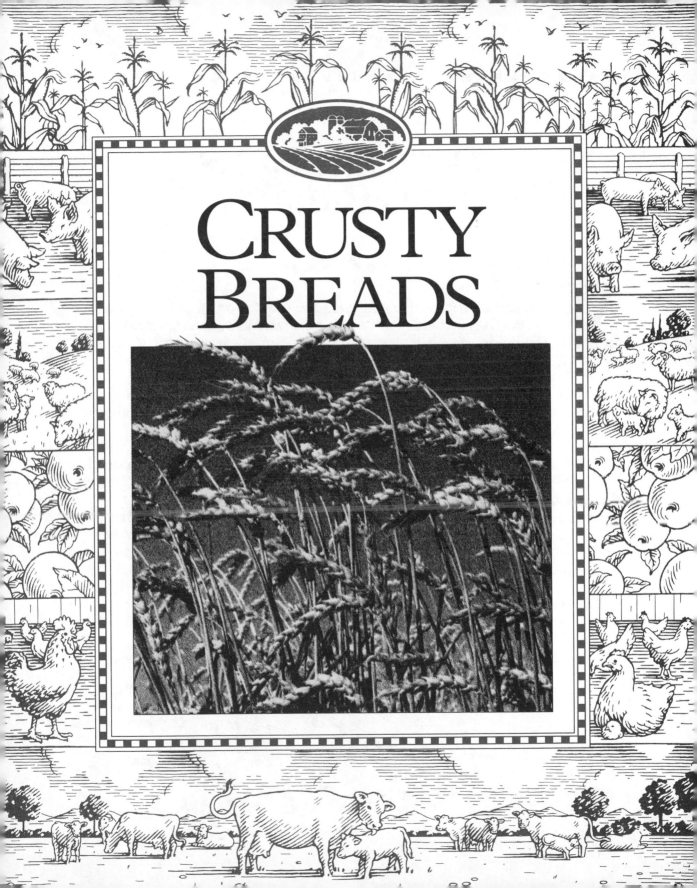

CRUSTY BREADS

BUTTERY BUNS AND BREADS

What can be more appealing than the yeasty aroma of freshly baking bread? It fills the air with a palpable warm sweetness, and when the golden results emerge from the oven, it's impossible to resist at least one steaming piece.

My repertoire of doughs increased dramatically through the hours I spent in warm farm kitchens, and I learned little tips and picked up hints that have given my baking an added richness of flavor and texture.

I learned when to let a yeast dough sit for 15 minutes before kneading, for a lighter result; I found that many contemporary recipes call for too much flour, and that old-fashioned doughs give more tender results. I've learned the feel of a good dough, the right time to add more flour, the perfect length of rising time. Never has my kitchen produced such fragrant delights, and I've passed them all along to you.

I wanted to find the best possible crescent roll, and a quick biscuit that floated off the plate. As you turn the pages, you'll find these and more. You'd best be prepared, because these recipes will have you in the kitchen, dusted with flour, before you can say "buttery buns and breads from the farmhouse bakery."

FARMHOUSE WHITE BREAD

H omemade bread is still a standard on many farms throughout America. More often than not, the loaves produced are like this one—simple, yeasty, and white. This fine-grained bread is wonderful fresh from the oven, sliced and used for sandwiches as is or toasted. And you can make it from start to finish in 2½ hours.

This is the recipe I use for the crust of an apple charlotte. The bread has a simple flavor, and it makes a perfect foil for the sweet golden apples (see page 485). When I'm baking it for the charlotte, I let the dough rise until it is almost at the edge of the loaf pan, but not quite. Then I cover the loaf pan with a piece of lightly buttered aluminum foil, fold it securely under the edges of the pan, and place several heavy baking sheets on top to keep the loaf flat while it bakes. That way, the cut slices are symmetrical, and there is little waste when trimming the bread for the charlotte. This method will impress your friends as well, because it results in a square bread that looks just as if it had come from the store!

1 package active dry yeast
1 cup lukewarm water
1 tablespoon sugar
2¾ to 3 cups unbleached all-purpose
 flour
2 tablespoons unsalted butter, at room
 temperature
1 teaspoon salt

1 In a large bowl, dissolve the yeast in the lukewarm water. Stir in the sugar, and mix well. When there are some bubbles on top of the liquid, after about 2 minutes, add 1 cup of the flour, the butter, and the salt, and mix well. Gradually add the remaining flour until the dough becomes too stiff to stir.

2 Turn the dough out onto a lightly floured surface, and knead until it is smooth and elastic, about 10 minutes. Add flour as you work if the dough is too sticky. Don't add too much, however—the dough should not be too firm.

3 Place the dough in a bowl or on a lightly floured surface in a warm spot (68°to 70°F), cover with a kitchen towel, and let it rise until doubled in bulk, about 45 minutes.

4 Preheat the oven to 375°F. Lightly oil a 9 x 5 x 3-inch loaf pan.

5 Punch the dough down, shape it into a loaf, and place it in the prepared loaf pan. Place the pan in a warm spot (68°to 70°F), and cover loosely with a towel. Let it rise either until it doesn't quite reach the edge of the pan (for a charlotte) or until it is just slightly over the edge, which will take about 30 minutes.

6 If you are using the bread for a charlotte, cover the pan with a piece of lightly oiled aluminum foil, tucking it securely under the edges of the pan. Place the pan in the center of the oven, and set several heavy baking sheets on top of it, to keep the bread from rising higher than the sides of the pan. Bake until the loaf sounds hollow when you tap the sides of the pan, about 30 minutes.

If you want to use the bread for toast or sandwiches, do not cover the pan. Using a sharp knife, slash the top of the loaf in several places, and bake until it sounds hollow when tapped, about 30 minutes.

7 Remove the loaf from the oven, and turn it out immediately onto a wire rack to cool.

1 loaf

HONEY CORNMEAL YEAST BREAD

M y husband, Michael and I had stopped in a small town outside Helena, Montana, for a lunch break on our way to the Berner farm in Loma, just north of Great Falls. As we wandered through town, stretching our legs, we were lured to a tiny storefront by the aroma of fresh bread.

A sandwich board out front advertised a slab of bread with butter just for walking in, so we did, and found an active bakery, a line of customers waiting, and a wooden butcher block with a loaf of corn bread on it. A young woman cut us slabs that were at least 2 inches thick and covered them with sweet butter. As we munched away, we tried to figure out what this place was.

It turned out to be one of the Great Harvest stores, a chain that began in Montana and has spread across the West. The couple who began Great Harvest mill all the grains for the breads and distribute them to the various stores. They insist that part of the advertising be an endless supply of samples, and that the quality of the breads—which is very high—never waver.

We were won over by the corn bread, which is sweet, yeasty, and cakey all at once. This is my version and there's nothing quite like it, toasted, with a morning cup of coffee.

3 cups milk
8 tablespoons (1 stick) unsalted butter
½ cup mild honey
2 teaspoons salt
2 packages active dry yeast
¼ cup lukewarm water
4 cups cornmeal
4 to 6 cups unbleached all-purpose
*   flour*

1 Place the milk, butter, honey, and salt in a medium-size saucepan over medium heat, and heat until the butter has melted. Remove from the heat and let cool to room temperature.

DOUGH HOOKS

▪▪▪▪▪

*I*f your electric mixer has a dough hook, use it in any recipe in this chapter calling for kneading the dough. It will certainly shorten kneading time and make your life a bit easier.

2 Dissolve the yeast in the lukewarm water in a large bowl, or in the bowl of an electric mixer.

3 Once the milk mixture has cooled to lukewarm, combine it with the yeast mixture.

4 Mix in the cornmeal. Then add the flour, about 1½ cups at a time, until the dough is too stiff to mix with a spoon or with the mixer. Turn the dough out onto a well-floured surface, knead it several times, and let it sit, loosely covered with a towel, for 15 minutes.

5 Knead the dough until is smooth and elastic, about 8 minutes, adding more flour if necessary to keep it from sticking to your hands. Don't use more than 6 cups of flour; the dough should be soft, not firm.

6 Place the dough in a bowl, cover loosely with a damp towel or a plate, and let rise in a warm spot (68° to 70°F) until it has doubled in bulk, about 2 hours.

7 Heavily flour two 10-inch metal or ceramic pie plates.

8 Punch the dough down, divide it in half, and shape each half into a round ball. Place the balls, seam side down, in the prepared pie plates, pressing down gently so the dough fills the pan. Cover loosely with a kitchen towel, and let rise in a warm spot until nearly doubled in bulk, about 30 minutes.

9 Preheat the oven to 375°F.

10 Using a sharp knife, make several slashes in the top of each loaf. Bake in the center of the oven until the loaves are golden and sound hollow when tapped sharply with a finger, about 35 minutes.

2 large (about 2½-pound) loaves

MILLET BREAD

This hearty bread makes you feel good with every bite. It's slightly sweet, dense and moist, and wonderful warm with cheese after supper, or for toast in the morning with butter and honey.

Millet bread rises quickly and can be made from start to finish in 3½ hours. The millet gives it a toothsome crunch, and the rye and whole-wheat flours combine to produce a rich, complex flavor.

2 packages active dry yeast
2 cups warm water
¼ cup molasses
2 tablespoons mild honey
2½ cups whole-wheat flour
1 cup rye flour
2½ teaspoons salt
1 cup millet
1½ to 2 cups unbleached all-purpose flour

1 Combine the yeast, water, molasses, and honey in a large mixing bowl, or in the bowl of an electric mixer, and mix until combined. Add the whole-wheat flour, and stir until combined. Then add the rye flour and the salt, and mix well. Add the millet, mix well, and then add enough of the all-purpose flour (about 1½ cups) to make a fairly firm dough.

2 Turn the dough out onto a lightly floured surface and let it rest for 15 minutes. Then, knead until it is elastic, adding more all-purpose flour as needed, 3 to 5 minutes. The dough will still feel somewhat sticky, and the millet grains will keep popping out as you knead; just corral them by kneading the dough right over them.

3 Place the dough in a bowl, cover with a kitchen towel, and let rise in a warm spot (68° to 70°F) until it has doubled in bulk, about 1½ hours.

4 Either line two 8½ x 4½-inch loaf pans with parchment paper, or lightly oil the pans.

5 Punch the dough down, divide it in half, and shape it into two loaves. Place them in the prepared pans, cover loosely

with a kitchen towel, and let rise until doubled in bulk, about 1 hour.

6 Preheat the oven to 400°F.

7 Using a sharp knife, make several slashes in the tops of the loaves. Bake the loaves in the center of the oven until they are golden and sound hollow when tapped sharply with a finger, about 35 minutes. Remove them from the oven and turn them out onto wire racks to cool.

2 loaves

CARYL'S MOLASSES BREAD

Caryl Smith, of Brighton, Iowa, gave me the recipe for this bread. It sounds hearty—and it is full of flavor—but it has a soft, delicate, sweet texture. It is good fresh from the oven, it makes excellent toast, and it is ideal to serve with cheeses, especially Greek teleme, a sharp New York Cheddar, or a fancy cheese like Gloucester or Wensleydale.

I use unsulphured molasses when I want its deep, hearty flavor. Otherwise I use regular molasses. This bread freezes very well.

2 cups boiling water
1 cup rolled oats
½ cup molasses
1 tablespoon unsalted butter, melted
½ cup lukewarm water
1 package active dry yeast
2 teaspoons salt
5 cups unbleached all-purpose flour

1 Combine the boiling water and the oats in a large bowl, stir, and set aside for 1 hour.

2 Stir the molasses, butter, and lukewarm water together in a small bowl. Then add the yeast, and stir until it dissolves. Stir in the salt, and then add the mixture to the oats. Mix well.

3 Add the flour, 1 cup at a time, stirring vigorously after each addition. When the dough becomes too stiff to stir, turn it out onto a floured surface and work the remaining flour into it. Let it rest for 15 minutes, then continue kneading the dough until it is smooth and elastic, 5 to 10 minutes more.

4 Lightly oil two 9 x 5 x 3-inch loaf pans.

5 Place the dough on a lightly floured surface or in a bowl, sprinkle it lightly with flour, cover with a kitchen towel, and set aside to rise in a warm spot (68° to 70°F) until it has doubled in bulk, about 2 hours.

6 Punch the dough down and knead it again for several minutes, to get all the air out. Divide the dough in half, and shape each piece into a loaf. Place each loaf in a prepared loaf pan, cover loosely with a kitchen towel, and set aside to rise in a warm spot until almost doubled, about 2 hours.

7 Preheat the oven to 375°F.

8 Using a sharp knife, slash the tops of the loaves in several places. Bake the loaves in the center of the oven until they are deep golden and sound hollow when tapped sharply with a finger, about 35 minutes.

9 Remove the loaves from the oven and turn them out onto wire racks. Let them cool for at least 10 minutes before slicing.

2 loaves

Note: To store the bread, wrap it in aluminum foil (don't put it in a plastic bag unless you don't mind if the crust becomes soft). To prepare it for freezing, let the loaves cool thoroughly. Wrap them in a double layer of foil, then seal them in plastic bags and freeze. They will keep for several weeks in the freezer.

BARNEY'S COUSIN'S HUSBAND'S LIGHT RYE BREAD

This bread—like most yeast breads—is so easy that it makes itself, particularly with the help of an electric mixer. It is a wonderful bread for sandwiches (if there is any left after it comes from the oven—it is uncommonly good when freshly baked).

The ample amount of yeast makes for quick rising and gives it a lightness despite the rye flour, which has no gluten and adds little bounce of its own accord. One thing I've found about rye flour is that it changes its personality in the summer, becoming somewhat ropey and stringy. The results, however, are just as good as they are in winter.

This bread will keep well for up to 4 days if tightly wrapped in aluminum foil. Don't refrigerate it, which will dry it out and shorten its life by several days.

By the way, Barney is farmer Barney Smith of Brighton, Iowa (see page 112). His cousin's husband I have yet to encounter—all I know is he makes a mean loaf of rye.

2 packages active dry yeast
2½ cups lukewarm water
¼ cup mild honey
4 tablespoons (½ stick) unsalted butter, melted and cooled
1 tablespoon salt
2 tablespoons caraway seeds
3 cups medium-ground rye flour
4 to 4½ cups unbleached all-purpose flour

1 Dissolve the yeast in the lukewarm water in a large bowl or the bowl of an electric mixer. Add the honey, butter, salt, and caraway seeds, and mix well, then add the rye flour, and mix well.

2 Add the all-purpose flour, 1 cup at a time, mixing until the dough begins to become elastic and somewhat stiff. At medium speed (about #6) on an electric mixer, this will take up to 5 minutes.

3 When the dough becomes too stiff to mix, turn it out onto a lightly floured surface and knead it until it is smooth, 5 to 10 minutes, incorporating more all-purpose flour if necessary to keep it from sticking.

4 Return the dough to the bowl, cover it with a kitchen towel, and let it rise in a warm spot (68° to 70°F) until it has doubled in bulk, 1½ to 2 hours.

5 Butter and flour two 8½ x 4-inch loaf pans.

6 Punch the dough down, and knead it for two or three turns. Divide it in half, shape each piece into a loaf, and place them in the prepared pans. Cover them loosely with a kitchen towel, and let them rise in a warm spot until doubled in bulk, about 1½ hours.

7 Preheat the oven to 375°F.

8 Using a sharp knife, make several slashes in the top of each loaf. Bake in the center of the oven until they are golden and sound hollow when tapped sharply with a finger, 30 to 40 minutes. Remove the loaves from the oven, and turn them out onto wire racks to cool.

2 loaves

FINN BREAD

I've been eating this bread for years, ever since my brother, John, and Stuart Yatsko became friends at school. Stuart would occasionally arrive at our house carrying a loaf, freshly baked by his mother, Ramona Takala Yatsko, who had learned the recipe from her mother Aili Takala.

I was lucky enough to visit Stuart's grandparents, Bill and Aili Takala, at their ranch near Great Falls, Montana. Aili treated me like one of her own, pulling out her favorite recipes, and cooking and baking as though it was a grand occasion.

I like to use graham flour in this bread, which is very finely ground whole-wheat flour. That, along with the addition of all-purpose flour and the cracked wheat releasing its heat and energy, makes the bread surprisingly light.

1 cup milk
2 tablespoons unsalted butter, melted
2 tablespoons honey
1½ teaspoons salt
1 cup water
1 package active dry yeast
½ cup wheat berries (available at natural
  foods stores)
2½ cups graham or whole-wheat
  flour
2½ to 3 cups unbleached all-purpose
  flour

1 Heat the milk with the butter in a small
saucepan over medium-high heat just
until little bubbles form around the edge of
the milk. Transfer it to a large bowl, add the
honey, salt, and ¾ cup of the water, and set
aside until lukewarm.

2 Dissolve the yeast in the remaining ¼
cup water in a large bowl, or in the
bowl of an electric mixer.

3 Place the wheat berries in a food processor, and process until they are
coarsely cracked. This makes a horrific
amount of noise and takes 2 to 3 minutes.
Most of the berries will be cracked in small
pieces, and some will be ground into flour.

4 When the milk mixture has cooled to
lukewarm, add the yeast mixture and
stir. Stir in the cracked wheat, and then add
the whole-wheat flour. Mix well, and set the
dough aside for 10 minutes, to allow the
gluten to relax.

5 Add the all-purpose flour, 1 cup at a
time, until the dough becomes too stiff

to stir. Turn it out onto a generously floured
surface, and knead in the remaining flour.
Let the dough sit for 15 minutes. Then continue kneading until it no longer sticks to
the surface or to your fingers, 8 to 10 minutes. The dough will become elastic, but it
will remain surprisingly soft for a whole-
wheat dough. Be careful not to add too
much flour—you don't want the dough to
be very hard or firm, but light and springy.

6 Form the dough into a ball, place it in
a bowl, cover it with a damp kitchen
towel, and let it rise in a warm spot (68° to
70°F) until it has doubled in bulk, about
1½ hours.

7 Generously flour two round cake pans
or two baking sheets.

8 Punch the dough down, and knead it
just enough to knock the air out of it.
Divide it in half, and form the halves into
balls. Place them in the prepared pans or on
the baking sheets, cover with damp towels,
and let rise just until they have doubled in
bulk, about 1 hour. (Don't let them rise too
much. It's better to catch them just before
they've doubled than just after, so check
them occasionally after 45 minutes. The
rising time will differ slightly, depending
on the room temperature.)

9 Preheat the oven to 350°F.

10 Poke the tops of the loaves in several
places with the tines of a fork, or
slash them with a sharp knife. Bake the
loaves in the center of the oven until they

are golden and sound hollow when tapped sharply with a finger, 35 to 45 minutes.

11 Remove the loaves from the oven, and turn them out on wire racks to cool.

2 loaves

PULLA
(FINNISH COFFEE BREAD)

This is Aili Takala's renowned coffee bread which she used to take out to the farmhands for their break. She often serves it at dinner too, for though it is sweet it goes well with a meal. The recipe makes three good-size loaves, so you can freeze some for a rainy day.

When you make this loaf, don't incorporate more than 9 cups of flour, though you may be tempted to do so. It is a very tender bread and the dough is meant to be soft, though not sticky. Be sure to let it rise the required amount of time so it doubles in bulk twice, which will add to its tenderness. Also be sure to let it rest the required 15 minutes before kneading, so it has a chance to relax.

1 package active dry yeast

½ cup warm water

1 cup warm milk

½ cup sugar

½ teaspoon salt

1 slightly heaping teaspoon freshly ground cardamom (seeds from about 10 pods)

3 large eggs, beaten

4½ to 5½ cups sifted unbleached all-purpose flour

4 tablespoons (½ stick) unsalted butter, melted

FOR THE TOPPING

¼ cup raw almonds

¼ cup sugar

1 large egg

2 teaspoons water

A LITTLE SAUNA COFFEE

Saturday nights on the farm were always a special occasion for Aili and Bill Takala—a respite from the week's work, a time to spend with other Finnish neighbors.

The Saturday gatherings followed Finnish tradition beginning with a steaming sauna followed by strong black coffee and delicate cakes and cookies. They were always held at the Takalas because Bill, who is a skilled carpenter, had transformed part of the original white clapboard homestead, which sits apart from the Takalas' house, into a roomy sauna.

"When everybody came here on Saturdays, we would sit around and talk about the homeland," Aili said. "I loved those times. It kept you close to everyone at home."

My husband and I got to experience our own version of sauna-coffee at the Takalas. The sauna was heated and waiting for us after supper our first night there, and we didn't hesitate a moment.

We quickly walked through the cold, quiet air to the small building at the end of the drive. Inside, it was warm from a wood stove surrounded by rocks that radiated intense heat, and fragrant with the aroma of the cedar benches that lined the walls. Pans of cold water were filled in readiness, and we poured some on the rocks to create clouds of soothing steam.

Our muscles softened as we relaxed on the benches. We jolted them by rinsing ourselves with the water, then relaxed and rinsed a few times more. Finally we dressed and made our way out into the night, whose chill now felt like a caress. Had it been winter, with its usual heavy blanket of snow, we would have been obliged to dash out and roll in it to cool off, in good Finnish fashion!

Our cheeks red from the heat, we walked into the kitchen, where Aili waited with a platter of a dozen varieties of cookies and a jug of strong coffee. Aili led us through some memories of her homeland, and through a few more about the warm friendship-filled Saturday nights on the farm.

1 Dissolve the yeast in the warm water. Stir in the milk and sugar. When there are some bubbles on top of the liquid, after about 2 minutes, add the salt, cardamom, eggs, and 3½ cups of the flour. Mix well, until the batter is smooth and elastic.

2 Add the melted butter, and stir until it is thoroughly combined and the dough is glossy. Then gradually add enough of the remaining flour to make a soft dough. Turn the dough out onto a lightly floured work surface, cover it with the mixing bowl, and let it rest for 15 minutes.

3 Knead the dough just until it is satiny, which should take just a few minutes. The dough will be somewhat soft, but it shouldn't stick to your hands or to the work surface. If it is very wet and sticks to your

fingers, add a bit of flour, using no more than ½ cup.

4 Place the dough in a lightly oiled mixing bowl, turn it to oil all sides, and cover lightly with a kitchen towel. Let rise in a warm spot (68° to 70°F) until it has doubled in bulk, about 2 hours.

5 Punch the dough down, return it to the bowl, cover, and let rise until it has doubled again, about 1½ hours.

6 Lightly oil two baking sheets.

7 Turn the dough out onto a lightly floured flat work surface. Punch the dough down, and divide it into 9 pieces. Roll each piece into a rope that is about 12 inches long. Braid three ropes together to form a loaf. Press the ends together and place the loaf on a baking sheet. Repeat with the remaining dough to form two more loaves. Two loaves will fit on one baking sheet, the third loaf on the other, so they

have room to rise. Let the loaves rise until they have increased by about one third, which should take 25 minutes.

8 Preheat the oven to 400°F.

9 Make the topping: Place the almonds and sugar in a food processor and process until the almonds are unevenly chopped—some should be fine, some in small chunks.

10 Whisk the egg with the water in another small bowl. Brush the loaves thoroughly with the egg glaze and sprinkle with the almond and sugar mixture. Bake in the center of the oven until the loaves are golden and sound hollow when tapped with a finger, about 30 minutes.

11 Remove the loaves from the oven and transfer them to a wire rack to cool.

3 loaves

OVEN-FRESH CRESCENT ROLLS

These rolls are so light that you have to hold them down to keep them from floating out of the basket. Well, almost. The recipe makes a lot, but the rolls are so good that leftovers are rare.

My grandmother made these for us at Thanksgiving, and they are as much a part of my memories of her, that day, and my childhood as anything. We all looked forward to them with anticipation, because that was the only time she made them during the year. No one else in my family tried to make them. It was as if that wouldn't have been possible—they were hers, she made them, and that was that.

It wasn't until my grandmother had died and my mother began making them that I discovered there was a recipe, and though my grandmother had a special touch, it was possible to attempt a re-creation of her rolls.

I now make crescent rolls several times a year. The first time my husband tasted one, he took a bite, thought for a moment, and said to the table at large, "These rolls taste like a memory." I knew just what he meant, and I think my grandmother would approve.

There is a secret to the tenderness of these rolls: Don't add a fleck more flour than the recipe calls for. You will want to, because the dough is very soft, but resist the temptation or they will toughen. Also, don't handle the dough too much—just knead it a few times, so the flour is thoroughly incorporated, then let it rise long and slowly. The final 4-hour rising is very important. Don't stint on it.

You can easily make these in an electric mixer. The trick is not to overbeat them, so mix them just until the flour is incorporated into the dough. Then turn the dough out onto a floured surface and finish the rolls by hand.

I like to bake these rolls right before we sit down at the table so they can be enjoyed warm from the oven. They are best eaten the day they are made.

1 cup milk
8 tablespoons (1 stick) unsalted butter, at room temperature
1 package active dry yeast
½ cup sugar
4½ cups all-purpose flour
2 large eggs
1 teaspoon salt

1 Heat the milk over medium-high heat just until tiny bubbles form around the edge of the milk. Pour the scalded milk into a large bowl, or the bowl of an electric mixer, and add the butter. Stir until the butter has melted. Then set the bowl aside until the mixture is lukewarm.

2 Stir the yeast and sugar into the milk. When there are some bubbles on top of the liquid, add 1 cup of the flour and mix well. Then add the eggs, one at a time, beating well after each addition. Add the salt and 1 more cup of flour, and mix vigorously until the dough is elastic and smooth, at least 6 minutes by hand, 3 minutes on medium speed (#6) in an electric mixer.

3 If you are mixing by hand, add the remaining 2½ cups flour, and mix until the dough is slightly firmer but still very soft and smooth. Turn it out onto a lightly floured surface, and knead just until it is smooth, which will take 2 to 3 minutes.

If you are using an electric mixer, add the 2½ cups flour and mix just until it is incorporated. Then turn the dough out onto a lightly floured surface, and continue kneading by hand until it is smooth.

4 Place the dough in a bowl, cover it with a kitchen towel, and set it aside to rise in a warm spot (68° to 70°F) until it has doubled in bulk, about 2 hours.

5 Lightly flour two baking sheets.

6 Turn the dough out onto a well-floured surface, divide it in half, and roll each half out to form a circle that is

⅛ inch thick and 16 inches in diameter. Cut each circle into quarters, and cut each quarter into four wedges. Roll the wedges up, beginning at the wide end, to form crescents.

7 Place the rolls on the prepared baking sheets, leaving 2 inches between them and arranging them with the tips rolled underneath, so they won't pop up during rising and baking. Cover the rolls with a kitchen towel, and let them rise in a warm spot (68° to 70°F) until they have nearly doubled in size, at least 4 hours.

8 Preheat the oven to 350°F.

9 Bake the rolls in the center of the oven until they are golden, 10 to 12 minutes. Remove, and serve immediately.

32 rolls

LaRene Reed's Idaho Potato Rolls

The recipe for these rolls is an old one from the Reed family (Idaho potato growers, see page 366), and it makes enough for crowd. I worried about taking LaRene's own handwritten copy, but she said, "Don't worry. I know it by heart."

Potato rolls are tender, moist, and slightly sweet. They go well with just about any meal, and they make a wonderful breakfast with fresh butter and honey.

You may be tempted to add extra flour because the dough is so soft and moist, but don't. Just add enough so that you can handle the dough without having it stick to your hands and the work surface, then dust it with plenty of flour to roll it out. These are quick to make, and you may find yourself with fresh-baked rolls on the table more often than you ever thought possible.

1 large Russet potato, boiled and well mashed
  (1 cup)
1 cup warm water
½ cup sugar
2 packages active dry yeast
4 to 4½ cups unbleached all-purpose flour
3 large eggs
8 tablespoons (1 stick) unsalted butter,
  melted
1 teaspoon salt

1 Lightly oil two 7 x 11 x 1½-inch baking pans.

2 Place the mashed potato, water, sugar, and yeast in a large bowl. Mix well with a wire whisk. Add 1 cup of the flour, and whisk until the mixture is quite smooth, about 2 minutes. (There may be some lumps from the potato, which is fine.) Add another ½ cup flour, and mix until smooth. Cover with a kitchen towel, set in a warm spot (68° to 70°F), and let rise until doubled in bulk, about 1 hour.

3 Add the eggs to this mixture, one at a time, mixing vigorously after each addition. Add the butter and salt, and mix well. Then gradually add 2½ cups flour, mixing quite vigorously. When the dough becomes too awkward to mix in the bowl, turn it out onto a lightly floured surface, and knead it until it is smooth, 5 to 10 minutes. Add flour (no more than an additional ½ cup) as you knead to keep the dough from sticking to the work surface and your hands. It will still be very soft—softer than bread dough.

4 Heavily flour the dough and the work surface, and roll the dough out until it is ¾ inch thick. Cut the dough into 2-inch squares and place them in the prepared pans, leaving about ¼ inch of space between them. Cover loosely with a damp kitchen towel and set aside to rise in a warm spot (68° to 70°F) until they have nearly doubled in bulk, 1½ to 2 hours.

5 Preheat the oven to 350°F.

6 Bake the rolls in the center of the oven until they are golden and puffed, about 12 minutes. Turn them out of the pans onto a wire cooling rack, let cool for 5 minutes, and then serve.

About 2 dozen

IF IT'S IDAHO, IT MUST BE POTATOES

LeRoy Reed started farming potatoes in Idaho with his father in 1955 and continued with his two brothers until 1982. Now retired, his son, Brian, has taken over.

The elder Reeds are never far away from potatoes, however. There's a lush, healthy field right beyond their backyard, and a sod-covered storage cellar is dug into the earth to one side of the house.

The Reeds grow Burbank Russets, the fluffy Idaho potato. "They're tricky to grow," LeRoy says. "All you have to do is go out and look at a Russet with a sour face, and it'll get a knot or a blemish."

Idaho has the ideal soil and climate for the Russet Burbank, but one problem the potato industry faces is getting an early jump on the market. The Burbank Russet isn't ready to harvest until late September, and all the potatoes seem to come in at the same time, which causes prices to drop. Plant breeders are at work developing an earlier potato. "It looks like it'll be called the Frontier Russet," LeRoy says. Once available, it will be ready to harvest by the end of August, which will extend the season and result in better prices to the grower.

THE PERFECT CLIMATE

The air is cool and moist inside the storage building. "Potatoes need moisture, so before we bring them in from the field, we water the floor of the building to create humidity," LeRoy explains. They pile the potatoes in the building and run huge fans on them at night, to bring in the cool Idaho air and reduce the temperature of the potatoes to about 40°F.

"A potato is a living organism, and it respires," LeRoy says. "It heats up in here, and they start to sweat and lose weight, so we put on a humidifier and it keeps them moist."

It's fortunate that the Reeds have a steady supply of potatoes, because they're never short of family to feed. LeRoy's two brothers and two sisters live within a 5-mile range and so do his sons, one of whom runs a dairy just a few miles away. One of the specialties there is low-fat ice cream and yogurt made with potatoes.

ALICE BERNER'S CORN BREAD

This recipe comes from Alice Berner, who farms 3,000 acres of wheat in northern Montana with her husband, Bud, and daughter, Bonnie. The Berners farm without fertilizers or pesticides, and their commitment to health follows through in the kitchen.

Alice has developed a repertoire of baked goods calling for honey and whole-wheat flour rather than sugar and white flour. This corn bread doesn't have a pinch of white flour in it, yet it is light and moist, and much more flavorful than traditional corn bread. It is a sweet bread, so take that into account when you consider what it will accompany. I like to serve it with roast chicken, the Hearty Vegetable Soup (see Index), or for breakfast with butter and honey.

1½ cups yellow cornmeal
2 cups whole-wheat flour
4 teaspoons baking powder
1¼ teaspoons salt
4 large eggs, separated
¾ cup honey
¼ cup mild vegetable oil, such as safflower
1⅓ cups milk

1 Preheat the oven to 425°F. Oil a 9 x 13-inch baking pan.

2 Combine the dry ingredients in a large mixing bowl. In a small bowl, mix together the egg yolks, honey, oil, and milk until thoroughly combined. Make a well in the dry ingredients, and pour the liquid ingredients into it. Gradually stir the dry ingredients into the liquids, working quickly and gently.

3 Add a pinch of salt to the egg whites, and beat them until they hold stiff peaks. Gently fold them into the batter, then pour the batter into the prepared pan. Bake until the corn bread is golden and springs back when lightly touched, about 20 minutes.

8 to 10 servings

ANNE FRIAR THOMAS'S HOT PEPPER CORN BREAD

There are as many recipes for corn bread, it seems, as there are southern cooks. This one is a favorite of Anne Friar Thomas, who makes it to serve to her ranch crew. She adds hot peppers to heat it up and fresh corn kernels to sweeten it. Even with the peppers and corn, however, it calls for butter and a drizzle of honey. Serve this with a hearty soup, salad, or stew—or as Anne does, with barbecued ribs.

1 cup yellow cornmeal
⅔ cup unbleached all-purpose flour
½ teaspoon salt
2 teaspoons baking powder
⅛ teaspoon baking soda
2 tablespoons sugar (optional)
2 tablespoons unsalted butter or lard
1 large egg
⅓ cup sour cream
¾ cup milk
2 serrano peppers, or 1 jalapeño pepper, stemmed and cut into thin rounds
1 cup corn kernels, fresh or frozen

1 Preheat the oven to 400°F.

2 Sift the dry ingredients together into a medium-size mixing bowl.

3 Place the butter in a 9-inch square baking pan, and put it in the oven to melt and to heat the pan, 3 to 5 minutes. While the butter is melting, whisk together the egg, sour cream, and milk in a small bowl. Stir the mixture quickly into the dry ingredients, just until all the ingredients are moistened. Do not overmix, or the corn bread will be tough. Fold in the chile peppers and the corn kernels.

4 Swirl the butter around in the hot pan, then pour in the batter, and bake in the center of the oven until the corn bread is golden and springs back when lightly touched, 20 to 25 minutes. Cool for 5 minutes before serving.

6 to 8 servings

SYLVIA'S JOHNNYCAKE

Sylvia Dufner lives with her husband, Don, and their three nearly adult sons on a farm in the northeast corner of North Dakota. Together they raise beans, everything from plain old navy beans to more exotic black beans, for the organic market (see page 161).

Until recently Sylvia worked in the fields alongside her husband and sons, stopping three to four times a day to drive home and prepare meals. She's been on strike for the past couple of years, however. "I used to bake and cook and bake and cook, and the more I did, the more everyone ate," she said. "I decided it was time to quit. I taught my sons how to cook and how to iron, and now, except for special occasions, if they're hungry and I've got something else to do, they cook their own meals."

We were sitting and talking about women on the farm, while Don and her sons showed off their John Deere tractor collection to my husband. "You know, it just didn't seem right that I worked alongside them all day, and they came home to relax and I was still cooking," she said.

Strong words from a loving mother, but easily understood. Despite her protestations there were sweet, soft brownies and freshly made sandwiches for the 6 o'clock lunch (a snack before a late-evening supper), and eager talk of her favorite recipes.

Johnnycake tops her list of favorites. She explains the name this way: "It was called journey cake because it lasted well on journeys in the old days." That was when fast-food restaurants weren't even a twinkle in a developer's eye. (Others say the name of this cakelike bread came from the South, where it was eaten with frequency and was named after the southern soldiers, Johnny Rebs.)

Sylvia makes her johnnycake with the buttermilk left over from making butter with milk warm from the family cow. If you can't get your buttermilk that fresh, don't worry—this tastes wonderful with the store-bought variety.

1 cup all-purpose flour
1½ cups yellow or white cornmeal
1 teaspoon baking soda
½ teaspoon salt
2 large eggs
½ cup light brown sugar, not packed
1½ cups buttermilk (see Note)
8 tablespoons (1 stick) unsalted butter, melted
and kept hot

1 Preheat the oven to 350°F. Lightly oil a 9 x 13-inch baking pan.

2 In a small bowl, mix together the flour, cornmeal, baking soda, and salt.

3 Mix the eggs and brown sugar together in a large bowl until they are light and fluffy. Add the buttermilk and mix well. Then add the dry ingredients, and mix gently and quickly until they are thoroughly combined. Add the hot butter, stirring just enough to incorporate it into the batter. Then transfer the batter to the prepared baking pan.

4 Bake in the center of the oven until the johnnycake is golden and springs back when touched lightly, 20 to 25 minutes. Cool for 5 minutes before serving.

8 to 10 servings

Note: If you don't have buttermilk on hand, add 1 teaspoon distilled white vinegar to 1½ cups milk, stir, and set aside until the milk curdles. Then use it instead of buttermilk. It won't have quite the buttery flavor, but it is an excellent substitute.

FEATHER-LIGHT BISCUITS

While I think of biscuits as the perfect breakfast food, farmhouse meals feature them at lunch and dinner too. They're welcome whenever they appear—hot, tender, and steaming from the oven. We had biscuits made with lard, and biscuits made with butter, and I liked them all. These biscuits, however, are my favorite. They're a combination of several recipes, including James Beard's famous cream biscuits. I'm partial to them at breakfast, with fresh preserves or honey.

Make these tender biscuits by hand, as they will suffer if made in a food processor or mixer.

2 cups all-purpose flour
1 teaspoon salt
2 teaspoons baking powder
1 tablespoon sugar
½ to ¾ cup heavy (whipping) cream
½ cup sour cream
4 tablespoons (½ stick) unsalted butter, melted

1 Preheat the oven to 425°F. Line a 10-inch cake pan with parchment paper.

2 Combine the flour, salt, baking powder, and sugar in a mixing bowl. Stir the ingredients with a fork.

3 In a small bowl, whisk together ½ cup of the heavy cream and the sour cream.

4 Slowly add the cream mixture to the dry ingredients, mixing lightly with a fork. Gather the dough together by hand, and if it doesn't completely come together, add a little more heavy cream until it does.

5 Pat the dough into a ball, and then roll it out on a lightly floured board to form a 9-inch square. Cut the dough into 12 squares, dip both sides of each square in the melted butter, and place them in the prepared pan so the sides are touching.

6 Bake in the center of the oven until the biscuits are lightly browned and puffed, 13 to 15 minutes. Remove from the oven, and serve immediately.

1 dozen

SPOONBREAD

This old-fashioned farm recipe was part of my childhood, introduced to me by my grandmother. She nearly always made spoonbread when I visited, and served it alongside lamb shanks and greens. I loved its warm, soft texture and full corn flavor.

The recipe directions, written in her hand, are rooted in her time: "Mix the water and the meal. Beat eggs and add with other ingredients to hot mush. A few dabs of butter on top before placing in oven helps, and plenty of butter on table for each serving. Honey or syrup by choice, too."

This is really more of a pudding than a bread, and I like to serve it with braised meats or stews. It is so plain and simple, yet so universally satisfying, and you'd think it was the most rarified dish on earth, the way it is greeted when set on the table. It looks gorgeous, with the golden crust that forms on top, and it smells as good.

I follow my grandmother's lead and sometimes make it to have by itself for a quick lunch when I'm in the mood for something warm, flavorful, and full of comfort.

2 cups milk
1 cup water
1 cup yellow cornmeal
2 tablespoons unsalted butter, at room
  temperature
2 large eggs
Salt to taste
Freshly ground black pepper (optional)

1 Preheat the oven to 400°F. Heavily butter a 6-cup ovenproof bowl or soufflé dish.

2 Combine 1 cup of the milk, the water, and the cornmeal in a medium-size saucepan, mix well, and bring to a boil over medium-high heat. Cook, stirring often, until the mixture thickens, bubbles, and comes away from the pan when you stir it, about 2 minutes. Add 1 tablespoon of the butter, stirring until it melts. Remove the pan from the heat.

3 In a small bowl, whisk the eggs with the remaining 1 cup milk. Add this to the warm cornmeal mixture, and season to taste with salt, and with pepper if desired.

4 Pour the batter into the prepared bowl, dot with the remaining 1 tablespoon butter, and bake in the center of the oven until a golden crust has formed on the top and the spoonbread is cooked through (it should not jiggle loosely when you move the dish), 30 to 35 minutes. Don't overcook it—the spoonbread is more of a pudding than a bread, and shouldn't be hard or solid. Serve immediately.

4 to 6 servings

COOKIES AND CAKES

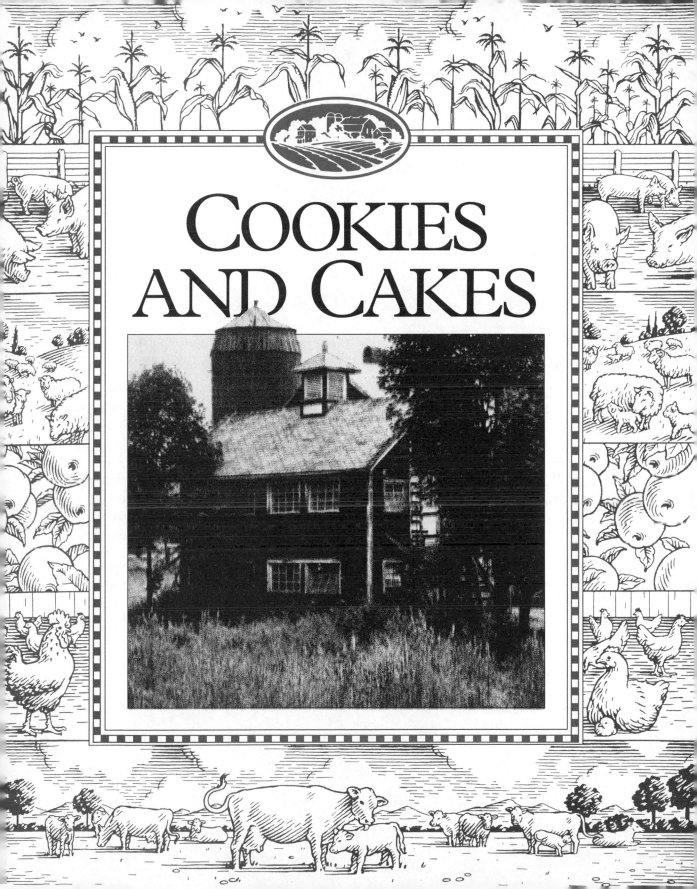

COOKIES, CAKES, AND A COUPLE OF CANDIES

Abundant and varied, the cakes, cookies, and candies produced in the farm kitchen are eaten at the farm table with full, lusty enjoyment. And, it's no wonder.

There have to be cakes and pies at the end of a meal to fill up hungry workers, and to make use of the farm's fruit trees. Cookies are a must for popping in lunch bags and satisfying mid-morning hunger, so batches of farmhouse cookies are big. A few farmers I visited even made their own candy, and I speak with authority when I say that since there is always an appetite around, candy doesn't last long. The caramels I sampled in Montana were gone before they even had time to set.

In many ways, farm desserts reflect what is easily available more than anything else. They are full of fruits and nuts grown on the farm. They also tend to be good "keepers," flavored with spices that mellow with age like ginger, cinnamon, cloves, nutmeg, allspice, cardamom, and vanilla. I found few chocolate cakes or cookies, perhaps because chocolate is a store-bought ingredient that may be easy to purchase now, but wasn't at the time that traditional farm food was developed. Never fear, chocolate is not altogether missing. You'll find the best chocolate cake in the world in these pages, and rich little chocolate whoopie pies too.

BONNIE SCHIMELPFENING'S PEANUT BRITTLE

Bonnie Schimelpfening makes pound after pound of this peanut brittle every year for Christmas. Some she sells at local crafts fairs, some she gives to friends as gifts. "People just love it, and I can hardly keep up with them," she says.

There are a couple of tricks to making it, though it is surprisingly simple. First, use the smallest peanuts you can (larger ones won't cook as thoroughly). If the peanuts have husks, don't remove them—they add color to the peanut brittle.

For more on the Schimelpfenings, see page 72.

3 cups sugar
1 cup light corn syrup
½ cup water
½ teaspoon salt
2 tablespoons unsalted butter
3 cups raw peanuts, preferably with husks
1 teaspoon vanilla extract
1 tablespoon baking soda

1 Mix together the sugar, corn syrup, water, and salt in a large heavy saucepan over medium-high heat. Bring it to a boil and cook, stirring occasionally, until the mixture turns golden and reaches the hard ball stage (about 265°F on a candy thermometer), up to 10 minutes.

2 Add the butter and the peanuts, stir, and return to a boil. Cook until it reaches the hard crack stage (about 310°F), another 5 to 10 minutes. Remove from the heat, add the vanilla and baking soda, and stir (it will bubble up and may need vigorous stirring to calm it down). Let the mixture sit for about 30 seconds, then pour it out onto a buttered, heat-resistant work surface such as Formica or marble (not wood).

3 Immediately spread the mixture out as thin as you can, using a metal or wooden spatula. Don a pair of thick rubber gloves, and as the peanut brittle cools but before it gets hard, begin pulling on it from every direction to stretch it, distribute the peanuts evenly, and give it a shiny gold luster, brittle texture, and improved flavor. It should stretch to almost double the original size. (Be sure to wear gloves, because the brittle is too hot to handle without them.)

4 When the peanut brittle is cooled and hard, break it up into pieces. It will keep for weeks in an airtight container stored in a cool place.

About 2½ pounds

ALICE BERNER'S CARAMELS

A lice Berner isn't a fan of white sugar—except where these buttery caramels are concerned. While we were staying with the Berners at their farm near Loma, Montana, a freak snowstorm hit. We all sat near the fire, playing cards, until Alice gave her hand to her grandson, Ashton, and disappeared into the kitchen. Not half an hour later she emerged with a pan of caramels. We couldn't wait to dig in.

These are simple to make, and they are sure to impress any caramel fans in the vicinity.

2 cups sugar
½ cup dark corn syrup
½ cup milk
4 tablespoons (½ stick) unsalted butter
1 cup heavy (whipping) cream
1 teaspoon vanilla extract

1 Butter a 7 x 12-inch baking dish.

2 Place all the ingredients except the vanilla in a large heavy saucepan, stir, and bring to a boil over medium-high heat.

Reduce the heat to medium, and cook at a slow boil until the mixture turns golden and reaches 246°F on a candy thermometer, 20 to 30 minutes. Then whisk in the vanilla, remove the pan from the heat, and pour the mixture into the prepared baking dish.

3 When the mixture has cooled, cut it in ½-inch squares and wrap them individually, in either waxed paper or aluminum foil. The caramels will keep about 2 weeks if stored in an airtight container in a cool place.

36 pieces

CRISP OAT COOKIES

Nearly every farmer I met who farmed more than a dozen acres had oats in the ground—a response to the recent demand for oat bran. Of course, not all the oats in this country are ground for bran. Thick, chewy rolled oats make a substantial bowl of oatmeal, as well as lending wonderful texture to cookies.

These simple crisp cookies are the most satisfying I've ever eaten. Buttery, slightly caramel-flavored from the brown sugar, and studded with chewy raisins, they go perfectly with a cup of tea or coffee and are a sweet, crisp foil to sharp Cheddar cheese.

They are satisfying to make, too, because they can be whipped up quickly and yield a substantial amount. Don't be concerned when you find yourself with more than fifty oat cookies on the cooling rack—they keep well.

1 cup raisins
2½ cups all-purpose flour
1 teaspoon baking soda
1 teaspoon salt
2½ cups rolled oats
12 tablespoons (1½ sticks) unsalted butter
1 cup (packed) dark brown sugar
½ cup heavy (whipping) cream
1 teaspoon vanilla extract

1 Preheat the oven to 375°F. Line two baking sheets with parchment paper.

2 Soak the raisins in hot water to cover for at least 30 minutes.

3 Sift the flour, baking soda, and salt together onto a piece of waxed paper. Add the rolled oats, and set aside.

4 Cream the butter in a large bowl until it is light and fluffy. Add the brown sugar, and mix until thoroughly blended and light. Then add the cream and the vanilla, stirring well after each addition. Drain the raisins, discarding the soaking liquid, and add them to the sugar mixture. Mix until they are distributed throughout. Add the dry ingredients, and mix well.

5 Divide the dough in half, and roll out one half so it is ¼ inch thick. Using 2-inch cookie cutters, cut out as many cookies as you can. Place the cookies ¼ inch apart

on one of the prepared baking sheets. Repeat with the remaining dough. Reserve any scraps, roll them out a second time, and cut out the remaining cookies. (Try to use up all the dough, as it will toughen if it is rolled out again.)

6 Bake the cookies in the center of the oven until they are golden, about 13 minutes. Transfer them to wire racks to cool.

About 55 cookies

HAZELNUT CRISPS

This is a magic cookie recipe—it produces buttery, nutty little discs with about as much effort as it takes to say "Yum." And if you don't want to bake all the cookies at once, the dough will keep in the refrigerator, well wrapped, for at least a week and in the freezer for several months. With that kind of versatility, freshly baked cookies are never more than moments away.

I like to make these with hazelnuts because I love their sweet flavor, but walnuts or pecans are tasty, too.

Serve these with Liz Clark's Brown Sugar Peach Ice Cream (see Index) for an ideal marriage of flavors and textures.

4 cups sifted all-purpose flour
1 tablespoon baking powder
¼ teaspoon salt
1 cup (2 sticks) unsalted butter, at room temperature
1 cup (packed) light brown sugar
¾ cup granulated sugar
2 large eggs, beaten
1 tablespoon vanilla extract
1 cup hazelnuts, toasted (see Note), skinned, and coarsely chopped

1 Mix the flour, baking powder, and salt together on a large piece of waxed paper, and set aside.

2 Place the butter and both sugars in a large bowl, and mix until fluffy. Add the eggs and the vanilla extract, and mix until they are thoroughly incorporated and the mixture is slightly lighter and fluffier. Then gradually incorporate the dry ingredients, mixing until thoroughly combined. Add the nuts and mix well.

3 Divide the dough into three portions, and form each one into a log 1½ inches in diameter. Wrap them (separately) in waxed paper, then in aluminum foil, and re-frigerate until ready to bake (at least 2 to 3 hours, so the roll is firm). The dough freezes well at this point and will keep, frozen, for several months.

4 Preheat the oven to 425°F. Line two baking sheets with parchment paper.

5 Cut the cookies into ¼-inch-thick slices, and place them ½ inch apart on the pre-pared baking sheets. Bake in the center of the oven until they are golden and have puffed slightly, 10 minutes. Remove from the oven, transfer to wire racks, and cool. Store in an airtight container. The cookies will keep well for 5 to 6 days.

About 13 dozen cookies

Note: To toast hazelnuts, preheat the oven to 350°F. Place the nuts in a baking pan large enough to hold them in a single layer, and toast, stirring once, until they give off a toasted aroma, 10 to 15 minutes.

GRANDMOTHER PIERSON'S MOLASSES SUGAR COOKIES

T hese are true farm cookies from my grandmother's family, who spent their early years on a farm in Michigan, then moved out west to an-other farm in Oregon. My grandmother made these for us, and like her mother she cut them out with a number 10 can so that they were huge, like small pizza pies. When we didn't live near her she would package them up and send them to us, and we would savor them for as long as they lasted.

This is still one of my favorite cookies. They have a wonderful cakey texture, and though I don't make them as large as my grandmother did, they are still a substantial and satisfying treat. These are good "dunkers," and about the only time I am tempted by an ice-cold glass of milk is when I eat these cookies. They are luscious with coffee, too.

These cookies are good for children because their flavor is mellow. If you want to jazz it up, add a tablespoon of finely chopped candied ginger.

If you don't have the time or desire to bake all the cookies at once, cut them out and arrange them on sheets of parchment paper. Place them in layers on a baking sheet, wrap the whole thing well with aluminum foil, and freeze. When you want fresh cookies, remove a sheet, let them thaw for several minutes, and bake according to the recipe.

1 cup sugar
1 cup molasses
1 cup (2 sticks) unsalted butter, melted
3 large eggs
1 teaspoon ground ginger
1 teaspoon ground cinnamon
1 teaspoon baking soda
Pinch of salt
5 cups all-purpose flour

1 Preheat the oven to 375°F. Line two baking sheets with parchment paper.

2 Place the sugar, molasses, and the melted butter in a large bowl, and mix well. Add the eggs, one at a time, mixing well after each addition.

3 Sift the spices and salt and 3 cups of the flour together onto a piece of waxed paper. Add this to the liquid mixture, and mix thoroughly. Add the remaining 2 cups flour, 1 cup at a time, mixing quickly but thoroughly to make a stiff dough. Gather the dough into a ball, wrap in waxed paper, then aluminum foil, and refrigerate for at least 2 hours or overnight. (You can refrigerate the dough for up to 2 days.)

4 Divide the dough into fourths so it is easier to work with, and roll one portion out on a lightly floured surface so it is ⅝ inch thick. Cut the dough with a 2½-inch round cookie cutter, and place the cookies 1 inch apart on the prepared baking sheets. Repeat with the remaining dough. Gather the scraps of dough together, roll out, and cut out the remaining cookies.

5 Bake the cookies in the center of the oven until they are puffed and golden, about 8 minutes. Transfer them to wire racks to cool. They will keep for 2 to 3 days in an airtight container.

80 cookies

NUTMEG SUGAR COOKIES

My grandmother learned to make these cookies from her mother. They're simple and full of good old-fashioned flavors like vanilla, nutmeg, and egg—the kind of cookie you want to settle down with while you read a good book and sip a cup of tea. As a girl my grandmother had little time for book reading, and I imagine she nibbled them when she was ironing or gardening, or taking care of her brothers and sisters on the family farm. But she loved these cookies, and as an adult she made them for us often.

This dough doesn't benefit from numerous rollings-out, which toughen it. To avoid that, I gather the scraps up to form a log, wrap it well, and refrigerate it. When it is chilled, I slice and bake the last cookies, and their texture suffers not a bit.

3½ cups unbleached all-purpose flour
1 teaspoon baking soda
2 teaspoons cream of tartar
1 teaspoon salt
½ teaspoon freshly grated nutmeg
1 cup (2 sticks) unsalted butter, at room
   temperature
1½ cups sugar
2 large eggs
1 teaspoon vanilla extract

1 Preheat the oven to 375°F. Line two baking sheets with parchment paper.

2 Sift the dry ingredients together onto a piece of waxed paper, and set aside.

3 Place the butter and the sugar in a large bowl, and mix until pale yellow and light. Add the eggs, one at a time, beating well after each addition. Then add the vanilla extract and mix well.

4 Add the dry ingredients, mixing just until they are incorporated. Transfer the dough to a lightly floured surface, and roll it out so it is about ¼ inch thick. Using a 2½-inch round cookie cutter, cut out the cookies. Place them about ½ inch apart on the prepared baking sheets.

5 Bake the cookies in the center of the oven until they are are pale gold and slightly puffed, about 12 minutes. Transfer them to wire racks to cool.

6 Meanwhile, roll the scraps into a log about 1½ inches in diameter, and wrap it well in waxed paper. Refrigerate the dough until it is firm, at least 2 hours (if keeping longer, wrap it also in aluminum foil). Cut the log into ¼-inch slices, and bake and cool as in Step 5.

About 3 dozen cookies

MORGAN HORSE COOKIES

This recipe comes from Caryl Smith, who, along with her husband, Barney, raises Morgan horses on their cattle farm near Brighton, Iowa (see page 112). The cookies got their name because Caryl cuts them out with a horse-shaped cookie cutter.

This is a crisp, sweet spice cookie, that transcends the ages. Both children and adults love them. All in all, this is a great crispy spice cookie.

The recipe makes a huge amount, but because the cookies are delicate, they disappear quickly.

3¾ cups sifted all-purpose flour
1¼ teaspoons baking powder
2½ teaspoons ground cinnamon
1¼ teaspoons ground cloves
1½ cups (3 sticks) unsalted butter, at room temperature
2 cups (packed) light brown sugar
1 large egg

1 Sift the flour, baking powder, and spices together onto a piece of waxed paper.

2 In a large bowl, cream the butter until it is light and fluffy. Gradually mix in the brown sugar, beating until it is fluffy. Then add the egg and mix well.

3 Gradually add the dry ingredients, and mix until combined. The dough will be fairly soft. Cover the bowl and chill the dough in the refrigerator until it is firm enough to roll out, about 1 hour.

4 Preheat the oven to 350°F. Line two baking sheets with parchment paper.

5 Divide the dough in thirds. Using one third, roll it out on a lightly floured surface so it is about ⅛ inch thick. Cut it out with a cookie cutter (I use a 2½-inch round one), and place the cookies ½ inch apart on the prepared baking sheets. Bake in the center of the oven until they are golden, 10 to 12 minutes. Save and refrigerate the dough trimmings, repeating the process with the remaining two thirds of the dough. As the cookies are baked, transfer them to wire racks to cool.

6 Gather all the dough trimmings together, and form them into logs 2 inches in diameter. Wrap them well in waxed paper and refrigerate. Then cut them into ⅛-inch-thick rounds, and bake as described in Step 5. (The dough will keep in the refrigerator for several days, or in the freezer for 2 to 3 months.) The cooled cookies will keep in an airtight container for at least 2 weeks.

About 12 dozen cookies

FARMHOUSE PILLOWS

T his recipe makes a huge batch of soft, pillowy cookies which, with their scents of vanilla and nutmeg, evoke a warm farm kitchen and a hungry crew ready to stick a couple of cookies in a shirt pocket for an afternoon snack on the tractor.

Like many old-fashioned cookie doughs, this one is so moist that you may be tempted to add more flour. *Don't!* Sprinkle a generous amount of flour on your work surface, and roll the dough out with the lightest possible hand. A soft, moist dough results in ethereally tender cake-like cookies.

Another secret to tenderness is not overworking the dough. Try to roll it out just once. Leave any scraps aside until all the cookies have been cut out, then quickly and gently roll out the scraps and cut cookies from that dough. Or take all the scraps and fashion them gently into a log, following the directions in Step 6, above.

These cookies are simple, plain, and rich, like the cookie version of a rich egg custard. For variety, add the minced zest of 1 lemon or 1 teaspoon ground cinnamon.

4½ cups all-purpose flour

4 teaspoons baking powder

½ teaspoon baking soda

½ teaspoon salt

1 teaspoon freshly grated nutmeg

1 cup (2 sticks) unsalted butter,
   at room temperature

2 cups sugar

2 large eggs

1 cup sour cream

2 teaspoons vanilla extract

1 egg mixed with 1 teaspoon water,
   for the glaze (optional)

½ cup finely chopped walnuts

1 Preheat the oven to 350°F.

2 Sift the dry ingredients together onto a piece of waxed paper, and set aside.

3 In a large bowl, cream the butter until it is pale yellow and light. Then add the sugar and mix vigorously until the mixture is nearly white. Add the eggs, one at a time, beating well after each addition. Add the sour cream and the vanilla, and mix well. Then stir in the flour mixture, mixing just until it is incorporated into the dough.

4 Sprinkle a generous amount of flour onto a work surface and onto the dough. Divide the dough into thirds, and roll out one third so it is about ⅜ inch thick. Using a 3-inch cookie cutter or a glass with a thin rim, cut out the cookies and place them about ½ inch apart on unoiled baking sheets.

5 Brush the cookies with the egg glaze if desired, and sprinkle each one with chopped nuts. Bake until the cookies have risen and spring back when touched, no longer than 15 minutes. They should be soft and thick, almost like small cakes. Transfer them to wire racks to cool, and store in an airtight container. They will keep for 3 to 4 days.

40 cookies

HERBFARM ROSEMARY SHORTBREAD

R on Zimmerman serves these cookies after lunch at the Herbfarm. The rosemary in them may seem unconventional, but it is a flavorful surprise. The herb's usual pungent flavor is softened by the butter and flour, and completely altered so that it seems a natural for sweet cookies.

I like to serve these in the afternoon with tea—or with any fruit dessert, particularly one made with apples. And I don't stop with rosemary. Sometimes I substitute nutmeg—I add a generous ¾ teaspoon—but you could try the same amount of mint, thyme, or lavender too.

These cookies improve with age. In fact, they are much better two days after they are baked, so plan accordingly.

1½ cups (3 sticks) unsalted butter,
    at room temperature
⅔ cup sugar
2 tablespoons fresh rosemary, or
    2 teaspoons dried
2¼ cups unbleached all-purpose
    flour
½ cup white or brown rice flour (available
    at natural foods stores)
¼ teaspoon salt
2 teaspoons sugar for topping
    (optional)

1 Preheat the oven to 375°F. Line two baking sheets with parchment paper.

2 Cream the butter in a large bowl until pale yellow and light. Add the sugar, and continue mixing until the mixture is fluffy.

3 If you are using fresh rosemary, mince it. If you are using dried rosemary,

crush it in a mortar and pestle, or by using a rolling pin on a flat surface, until it is fine but not a powder.

4 Add both flours, the salt, and the rosemary to the butter mixture, and mix until thoroughly combined. The dough will be somewhat soft. Refrigerate it for 1 hour, if necessary, so that it is firm enough to roll.

5 Roll the dough out to form a rectangle about 10 x 14 inches, and ¼ inch thick. Cut the cookies into 1½ x 2-inch rectangles or any other shape you like. Place them about ½ inch apart on the prepared baking sheets. Sprinkle them with the sugar topping if desired, and bake in the center of the oven until they are gold at the edges, 12 to 15 minutes.

6 Remove the cookies from the oven, and transfer them to wire racks to cool. Pack in an airtight container. The cookies will keep, their flavor improving, for at least a week.

About 3 dozen cookies

PETE YAMAMOTO AND HIS ALMONDS

Pete Yamamoto grows almonds in California's San Joaquin Valley, 7 miles east of the town of Turlock. It's the heart of almond country, which runs from Chico to Bakersfield.

Pete's parents came to California from Japan in the 1920s and started farming. Japanese couldn't buy land under the "Alien Land Law," which allowed only citizens to own land. And they weren't allowed to become citizens. But attorneys helped them form a corporation composed of the first of their children born in the United States. "A bunch of infants bought the land," Pete said, chuckling. "You know how those attorneys are!"

The elder Yamamotos acquired land prior to World War II and used it to farm strawberries. In 1942 the family, along with all the Japanese farmers in the valley, was sent to an internment camp in Colorado. Instead of losing their land and possessions, however, they were lucky. "We had a sympathetic attorney who held our farms. He hired a manager and leased out the farms while we were gone, then we got them back when we returned," Pete said.

After the war, when Pete's parents had built up their financial resources, they added permanent crops to their strawberries, beginning with grapes, then going into peaches and almonds. Pete worked alongside them until he went to the University of California at Davis and got a degree in pomology, the study of tree fruit.

AN ALMOND EXPERT

Pete is a conservative farmer who now owns 75 acres of almond groves and who leases another 230. Every now and then he considers organic farming. "I don't want to use chemicals, but there's a limit you don't want to go beyond," he said. "When we spray for insects we don't treat to kill them, we just have to keep them below a certain level. We also introduce a predacious mite to feed on harmful mites. The problem I see with using chicken or cattle manure for fertilizer is that it has salmonella, and if you don't dig it under real well I'd worry about the fruit. And if we went organic, our production might be half, and think about what prices would be."

With those views in mind Pete, along with his two brothers and four hired hands, grows almonds conventionally, relying heavily

on county extension agents and chemical companies for advice.

Pete markets his almonds through the Blue Diamond Growers cooperative, and he thinks cooperatives are the way to go. "As a member of the co-op I don't have to worry about marketing my almonds, because they do all that for the growers," he said. Pete also keeps busy as one of two growers who represent the cooperative's 5,000 members on the Almond Board of California.

TOURING THE FARM

Pete wanted us to see his farm, so we followed him out Santa Fe Avenue, a long, flat strip bordered on both sides by almond groves. Summer temperatures can soar above 105°F in the valley, making it too hot to work, though today it was merely in the high 80s. Relief comes in fall and winter, when temperatures drop to the 20s. Without that coolness, there would be no fruit trees in the valley. "Deciduous trees have a certain cold hour requirement, and if they didn't get it they wouldn't grow and bear fruit," Pete said. "The winter does it for us."

Pete grows three varieties of almonds for purposes of cross-pollination. The largest and most common are the Non-pareils, then the Neplus and the Carmels. The trees look the same to the novice, but an expert can tell them apart at a glance. "The Non-pareils have small pointed leaves, and the Neplus have a much bigger leaf. The other ones are the Carmels," Pete said.

When the trees bloom in February, the orchard is transformed by fluffy pink-tinged blossoms. A beekeeper who comes all the way from South Dakota, hives in tow, sets them up in the orchard to pollinate the blossoms.

The almonds develop throughout the spring and summer. Harvest begins at the end of August and usually lasts through September. The nuts dry almost entirely on the trees, and the green hulls open. A hydraulic shaker—a long, snaky arm with two pincers at the end—grabs hold of the trunk of the tree and shakes it to dislodge the nuts, which fall and lie on the flat bare ground for 10 days to finish drying. They are then raked, gathered, and picked up by machine.

Once dry, the raw almonds will keep for a year, though most of them are processed sooner at the co-op—into everything from skinned whole almonds to slivers, chunks, and those that are roasted and dusted with barbecue salt. The shells are burned to power the processing plant, and the hulls are sold for cattle feed.

More than 60 percent of the cooperative's almonds are exported. "We started exporting in the 1950s," Pete said. "Until then it was a domestic market, but it just wasn't big enough." Germany takes the bulk, then Japan, France, and Canada. The cooperative competes in this international market with Spain, Italy, and Morocco.

As we prepared to leave, Pete and his wife Irene accompanied us to the car, via their garage. Stacked high on a shelf were gallon-size cans of roasted almonds, and Pete pulled one down to give to us. "In case you get hungry on the road," he said.

GREG'S FAVORITE RUSKS

This is a recipe from Irene Yamamoto, wife of Pete Yamamoto, an almond grower in Turlock, California, the heart of California almond country (see page 386).

The crisp rusks flood your mouth with the subtle flavor of fresh almonds. They are perfect for dunking in coffee and are a favorite of Irene and Pete's son Greg.

2 cups whole almonds, toasted (see Note)

2 cups sugar

5½ cups unbleached all-purpose flour

¾ teaspoon salt

1 teaspoon baking soda

1 cup (2 sticks) unsalted butter, at room temperature

1 cup sour cream

2 large eggs

1 Preheat the oven to 375°F. Line two baking sheets with parchment paper.

2 Combine the almonds and 2 tablespoons of the sugar in a food processor, and grind to a fine powder.

3 Sift the flour, salt, and baking soda together onto a piece of waxed paper.

4 Cream the butter and the remaining sugar in a large bowl until pale yellow and light. Add the sour cream and the eggs, one at a time, mixing well after each addi-

tion. Stir in the flour mixture and the almonds just until incorporated.

5 Turn the dough out onto a lightly floured surface, and pat it out to form a 13 x 4-inch rectangle that is ¾ inch thick. Cut the rectangle in half lengthwise, so you have two pieces of dough measuring 13 x 2 inches, and transfer them to the prepared baking sheets. Bake in the center of the oven until golden, puffed, and firm, about 35 minutes. Slide the parchment paper onto wire racks, and cool the strips until they are lukewarm, about 15 minutes. Lower the oven temperature to 300°F.

6 Slice the strips crosswise into ½-inch-thick slices, and lay them on their side on the parchment. Return the paper to the baking sheets, and bake the slices until they are golden, 15 to 20 minutes. Turn and bake until golden on the other side, another 15 to 20 minutes. Transfer the rusks to wire racks to cool. Tightly covered, these will keep for at least a week.

About 80 rusks

Note: To toast almonds, preheat the oven to 350°F. Place the nuts in a baking pan large enough to hold them in a single layer, and toast, stirring once, until they give off a toasted aroma, 10 to 15 minutes.

JILL'S SORGHUM COOKIES

The recipe for these cookies was given to me by Jill Jones, whose husband, Herman, makes sorghum molasses each fall (see page 390). If you can't find sorghum molasses, use regular molasses. The flavor won't be quite as delicate, but the cookies will still be delicious.

12 tablespoons (1½ sticks) unsalted butter,
    at room temperature
1 cup (packed) light brown sugar
¼ cup sorghum molasses
1 large egg
2¼ cups all-purpose flour
2 teaspoons baking soda
½ teaspoon salt
1 teaspoon ground ginger
1 teaspoon ground cinnamon
½ teaspoon ground cloves
½ cup granulated sugar

1 Preheat the oven to 400°F. Line two baking sheets with parchment paper.

2 Cream the butter and brown sugar together in a large mixing bowl until light and fluffy. Add the sorghum molasses, and then the egg, mixing well after each addition.

3 Sift the flour, baking soda, and spices together into a medium-size bowl, and then stir into the molasses mixture. The dough will be quite stiff.

4 Pour the sugar into a shallow bowl. Form the dough into ¾-inch balls, roll them in the sugar, and place them about 2 inches apart on the prepared baking sheets. Bake the cookies in the center of the oven until they are puffed and golden, about 10 minutes. Transfer them to wire racks to cool. Store in airtight containers. They will keep for about 1 week.

5 dozen cookies

THE BEST KIND OF MOLASSES

Herman Jones of Fayetteville, Arkansas, is one of the few farmers left in his area who still make sorghum molasses, and he uses a time-honored method he learned from his father.

Every spring Herman plants a small patch of sugar sorghum, which resembles short corn with a dark brown tassle, and in October he cleans out his sorghum shack, polishes his press, and goes to work.

He cuts the sorghum stalks by hand, then runs them through an old iron press, which in his father's day was run by mules. Herman's, though arcane looking, is a modern invention powered by a gas engine. As the press turns, the sorghum yields a sticky liquid that runs into a pipe and in turn fills a 50-gallon tank inside the nearby sorghum shack.

Herman builds a wood fire under a specially designed trough, which is separated into three sections. The sorghum drips into the trough, and is held in the first section until it bubbles and boils and begins to turn golden. Then Herman spoons it into the second section, where it cooks down further. As it cooks, filling the air with its sweet aroma and the shack with nearly impossible heat, impurities rise to the surface, and Herman is in constant motion as he skims them off.

After many hours, when the sorghum is darker and thicker and impurities no longer boil to the top, Herman spoons it into the third section, where it cooks slowly to a deep, thick golden brown. From there it is strained several times before being bottled in pint jars. It takes Herman about three long, hot, sticky days to make the molasses, from cutting the sorghum to canning the syrupy liquid.

Sorghum—properly called sorghum molasses—is very different from the molasses most of us are used to. As Herman puts it, "It doesn't have that bittery wang to it that molasses does." Traditional molasses is a by-product of sugar, which may account for its bitterness and nearly black color. Sorghum molasses is deep brown, mild, sweet.

Labeling is important in sorghum molasses. If a label reads "sorghum," it isn't sorghum molasses, but a by-product of sugar. True sorghum molasses is called by both names. A taste will tell you if all else fails, because Herman is right, there is no bittery wang to sorghum molasses.

OLD-FASHIONED SPICE COOKIES

This is a simple, old-fashioned spice cookie that my grandmother made often. It calls for ingredients that were common on the farm, and it goes together so quickly that she could have fresh cookies for her brothers and sisters within about half an hour after they'd all come in from work. There is nothing better with a cup of hot tea or a glass of cold milk.

8 tablespoons (1 stick) unsalted butter,
   at room temperature
½ cup (packed) dark brown sugar
¼ cup molasses
1 large egg
2½ cups unbleached all-purpose flour
1½ teaspoons ground ginger
1 heaping teaspoon ground cinnamon
¼ teaspoon salt
2 teaspoons baking soda
2 tablespoons hot water
6 tablespoons cold water
1 cup dried currants

1 Preheat the oven to 375°F. Line two baking sheets with parchment paper.

2 In a large bowl, mix the butter and the brown sugar until light and fluffy. Add the molasses and stir. Then add the egg and mix well.

3 Sift the flour, the spices, and the salt together onto a piece of waxed paper.

Mix the baking soda and the hot water in a small bowl or measuring cup.

4 Gradually add the dry ingredients to the creamed ingredients. Then add the cold water and the baking soda mixture. Mix quickly but thoroughly. Fold in the currants.

5 Drop the dough by tablespoons 2 inches apart on the prepared baking sheets, and bake in the center of the oven until golden and puffed, about 10 minutes. Remove from the oven and transfer to wire racks to cool. These keep in an airtight container for 2 to 3 days.

30 cookies

SNOW MOUNDS

This delicate little cookie comes from my grandmother's repertoire. Every year she would bake a batch at Christmas and bring them to our house in an old-fashioned cardboard box with a bright poinsettia design stamped on it. Waiting for her arrival vied with waiting for Santa to come down the chimney, and I'll never forget the suspense and excitement as she pulled box after box from the bags she carried. Even though each year she made the same cookies, the pitch of excitement was always the same, and I'm sure it would still be so today.

2½ cups all-purpose flour
½ teaspoon salt
1 cup (2 sticks) unsalted butter, at room
  temperature
2 cups confectioners' sugar, sifted
1 teaspoon vanilla extract
¾ cup finely chopped walnuts

1 Preheat the oven to 400°F.

2 Sift the flour and the salt together onto a piece of waxed paper.

3 Cream the butter in a medium-size mixing bowl until it is pale yellow and light. Add ½ cup of the confectioners' sugar, and mix until it is fluffy. Add the vanilla and mix well. Then gently stir in the flour mixture. Stir in the nuts, working carefully. Do not overmix the dough, or the cookies may be tough.

4 Form the dough into 1-inch balls, place them about ¾ inch apart on unoiled baking sheets, and bake in the center of the oven until they are golden, 14 to 17 minutes.

5 Meanwhile, sift the remaining 1½ cups confectioners' sugar into a shallow bowl or plate.

6 Remove the cookies from the oven, and while they are still hot, roll them in the confectioners' sugar. Let them cool on wire racks. When they are cool, roll them in confectioners' sugar again, and store them in an airtight container. Stored in a cool place, these cookies will keep for 4 to 5 days.

4 dozen

BUTTERY PECAN DROPS

These elegant little cookies come not from a farm, but from a Santa Rosa (California) pastry chef, Cathy Burgett. I couldn't resist including them here because of all the pecan cookie recipes I tried, these make the most of fresh pecans. They highlight the pecan's buttery texture and do justice to its rich nutty flavor.

Pecan Drops improve with age. In fact, they are much better one to two days after they are made, when they have had a chance to mellow.

Don't reserve these for Christmas—they're a nice buttery mouthful after dinner, with coffee, any time of the year.

2 cups pecan halves
1 cup plus 2 tablespoons sugar
1¾ cups all-purpose flour
¼ teaspoon salt
1 cup (2 sticks) unsalted butter, at room temperature
1 teaspoon vanilla extract
1 tablespoon strong brewed coffee or brandy

1 Preheat the oven to 350°F. Line two baking sheets with parchment paper.

2 Place the pecans in a food processor along with 2 tablespoons of the sugar, and process until very fine, almost like flour. Transfer the mixture to a medium-size bowl, stir in the flour and salt, and set aside.

3 Cream the butter and ½ cup of the sugar in a large bowl until pale yellow and light. Add the vanilla and the coffee, and mix well. Then gradually add the flour mixture, stirring just until it is combined. Do not overmix, or the batter will become oily and too soft.

4 Place the remaining ½ cup sugar in a plate or shallow bowl. Using your hands, quickly form the dough into pieces the size of a small walnut, and roll them in the sugar. Place them ½ inch apart on the prepared baking sheets, and bake in the center of the oven until they are golden and puffed, 12 to 15 minutes. Transfer the cookies to wire racks to cool. They will keep in an airtight container for at least 1 week.

About 50 cookies

AMISH PEANUT BUTTER OATMEAL COOKIES

These are a slight variation on an old Amish recipe, and they are the peanuttiest cookies I've ever had. If you're a peanut fan the way I am, you will love their nutty crunch. The addition of spices adds a delicate, aromatic undertone. You may want to double the recipe, because these disappear quickly.

1½ cups all-purpose flour
½ teaspoon salt
½ teaspoon baking soda
1 teaspoon baking powder
1 teaspoon ground cinnamon
¼ teaspoon ground cloves
¼ teaspoon freshly grated nutmeg
2 cups rolled oats
1 cup (2 sticks) unsalted butter,
   at room temperature
1 cup unsalted chunky peanut
   butter
1 cup sugar
1 teaspoon vanilla extract
2 large eggs
1 cup raw peanuts, preferably Spanish

1 Preheat the oven to 375°F. Line two baking sheets with parchment paper.

2 Sift together the flour, salt, baking soda, baking powder, and spices onto a piece of waxed paper. Add the oats and mix together.

3 Cream the butter in a large bowl until pale yellow and fluffy. Add the peanut butter, and cream until thoroughly incorporated. Then slowly add the sugar, and mix until the mixture is pale golden and fluffy. Add the vanilla and mix well. Then add the eggs, one at a time, mixing until combined.

4 Slowly add the flour mixture, and stir just until it is incorporated into the butter mixture. Fold in the peanuts, mixing them in thoroughly.

5 Drop the dough by tablespoons 1 inch apart on the prepared baking sheets. Using the back of a fork, mark the top of each cookie in a crisscross pattern, flattening it out as you do. Bake the cookies in the center of the oven until they are golden, about 15 minutes. Transfer them to wire racks to cool. These will keep in an airtight container for 3 to 4 days.

About 4 dozen cookies

ANNE FRIAR THOMAS'S COWBOY COOKIES

This recipe comes from Anne Friar Thomas, owner of the J. Carter Thomas Ranch in Cuero, Texas. For the past four decades she has cooked for the dozen or so ranch hands who keep her 17,000-acre cattle ranch in smooth working order. She isn't your typical ranch or farm cook, according to ranch foreman Joe Adams, who says, "Mrs. Thomas's food is some of the best around."

I found several versions of the Cowboy Cookies recipe in my travels, but this was my all-time favorite. They'll please you, but you'll need to hide them if you want more than one or two, because they will please everyone else within range, too.

2 cups all-purpose flour

1 teaspoon baking soda

½ teaspoon salt

1 teaspoon baking powder

1 cup (2 sticks) unsalted butter, at room temperature

1 cup granulated sugar

1 cup (packed) dark brown sugar

2 large eggs

1 teaspoon vanilla extract

2 cups rolled oats

1 package (6 ounces) semisweet chocolate chips

¾ cup pecan halves, chopped

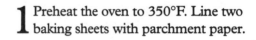

1 Preheat the oven to 350°F. Line two baking sheets with parchment paper.

2 Sift the flour, baking soda, salt, and baking powder together onto a piece of waxed paper, and set aside.

3 Cream the butter and both sugars together until light and fluffy. Add the eggs, one at a time, mixing thoroughly after each addition. Stir in the vanilla, and then add the flour mixture and mix well. Add the oats, the chocolate chips, and the nuts, mixing well after each addition.

4 Drop the dough by teaspoons ½ inch apart onto the prepared baking sheets, and bake in the center of the oven until the cookies are golden, about 15 minutes. Transfer them to wire racks to cool. These cookies will keep in an airtight container for 5 to 6 days.

4 dozen cookies

MY MAN'S COOKIES

Though Anne Friar Thomas cooks all year, roundup time in the fall is crucial, because the crew works extra-long hours and is in need of big, filling meals. According to a roundup menu she sent me after I'd visited her at the ranch, these cookies were the finale of a meal starring roast brisket, mashed potatoes, steamed carrots with butter and parsley, bread, and fruit.

1⅓ cups unbleached all-purpose flour
½ teaspoon baking soda
½ teaspoon salt
½ teaspoon baking powder
1 cup rolled oats
8 tablespoons (1 stick) unsalted butter, at room temperature
½ cup granulated sugar
½ cup (packed) dark brown sugar
1 large egg
1 teaspoon vanilla extract
1 cup toasted pecans (see Note), coarsely chopped

1 Preheat the oven to 350°F. Line two baking sheets with parchment paper.

2 Sift the flour, baking soda, salt, and baking powder onto a piece of waxed paper. Place the oats on top.

3 Cream the butter in a large mixing bowl until it is pale yellow and light. Add both sugars and mix well. Then add the egg and the vanilla, mixing well after each addition. Stir in the dry ingredients, mixing until combined. Mix in the nuts by hand.

4 Drop the dough by level tablespoons about ½ inch apart on the prepared baking sheets, and bake in the center of the oven until golden, about 15 minutes. Transfer them to wire racks to cool. These will keep for several days if stored in an airtight container.

About 4 dozen cookies

Note: To toast pecans, preheat the oven to 350°F. Place the nuts in a baking pan large enough to hold them in a single layer, and toast, stirring once, until they give off a toasted aroma, 10 to 15 minutes.

NUTMEG LOGS

I thought Nutmeg Logs were one of my family's specialties, but I found similar recipes in many farm collections. They are simple, buttery, and redolent of nutmeg—a good, old-fashioned cookie with great flavor.

This recipe makes a large quantity, but they are bite-sized and disappear quickly.

3 cups all-purpose flour
½ teaspoon salt
1 teaspoon freshly grated nutmeg
1 cup (2 sticks) unsalted butter, at room
temperature
¾ cup granulated sugar
1 egg
2 teaspoons vanilla extract
¾ cup confectioners' sugar, sifted

1 Preheat the oven to 350°F.

2 Sift the flour, salt, and nutmeg together onto a piece of waxed paper.

3 In a large mixing bowl, cream the butter until it is light. Then add the sugar and mix until light and fluffy. Add the egg and the vanilla, and mix well. Gradually stir in the flour mixture. Chill the dough, covered, for about 30 minutes, so it is easy to work with.

4 Shape the dough into logs about ½ inch in diameter. Cut the logs into 1-inch lengths, and place them on unoiled baking sheets about ¼ inch apart. Bake in the center of the oven until the logs are beginning to turn gold at the edges, about 15 minutes.

5 Place the confectioners' sugar in a plate or shallow bowl, and while the logs are still hot, roll them in the sugar. Cool them on wire racks, and then store them in an airtight container. These cookies improve with age if stored in a cool place. They will keep well for a month.

About 7 dozen cookies

CHOCOLATE-TIPPED CRESCENT COOKIES

My grandmother grew up on a farm with eight brothers and sisters, and she emerged from this experience with, among other things, a packet of wonderful recipes and a cooking talent that was simple, skilled, and resulted in the most flavorful food I've ever tasted.

These cookies were one of our favorites. The only trick is to thoroughly mix the flour into the butter mixture, and to use the dough at room temperature.

The result is a simple, short, buttery cookie that looks as though it took many more hours to make than it did. You can vary it with a touch of orange zest, for a completely different and equally delicious cookie.

2 cups all-purpose flour, sifted

½ teaspoon salt

1 cup "quick" oats

1 cup (2 sticks) unsalted butter, at room temperature

½ cup confectioners' sugar, sifted

2 teaspoons vanilla extract

Zest of 1 orange, minced (optional)

¼ cup milk

4 ounces good-quality semisweet chocolate, preferably Lindt or Tobler brand, cut into small pieces

1 cup toasted (see Note) almonds or untoasted pistachios, finely chopped

1 Preheat the oven to 325°F. Line two baking sheets with parchment paper.

2 Sift the flour and salt together onto a piece of waxed paper. Add the oats, and mix together.

3 Cream the butter in a large bowl until it is pale yellow and light. Then add the confectioners' sugar, and mix until light and fluffy. Stir in the vanilla, and the orange zest if desired. Then add the flour mixture and mix thoroughly.

4 Take 1 level tablespoon of dough and shape it into a small log, tapering it slightly at the ends. Repeat with the remaining dough, placing them ½ inch apart on the prepared baking sheets. Bend each log gently into a crescent shape.

5 Bake the crescents until they are pale gold at the edges, 25 to 28 minutes. Remove them from the oven, and transfer them to wire racks to cool.

6 Combine the milk and the chocolate in a small heavy saucepan over low heat, and melt the chocolate, whisking constantly. Remove the pan from the heat. Place the nuts in a small bowl.

7 Dip each end of the cookies into the warm chocolate mixture, then into the chopped nuts. Return the crescents to the wire racks, and let the chocolate harden, about 30 minutes. Store in an airtight container. The cookies will keep for at least 5 days.

About 4 dozen cookies

Note: To toast almonds, preheat the oven to 350°F. Place the nuts in a baking pan large enough to hold them in a single layer, and toast, stirring once, until they give off a toasted aroma, 10 to 15 minutes.

THUMBPRINT BUTTER COOKIES

Here's another recipe from my childhood that I thought was a Bain (my mother's maiden name) family exclusive. But no, I found this cookie on my plate at several farms. The nuts and filling varied, but all were delicious.

My mother claims that it hurts her thumb to press the cookies when they're hot, so her current tool for making the indentation is the end of a wooden spoon, which she quickly jabs into the cookies. It works quite well, though you don't have the same control as you do if you use your thumb. It is, however, an ideal solution for the tender-skinned!

Try varying the nuts used in these cookies. I like walnuts, and hazelnuts for a change. Also, although red currant jelly is a gorgeous, bright, clear red filling and its tartness is a foil to the sweet cookie, raspberry jelly adds a nice flavor.

8 tablespoons (1 stick) unsalted butter,
   at room temperature
¼ cup (packed) light brown
   sugar
1 large egg, separated
½ teaspoon vanilla extract
1 cup all-purpose flour
¼ teaspoon salt
¾ cup pecan halves, finely chopped
¼ cup red currant jelly

1 Preheat the oven to 350°F. Line two baking sheets with parchment paper.

2 In a medium-size mixing bowl, mix the butter until it is pale yellow and light. Add the brown sugar, and mix vigorously until it is fluffy. Add the egg yolk and the vanilla extract, and mix well. Then stir in the flour and the salt by hand, just until combined. Be careful not to overmix the dough. If you do and the dough becomes soft, refrigerate it, covered, for 30 minutes so it firms up.

3 In a shallow bowl, whisk the egg white with a pinch of salt just until it begins to turn foamy. Place the pecans in another shallow dish.

4 Using your hands, form the dough into 1-inch balls. Roll the balls in the egg white, then quickly in the pecans. Place them 1 inch apart on the prepared baking sheets, and bake in the center of the oven for 5 minutes. Remove them from the oven, and using your thumb (or the handle of a wooden spoon), make an indentation in the top of each cookie, slightly flattening it. Work quickly so you don't burn your thumb. Return the cookies to the oven, and continue baking them until they are golden, about 15 more minutes. Transfer them to a wire rack to cool.

5 While the cookies are cooling, place the red currant jelly in a small heavy saucepan over very low heat, just to melt. Allow the jelly to cool to lukewarm.

6 When the cookies are cool, fill each indentation with ½ teaspoon red currant jelly. Let the jelly solidify, then store the cookies in an airtight container. They will keep in a cool place for 2 to 3 days.

2 dozen cookies

APRICOT BARS

I love to make these bars at Christmas because they are a tart, fruity foil to the usual selection of sweet cookies. They are simple to make, and when cut in 1-inch squares make a luscious tidbit.

Try to use unsulphured apricots, which are darker in color but much superior in flavor to those that have been treated with sulphur. The confectioners' sugar is only for appearance, not at all necessary to the flavor of these tasty little bars.

⅔ cup dried apricots, preferably
   unsulphured
8 tablespoons (1 stick) unsalted butter,
   at room temperature
¼ cup granulated sugar
1⅓ cups all-purpose flour
½ teaspoon baking powder
¼ teaspoon salt
2 large eggs
1 cup (packed) dark brown sugar
½ teaspoon vanilla extract
½ cup walnuts, chopped
½ cup confectioners' sugar (optional)

1 Rinse the apricots, place them in a medium-size saucepan, and cover with water. Bring them to a boil over medium-high heat, then reduce the heat to medium-low and simmer until they have softened, 10 minutes. Drain the apricots, and allow them to cool. Then dice them.

2 Meanwhile, preheat the oven to 350°F. Lightly oil an 8-inch square baking pan.

3 Place the butter, sugar, and 1 cup of the flour in a medium-size bowl, or in a food processor, and mix until crumbly. Press the mixture into the bottom of the prepared baking pan, making a firmly packed layer. Bake in the center of the oven until pale golden, about 25 minutes. Remove the pan from the heat and let it cool on a wire rack.

4 Sift the remaining ⅓ cup flour with the baking powder and the salt into a small bowl. Set aside.

5 In a large bowl, or in the bowl of an electric mixer, whisk the eggs to break them up. Gradually add the brown sugar, and whisk until slightly foamy. Add the flour mixture (with the paddle attachment if using the electric mixer), and mix until incorporated, being careful not to overmix. Add the vanilla, the nuts, and the apricots, and mix until blended.

6 Spread the mixture over the baked layer. Return the pan to the oven, and

bake until the top is golden and springs back when you touch it, 30 minutes.

7 Remove the pan from the oven and let it cool on a wire rack. Cut the apricot bars into squares. If desired, spread the confec-tioners' sugar on a sheet of waxed paper, and roll the bars in it to cover the top and sides. They will keep for 2 weeks if stored in an airtight container in a cool place.

About 5 dozen 1-inch squares

BARBARA FISCHER'S WHOOPIE PIES

T hese deep chocolate, pillowy cookies might be considered the official Amish snack. They're a common after-school treat, and one that's proffered to visitors as well, along with a cup of coffee. I got this recipe from Barbara Fischer, a horseradish farmer who makes them often for her large family. The recipe is a big one, but don't be concerned—no matter what size your family is, these won't be around for long.

1 cup (2 sticks) unsalted butter, at room temperature
2 cups sugar
2 eggs, at room temperature
2 teaspoons vanilla extract
4 cups all-purpose flour
2 teaspoons baking soda
½ teaspoon salt
1 cup good-quality unsweetened cocoa, such as Droste
1 cup sour cream
1 cup hot water

FOR THE FILLING
12 tablespoons (1½ sticks) unsalted butter, at room temperature
2 cups confectioners' sugar
Pinch of salt
4 teaspoons vanilla extract
2 egg whites
2 teaspoons freshly squeezed lemon juice, or more to taste

1 Preheat the oven to 350°F. Lightly oil two baking sheets, or line them with parchment paper.

2 In a large bowl, cream the butter until it is pale yellow and light. Add the sugar, and continue beating until the mixture is light and fluffy. Then add the eggs, one at a time, mixing well after each addition. Add the vanilla and mix well.

3 Sift the flour, baking soda, salt, and cocoa together onto a large piece of waxed paper. Add the dry ingredients in thirds to the creamed mixture, alternating with the sour cream and the hot water, beginning and ending with the dry ingredients.

4 Drop the dough by tablespoons about 1 inch apart on the prepared baking sheets. Bake until the cookies are puffed and spring back when touched, 10 to 12 minutes. Transfer them to wire racks to cool.

5 To make the filling: In a large bowl or the bowl of an electric mixer, whisk the butter until light, then whisk in the confectioners' sugar until light and fluffy. Add the salt and mix well, then whisk in the vanilla. Add the egg whites, whisking vigorously. The mixture will appear to separate, but continue whisking vigorously until it comes back together in a smooth cream. Whisk in the lemon juice, adding more to taste, if desired.

6 When the cookies are cool, spread one with a thin layer of filling, and top with another cookie to make a whoopie pie. Continue with the remaining cookies, until all the cookies and filling are used up.

34 whoopie pies

PUMPKIN WHOOPIE PIES

We tasted these whoopie pies—sandwich cookies that fall somewhere between a cookie and a tiny cake—at the home of an Amish farmer near Gettysburg, Pennsylvania. They were wrapped individually and stored in a large cookie jar, which was hidden behind a chair in the kitchen so the youngest in the family wouldn't eat them all. As we savored their cakey spiciness, the youngest son ran in and went right to the whoopie pie hiding place to get one of his own. So much for trying to outsmart a child!

These whoopie pies should rest for at least 24 hours before being eaten, as their flavor deepens and becomes richer.

FOR THE COOKIES

2½ cups all-purpose flour
¾ teaspoon ground cloves
1 teaspoon ground cinnamon
1½ teaspoons ground ginger
1 teaspoon salt
1 teaspoon baking powder
1 teaspoon baking soda
1 cup (2 sticks) unsalted butter,
    at room temperature
2 cups (packed) light brown sugar
3 large egg yolks
2 cups puréed pumpkin, canned
    or fresh
1 teaspoon vanilla extract

FOR THE FILLING

6 tablespoons (¾ stick) unsalted butter,
    at room temperature
1 cup confectioners' sugar
Pinch of salt
2 teaspoons vanilla extract
1 egg white
1 tablespoon milk

1 Preheat the oven to 350°F. Line two baking sheets with parchment paper.

2 Sift the dry ingredients together onto a large piece of waxed paper.

3 In a large bowl, or the bowl of an electric mixer, cream the butter until it is light. Add the brown sugar and mix until it is incorporated and light. Then add the egg yolks, one at a time, mixing well after each addition. Add the pumpkin purée and the vanilla, and mix well. Then slowly add the dry ingredients, and mix until thoroughly combined. Be careful not to overmix, or the cookies will be tough.

4 Drop the batter by tablespoonfuls about 1 inch apart on the prepared baking sheets. (Or pipe them, using a ½-inch tip.) Bake until they are puffed and spring back when touched, 10 to 12 minutes. Transfer the cookies to a wire rack to cool.

5 Make the filling: In a large bowl, or the bowl of an electric mixer, whisk the butter until light, then whisk in the confectioners' sugar until light and fluffy. Add the salt and mix well, then whisk in the vanilla. Add the egg white, whisking vigorously. The mixture will break and separate, but continue whisking vigorously until it comes back together and forms a smooth cream. Then whisk in the milk.

6 When the cookies are cool, spread one with a thin layer of filling and top it with another cookie to make a whoopie pie. Continue with the remaining cookies and filling. Store the cookies in an airtight container. They will keep for at least 1 week.

34 whoopie pies

BEST-EVER CHOCOLATE CAKE

I discovered this cake recipe among a collection of Amish recipes. In my opinion, it is the most delicious chocolate cake in the world. I feel eminently qualified to judge, since from a tender age, I've been on a campaign to find the best chocolate cake with chocolate icing.

This cake satisfies on all levels. It is dense, rich with chocolate flavor, moist and springy at the same time, plus it is big, tall, and slightly mounded so that when you serve it, guests can't help oohing and aahing. And with its thin layer of icing, it makes a perfect, and gorgeous, dessert.

Just remember, the cake is best when made the day before, so it has a chance to ripen. Cover it with a bowl, or place it in an airtight container to keep.

4 cups unbleached all-purpose flour
2 teaspoons baking soda
1 cup good-quality unsweetened cocoa,
    such as Droste
1 cup (2 sticks) unsalted butter, at room
    temperature
2 cups sugar
2 large eggs
2 teaspoons vanilla extract
1 cup sour cream
1 cup hot water

FOR THE ICING

8 tablespoons (1 stick) unsalted butter,
    at room temperature
5 ounces bittersweet chocolate, such as
    Lindt or Tobler
6 tablespoons heavy (whipping) cream
1¾ cups confectioners' sugar, sifted
1 teaspoon vanilla extract

1 Preheat the oven to 350°F. Lightly oil two 9-inch round cake pans. Line them with parchment paper, and lightly oil and flour the paper.

2 Sift the flour, baking soda, and cocoa together onto a large piece of waxed paper.

3 In a large bowl, or the bowl of an electric mixer, mix the butter until it is pale yellow and fluffy. Add the sugar, and continue mixing until light. Then add the eggs, one at a time, and mix until they are thoroughly incorporated. Add the vanilla and mix well.

4 Add the dry ingredients to the creamed mixture in thirds, alternating with the sour cream and the hot water, beginning and ending with the dry ingredients.

5 Divide the batter between the prepared pans, and tap the pans once, sharply, on the counter. Bake in the center of the oven until the cakes are puffed and spring back when lightly touched, 45 to 50 minutes.

6 While the cakes are baking, make the icing: Combine the butter, chocolate, and cream in a medium-size heavy saucepan over low heat. Heat until melted, stirring occasionally. Remove the pan from the heat, and whisk in the confectioners' sugar until smooth. Whisk in the vanilla, and set the icing aside to cool to lukewarm.

7 Transfer the cakes to a wire rack to cool. When they are cool, turn them out of the baking pans. Trim the domed top off of one layer so that it is flat. Place that layer on a serving plate.

8 When the icing has cooled but is still runny, spread it over the bottom layer, including the sides. The icing will run down the sides of the cake, but you can easily catch and spread it, using a spatula or a wide knife. Place the second layer of cake, right side up, on the first and ice it with the remaining icing, making a nice even layer. Serve the following day.

One large cake (10 to 12 servings)

KING-SIZE APPLE CAKE

T his is one of my favorite desserts, and I am grateful to Alice Berner, of Big Sandy, Montana, for sharing it with me. Like Alice, it is lively and solidly good.

Whatever time of year I make this cake, it brings to mind the holidays. It's moist and dense from the generous amount of fresh apple, and its flavor and texture are festive from the spices and the liberal amount of fruits and nuts. It's simple to make, and so versatile that you can serve it in the morning with coffee or tea, or dress it up with a Lemon Glaze (page 421) or Caramel Frosting (page 414) and present it after a lovely supper—accompanied by a small glass of port, perhaps.

This cake will keep at least a week if it is tightly covered. It is best to make it at least the day before you plan to serve it, as the flavors mellow overnight.

1 cup (2 sticks) unsalted butter, at room
temperature
2 cups sugar
3 large eggs
2⅔ cups sifted all-purpose flour
3 tablespoons good-quality unsweetened
cocoa, such as Droste
1 teaspoon salt
1 teaspoon ground cinnamon
1 teaspoon ground allspice
2 teaspoons baking soda
¼ cup hot water
3 cups grated fresh apple (from about
2½ medium-size peeled apples)
1 cup raisins
1 cup chopped walnuts or pecans

1 Preheat the oven to 350°F. Heavily butter and flour a 10-inch bundt pan.

2 Cream the butter and sugar together in a large mixing bowl, or in the bowl of an electric mixer, until pale yellow and light. Add the eggs, one at a time, mixing well after each addition. Beat the mixture until it is light and fluffy.

3 Sift the flour, cocoa, salt, cinnamon, and allspice together onto a piece of waxed paper.

4 Add the baking soda to the hot water, and mix until it is dissolved. Add the dry ingredients to the butter mixture alternately with the soda and water mixture, beginning and ending with the dry ingredients.

5 Stir in the apples, raisins, and nuts. Spoon the batter (which will be very thick) into the prepared pan. Bake until the cake is deep brown and springs back when lightly touched, about 1 hour and 10 minutes. Cool on a wire rack for 10 minutes, then unmold from the pan and allow to cool thoroughly before serving.

One 10-inch cake (10 to 12 servings)

WHAT ARE THOSE BERRIES DOING DOWN SOUTH?

When we left the city of Lakeland, Florida, which sprawls amoeba-like into the surrounding farm-land, it was sunup on a cool December morning, and the sun was at our backs. The sun glinted off irrigation water shooting over the fields; it had been on since the middle of the night to protect the crops from an unseasonable frost. We passed a field of limp, blackened squash plants that some unlucky farmer hadn't irrigated in time.

The sun was fully up by the time we reached the Joyner farm, halfway between Lakeland and Plant City, the strawberry capital of Florida, though a chill wind chased clouds across the sky. Pickers worked in one field, and a knot of others stood near the truck where berries were weighed, waiting for the sun to dry the remaining fields so they could begin their day.

The fields were ribbed with straight rectangular rows covered in black plastic and topped with bushy little plants. The berries were hidden underneath the leaves, flashing brilliant red when they showed, making the field look as if it were decorated for Christmas.

John Joyner was helping his children hang Christmas lights on their house. He turned the job over to his wife and took us on a tour of the fields.

"The black plastic came in the '60s," he explained, kneeling down to break through it and finger the soil it covered. "It's industry standard now. It heats the soil, keeps down weeds, and holds moisture, which helps the berries grow faster."

John lives in the family farmhouse, which is surrounded by 32 lush, productive acres. He learned farming from his father, who farmed with his father before him. Though only in his mid-thirties, John has seen many changes in the Florida strawberry industry.

Not all his farmland is in berries, though they are the major crop and represent his major investment and risk. If the crop can make it through the hazardous start of the

growing season without a killing frost or wind, the profit makes the risk worthwhile.

BERRIES FROM UP NORTH

John begins every season with new plants, which he imports from Canada at considerable cost because there is no commercial source any closer. That's where his risk begins. Sometimes he's gotten bad bunches from Canada, which either wouldn't produce or were infected by disease.

"The plants cost about $75 per 1,000, which is enough for one row," he said. Shading my eyes and looking out at the fields, I lost track of the rows after about forty. "We've got $4,000 invested in each acre until the berries are picked," he said. Why not cut the startup costs and leave the plants—which will bear again—in the ground? "It doesn't make sense for a commercial operation, because they don't produce enough after the first year," he said. "But we're looking at producing our own bedding plants."

The berry season runs until May, with a small peak in January and another major peak in March, when the berries are at their sweet, juicy best. "We try to plan it so our strawberries are finished producing by the time those from California are on the market," John said.

California is the Florida industry's major competition. "We're nothing compared with California; they dwarf us. This whole area only has 5,000 acres—but we have berries when they don't."

By mid-May the plastic is pulled off the rows, the plants are mowed down to the ground, and peas are planted for a summer crop and to fix nitrogen in the soil.

"The plastic is recycled and made into garbage bags," John said. "I guess there will be biodegradable plastic too, though right now it's got problems because it starts decomposing too soon in the sun."

John uses pesticides for spider mites and the gray and downy molds that plague his plants. "I don't like to use 'em, but I can't sit and watch my plants go," he said. "We try to irrigate before we harvest, to rinse off the plants and berries."

Pickers start in the fields at sunup as long as there hasn't been a heavy dew. If the berries

are wet, they wait until the sun has dried them off. Then, equipped with little rolling carts, they skitter across the fields sideways like crabs, picking in a blur. "We like to get everything picked by noon if we can," John explained.

FASHIONABLE VARIETIES

The variety they were picking is called Selva; it comes in early and bears longer

▶ ▶ ▶

than older varieties. John is experimenting with another called Osso Grande, which is just beginning to ripen and is sweeter than any other strawberry. A later variety, Pajaro, picks up in January. It falls somewhere between Selva and Osso Grande on the sweetness scale.

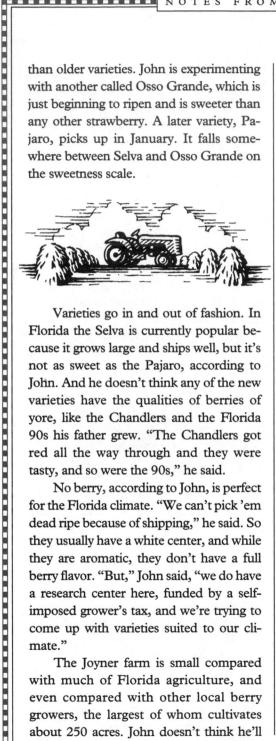

Varieties go in and out of fashion. In Florida the Selva is currently popular because it grows large and ships well, but it's not as sweet as the Pajaro, according to John. And he doesn't think any of the new varieties have the qualities of berries of yore, like the Chandlers and the Florida 90s his father grew. "The Chandlers got red all the way through and they were tasty, and so were the 90s," he said.

No berry, according to John, is perfect for the Florida climate. "We can't pick 'em dead ripe because of shipping," he said. So they usually have a white center, and while they are aromatic, they don't have a full berry flavor. "But," John said, "we do have a research center here, funded by a self-imposed grower's tax, and we're trying to come up with varieties suited to our climate."

The Joyner farm is small compared with much of Florida agriculture, and even compared with other local berry growers, the largest of whom cultivates about 250 acres. John doesn't think he'll get any bigger and is worried about increasing land values and competition from agribusiness. Nonetheless, John doesn't want to do anything but farm, and he has found a solution in the increasing traffic along the road that cuts through his property. "We saw all these tourists driving by and we thought it might be kind of nice to offer strawberry shortcake and milkshakes, so we set up a concession stand," he said. It has become a land-office business. The stand became Joyner's Restaurant, with an adjoining produce section where John's wife and mother sell the onions, peas, eggplants, and squash he grows, as well as some imports. As the Lakeland sprawl develops, so will the Joyner business.

By 11 A.M. the Joyner Restaurant begins to fill with traveling businessmen, workers from nearby warehouses, neighbors, and tourists. The fried Cuban sandwiches and tasty soups are good, but the crowds come for the mound of strawberry shortcake, made with field-ripened berries.

"These berries were picked here this morning," the waitress said, as she set down a plate heaped with juicy berries and cream that obscured the buttery shortcake. As I ate it, savoring the sweet berry flavor, I thought a person could do worse than stake his future success on a plate of strawberry shortcake.

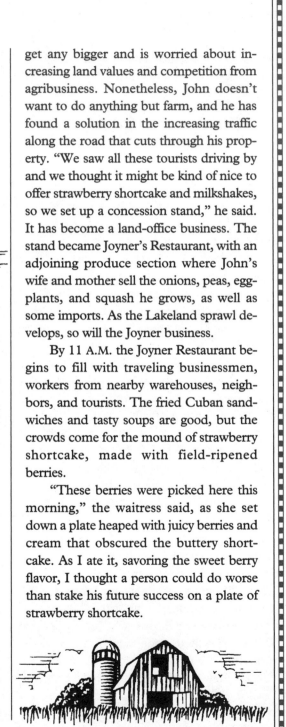

BEST-EVER STRAWBERRY SHORTCAKE

This shortcake is inspired by the one I tasted at the Joyner Restaurant outside Lakeland, Florida (see page 408). I've taken liberties with their version—a recipe they were loath to share. It is tinged with orange zest, and full of buttery flavor. It is so easy to make that you can do it in your sleep—the only requirement is a light hand. It is treated much like puff pastry without all the chilling, and you'll find it surprisingly light.

The best time to make the shortcake, is when local berries are ripe, full of color and sun. If you can't find strawberries or want a little change, try blackberries, blueberries, or raspberries.

Whichever berries you use, cut and toss them with a touch of sugar several hours before you plan to serve them, so they release their fragrant juices.

4 pints ripe strawberries, stemmed

7 tablespoons granulated sugar

1 cup all-purpose flour

¾ cup plus 2 tablespoons cake flour

½ teaspoon salt

2½ teaspoons baking powder

Minced zest of 1 orange

6 tablespoons (¾ stick) unsalted butter, chilled

2 cups heavy (whipping) cream, chilled

1 teaspoon vanilla extract

1 tablespoon confectioners' sugar

1 Preheat the oven to 425°F. Line a baking sheet with parchment paper. Chill a medium-size bowl and a whisk or whisk attachment or rotary blades of an electric mixer (for whipping the cream).

2 Cut the berries into ¼-inch-thick slices, and place them in a large bowl. Toss them with 2 tablespoons of the sugar, and set aside.

3 In a large bowl, or in a food processor, combine both flours with the salt, baking powder, 4 tablespoons of the sugar, and the orange zest. Stir well, or process once or twice, to mix. Add the butter and process, or cut it in with a pastry blender or two knives until it ranges from the size of coarse cornmeal to the size of a pea.

4 Add 1 cup of the cream all at once, and lightly mix until the dough gathers together but does not completely adhere. Be

very careful not to overmix. If you are using a food processor, pulse just two or three times.

5 Turn the dough out onto a well-floured surface, dust it lightly with flour, and press it down with a rolling pin until it is somewhat rectangular in shape and about ½ inch thick. Fold it in thirds like a business letter, and turn it one quarter turn (90 degrees). Lightly flour it and gently press it out again until it is an even rectangle about ½ inch thick, fold it in thirds, and turn it another quarter turn.

6 Lightly flour the dough again if necessary to keep it from sticking to the rolling pin, and roll it out to form a very even rectangle measuring about 6 x 12 inches; straighten the edges by pushing the rolling pin up against them. Cut it in half, crosswise, then cut an X through each half

so that you have eight triangular pieces. Transfer them to the prepared baking sheet, leaving about ¼ inch between them. Sprinkle the pieces with the remaining 1 tablespoon sugar. Bake in the center of the oven until the shortcakes are golden and puffed, about 12 minutes. Slide the parchment paper off the baking sheet and onto a wire rack to cool.

7 Using the chilled whisk or electric mixer attachment and bowl, whip the remaining 1 cup cream with the vanilla and the confectioners' sugar until it holds soft peaks.

8 Place a shortcake in the center of each dessert plate, and top it with berries and a dollop of whipped cream. Serve immediately.

8 servings

GREAT-GRANDMA'S SHEEP WAGON CARROT CAKE

A lice Berner's great-grandmother was the magician who made this cake out on the trail when she went along to move the sheep from one pasture to another in the plains of Montana.

As I'm preparing the ingredients, I like to imagine the woman who wrote this recipe down, and think of how many times she must have stood over a wood fire—maybe built right on the ground, or in a pit, or in a wagon pulled along on the trail—and gone through a similar process. She probably didn't have any butter—more likely it was lard. Nevertheless, this cake probably tastes much the way it did on the trail, and what a treat it must have been after a hard day's ride, with its rich, delicious flavors.

This cake is good the day it is made, but, tightly wrapped, it becomes more mellow and moist as the days go by.

If you want to turn it into a holiday cake, substitute ⅔ cup brandy for the same amount of water when you are cooking the fruit and carrot mixture.

1⅓ cups water
1⅓ cups sugar
1 cup raisins or chopped candied fruit
1 tablespoon unsalted butter
1½ cups finely grated carrots
2½ cups all-purpose flour
1 teaspoon ground cinnamon
1 teaspoon ground cloves
1 teaspoon freshly grated nutmeg
½ teaspoon salt
1 teaspoon baking soda
2 teaspoons baking powder
1 cup coarsely chopped walnuts or pecans
Caramel Frosting (recipe follows) or
  confectioners' sugar (optional)

1 Combine the water, sugar, raisins, butter, and carrots in a medium-size saucepan, and bring to a boil over medium-high heat. Reduce the heat to medium and simmer the mixture, uncovered, for 5 minutes. Remove the pan from the heat, cover, and let sit for 12 hours.

2 Preheat the oven to 275°F. Butter a 10-inch tube pan.

3 Sift the flour, spices, baking soda, and baking powder together onto a piece of waxed paper.

4 Transfer the carrot mixture to a large bowl, or the bowl of an electric mixer. Add the dry ingredients and mix until thoroughly combined. Then stir the nuts in well. Transfer the batter to the tube pan, smooth it out, and place the pan on a baking sheet. Bake in the center of the oven until the cake is a dark brown and springs back when lightly pressed, about 1¾ hours. It will feel firmer than other cakes.

5 Transfer the pan to a wire rack, and let the cake cool for 10 minutes. Then remove the cake from the pan and return it to the rack. When it is fully cool, frost the cake or dust it with confectioners' sugar.

One 10-inch cake (about 12 servings)

CARAMEL FROSTING

■■■■■■

This frosting, from Alice Berner in Montana, is everything a frosting should be. It is very, very sweet and has a deep caramel flavor. Every time I make it, usually for a spice cake, it gets so much attention I wonder if next time I shouldn't just serve it with cake on the side! If you ever have any frosting left over, just store it in the refrigerator. It is amazing what you can eat it on—we had a guest who spread it on saltines!

8 tablespoons (1 stick) unsalted buter
½ cup (packed) dark brown sugar
2 tablespoons milk
1 cup plus 2 tablespoons confectioners' sugar
½ teaspoon vanilla extract

1 Melt the butter in a medium-size heavy saucepan over medium heat. When the butter is melted, stir in the brown sugar, reduce the heat to low, and cook just until the sugar melts and begins to get slightly ropy, about 2 minutes, stirring occasionally.

2 Stir in the milk and raise the heat to medium. Cook just until the mixture comes to a boil, stirring frequently. Remove the pan from the heat and cool to lukewarm.

3 Either transfer the mixture to a medium-size mixing bowl or leave it in the saucepan if it is large enough. Add the confectioners' sugar to the mixture, about ½ cup at a time, whisking vigorously until it is smooth and spreadable. Whisk in the vanilla extract and use immediately.

*1 cup (enough to glaze a
10-inch bundt cake)*

SPICY HALLOWEEN GINGER CAKE

■■■■

This recipe was given to me many years ago by Susan Kobos, who lives on a farm in Molalla, Oregon, not far from Portland, with her husband, David, and their three children.

Susan and David are a complementary couple in every way, right down to their cooking preferences. Susan loves to bake, David loves to prepare meat and vegetables, and the harmonious meals served at their home reflect their dual skills.

Susan said she makes this cake for Halloween. It's studded with chocolate chips, tart with caramelized apples, and sparkling with molasses and spice. It tastes wonderful the first day, cooled just to lukewarm from the oven, and is even better the second.

2 cups dark molasses
1 cup (2 sticks) plus 2 tablespoons
   unsalted butter, at room
   temperature
¼ cup strong brewed coffee
4¾ cups cake flour
½ teaspoon salt
1 teaspoon ground allspice
1 teaspoon ground cloves
4 teaspoons ground cinnamon
4 teaspoons ground ginger
2 teaspoons ground mace
2 teaspoons freshly grated nutmeg
1½ teaspoons baking soda
4 tart medium apples, such as Granny Smith
½ cup (packed) dark brown sugar
2 large eggs
2 cups sour cream
½ cup semisweet chocolate chips or baking
   chocolate cut into small pieces

1 Preheat the oven to 350°F. Lightly oil a
13 x 9 x 2-inch baking pan.

2 Combine the molasses, butter, and coffee in a medium-size saucepan, and bring to a boil over medium-high heat, stirring occasionally. As soon as it boils, remove from the heat. Transfer the mixture to a large bowl, or the bowl of an electric mixer, and let cool to lukewarm.

3 Sift the flour, salt, spices, and baking soda together onto a large piece of waxed paper.

4 Core, peel, and halve the apples, then slice them into ¼-inch-thick slices. Line the prepared pan with the apple slices slightly overlapping them. Sprinkle them with the brown sugar.

5 Whisk the eggs into the molasses mixture. Add the dry ingredients and mix quickly but thoroughly. Then add the sour cream, mixing just until it is incorporated. Fold in the chocolate chips, and then pour the cake batter over the apple slices.

6 Bake in the center of the oven until the cake springs back when touched lightly and a knife inserted in the center comes out clean, about 55 minutes. Remove the pan from the oven, and transfer it to a wire rack to cool at least to lukewarm before serving.

7 To serve, cut the cake in pieces and turn them out of the pan upside down, so the apple slices are on top. Or turn the whole cake out onto a large serving platter, and serve.

One 13 x 9-inch cake
(12 to 14 servings)

AILI TAKALA'S RHUBARB CAKE

An unforgettable meal greeted us when we arrived at the home of Aili and Bill Takala, in Stockett, Montana, and along with the Takalas' grandson Stuart, a longtime friend, we did our best to eat it all. Aili urged us along from her customary chair to the side of the table and Bill rested in an armchair in the adjoining living room.

The Takalas eat very early—a habit developed during 40 years of farming—and when they have guests they still eat at their usual time, preferring to enjoy their guests' dinner from the sidelines. It's the old-fashioned way—it leaves Aili free to clear away empty dishes, urge more delicious food on her guests, fill glasses of milk or water, and generally participate in the lively conversation while making sure everyone is well fed and comfortable. Bill contributes from his chair, and together they are hosts without peer.

When I asked Aili for the recipe for this tart rhubarb-studded cake (which disappeared in its entirety at the end of that meal, with only symbolic help from Bill and Aili), she gave it to me and suggested the coconut be left out. I like it in.

This cake will keep for several days if well covered.

2 cups diced fresh rhubarb (¼-inch cubes)
1½ cups sugar
8 tablespoons (1 stick) unsalted butter
1 large egg, beaten
1 teaspoon vanilla extract
2 cups plus 2 tablespoons all-purpose flour
1 teaspoon baking soda
1 teaspoon ground cinnamon
½ teaspoon salt
1 cup buttermilk
½ cup unsweetened shredded coconut
   (available at natural foods stores)
Confectioners' sugar, for dusting (optional)

1 Preheat the oven to 350°F. Lightly butter a 7 x 12-inch glass baking dish.

2 Place the rhubarb and ¼ cup of the sugar in a small bowl, stir, and set aside while you prepare the cake.

3 In a large bowl, or the bowl of an electric mixer, mix the butter with the remaining 1¼ cups sugar until pale yellow and light. Add the egg and the vanilla, and mix well.

4 Sift the flour, baking soda, and spices together onto a piece of waxed paper.

5 Add the dry ingredients in thirds to the butter mixture, alternating with the buttermilk, beginning and ending with the dry ingredients. Fold in the rhubarb mixture, and then the coconut. Spoon the batter, which will be fairly thick, into the prepared baking dish.

6 Bake until the cake is golden and puffed, and springs back when pressed gently, 45 to 50 minutes. Remove the pan from the oven and set it on a wire rack to cool. When the cake is cool, dust it with confectioners' sugar if desired. Cut it into ten pieces and arrange them on a serving platter, or place the pieces on individual dessert plates, and serve.

One 7 x 12-inch cake (10 servings)

MAE POIROT'S FRUIT CAKE

I think this cake given to me by Mae Poirot (see page 419), which I've eaten barely cooled from the oven, goes down so easily, it's hard to even think about wrapping it and saving it until Christmas.

2 cups walnuts or pecans, coarsely chopped
3 cups pitted dates
3 cups seedless raisins
1½ cups (8 ounces) dried apricots
1½ cups (8 ounces) dried pitted
  prunes
¼ cup honey
¼ cup dry sherry
2 cups sifted all-purpose flour

½ teaspoon salt
¼ teaspoon baking soda
1 teaspoon ground cinnamon
½ teaspoon ground cloves
2 cups (4 sticks) unsalted butter
1¼ cups (packed) dark brown sugar
4 large eggs
¼ cup bourbon

1 Preheat the oven to 350°F.

2 Spread the nuts on a baking sheet, and toast them in the oven until they are golden and somewhat crisp, 10 to 15 minutes. Remove them from the oven and let them cool. Reduce the oven temperature to 275°F.

3 Line two 9 x 5 x 3-inch loaf pans completely with parchment paper, and then heavily oil the paper.

4 Cut the dates in half lengthwise, then in quarters. Rinse the raisins under very hot water, to plump them up, and pat them dry with paper towels. Slice the apricots into ¼-inch-thick strips, and coarsely chop the prunes. Place all the dried fruits in a large bowl.

5 In a small bowl, whisk together the honey and the sherry. Pour this over the dried fruit, and toss. Set aside until ready to use. (You may do this the night before you plan to make the fruitcake. Cover the bowl tightly.)

6 Sift together the flour, salt, baking soda, and spices onto a piece of waxed paper.

7 In a large bowl, or the bowl of an electric mixer, beat the butter until it is light and fluffy and will hold soft peaks. (If you are doing this by hand, it will take 5 minutes of solid beating. It will take about 3 minutes in an electric mixer.) Add the brown sugar, and continue beating until the mixture is very light and fluffy.

8 Beat in the eggs, one at a time. Then add the dry ingredients, mixing just until they are incorporated. Stir the nuts into the fruit mixture, then stir that into the cake batter, working quickly but making sure that the fruit and nuts are evenly dispersed throughout the batter.

9 Divide the batter between the loaf pans, smoothing it on top. Place a pan full of water on the bottom rack of the oven, and place the loaf pans on the center rack. Bake until the cakes are golden and spring back when lightly touched, 2 hours and 30 to 50 minutes. Remove the pans from the oven and transfer them to a wire rack to cool for 20 minutes. Then turn the cakes out from the pans, and cool them completely on the rack. Remove the paper from the cakes.

10 Cut two pieces of cheesecloth large enough to wrap around a cake at least once. Dip them into the bourbon, wring them out lightly, and wrap them around the cakes. Then wrap the cakes with waxed paper, and seal in a plastic bag until ready to serve. You may want to pour more bourbon over the cheesecloth at 2- or 3-week intervals until you serve the cakes.

Two 9 x 5 x 3-inch loaves (10 to 12 servings each)

THE FARMER PROPHET

Eugene Poirot was something of a prophet among farmers and ecologists. Long ago, before anyone was talking about global warming and other insidious environmental developments, Poirot would walk the prairie that abutted his farm near Golden City, Missouri, paying attention to the natural cycles. He believed strongly in the lessons of what he observed, and he ordered his farming around them. He never tilled the 800 acres of virgin prairie that formed a part of his land, nor has his son, Severin, and the prairie is rapidly becoming a living relic.

Over the many years that Gene farmed his land, he transformed it from abused, exploited, nearly dead acreage to rich and productive soil. Whenever something puzzled him, he went to the prairie for the answer. He built irrigation ditches, rotated crops, raised cattle and catfish, using lessons he learned from the prairie.

He wrote about his work in a book called *Our Margin of Life*, and filmmaker Tom Putnam recorded his work in a moving documentary. Both works have influenced a generation of farmers, as I discovered in my visits—Gene Poirot's name came up often and with reverence.

I was lucky enough to visit the Poirot farm. Gene died several years ago, but I met his wife, Mae, and Severin, who took over the farm from his father. Severin, who grows sweet corn and popcorn, doesn't wander the prairie in quite the same fashion as his father, nor listen to its lessons in quite the same way—because he learned them from his father and practices them automatically.

He took us on a tour of his fields. Walking into one, he opened his arms wide. "This," he said, pointing to one side, "is theater popcorn. This," pointing to the other, "is microwave popcorn." They both looked like corn to me, but were different varieties developed for specific uses.

After a long afternoon with Severin, we returned to the Poirot family home and Mae served us muffins and tea. When pressed for a recipe, she gave me one for a deliciously old-fashioned fruitcake (see page 417).

"My husband loved that cake," she said. "He used to take a hypodermic needle filled with bourbon, and stick the cake with it, and he insisted that was what made it taste so good."

ANNE FRIAR THOMAS'S HARVEST PECAN CAKE

T his golden, softly nutty cake comes from Texas, where pecans grow in profusion. It is chock full of nuts, so that every mouthful has its rewarding crunch.

Harvest Pecan Cake is equally good for dessert and for breakfast. Anne Friar Thomas's other recipes are on pages 395 and 396.

2 cups pecans, toasted until deep golden
  (see Note) and cooled
2¼ cups sifted all-purpose flour
¼ teaspoon salt
1 teaspoon baking powder
1 cup (2 sticks) unsalted butter, at room
  temperature
¾ cup granulated sugar
¾ cup (packed) light brown sugar
6 large eggs, separated
¼ cup milk
½ teaspoon vanilla extract
1½ tablespoons very strong brewed coffee
Lemon Glaze (recipe follows)

1 Preheat the oven to 350°F. Generously butter a 10-inch tube or bundt pan.

2 Coarsely chop the pecans.

3 Sift the flour, salt, and baking powder together onto a piece of waxed paper.

4 In a large bowl, or the bowl of an electric mixer, cream the butter until it is pale yellow and light. Add both sugars, reserving 1 tablespoon of the granulated sugar, and mix until they are thoroughly incorporated and the mixture is light and fluffy. Add the egg yolks, one at a time, mixing well after each addition.

5 In a small bowl, stir together the milk, vanilla, and coffee. Add this to the butter mixture alternating with the dry ingredients, beginning and ending with the dry ingredients. Quickly fold in the pecans.

6 Beat the egg whites with a pinch of salt until they are foamy and beginning to thicken. Add the remaining 1 tablespoon sugar, and continue beating until they are glossy and hold stiff peaks. Fold them into

the cake batter until they are thoroughly incorporated.

7 Pour the batter into the prepared pan, and bake until the cake is golden and puffed, and springs back when touched lightly, about 55 minutes.

8 Poke several holes in the top of the cake, and pour the warm lemon glaze over it. Allow to cool before serving. This cake will keep for several days in an airtight container.

1 cake (10 to 12 servings)

Note: To toast pecans, preheat the oven to 350°F. Place the nuts in a baking pan large enough to hold them in a single layer, and toast, stirring once, until they give off a toasted aroma, 10 to 15 minutes.

LEMON GLAZE

This is a simple glaze that takes only a moment to prepare and adds a refreshing tang to a spice or fruit cake.

½ cup confectioners' sugar
1 tablespoon freshly squeezed
  lemon juice

Sift the confectioners' sugar into a small bowl. Whisk in the lemon juice until the mixture is smooth. Drizzle the glaze over the cake.

½ cup

FRESH BANANA BREAD

This recipe—and the Banana Bread Pudding (see page 474)—was inspired by a fresh bunch of small, sweet bananas that was handed to me by Wayne Boynton, a sugar cane farmer in Florida who also has a row of banana trees on his land.

This banana bread is hearty, not too sweet, and ideal for a bread pudding because it bakes up firm, slightly less moist than traditional banana bread. If you want to use this recipe for Banana Bread Pudding, omit the walnuts, nutmeg, and lemon zest, and increase the baking time to 1 hour.

1¾ cups all-purpose flour

1 teaspoon freshly grated nutmeg

1 teaspoon baking soda

½ teaspoon baking powder

½ teaspoon salt

5 tablespoons plus 1 teaspoon (⅓ cup) unsalted butter, at room temperature

⅔ cup sugar

2 large eggs

1 cup mashed banana (from 2 large bananas)

1 tablespoon vanilla extract

2 teaspoons minced lemon zest

½ cup chopped walnuts

1 Preheat the oven to 350°F. Lightly oil a 9 x 5 x 3-inch loaf pan.

2 Sift the flour, nutmeg, baking soda, baking powder, and salt together on a sheet of waxed paper, and set aside.

3 Cream the butter in a medium-size bowl until light. Add the sugar and beat until thoroughly mixed and light. Add the eggs, one at a time, beating thoroughly after each addition. Add the mashed bananas, vanilla, and lemon zest. Mix well, then fold in the walnuts. Fold in the dry ingredients until thoroughly incorporated.

4 Pour the batter into the prepared pan, run the blade of a knife lengthwise through the batter (to prevent the bread from cracking on top as it rises during baking), and bake until the bread is golden and springs back when lightly touched, 45 minutes. Remove the pan from the oven, unmold the bread onto a wire rack, and let it cool before serving.

6 to 8 servings

LILLIAN'S LEMON BREAD

W hen we visited the Coach Farm, in the Hudson Valley about two hours north of New York City, owners Miles and Lillian Cahn greeted us and led us directly to the lunch table. We had a rousing meal, and this lemon bread was served as dessert.

It is sweet, tart, and tender, and when I remarked on it, Lillian said it's been a favorite in their

family since they first had it when they were staying at the home of their friend Flo Schmalzl. "That was twenty-five years ago, and I've made it for my family ever since," she said. "But you can't have the recipe unless you promise to give Flo credit."

So the credit goes to Flo, though I will always associate this bread with the Cahns. The recipe makes two loaves, so you can serve one and freeze the other.

3 cups all-purpose flour
2 teaspoons baking powder
1 teaspoon salt
1 cup (2 sticks) unsalted butter, at room
   temperature
2 cups sugar
4 large eggs
Minced zest of 2 lemons
1 cup milk
¾ cup coarsely chopped walnuts
½ cup freshly squeezed lemon juice

1 Preheat the oven to 350°F. Line two 9 x 4-inch loaf pans with parchment paper. Generously butter the paper.

2 Sift the flour, baking powder, and salt together onto a piece of waxed paper.

3 In a medium-size bowl, or the bowl of an electric mixer, cream the butter until it is pale yellow and light. Add 1½ cups of the sugar, and beat until it is incorporated and the mixture is fluffy. Add the eggs, one at a time, beating well after each addition. Then add the lemon zest and mix well. Add the dry ingredients in thirds, alternating with the milk, beginning and ending with the dry ingredients. Mix just until the dry ingredients are incorporated. Do not over-mix, or the bread will be tough. Fold in the walnuts.

4 Spoon the batter into the prepared loaf pans, smoothing it out on top. Bake in the center of the oven until the breads are golden and spring back lightly when touched, 45 to 50 minutes.

5 While the breads are baking, mix the lemon juice with the remaining ½ cup sugar in a small bowl. Set it aside.

6 When the breads are baked, transfer the pans to wire racks to cool. While the loaves are still hot, poke several holes in the top of the breads with a fork or a cake tester, and pour the lemon juice mixture over them. Let the loaves cool, then turn them out of the pans. Remove the parchment paper if you plan to serve them immediately. Otherwise, leave the paper on the breads, wrap them tightly in aluminum foil, and freeze.

Two 9 x 4-inch loaves
(6 servings each)

FUNNY CAKE

This recipe has a strong Pennsylvania Dutch influence and was given to me by a co-worker many years ago. Funny Cake originated with her husband's farming family and she always made it for get-togethers. It was usually the most popular dessert on the buffet table.

The cake lives up to its name because it's a funny, quirky recipe that doesn't make sense until you bite into the finished product.

FOR THE SYRUP
½ cup milk
¼ cup sugar
¼ cup good-quality unsweetened cocoa,
  such as Droste
1 teaspoon vanilla extract

FOR THE CAKE BATTER
1 cup all-purpose flour
1 teaspoon baking powder
¾ cup sugar
4 tablespoons (½ stick) unsalted butter,
  at room temperature
1 large egg, beaten
½ cup milk
1 teaspoon vanilla extract
2 teaspoons grated orange zest

1 prebaked 9-inch pie shell (page 431)

1 Preheat the oven to 350°F.

2 Make the syrup: Bring the milk to a boil in a small heavy saucepan. Combine the sugar and the cocoa in a medium-size bowl, and add the hot milk. Stir gently with a wire whisk until the ingredients are well mixed. Then add the vanilla, mix well, and set aside (if you are making this more than 1 hour in advance, cover and refrigerate).

3 Make the batter: Sift the flour and the baking powder together onto a sheet of waxed paper. In a medium-size bowl, or the bowl of an electric mixer, mix the sugar and the butter until pale yellow and light. Add the egg and mix well. Then add the milk and the vanilla, and mix until smooth and thoroughly combined. Fold in the dry ingredients and the orange zest.

4 To assemble the cake, pour the syrup mixture into the baked pie shell, then spread the cake batter over the syrup (do not mix the two). Place the cake on a baking sheet, and bake in the center of the oven until the cake springs back when touched gently, about 45 minutes. Transfer the Funny Cake to a wire rack to cool before serving.

One 9-inch cake (6 to 8 servings)

GYPSY'S ARM CAKE

Gypsy's Arm Cake, a recipe from Juanita Hormachea of Boise, Idaho, is a Basque version of a genoise, and much more rustic in texture. It is rich with egg and filled with a delicately cinnamon-flavored pastry cream that will win your heart. And it is so easy to make, you'll be amazed. Serve it as dessert, or at brunch with a pot of strong steaming coffee.

FOR THE PASTRY CREAM
5 egg yolks
6 tablespoons granulated sugar
¼ cup all-purpose flour
Pinch of salt
1½ to 1¾ cups milk
1 cinnamon stick, 3 inches long

FOR THE CAKE
7 large eggs, separated, at room temperature
1 cup granulated sugar
1¼ cups cake flour
1 teaspoon baking powder
½ teaspoon salt
1 teaspoon vanilla extract
3 tablespoons confectioners' sugar
¼ teaspoon ground cinnamon

1. Make the pastry cream: Whisk the egg yolks with the sugar in a medium-size bowl until they are thick and lemon-colored. Whisk in the flour and the salt, and set aside.

2. Place 1½ cups of the milk and the cinnamon stick in a medium-size saucepan over medium-high heat. Scald the milk by heating just until little bubbles form around the edge of the milk. Remove the pan from the heat, cover, and set aside to infuse for 15 minutes.

3. Remove the cinnamon stick from the milk and discard. Return the milk to the scalding point over medium-high heat, and then gradually whisk it into the egg yolk mixture. Return this mixture to the saucepan, and cook over medium heat, stirring constantly, until it comes to a boil. Continue cooking for at least 2 minutes, until the pastry cream thins slightly and the flour taste has cooked out of it. Remove the pan from the heat, transfer the pastry cream to a bowl, cover, and set aside to cool.

4. Preheat the oven to 375°F. Line a 17 x 11 x 1-inch jelly roll pan with parch-

ment paper. Brush it with a mild vegetable oil or melted butter, and dust with flour.

5 Prepare the cake: Beat the egg yolks and ¾ cup of the sugar with the whisk attachment in an electric mixer until the mixture is thick and lemon-colored.

6 Sift the flour, baking powder, and salt together onto a sheet of waxed paper. Remove the whisk, and using the paddle attachment, add the dry ingredients to the egg mixture at low speed, mixing until just incorporated. Add the vanilla, mix quickly and thoroughly, and set aside (the mixture will be quite thick).

7 In a separate bowl, whisk the egg whites with a pinch of salt until they form stiff points. Add the remaining ¼ cup sugar, and whisk until the egg whites are glossy, 30 seconds. Fold one-fourth of the egg whites into the batter until incorporated, then fold in the remaining egg whites, working quickly. They should be incorporated into the batter, but be careful not to overmix.

8 Spread the batter in the prepared pan, and bake until the cake is golden and

the top springs back when lightly pressed, 8 to 10 minutes.

9 While the cake is baking, sift 1 tablespoon of the confectioners' sugar over a clean kitchen towel.

10 Remove the cake from the oven, and immediately invert it onto the sugar-dusted towel. Peel the parchment paper from the cake, and starting from one long side, gently roll the cake up in the towel. Allow it to cool for about 30 minutes.

11 When the cake has cooled, unroll it. Trim off the edges of the cake. If necessary, thin the pastry cream slightly with additional milk to easy spreading consistency. Spread an even layer on the cake. Carefully reroll the cake and place it, seam side down, on a serving platter.

12 Mix the cinnamon and the remaining 2 tablespoons confectioners' sugar together, and sift over the top of the cake. Serve immediately.

One cake roll (10 to 12 servings)

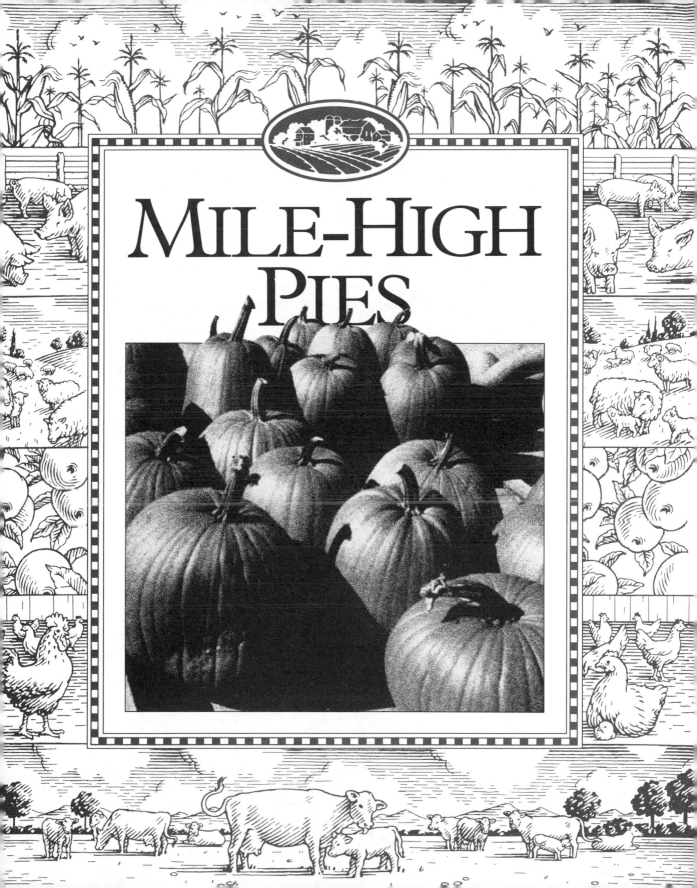

MILE-HIGH
PIES

PIES, PIES, PIES

Pies, pies, and more pies—and tarts and turnovers—cooling on the proverbial farmhouse windowsill, counter, and tabletop, is more than a farm cliche. It is a fact. Farmers eat them for breakfast, lunch, and dinner, and so did I.

It would be hard to rank the most memorable farmhouse pie I ate. Sometimes I'm convinced it's Elizabeth Ryan's Cranberry Pie, then I remember Linda Stoltzfus's Pumpkin Custard Pie and Caryl Smith's Best-Ever Apple Pie. As summer rolls around I can hardly wait to make Velma Williams's Peach Pie with pecans. Grape pie is a festive change of pace in winter, and so is the Pear Maple Syrup Pie. So you see, it really is much too difficult to pick a favorite. They're all delicious, and that's why they are here.

I spent much of my time in farmhouse kitchens watching experts bake their pies, picking up tips as they worked along. I learned to roll pastry out from the center until it was nearly see-through thin; to heap fillings high above the edge of the pastry so that each piece would be thick and luscious with fruit when cut; to slit the top pastry at least eight times to ensure it rising evenly.

I took dozens of notes because having become accustomed to eating delicious pies, I wanted to become an expert myself. If experimentation and repetition lead to expertise, then I have it because now I make pies every chance I get. I've become convinced that they are the jewel of farmhouse cooking and, as I learned on the farm, delicious any time, particularly for breakfast.

PASTRY FOR A TWO-CRUST PIE

This makes a beautiful, and very forgiving, pie crust. It is easy to roll, even if you have a heavy hand. Use it for any sweet or savory 9-inch pie. It has less fat than the other pastry recipes included and as a result has a less buttery flavor, but it fits in well with many people's dietary requirements.

The amount of water you will need varies according to the texture of the flour and the humidity in the air. Use the smallest possible amount, and don't process it too much. The dough shouldn't form a ball, but should just begin to come together.

2 cups unbleached all-purpose
  flour
¼ teaspoon salt
⅓ cup unsalted butter, chilled, cut
  into small pieces
⅓ cup lard, chilled, cut into small
  pieces
⅓ to ½ cup ice water

1 Place the flour and the salt in a food processor, and process briefly just to mix them together.

2 Add the butter and the lard, and using short pulses, process until the mixture ranges in size from peas to coarse cornmeal.

3 Slowly pour in the water, using short pulses to incorporate it into the flour mixture. The mixture should be moist enough to hold together, but don't process it to the point of forming a ball. The dough should still look crumbly, but it should adhere when you press it between your fingers.

4 Transfer the pastry to a large piece of waxed paper. Divide it in half and press each half out to form a flat round about 5 inches across. Wrap each round tightly in waxed paper and refrigerate for at least 1 hour. If you make this pastry the night before you plan to bake it, wrap the waxed-paper-covered rounds in aluminum foil so they don't dry out. Proceed with the specific pie recipe.

Pastry for a 9-inch 2-crust pie

FARMHOUSE PASTRY

I got this pastry recipe from Cathy Burgett, who lives in Santa Rosa, California. A pastry chef, Cathy is the one I turn to whenever I have a question or need assistance with a pastry recipe. Cathy isn't a farmer, but she makes the best pie pastry around. This pastry is buttery and flaky, and it bakes up lighter and more golden that any I've had.

You must chill the dough for at least an hour before rolling it out, as it is quite delicate; if it is the least bit warm, it will be difficult to work with. I often make it the day before and refrigerate it overnight.

2 cups unbleached all-purpose flour
1 teaspoon salt
1 tablespoon sugar
12 tablespoons (1½ sticks) unsalted
  butter, chilled, cut into small pieces
3 tablespoons lard, chilled, cut into
  small pieces
3½ tablespoons ice water

1 Place the flour, salt, and sugar in a food processor, and process briefly to mix together.

2 Add the butter and the lard to the flour, and using short pulses, process until the mixture ranges in size from peas to coarse cornmeal.

3 Slowly pour in the water, and using short pulses, incorporate it into the flour mixture. Add enough water so the pastry holds together in a loose ball.

4 Transfer the pastry to a large piece of waxed paper. Divide it in half and press each half out to form a flat round about 5 inches across. Wrap them tightly in waxed paper, and refrigerate for at least 1 hour. (If you make this the night before, wrap the dough in waxed paper, then in aluminum foil, so it doesn't dry out.) Proceed with the specific recipe.

Pastry for a 9-inch 2-crust pie

BUTTERY PASTRY
(PATE BRISEE)

T his buttery pastry, which is extremely easy to work with, is as delicious for savory tarts as it is for sweet desserts. As with any pastry,
once the liquid is added to the flour mixture, it should be handled
just enough to make it hold together. Then chill it for at least an hour, and
preferably overnight.

1½ cups all-purpose flour
¼ teaspoon salt
12 tablespoons (1½ sticks) unsalted butter,
  chilled and cut into 12 pieces
2 tablespoons ice water

1 Place the flour and salt in a food processor, and process briefly to mix. Add the
butter, and using short pulses, process until
the mixture ranges in size from sand to
small peas. Add the water and process,
using several pulses, until the pastry holds
together but doesn't form a ball.

2 Turn the pastry out onto a smooth
lightly floured work surface. Using the
heel of your hand, push the crumbly dough
away from you in small sections. This way
you will mix it quickly without handling it
too much. Use long strokes. Then gather the
pastry into a ball, pat it out to form a 6-inch
disc, and wrap it well in waxed paper. Refrigerate for at least 1 hour, or overnight if possible. Proceed with the specific pie recipe.

Pastry for a 10½-inch tart

ONE-CRUST PASTRY

L ight and tender, this pastry is good to have on hand for any single-
crust need. You can make it, roll it out, fit it in a pie plate, and freeze
it, well wrapped for up to three months.

1½ cups unbleached all-purpose flour

1 teaspoon salt

1 tablespoon sugar

10 tablespoons (1¼ sticks) unsalted butter, chilled, cut into small pieces

2 tablespoons lard, chilled, cut into small pieces

2 to 3 tablespoons ice water

1 Place the flour, salt, and sugar in a food processor, and process briefly to mix together.

2 Add the butter and the lard, and using short pulses, process until the mixture ranges in size from peas to coarse cornmeal.

3 Slowly pour in the water, and using short pulses, incorporate it into the flour mixture. Add enough water so the dough holds together but does not form a ball.

4 Transfer the pastry to a large piece of waxed paper, and press it out to form a flat round about 5 inches across. Wrap it tightly in waxed paper, and refrigerate for at least 1 hour, or preferably overnight. If leaving overnight, wrap the pastry also in aluminum foil.

5 For a 9-inch pie plate, roll out the pastry on a lightly floured surface to form a 10-inch circle (for a 10-inch pie plate, roll it out to form an 11-inch circle). Line the pie plate with the pastry, pressing it gently into the plate, and carefully crimp the edges. Chill for 30 minutes.

6 To prebake the pie shell, preheat the oven to 400°F.

7 Line the pastry with parchment paper, and fill it with pastry weights or dried beans. Bake until the edges begin to turn golden, 12 to 15 minutes. Remove the weights and the paper, and continue baking until the bottom of the pastry is golden, another 10 minutes.

8 Cool the pie shell on a wire rack, and proceed with the recipe.

Pastry for a 9- or 10-inch pie or a 10½ inch tart

BEST-EVER APPLE PIE

I learned the secret to a good apple pie from Barney and Caryl Smith, who live in Brighton, Iowa (see page112). Barney and Caryl were talking about Barney's mother and the pies she made every week

and delivered to her children, long after they'd left home. After tasting Caryl's pie, she looked up and said, "I'm not bringing pies here anymore. I don't need to." Caryl took that as a supreme compliment, and she is rightfully proud.

The secret to Caryl's apple pie? Always use at least three different kinds of apples, for depth and flavor; try to use a combination of sweet and tart, crisp and soft. If you have a batch of Golden Delicious apples, throw in a Granny Smith and a Jonagold or two. If you're lucky enough to have a cornucopia of varieties, try any combination of Cortland, Macoun, Red Stayman, York Imperial, McIntosh, Gravenstein, Melrose, and Mutsu.

Pastry dough for a two-crust pie
  (pages 429 and 430)
½ cup (packed) light brown sugar
¼ cup granulated sugar
2 tablespoons all-purpose flour
1 teaspoon ground cinnamon
Pinch of salt
1 large egg
2 tablespoons water
8 cups sliced peeled apples (about 3½
  pounds)
1 tablespoon freshly squeezed lemon juice
1 teaspoon vanilla extract
2 tablespoons unsalted butter, cut into
  small pieces
1 tablespoon granulated sugar for the
  crust (optional)

1 Preheat the oven to 425°F.

2 Roll out half the pastry to fit a 9- or 10-inch pie plate, and line the plate leaving an inch of dough hanging over the edge.

3 Mix both sugars with the flour, cinnamon, and salt in a small bowl. In another small bowl, whisk together the egg and the water.

4 Toss the apples with the lemon juice, then the sugar mixture, then the vanilla in a large bowl.

5 Place the apples in the pie plate and dot with the butter. Brush the edges of the pastry with the egg glaze. Roll out the top pastry quite thin, and lay it over the apples, pressing it onto the glazed portion of the bottom pastry. Fold the edges of the bottom pastry over the top edge, and crimp closed. (The egg glaze helps hold the top and bottom pastry together.)

6 Brush the top crust with egg glaze, but don't attempt to use all of the glaze, or the crust may get soggy. Cut at least 8 slits in the top of the pie, and sprinkle with the sugar if desired.

7 Place the pie plate on a baking sheet, and bake it in the bottom third of the oven until the pastry is golden on top and the apples are tender, about 50 minutes. Remove it from the oven and let it cool for at least 15 minutes before serving.

One 9- or 10-inch pie (6 to 8 servings)

NOTES FROM AN APPLE PIE EXPERT

In Brighton, Iowa, Caryl Smith is baking an apple pie for her husband, Barney, and her son, Nelson. Nelson is visiting now, but when he lived at home, Caryl made an apple pie every day, and the three of them would eat it after lunch. They weren't over eating—it would be hard to find a more fit trio than the Smiths—they just love apple pie, and they don't tire of it.

Apple pies are not a simple matter in the Smith household. "You've got to have at least three types of apples in a pie for it to be any good," Barney says. Caryl prefers Jonathan, Winesap, Ramared, and an apple that grows on a shoot from one of their trees, so dark red it's almost black. "I like a lot of apples in my pie, so I cut them thin, toss them with flour,

sugar, and cinnamon, and fill them way over the edge of the pan," she says.

Lard pastry is another absolute in the Smith household. Caryl used shortening once, and got complaints that the pie tasted as if it had come from the supermarket. "If the pastry doesn't have lard in it, it doesn't taste good," Caryl says. She concedes that a mixture of lard and butter works well, too.

Caryl bakes her pies a long time. "I put the pie on a baking sheet because they always boil over," she says. "In fact, that's how I know it's done." The average baking time is just over an hour, with the oven set at about 375°F. "I know you're supposed to start a pie out in a hot oven and turn it down, but I'd forget, so I just keep it at the same temperature," she says.

APPLE TART WITH CIDER SAUCE

This dessert speaks of the Pacific Northwest, with its old-fashioned apple varieties that grow in abundance in the mild, maritime climate. The eastern part of the state is most widely known for apples—

Golden and Red Delicious, Granny Smith, Jonagold, and several others—but it's the west that produces the apples with the most character, gems like sweet-tart Gravenstein, Macoun, and Criterion.

I like to use Gravensteins in this recipe, though any good, flavorful, slightly tart cooking apple works well. The fragrant mellow flavors of the apples, the lightly caramelized sugar, the lemon zest, and the vanilla bean are balanced here by the assertive pungency of the golden cider sauce. And if you can't find any hard cider, make your own: Buy some good unfiltered apple cider and let it sit in a glass container (a plastic container can give an "off" flavor to the cider) until it "turns" and becomes slightly fizzy, which shouldn't take much longer than a couple of days.

FOR THE CIDER SAUCE

3 cups medium-dry hard cider
½ cup heavy (whipping) cream
1 tablespoon sugar
4 tablespoons (½ stick) unsalted butter, chilled,
  cut into pieces

FOR THE APPLE TART

6 medium-size firm tart apples (about 2½
  pounds), such as Criterion, Gravenstein,
  or Granny Smith
4 tablespoons (½ stick) unsalted butter,
  cut into 4 pieces
½ cup sugar
1 vanilla bean, slit lengthwise
Zest of 1 lemon, cut off in ¼-inch-wide
  strips with a vegetable peeler
1 teaspoon freshly squeezed lemon
  juice
1 tablespoon medium-dry hard cider
1 prebaked 10½-inch tart shell
  (page 431)

1 Make the cider sauce: Bring the cider, cream, and sugar to a boil in a medium-size saucepan over medium-high heat. Cook until reduced by two thirds, to 1 cup (it will turn a lovely golden brown). Reduce the heat to low, and whisk in the butter piece by piece, working on and off the heat so the butter melts slowly and emulsifies into the sauce. Remove the sauce from the heat and pour it into a bowl to cool to room temperature. It will thicken slightly as it cools. If you aren't serving the pie for several hours, cover, and let sit at room temperature.

2 Make the tart filling: Peel, core, and thinly slice the apples.

3 Melt the butter in a large skillet over medium heat, and add the apples, sugar, vanilla bean, lemon zest, and lemon juice. Cook, stirring occasionally, until the apples are soft but still slightly crunchy, the sugar has lightly caramelized, and the liquid has evaporated, 8 to 10 minutes. Stir in the cider, remove the skillet from the heat, and discard the lemon zest and the vanilla bean. Let the filling cool to lukewarm.

4 When the apple mixture has cooled, spread it evenly in the pastry shell, and serve immediately. Serve the cider sauce on the side.

One 10½-inch tart
(8 servings)

APPLE AND CRANBERRY PIE

T his pie was inspired by Elizabeth Ryan, an expert in both apples and pies. Elizabeth and her husband, Peter, sell their apples at the Manhattan Greenmarket two days a week (see page 482), and alongside their bushels in the fall are luscious pies. She fills her pies with apples, of course, but also with all sorts of other fruits.

When it comes to pie, Elizabeth is very opinionated, but she has earned the right because her pies are in high demand. She adds as much fruit to her pies as she can, pressing down "with every ounce of strength I've got" as she puts the fruit in the pan.

Elizabeth's favorite pie apples are Rhode Island Greening and Baldwin, though she always uses a mix. If she doesn't want to use sugar, she chooses sweeter apples like Jonagold, Golden Delicious, Cortland, Spi-Gold (King Luscious), or Mutsu, with some Rhode Island Greenings, which are firm and very tart, thrown in for character, and she doubles the amount of cinnamon called for here. If she uses sugar, she will stick with tart varieties such as Gravenstein, Greenings, Winesap, and Spy.

If you don't have such a variety of apples at hand, try combining Granny Smith or Newton Pippin (also called Newton) with

Golden Delicious. The cranberries, along with the spices give the pie character.

Pastry dough for a two-crust pie (pages 429 and 430)
½ cup sugar
½ teaspoon ground cinnamon
2 tablespoons all-purpose flour
1 teaspoon grated orange zest
3 to 3½ pounds mixed apples, peeled, cored, and cut in slices just over ⅛ inch thick
1 cup fresh or frozen cranberries (do not thaw)
2 tablespoons unsalted butter, cut into 4 small pieces
1 egg mixed with 1 teaspoon water

1 Preheat the oven to 400°F.

2 Roll out half the pastry to fit a 9-inch pie plate, and line the plate leaving an inch of pastry hanging over the edge. Place it in the refrigerator to keep cold. Roll the remaining pastry out to form a 12-inch circle. Lay it on a baking sheet, and place it in the refrigerator while you prepare the pie filling.

3 In a large bowl, mix together the sugar, cinnamon, flour, and orange zest. Add the apple slices, and toss until they are thoroughly coated with the mixture.

4 Place the apples in the pie plate in thirds, alternating with half the cranberries. Press down firmly on each layer, even though you may pop some of the

cranberries. The fruit will mound well above the edge of the pie plate. Dot it with the butter.

5 Place the top crust over the pie, and trim it so it extends about ¼ inch beyond the edge of the pie plate. Fold the bottom crust up and over the edge, pressing them together gently. Crimp the edges of the crust so they look attractive. Roll out any remaining scraps of dough and cut them into an apple shape, cutting out a stem and a leaf as well. Brush the top crust with egg glaze, arrange the cut-out apple decoration on it, and then brush with egg glaze again. Make at least 8 slits in the top crust for the steam to escape, and to prevent the crust from falling unevenly if the apples shrink during cooking.

6 Place the pie on a baking sheet, and bake in the bottom third of the oven until the crust is golden and the filling is beginning to bubble up out of the slits, 45 minutes to 1 hour.

7 Transfer the pie to a wire rack, and let it cool to room temperature before serving.

One 9-inch pie (6 to 8 servings)

CRANBERRIES

With the Thanksgiving season come those familiar cellophane bags of glistening fresh cranberries—but where do they come from?

Cranberries, reputedly dubbed "cranberries" by the Pilgrims, who thought their pale pink blossoms resembled cranes, don't, of course, originate in those bags. They grow on vines in marshy areas or bogs, rooted in up to 8 feet of peat (decomposed plant matter) and high-acid sandy soil. They ripen in the fall, and thus have been present at every Thanksgiving since the first one.

The small round berry is native to North America, and it has been a food source since there were people to consume it. It was an ingredient in pemmican, a mixture of dried fruits and berries that sustained Native American tribes. They treasured the cranberry so much that when the Pilgrims arrived, they quickly introduced them to it. The berry was well received and became a part of the Pilgrims' seasonal diet as well as a standard provision on

American ships, where its high vitamin C content kept scurvy at bay. By the 18th century, the berries were being exported to Europe.

NOT JUST MASSACHUSETTS

The cranberry industry began in Cape Cod, which is still the major region of production. Wisconsin, New Jersey, Washington, and Oregon all produce cranberries too, as do several Canadian provinces.

Though Massachusetts produces the bulk of the crop, berries from Washington—which account for about 5 percent of the total grown in the country—are considered the highest quality. They're plump and juicy and a particularly vivid red (because the growing season is longer in the Northwest, anthocyanin, the pigment that produces the red color in the berries, has more time to develop). Washington's berries are reserved for the fresh market, where they are packaged in plastic bags and displayed in produce sections.

Wild cranberries grow in Washington, but domesticated vines were imported from Cape Cod in 1883, and many have produced

continually since then. "They will produce forever if they're properly cared for," says Don Hatton, a grower and director for Ocean Spray, a cranberry and citrus fruit growers' cooperative.

Most of Washington's more than 1,200 acres of cranberry bogs are tucked away on the southern coast in Grayland or on the nearby Long Beach Peninsula—acre after flat, purple-tinged acre, inland from the pebbled beaches. These tidy bogs are offset by drainage ditches, dikes, or neat wooden barriers that prevent the land from reverting to its natural marshy state.

The small bushy vines resemble heather, to which they are related, and they grow so close together that they create an undulating blanket that looks soft enough to roll on. It isn't, though the snaky branches make a ground cover so firm it springs back when you step on it. The plump berries are hidden beneath the thick foliage and are almost impossible to spot, even when they're ripe.

PICKING THE BERRIES

▪▪▪▪▪

Come October, the cranberry bogs jump with activity as harvest begins. Many growers dry-pick the berries with a machine called a Furford Picker. Invented in the 1950s by Julius Furford of Grayland, the Furford Picker is state-of-the-art because it picks and prunes the vines simultaneously. Dull metal teeth right near the ground gently knock the berries onto a conveyor belt that deposits them in a canvas bag. It's somewhat painstaking work, but it ensures undamaged berries that can be sold for a high price. It's more efficient than the old method, when growers worked on their hands and knees using wooden scoops, like rakes, to comb through the vines.

Though mechanical dry-pickers are efficient, they are expensive and labor-intensive, and most growers water-harvest the berries. In water-harvesting, individual bogs are flooded with about 8 inches of water, and a large machine referred to as an "egg beater" is pushed or ridden through the vines, churning up the water and jostling the berries loose. As they're freed they bob to the surface, transforming the bog into a brilliant magenta pool.

Malcolm and Ardell McPhail, owners of CranMac farms near Ilwaco, Washington,

▶ ▶ ▶

usually spend ten days harvesting their 28 acres. With friends and neighbors they don hip boots, grab long-handled pushers, and wade in after the egg beater. They work fast, because although ripe berries will keep on the vine for a month, once the bog is flooded they must be harvested within a day.

Using the pushers, they corral the berries in wooden booms, then sweep them into an elevator that conveys them into huge wooden boxes. With the brilliant sun bouncing off the glistening berries and the camaraderie, it seems more like a party than a harvest.

Water-harvesting is a simpler process than dry-picking, and it results in a higher yield, but it is rougher on the berries. The McPhails sell their cranberries for processing. "Growers get a premium for fresh fruit, but I guess I'm not interested," Malcolm said. "You can load them five feet high without worrying, and carry them in one hundred tons at a time," he said. Most newly planted bogs are designed to accommodate water-harvesting.

More than 27,000 of the nation's 30,000 cranberry bogs are under contract

to Ocean Spray, and most of Washington's cranberries are processed at the Ocean Spray plant in Markham. There they undergo a series of tests to determine whether they will be packaged fresh or made into whole sauce, jellied sauce, or juice.

PASSING THE FRESH-TEST PHYSICAL

To qualify for the fresh market, the berries must first pass a "bounce test." They are poured into a low-tech wooden contraption that forces them to bounce over a series of 2½-inch-high barriers. Those that bounce all the way to the end are the cream of the crop, and after hand-sorting and exposure to ultraviolet light to reveal any defects, they are packaged in cellophane bags.

Cranberries destined for processing are frozen, which increases their juice yield, and then cooked in huge stainless steel vats and processed as needed.

Cranberries are delectably versatile. They add vibrant color and tart flavor to everything from breads to meats. Don Hatton suggests dipping them in chocolate or caramel, and Ardell McPhail puts them in muffins and cakes, cooks them with chicken, or pops raw cranberries in her mouth. "There's nothing like it for quenching your thirst," she says.

ELIZABETH RYAN'S CRANBERRY PIE

This recipe is another from Elizabeth Ryan, an apple grower in New York's Hudson Valley. Elizabeth is not only an experienced farmer, she's a passionate baker too, and anyone who visits Manhattan's Union Square Greenmarket on Saturdays has probably been tempted by her pies.

This is one of Elizabeth's most popular Thanksgiving pies, vying with apple and pumpkin. "It's my version of mince pie," she says, "and I like it a lot better."

This may well be one of the best pies I have ever tasted, and because of it, my freezer is never without a bag or two of cranberries, so I can make it year-round. (Freezing cranberries releases more of their juice too, which is a tip worth knowing.) The cranberries are sweetened just enough to calm their tartness and let the flavors in the filling come through.

Pastry dough for a two-crust pie (pages 429 and 430)
1 cup sugar
¼ cup all-purpose flour
3½ cups fresh or frozen cranberries (do not thaw frozen berries)
Grated zest of 1 orange
¼ cup freshly squeezed orange juice
⅓ cup walnuts, coarsely chopped
½ cup raisins
3 tablespoons unsalted butter, melted
1 egg mixed with 2 teaspoons water

1 Preheat the oven to 400°F.

2 Roll out half the pastry to fit a 9-inch pie plate, and line the plate, leaving an inch of dough hanging over the edge. Roll out the remaining pastry to cover the pie, transfer it to a baking sheet, and

refrigerate both top and bottom, at least 1 hour.

3 Mix the sugar and flour together in a small bowl.

4 Chop the cranberries in a food processor until they are in uneven pieces ranging from the size of a pea to finely ground. This will take about 2 minutes for frozen berries, and several pulses for fresh.

5 Transfer the cranberries to a medium-size bowl, and add the orange zest, orange juice, walnuts, raisins, and melted butter. Mix until they are thoroughly combined.

6 Sprinkle about ¼ cup of the sugar mixture on the bottom crust, and pile the cranberry mixture on top. Sprinkle the remaining sugar mixture over the berries, and cover with the top crust. Fold the edges of the bottom crust up and over the top crust, and crimp the edges. Brush the top crust with the egg wash, make at least 8 slits in it for steam to escape, and place the pie on a baking sheet.

7 Bake the pie in the center of the oven until the pastry is golden and the filling is bubbling up through the slits, about 50 minutes. Remove the pie from the oven and let it cool to room temperature before serving.

One 9-inch pie (6 to 8 servings)

SOUR CHERRY CRUMB PIE

O n the East Coast, sour cherries appear at farm stands and farmers' markets around the end of June, their vivid red translucence keeping company with sweet cherries and strawberries, and making cheery spots of color among the early summer greens.

Sour cherries make delectable, delicately flavored desserts, and this sugar-and-almond-crusted pie is one of them. It is simple to make, not too sweet, and as lovely to look at as it is to eat.

If you've ever sucked on a sour cherry pit, you have noticed their distinct almond taste. Rather than leave the pits in the cherries to waylay eager eaters, the almonds added here give the same subtle flavor.

1 prebaked 9-inch pastry shell
   (page 431)

FOR THE TOPPING
¾ cup all-purpose flour
½ cup sugar
Pinch of salt
6 tablespoons (¾ stick) unsalted butter, cut into small pieces
½ cup raw almonds, chopped so that some pieces are coarse and others are fine

FOR THE CHERRIES
1 tablespoon quick-cooking tapioca
3 tablespoons sugar
4 to 4½ cups sour cherries, pitted

1 Preheat the oven to 375°F.

2 Prepare the topping: Mix the flour, sugar, and salt together in a small bowl. Add the butter, working it in quickly and lightly with the tips of your fingers. (Or mix the ingredients together in a food processor, using short pulses, until the mixture resembles coarse crumbs. Stir the almonds in by hand, and set aside.

3 In another small bowl, mix together the tapioca and sugar. Layer the cherries into the prebaked pie crust in thirds, alternating them with a sprinkling of the tapioca mixture. Cover the cherries completely with the topping, pressing down on it gently.

4 Bake the pie on the bottom rack of the oven until the topping is golden and juice is beginning to bubble through it, about 45 minutes. Remove the pie from the oven and let it cool to room temperature before serving.

One 9-inch pie (6 to 8 servings)

ALMONDS

The almond, native to western Asia, is closely related to the peach. Sweet almonds, the eating almonds, are the most common variety. Bitter almonds are pressed to make almond extract.

It's best to buy raw whole almonds for cooking; they will be fresher than any processed nuts.

AN EDUCATION IN BLUEBERRIES

Nate Pennell sits surrounded by a cluster of co-workers at the Washington County Soil and Water Conservation District in Machias, Maine. He's talking about blueberries and farming, and everyone is laughing.

We leave to board Nate's pickup and drive through undulating fields of low scrubby bushes. These are blueberry barrens, and they stretch for miles with little relief. The picking season has just begun, and there are already a few "rakers," bent low to "comb" berries from the bushes with rakes that look like dustpans with teeth.

Nate follows a maze of roads through the barrens, searching for a particular field. There is nothing to indicate direction. "People get lost in here all the time," he says casually. "But I grew up here, so I know where I'm going."

Nate lives several lives. During the week he's the manager for the conservation district, which means he is the local expert and troubleshooter for the county's 600 berry growers. On summer evenings and weekends he's a farmer, tending his own blueberries and vegetables. On weekends he's a merchant, selling his produce at the Machias farmers' market.

Nate is devoted to food in all of his lives,

as evidenced by his comfortable roundness. He does a lot of the cooking at home, assisting his wife, who works full-time as an auto mechanic at a local garage. And he doesn't just whip up hamburgers and frozen pizza—Nate goes more for fresh garden foods, hearty slow-cooked stews, and a blueberry pie or two.

We stop near a field and Nate pulls back some branches to look for berries hanging near the ground. Most are blue but some are white, still unripe. He eats a few ripe berries, and their taste triggers a recipe. "I make blueberry syrup every year," he says. "I take berries, add water and sugar, some nutmeg and cinnamon, and cook 'em 'til they pop," he said. "I'm supposed to be on a diet, but I eat quite a lot anyway." (See page 343 for the recipe.)

ONE SINGULAR DEVOTION

It figures that he loves blueberries. Everyone in Washington County does—after all, it's the second-largest blueberry producing county in Maine. Those who work with the

berries even tend toward clothing in shades of blue, a conscious effort, according to Nate, to foster local blueberry pride.

As we drive out of the barrens, a rabbit sprints across in front of the truck. "I make mulligan stew with rabbit and chicken, and I like to use partridge and squirrel," Nate says. "I add a rutabaga and parsnips and carrots, and boil them all together. Then I make dumplings and stir in a few blueberries." (For a tamer version of this recipe, see page 159.)

He swings into the yard of a metal building where trucks are unloading berries. Inside it's cool, dark, and heady with the scent of blueberries. These are not the big, round pulpy ones that are commonly available in supermarkets. Those are hybrid high-bush berries, bred for vigor and growing ability, not flavor. These berries, still mixed with chaff from the fields, are tiny and dark. When you bite them they pop and release tart, tangy juice. "Forty years ago the berries were loaded on the train and were in Boston the next day," Nate said. "Now the Japanese buy the biggest, we send some fresh to markets along the East Coast, and we freeze 90 percent of them."

REST STOP

It is nearly noon, and we return to Machias, passing berry-laden trucks. In Machias, we go into Graham's Restaurant, and owner Amy Graham exchanges news with Nate. "I brought her here to try your pie," he says, nodding toward me. She takes our order for fried clams and returns with carefully typed recipes for Blueberry Glacé Pie (see page 447), a piece of which was delivered directly by the waitress, and another for a cooked double-crust pie. "I don't always follow these exactly," she says. "Sometimes I use more berries."

Nate is already well into his cream-topped pie. "She makes one of the best," he whispers. "And her family grows all their berries."

Still full from lunch, there is another stop. "I've got to show you where my friends the Perlmans have farmed organically for fourteen years," he says. "You won't believe it."

We drive down a rutted road and turn into Crossroads Organic Farm, parking alongside several other cars. Delia Pearlman, the couple's 15-year-old daughter, harvests vegetables as people request them. Nate sighs. "I don't know how they do it," he says, fingering a frond of fennel that nearly reaches his shoulder and gazing wistfully at tall cornstalks.

We walk back to the truck, hugging huge bags of truly garden-fresh produce. Nate is uncommonly knowledgeable about the area, the blueberries, and just about everything else, and I ask him why. "Before I went to work for the county I was a schoolteacher. They still beg me to come back and teach," he says. Instead he prefers to work with blueberry growers, find solutions to their problems, and dream up ideas for his next meal.

BLUEBERRY PIE

This might be considered the state dessert of Maine, along with the Blueberry Glacé Pie on the facing page. It can be made year-round with the good-quality quick-frozen blueberries that now seem to be produced in nearly every state in the Union. Though Maine blueberries are best here, the larger blueberries, which aren't as great fresh but are delicious cooked, give lots of spicy flavor to this pie.

Pastry for a two-crust pie (pages 429 and 430)
⅓ cup sugar
2 tablespoons all-purpose flour
Pinch of salt
¼ teaspoon freshly grated nutmeg
¼ teaspoon ground cinnamon
5 cups fresh or frozen blueberries (do not thaw)
1 tablespoon unsalted butter, cut into 4 pieces
1 tablespoon milk

1 Preheat the oven to 400°F.

2 Roll out half the pastry to fit a 9-inch pie plate, and line the plate leaving an inch of pastry hanging over the edge.

3 In a small bowl, mix together the sugar, flour, and spices. Sprinkle about 2 tablespoons of the mixture over the crust. Pour half the berries into the crust, sprinkle them with about 4 tablespoons of the sugar mixture, and top with the remaining berries and sugar mixture. Dot with the butter.

4 Place the top crust over the pie, and trim it so it extends about ¼ inch beyond the edge of the plate. Fold the bottom crust up and over the edge, pressing them together gently. Crimp the edges, and brush the pastry lightly but thoroughly with the milk.

5 Make at least 8 slits in the top crust to allow steam to escape and the pastry to bake evenly, and bake in the bottom third of the oven until the crust is golden and the berries are bubbling up through the slits, about 50 minutes.

6 Remove the pie from the oven, and let it cool slightly before serving.

One 9-inch pie (6 to 8 servings)

BLUEBERRY GLACE PIE

This pie is ubiquitous in northern Maine during blueberry season, which arrives about mid-August. As pickers bend low in the fields to comb the tiny purple-blue berries from their plants, cooks in home and restaurant kitchens prepare this fresh, juicy pie.

I had it at Graham's Restaurant in Machias, Maine, and loved it so much that owner Amy Graham gave me her recipe. It is very simple, and best made with wild Maine blueberries, which are more flavorful and sprightly than the cultivated variety. However, use whatever fresh blueberries are available, or substitute wild huckleberries. This pie won't succeed with frozen berries.

2 tablespoons cornstarch
¾ cup water
1 teaspoon freshly squeezed lemon juice
4 cups fresh blueberries
1 tablespoon unsalted butter
¾ cup sugar
Pinch of salt
1 prebaked 9-inch pastry shell (page 431)
¾ cup heavy (whipping) cream
1 tablespoon confectioners' sugar

1 Mix the cornstarch, 2 tablespoons of the water, and the lemon juice together in a small bowl, and stir until the cornstarch has thoroughly dissolved.

2 Place 1 cup of the blueberries and all the remaining water in a medium-size saucepan over medium-high heat, and bring to a boil. Cook until the berries begin to pop, about 4 minutes. Add the cornstarch mixture along with the butter, sugar, and salt. Cook, stirring, until the mixture is thick and clear, about 2 minutes. Remove the pan from the heat.

3 Fold the remaining 3 cups berries into the cooked berry mixture, and pour into the prebaked pie shell. Refrigerate, at least 2 hours but no more than 4. Just before serving, whip the cream until it forms soft peaks, gradually incorporating the confectioners' sugar as the cream thickens. Either spread the cream over the pie or serve it on the side. Serve immediately.

One 9-inch pie (6 to 8 servings)

THE PAVICH GRAPE STORY

The Pavich farmhouse sits amid 480 acres of lush grapevines in California's San Joaquin Valley. Here the matriarch of the family, Helen, holds court—which for her means advising her two sons, Stephen Paul and Tom, who now run the farm since her husband, Stephen Sr., passed away, caring for the kitchen garden she's kept for the past forty years, making sure the juice oranges are picked off the laden tree out front, and cooking for the family, who make regular appearances at her dining table.

The elder Pavichs moved to the San Joaquin Valley in 1953 from the California coast, where Stephen had tried his hand at fishing. They rented land for two years, then bought what is now referred to as the home ranch, an existing vineyard at the time.

"My husband would prune and I'd take the kids in the field and they'd pull the canes (vine shoots)," she said. "They did that for about six years, and that's how we taught them, by taking them right out in the vineyards."

They learned well, as Pavich Family Farms has grown into the world's largest grower of organic table grapes and is often mentioned as an example of what can be accomplished through alternative farming methods.

THE PAVICHS GO ORGANIC

The Pavich's road to organic farming began one day when Stephen Paul was working on a cleaned-out chemical rig. He dropped a wrench inside, and when he leaned in to pick it up, he was nearly overcome by the fumes. Stephen Paul was shocked at the volatility of the chemical residue, and the experience changed his life and the Pavich farms forever. "He knew the rig had been cleaned, but it still smelled so strong that he got to wondering what the chemicals were doing to his land and his crops," Tonya Pavich, his wife, said. "He wondered how he could strengthen the soil and the plants so they would have a better immune system and wouldn't need chemicals."

Stephen Paul took the matter up with his father, suggesting that they try biological pest

and weed control methods instead of chemicals on their land. "You've got to understand that chemicals were considered the silver-bullet method for quick-fixing production problems," Tonya said. "But Stephen's father was incredibly foresighted and he said he could try it if he wanted, but if it didn't work they'd go back to the old way."

They began biological farming—the precursor to organic farming—in 1968 and sold their first organic grapes to natural foods stores in 1971. "All through the seventies we didn't sell more than one percent of our crop as organic, even though all of it was," Tonya said. "Even into the eighties we couldn't find a market for it, so we sold it through the commercial market." By the mid-1980s, however, the public's interest in organic foods had expanded the market, and in 1989 the Pavichs sold 60 percent of their crop as organic.

The Pavichs now farm 1,800 acres that are certified organic by the California Certified Organic Farmers, with another 200 in transition, or in the process of becoming organic. They ship 1.3 million boxes of half a dozen grape varieties all over the country, under the labels Normandie and Pavich. Some years ago they branched out and bought a 200-acre farm in Arizona where they raise organic melons, cotton, and grapes.

THE PAVICH BLEND

■ ■ ■ ■

The Pavich home farm is flanked to the east by the Sierra mountains, and is surrounded by acre after acre of gnarly vines that twist out of the ground, their leaves forming a canopy over the space between the rows. The Pavichs' acreage stands out because instead of bare ground between the rows, there's a lush green bed of grasses and pea-family plants called the "Pavich blend." This cover crop is part of their organic system. It keeps the weeds down and the soil in place, and provides shelter for the insects that are part of the Pavichs' biological control system. By harboring insects, a natural predation system is set up. Helpful insects, such as ladybugs and lacewings, keep harmful insects, such as aphids, at bay. Chemicals have no function in this system.

The Pavichs pipe fish emulsion fertilizer to their vines and cover crops along with the irrigation water, which sprays out through a fan jet system in a 360-degree range. Their organic program also includes inoculating the soil with helpful bacteria and spreading it with homemade compost.

In general the vineyards are ploughed before the grapes develop, which helps send the nitrogen in the soil to the plants. The compost is applied, then the cover crop is planted. During the summer, the soil (or "berm") directly under the vines is kept clean by hand tilling, or with the help of a weed badger, which yanks up weeds by the roots. After harvest, the cover crop is generally disked under for green manure.

Like most organic farmers, the Pavichs find organic farming to be more labor-intensive than conventional farming. But the dividends are the quality of their fruit and their healthy vines, which now fight off disease and insects by themselves. They are paid a premium in the marketplace as well, which helps justify their costs.

GRAPE PIE

The idea for this pie comes from Helen Pavich, who has spent the past forty-plus years surrounded by vineyards and blessed with an abundance of fresh, flavorful grapes (see page 448). Because she has grapes to spare, she uses them in ways others might not—adding them to soups (see page 65), freezing them for a snack, or putting them in this fresh, surprising pie.

I was a little dubious about grape pie, but the fruit truly comes into its own here. It is surprisingly similar to a gooseberry pie, though not as tart, and the nutmeg gives it a pepperiness that I find irresistible.

Pastry dough for a 2-crust pie (see pages 429
   and 430)
¼ cup all-purpose flour
¼ cup sugar
½ teaspoon freshly grated nutmeg
6 cups green, or mixed red and green, seedless
   grapes, rinsed and drained
1 tablespoon unsalted butter, cut into 4 small
   pieces
1 to 2 teaspoons milk

1 Preheat the oven to 400°F.

2 Roll out half the pastry to fit a 9-inch pie plate, and line the plate leaving an inch of pastry hanging over the edge.

3 Mix the flour, sugar, and nutmeg together in a small bowl.

4 Sprinkle about 1 tablespoon of the flour mixture over the bottom crust, and top it with one third of the grapes. Sprinkle half the remaining flour mixture over the grapes and repeat, ending with the remaining third of the grapes. Dot with the butter.

5 Roll out the remaining pastry, and cover the pie with it. Trim the edges, then bring the bottom edge up and over the top edge, and crimp it closed. Brush the top crust with the milk, and make at least 8 cuts in the top for steam to escape.

6 Place the pie on a baking sheet, and bake in the bottom third of the oven until the pastry is golden and the juice is bubbling up through the cuts, about 55 minutes.

7 Remove the pie from the oven, and let it cool for at least 10 minutes before serving.

One 9-inch pie (6 to 8 servings)

TEXAS PEACH PIE

T his pie—made with sweet, juicy, fragrant peaches, crisp golden pecans, and a touch of nutmeg—is the essence of Texas. It is so good, so flavorful, that it will tempt you over and over again. It comes from Velma Williams, who, with her husband, Walter, owns a pecan and cattle ranch near Yoakum, Texas. I spent several days at the Williams's, learning about pecans, meeting the individual cattle and trying to learn their names, and eating the special dishes that Velma prepared for lunch and dinner each day. It was high peach season, and Velma always has an ample supply of pecans on hand. When she produced this pie, I knew it would become one of my favorites. I like to serve Peach Ice Cream (see Index) alongside.

Pastry dough for a 2-crust pie (see pages 429
  and 430)
10 to 12 ripe peaches, peeled, pitted, and
  thinly sliced (6 cups)
2 teaspoons freshly squeezed lemon juice
⅓ cup (packed) dark brown sugar
2 tablespoons all-purpose flour
½ teaspoon freshly grated nutmeg
½ cup pecans, toasted (see Note)
3 tablespoons butter, cut into small pieces
1 large egg mixed with 1 tablespoon water

1 Preheat the oven to 425°F.

2 Roll half the pastry out to fit a 10-inch pie plate, and line the plate leaving an inch of dough hanging over the edge.

3 In a medium-size bowl, combine the peaches, lemon juice, brown sugar, flour, nutmeg, and pecans, and toss to combine thoroughly. Pile the mixture into the lined pie plate, and dot with the butter. Brush the edges of the pastry with the egg glaze.

4 Roll out the remaining pastry to form a 12-inch circle, and lay it over the peach mixture, pressing it down gently but firmly. Trim the edges, and fold the over-

hanging pastry from the bottom crust up and over the edge of the top crust, crimping the two together. Brush the top and the edges of the pastry with some of the egg glaze (don't use too much, or the crust may become soggy). Cut at least 8 slits in the top of the pie. Roll out any remaining dough ⅛ inch thick, cut out attractive shapes, and arrange them on the top crust. Brush with the egg glaze.

5 Place the pie on a baking sheet, and bake in the bottom third of the oven until the crust is golden and the peaches are bubbling, about 55 minutes. Remove the

pie from the oven, and let it cool for 10 minutes before serving.

One 10-inch pie (6 to 8 servings)

Note: To toast pecans, preheat the oven to 350°F. Place the nuts in a baking pan large enough to hold them in a single layer, and toast, stirring once, until they give off a toasted aroma, about 10 minutes.

PEAR MAPLE SYRUP PIE

T his recipe evolved after a visit to the Northeast, where the sugar maples flow freely and pears are grown by the bushel. These ingredients, both earmarked by their subtlety, are common in the supermarkets of New England, and I couldn't resist bringing them home and combining them in a pie. They are a perfect match, along with a touch of lemon juice to elevate the flavor of both.

I like to use grade B maple syrup because it has a darker, more intense flavor. But I've made the

pie with the more common Grade A, and it was luscious.

6 medium pears, peeled, halved, and cored
Pastry dough for a 2-crust pie (see pages 429
   and 430)
2 tablespoons all-purpose flour
1 tablespoon freshly squeezed lemon juice
¼ cup maple syrup
1 large egg mixed with 2 teaspoons water

1 Preheat the oven to 400°F.

2 Slice the pears crosswise into ¼-inch-thick slices.

3 Roll out half the pastry to fit a 9- or 10-inch pie plate, and line the plate leaving an inch of pastry hanging over the edge.

4 Pile one third of the pear slices in the pie plate, and sprinkle with one third of the flour. Repeat with the remaining pears and flour. Stir the lemon juice and maple syrup together in a small bowl, and pour the mixture over the pears.

5 Roll out the top pastry quite thin. Brush the edges of the bottom pastry with some of the egg glaze, and lay the top pastry over the pears, pressing it onto the glazed edges. Fold the edges of the bottom pastry up and over the top edge, and crimp closed attractively. Brush the top crust generously with egg glaze, prick it at least eight times with the point of a sharp knife, and place the pie on a baking sheet.

6 Bake in the bottom third of the oven until the crust is golden and the pears are tender but not soft, about 55 minutes. If the crust begins to brown too quickly, lay a piece of aluminum foil loosely over it.

7 Remove the pie from the oven and let it cool for 10 minutes before serving.

One 9- or 10-inch pie (6 to 8 servings)

PEAR TART

In the fall there is nothing quite as good as the delicate perfume and juicy firm texture of pears. This tart makes the most of them by enhancing their flavor with lemon and hazelnuts, and nesting them in a crisp, nutty pastry.

Don't be daunted by this tart—it does take time, but the results are spectacular when it all comes together in a lovely, luscious dessert.

FOR THE HAZELNUT PASTRY

¾ cup all-purpose flour
¼ cup hazelnuts, toasted and skinned
    (see Note), finely ground
½ teaspoon salt
⅓ cup sugar
7 tablespoons unsalted butter, cut into small
    pieces, at room temperature
4 egg yolks
½ teaspoon vanilla extract

FOR THE PEARS AND POACHING
LIQUID

6 firm medium Bosc pears
½ lemon
4 cups water
½ cup (lightly packed) light brown sugar
½ cup granulated sugar
3 whole cloves
1 vanilla bean, slit lengthwise
1 slice candied ginger, coarsely chopped
    (1 teaspoon)
3 long strips (3 inches each) lemon zest

FOR THE TART FILLING

2 large eggs
¼ cup (packed) dark brown sugar
¼ cup granulated sugar
4 tablespoons (½ stick) unsalted butter,
    melted
Minced zest of 1 lemon
2 tablespoons freshly squeezed lemon juice
⅓ cup hazelnuts, toasted and skinned
    (see Note), coarsely chopped

1 Make the pastry: Place the flour, ground hazelnuts, salt, and sugar in a food processor and pulse once to mix. Add the butter, and process until it is mixed with the flour and cut into pieces smaller than a pea. Add the egg yolks and the vanilla, and process with short pulses. Continue with longer pulses until the dough holds together but isn't overmixed, 2 to 3 minutes total. Flatten the pastry to form a small disc, wrap it in waxed paper, and refrigerate for 1 hour.

2 While the pastry is chilling, prepare the pears: Peel, halve, and core the pears. Rub each piece with the lemon to prevent its browning while you prepare the remainder.

3 Combine the water, both sugars, cloves, vanilla bean, candied ginger, and lemon zest in a large heavy saucepan. Cover, bring to a boil over high heat, and cook until the sugar has dissolved, stirring once, 3 to 5 minutes. Add the pear halves to the poaching liquid. If it doesn't completely cover them, add more water. (If you are adding more than ½ cup, add an extra tablespoon of sugar.) Let the liquid return to a boil, then reduce to a brisk simmer, cover, and poach the pears until they are tender, 30 minutes. Test them occasionally by piercing the thickest part of the pear with a sharp knife. Using a slotted spoon, remove the pears from the liquid, drain them, and arrange them in a single layer on a plate or a clean work surface; let them cool. Reserve the poaching liquid.

4 Preheat the oven to 375°F.

5 Place the poaching liquid over medium-high heat, and cook, uncovered, until it is reduced by about three fourths, 8 to 10 minutes. It should be thick and syrupy. Strain, and keep warm.

6 Using your fingers or the back of a spoon, press the chilled pastry into a 10-inch tart tin with removable bottom. Pierce the pastry several times with a fork, and bake it in the center of the oven until it is golden and cooked through, about 20 minutes. If the edges begin to brown too quickly, loosely cover the entire pastry with aluminum foil. When the pastry is baked, remove it from the oven and let it cool on a wire rack.

7 Make the tart filling: In a medium-size bowl, whisk together the eggs and both sugars until pale yellow. Add the butter and the lemon zest, and whisk thoroughly. Combine three of the poached pear halves with the lemon juice in a food processor, and purée. Add the purée to the egg mixture, whisking thoroughly. Stir in the hazelnuts, and set aside.

8 Cut all but one remaining pear half lengthwise into ¼-inch-thick slices, leaving them attached at the stem end. Thinly slice the remaining pear half crosswise (these slices should be completely cut through).

9 Assemble the tart: Stir the filling mixture once, and pour it into the cooled tart shell. Place a knife under each pear half, and press gently on the pear to fan it out slightly. Transfer the pears on the knife to the tart shell and arrange them with the blossom end right next to the edge and the stem end toward the center. Crowd the pears slightly if necessary to fit them in. Place a knife under the pear that is cut across the width, and press on it gently so it spreads out. Place it in the center of the tart. Bake in the center of the oven until the filling has set, 25 to 30 minutes. Again, if the edges begin to brown too much, loosely cover the tart with aluminum foil. Cool to room temperature.

10 Just before serving, brush the pears with some of the thickened poaching liquid to shine them up. Serve the tart, passing the additional poaching liquid alongside.

One 10-inch tart (6 to 8 servings)

Note: To toast hazelnuts, preheat the oven to 350°F. Place the nuts in a baking pan large enough to hold them in a single layer, and toast, stirring once, until they give off a toasted aroma, about 10 minutes. Wrap the nuts in a kitchen towel and rub them between your hands to remove the skin.

PLUM PIE

This is a pie to make Jack Horner proud. Loaded with plums and spiked with vanilla sugar and allspice, it is full of warm, rich, fruity flavors. You can use either fresh or frozen plums. If using frozen, thaw and drain them first, discarding the liquid.

The juiciness of this pie will vary with the ripeness of the plums. You can adjust the amount of flour if you like, but don't use too much or the pie will be less tasty. I prefer to go with the prescribed amount of flour, and if the pie is juicier than usual, so be it.

Pastry dough for a 2-crust pie (see pages 429 and 430)
½ teaspoon ground allspice
7 tablespoons Vanilla Sugar (recipe follows)
8 cups pitted fresh Italian prune plums
¼ cup all-purpose flour
1 egg mixed with 1 teaspoon water

1 Preheat the oven to 400°F.

2 Roll half the pastry out to form a 12-inch circle about ¼ inch thick. Fit it into a 9-inch pie plate, leaving 1 to 2 inches of dough hanging over the edge of the plate.

3 Mix the allspice with the vanilla sugar in a small bowl. Remove 1 tablespoon and set it aside for the crust.

4 Place one-third of the plums in the pie shell, and sprinkle them with one-third of the flour and one-third of the sugar mixture. Repeat the layers, using up the remaining plums, flour, and sugar mixture. Paint the edge of the pastry shell, with some of the egg glaze.

5 Quickly roll out the remaining dough to form a 10-inch round, and lay it over the fruit. Press the edges gently onto the glazed edges of the bottom crust. Fold the edges of the bottom crust up and over the top edges and crimp them together, using your fingers or the tines of a fork.

6 Paint the top crust with egg glaze, and cut at least 8 slits in it for steam to escape. Sprinkle the remaining 1 tablespoon of sugar mixture over the crust, and bake in the bottom third of the oven until the top crust is golden and cooked through and the juice is bubbling up through the pastry, 45 to 55 minutes.

One 9-inch pie
(6 to 8 servings)

VANILLA SUGAR

■ ■ ■ ■ ■ ■

After I've used the seeds from a vanilla bean, I hate to throw the bean away because it is still potent with sweet vanilla flavor. So instead I push it down into a jar full of sugar, leave it for a week or so until the sugar has absorbed the vanilla flavor, then use the sugar in baked goods, to sprinkle atop a cake or pie, or sometimes for use in tea. It keeps indefinitely.

4 cups sugar
1 vanilla bean

Pour the sugar into a 1-quart jar or container. Push the vanilla bean (either a whole one or one with the seeds removed) down into the sugar, cover, and let ripen for at least 1 week. Replenish the sugar as you use it, and replace the vanilla bean every couple of months.

4 cups

VELMA WILLIAMS'S NOT-SO-SWEET PECAN PIE

I love pecan pie because I love pecans, but I usually find it just a touch too sweet. Velma Williams, who contributed the peach pie on page 451, had the same problem. She gave me this recipe, which does justice to the pecans and doesn't bowl you over with sugar. She suggested adding sour cream to the sugar mixture as well, which gives it a smooth richness. This has become the pecan pie of choice in our household.

3 large eggs, lightly beaten
½ cup sugar
1 cup dark corn syrup
¼ cup sour cream
2 teaspoons vanilla extract
¼ teaspoon salt
1¼ cups pecan halves
1 prebaked 9-inch pie shell (see page 431)

1 Preheat the oven to 400°F.

2 Whisk the eggs, sugar, and corn syrup together in a large bowl until thoroughly combined. Then vigorously whisk in the sour cream, vanilla extract, and salt, and set aside.

3 Place the pecans in an even layer in the pastry shell (arrange them in a pattern, rounded side up, if you like). Carefully pour the egg mixture over them (don't disturb the pattern), transfer the pie to a baking sheet, and place it in the bottom third of the oven.

4 Bake the pie for 10 minutes. Then reduce the heat to 350°F and continue baking until the filling is set, another 35 minutes. Remove it from the oven and let it cool to room temperature on a wire rack before serving.

One 9-inch pie (6 to 8 servings)

LINDA STOLTZFUS'S PUMPKIN CUSTARD PIE

It was dinnertime at the Stoltzfus Farm. Dusk was falling, and the rooms were softly shadowed from the weakening light that came in the windows. Amos and Linda Stoltzfus prefer not to bring electricity inside the house, and Amos lit a gas lamp that hung over the large kitchen table, which was set for supper and nearly groaning under dishes, bowls, pots, and baskets. There was homemade beef stew (see page 91), ham and cheese buns, pickles, and applesauce. After a short prayer we dove in and ate our fill, with everyone cheerfully vying for the last ham and cheese bun.

AT THE STOLTZFUS FARM

Linda and Amos Stoltzfus are a young Amish couple who live in northwestern Pennsylvania. I wanted to talk with Amos about his tomato farm and onion processing facility—he slices onions, shipped to him from Colorado, for pizza parlors and other fast-food restaurants.

When we arrived, Amos was in the barn across the farmyard from the house, with four of the couple's five children, who were helping to slice onions. Steven, who is 10, was feeding the "topped and tailed" onions through a gleaming stainless-steel hydraulically powered slicer, which spat them out in fat slices. Lena, 4, and Ben, 5, were separating the slices, between giggling fits, and young Amos Jr., 2½, was bravely inching a box half full of onions across the floor, getting more frustrated by the second.

Marian, 7, was in the house with Linda, and they came out to meet us and to rescue Amos Jr. from his plight.

Amos left Steven in charge of the work and took us out to his "power plant," a generator run by a Honda engine. He explained that although the Amish eschew electricity, they have nothing against mechanization (for instance they can ride in but not drive cars) but merely want to remain independent. Each Amish home, if they desire, has such a generator, and with it they power everything from specially adapted lights to mechanical dough mixers. If a generator breaks down they fix it, and they buy their fuel from a number of places, so they aren't dependent on any one source of power.

Marian came running out to invite us to supper, which we gladly accepted. "It will be ready in forty minutes," she said, then whispered something to her father. After she'd left he turned to us and said, "She didn't want you to know that Linda was making a special dessert in your honor, and that's why we have to wait for supper." Her Pumpkin Custard Pie was the delicious result.

We loved everything we tasted, but our favorite, and Linda confessed one of hers, was this light pumpkin pie with its hint of vanilla and cinnamon. It is best when made with freshly cooked pumpkin, preferably the pink-skinned long-necked "neck pumpkin" variety common on the East Coast. But traditional jack-o'-lantern pumpkins work well, as does the pumpkin from a can. If you cook your own, the purée will be quite wet, so be sure to cook it down until it is thick enough to sit up on a spoon.

There is a wide range in the cooking time because ovens vary. Linda's direction was to cook it so it is still "wiggly in the center," which I find guarantees a good result.

¾ cup plus 2 tablespoons pumpkin purée
2 large eggs, separated
6 tablespoons (lightly packed) light brown
   sugar
6 tablespoons granulated sugar
Pinch of salt
1⅓ cups milk
¾ teaspoon vanilla extract
1 tablespoon unsalted butter, melted
3 tablespoons all-purpose flour
1 prebaked 9-inch pie crust (see page 431)
¼ teaspoon ground cinnamon

1 Preheat the oven to 425°F.

2 In a medium-size bowl, whisk together the pumpkin and the egg yolks until combined. Whisk in both sugars, and the salt, milk, vanilla, and melted butter. Then whisk in the flour until the mixture is smooth.

3 In another medium-size bowl, lightly whisk the egg whites, until they are foamy but not stiff. Whisk them lightly into the pumpkin mixture, then pour it into the prebaked pie shell. Sprinkle the cinnamon over the top.

4 Bake the pie in the bottom third of the oven for 10 minutes. Then reduce the heat to 350°F and continue baking until the pie is nearly set but still moves slightly in the center, 25 to 35 minutes. Let it cool to room temperature before serving.

One 9-inch pie (6 to 8 servings)

SEVEN A.M. BANANA CREAM PIE

I had the best banana cream pie I've ever eaten at Cooky's Cafe in Golden City, Missouri. When I walked in there one early spring morning, every single surface was covered with fresh-baked pies. Farmers and hunters crowded the tables and the bar, and many were eating big slices. So I ordered banana cream, and it came to the table still warm, the pastry cream oozing out the side, the meringue tender and vanilla-scented.

I've re-created that pie here, and it takes me right back to Cooky's. The secret is simple: Use ripe, flavorful bananas and add them to the pastry cream while it is still warm.

This pie should be eaten within about 3 hours of baking, or the meringue will begin to "weep" and become runny.

FOR THE PASTRY CREAM
3 cups milk
1 vanilla bean
4 egg yolks, at room temperature
⅓ cup sugar
6 tablespoons all-purpose flour
2 medium-size fully ripe bananas, sliced into
*   thin rounds*

FOR THE MERINGUE
4 egg whites, at room temperature
Pinch of salt
2 tablespoons sugar
½ teaspoon vanilla extract

1 prebaked 9-inch pie shell (see page 431)

1 Make the pastry cream: Combine the milk and the vanilla bean in a medium-size heavy saucepan. Scald the milk over medium heat by heating just until little bubbles form around the edge of the pan.

Remove the milk from the heat, cover the pan, and let it infuse for 10 minutes. Then remove the vanilla bean (you can rinse, dry, and reserve it for vanilla sugar, see page 457).

2 While the milk is infusing, whisk together the egg yolks and the sugar in a large bowl until pale yellow and light. Whisk in the flour, then slowly add the hot milk, whisking constantly. Return the mixture to the saucepan and cook over medium heat, whisking constantly, until it bubbles. Continue cooking, stirring constantly, until the mixture thickens, then becomes slightly thinner (which shows the flour is cooked), at least 2 minutes. Remove the pan from the heat and pour the pastry cream into a mixing bowl.

3 Stir the banana slices into the warm pastry cream, cover, and set aside to cool. (You can prepare the pie up to this point a day ahead. Refrigerate the cooled pastry cream. Any bananas that come to the surface of the pastry cream may brown slightly.)

4 Make the meringue: Place the egg whites and the salt in a large mixing bowl, or in the bowl of an electric mixer fitted with a whisk. Whisk slowly at first to break up the egg whites, then more quickly until the egg whites become white and foamy. Slowly add the sugar, then the vanilla, and continue whisking until the egg whites form stiff peaks.

5 Preheat the broiler.

6 Pour the banana custard into the pre-baked pie shell, and mound the meringue over it. Either smooth it out, or using a flexible knife blade, make little peaks all over the meringue. Make sure the meringue reaches the edge of the crust all around.

7 Place the pie 3 inches below the broiler and broil just until the meringue is golden, 3 to 5 minutes.

8 Remove the pie from the oven, let it cool on a wire rack, and serve within 2 to 3 hours.

One 9-inch pie (6 to 8 servings)

OLD-FASHIONED INDIANA CREAM PIE

Though the Berner family of Loma, Montana, eschews sugar most of the time, this pie is a favorite at Christmas, when all the stops come out. The women of this extended family bake all the family special-ties and everyone enjoys the yearly indulgence.

This pie resembles cheese-cake in texture and flavor though it is simpler, less rich, and much eas-ier to make. Be sure to prebake the pastry until it is pale gold, and ei-ther serve the pie after it has cooled to room temperature or chill it overnight and let it return to room temperature, which allows the flavors to mellow.

Try this with fresh berries in season or Blueberry Syrup (see Index).

¾ cup sugar

3 tablespoons all-purpose flour

1 teaspoon freshly grated nutmeg

⅛ teaspoon salt

1 large egg

1½ cups sour cream

1 tablespooon unsalted butter, melted

1 teaspoon vanilla extract

1 prebaked 9-inch pie shell (see page 431)

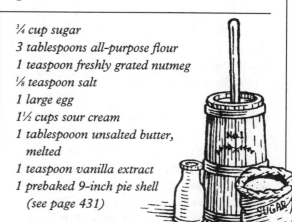

1 Preheat the oven to 400°F.

2 Sift the sugar, flour, nutmeg, and salt together onto a piece of waxed paper.

3 In a large bowl, whisk the egg with the sour cream. Add the dry ingredients to the egg mixture and mix well. Then add the melted butter and the vanilla, and whisk until smooth. Pour the filling into the pre-baked pie shell, and place the pie plate on a baking sheet.

4 Bake the pie in the bottom third of the oven for 10 minutes. Then reduce the heat to 300°F and continue baking until the filling is set, 20 to 25 minutes.

5 Remove the pie from the oven and let it cool to room temperature on a wire rack. Serve immediately, or refrigerate and serve the next day.

One 9-inch pie (6 to 8 servings)

APPLE STRUDEL

This is a version of Elizabeth Ryan's apple strudel, which she adapted from her grandmother's recipe. It is loaded with an aromatic mixture of apples and spices, and although it takes time to put together, there is nothing complex about it. One thing to remember when working with phyllo pastry is to work quickly because the sheets dry out when exposed to air. Once they are brushed with butter, however, all is well. The bread crumbs in this recipe are traditional, and they give the strudel a crisp lightness.

For more on Elizabeth, turn to page 482.

½ cup walnuts
1½ pounds tart apples, peeled, halved, cored, and sliced very thin (less than
   ⅛ inch)
½ cup (lightly packed) light brown
   sugar
½ cup raisins

¾ teaspoon ground cinnamon
½ teaspoon ground mace
2 tablespoons chopped candied ginger
Pinch of salt
8 ounces (½ package) phyllo dough
8 tablespoons (1 stick) unsalted butter,
   clarified (see Note)
¾ cup fresh bread crumbs
Whipped cream (optional)

1 Preheat the oven to 350°F.

2 Place the walnuts in a baking pan large enough to hold them in a single layer and toast, stirring once, until they give off a toasted aroma, about 10 minutes. Let them cool, then coarsely chop them. Raise the oven temperature to 375°F.

3 In a large bowl toss together the apple slices, brown sugar, raisins, cinnamon, mace, candied ginger, salt, and walnuts so they are thoroughly mixed.

4 Place two sheets of waxed paper that are at least 24 inches long on a work surface, with their long edges overlapping about 2 inches. Cover the phyllo with a damp (not wet) towel, and place it nearby.

5 Place one sheet of phyllo on the waxed paper, about 2-inches left of the center. Brush it with clarified butter, and sprinkle it lightly with bread crumbs. Place the second sheet of phyllo on top of the first but about 2 inches to the right, leaving a 2-inch border of the first sheet showing. Brush the second layer with butter, and sprinkle it with bread crumbs. Repeat with the remaining layers of phyllo, so that alternate layers sit either flush with the first or second layer. Use all of the bread crumbs and all but 1 tablespoon of the butter.

6 Toss the apple mixture briefly, and then mound it in a long, high mound leaving a 3-inch border at one of the ends and a 2-inch border on each long side. Fold both long sides of the phyllo over the apple mix-ture to enclose it, then fold the unfilled end of phyllo over the apple mixture. Working from that end, roll the phyllo up jelly-roll fashion. Make sure the long sides of the phyllo remain folded over the apple mixture to keep it enclosed. Press gently but firmly as you work so the roll is tight and firm.

7 Cover a baking sheet with parchment paper. Using the remaining 1 table-spoon clarified butter, brush the paper and the strudel (being sure to brush plenty of butter on the ends). Bake the strudel in the center of the oven until it is deep golden, 45 to 55 minutes. Some liquid from the apple mixture may bubble out onto the baking sheet.

8 Remove the strudel from the oven, and let it cool on a wire rack for about 30 minutes or until room temperature, before serving. Use a finely serrated knife to cut the strudel into pieces about 1½ inches thick. Serve with whipped cream if desired.

About 12 servings

Note: To clarify butter, place it in a heavy saucepan over high heat. When the butter has melted, remove the pan from the heat and skim off any white foam that has boiled to the top. Strain the butter through a very fine strainer to remove any milk solids.

BREAD TART WITH APPLE COMPOTE

This dessert was inspired by the abundance of apples that tumble into East Coast markets beginning in early August. By September the temperatures have cooled and the time is ripe for making homey desserts that take best advantage of the season.

This is one of my favorites because it has everything going for it—speed, ease, flavor, and style. If you have unexpected guests, this is a good dessert to choose.

This also makes a spectacular breakfast or brunch dish. It is best eaten right after it is made, so if you plan to make it for morning, mix up the dough the night before and bake it in the morning. In fact, the apples can be cooked the night before, too.

FOR THE BREAD DOUGH

1 cup lukewarm water
1 package active dry yeast
1 tablespoon sugar
2 to 2½ cups unbleached all-purpose flour
½ teaspoon salt
1 large egg, at room temperature

FOR THE APPLE COMPOTE

6 small, tart, crisp apples (about 1¾ pounds), such as Milton, Newton, or Winesap, cored, peeled, and quartered
3 tablespoons unsalted butter
½ cup sugar
1 teaspoon vanilla extract

1½ cups Crème Fraîche (recipe follows) or sour cream

1 Make the bread dough: Combine the water, yeast, and sugar in a large bowl and mix well. When there are some bubbles on top of the liquid, after about 2 minutes, add 1 cup of the flour and the salt, and mix well. Whisk the egg in a small bowl, then add it to the flour mixture, mixing well. Add enough of the remaining flour to make a smooth somewhat stiff dough. Turn it out on a well-floured surface and knead the dough, adding more flour as necessary, until it is

smooth and elastic, about 10 minutes. The dough should be somewhat moist, not stiff and dry. Place it in a bowl, cover with a damp towel, and let rise in a warm place (68° to 70°F) until doubled in bulk, about 1 hour.

2 Punch the dough down, return it to the bowl, and let it rise again until nearly doubled in bulk, about 1 hour.

3 Preheat the oven to 425°F. Line a baking sheet or a 10 x 15-inch jelly roll pan with parchment paper.

4 Make the compote: Cut each apple half in three vertical sections, then in very thin horizontal slices.

5 Melt the butter in a skillet over medium-high heat. Add the apples, sugar, and vanilla, and stir until the apples are coated with the mixture. Reduce the heat to medium-low, and cook just until the apples begin to soften, about 10 minutes. Remove the skillet from the heat and set it aside.

6 Roll out the bread dough until it is about ¼ inch thick, and transfer it to the prepared pan. Spread the apple compote on top of the dough to within 1 inch of the edges. Spread the liquid from the apples, which will make a glaze for the dough, all the way to the edges.

7 Bake the tart in the center of the oven until the dough and the apples are golden, 20 to 25 minutes. Remove it from the oven, let it cool for about 5 minutes

on a wire rack, and then serve with the crème fraîche alongside.

6 servings

CRÈME FRAÎCHE

■ ■ ■ ■ ■ ■

2 cups heavy (whipping) cream, preferably not ultra-pasteurized
3 tablespoons cultured buttermilk

1 Whisk the cream and the buttermilk together in a medium-size bowl. Cover with a cotton towel, and let stand in a warm spot—on top of the refrigerator or in a gas stove with the pilot light on—until it thickens, about 12 hours, depending on the temperature.

2 Cover the crème fraîche and refrigerate it for several hours, until it thickens. It will keep in the refrigerator, tightly covered, for up to 2 weeks.

2 cups

BLATSCHINDAS
SPICED PUMPKIN TURNOVERS

These delicate little pastries come from Pauline Kirschenmann, of Medina, North Dakota (see page 116). She bakes as easily as most people drink water, and nearly every day there is something fresh from the oven on the Kirschenmann table.

These are one of her family's favorites, and they have become one of mine as well. I make mine smaller than Pauline does, because I like to serve them after dessert, with coffee, to finish a good meal.

Blatschindas are a real treat any time of day, however, particularly during the holidays when visitors drop in. Enjoy them fresh the day they are made, or frozen and reheated. You can also freeze them before they are baked, and then bake them when you need them.

FOR THE PASTRY

2 cups all-purpose flour
1 tablespoon sugar
¾ teaspoon salt
8 tablespoons (1 stick) unsalted butter,
  chilled, cut into small pieces
1½ teaspoons
  cider vinegar
¼ cup cold water
1 large egg

FOR THE PUMPKIN FILLING

1 cup puréed pumpkin
¼ teaspoon salt
½ teaspoon ground cinnamon
¼ teaspoon vanilla extract
½ teaspoon freshly squeezed lemon juice
1 tablespoon sugar, or to taste

FOR FINISHING AND SERVING

1 egg mixed with 1 tablespoon cool water
2 tablespoons mild honey, or to taste
½ teaspoon freshly grated nutmeg, or to taste

1 Make the pastry: Place the flour, sugar, and salt in a food processor, and process just to mix. Add the butter and process, using short pulses, until the mixture ranges in size from peas to coarse cornmeal.

2 In a small bowl, combine the vinegar, the water, and the egg. Whisk thoroughly, and add to the flour mixture, using short pulses to incorporate it. Process just until the mixture begins to hold together but is still in pieces. The dough should hold

together when you press it between your fingers, but it should not feel damp. Press the dough lightly to form a flattened disc, wrap it in waxed paper, and chill it for at least 1 hour.

3 Make the pumpkin filling: Mix all the ingredients except the sugar in a small bowl. Season to taste with the sugar.

4 Preheat the oven to 400°F.

5 Roll the pastry out on a lightly floured surface so it is very thin, about ⅛ inch thick. Cut out twenty-four 3-inch rounds. Work with six at a time, and place the others in the refrigerator so they don't soften.

6 Brush the edge of one pastry round with some egg wash, and then place 1 teaspoon of the filling on the bottom third of the round. Fold the top half over the filling, and gently press the edges together. Using the tines of a fork, press the edges together again, more firmly, to seal them thoroughly and to make a design on the edge. Brush the pastry lightly with egg wash, and poke several holes in it to allow steam to escape. Refrigerate it while you repeat with the remaining rounds of dough. (You can prepare the blatschindas to this point and then freeze them, well wrapped, for up to 2 months. Let them thaw slightly, then proceed with the recipe.)

7 Arrange the blatschindas about ½ inch apart on a baking sheet, and bake until they are golden and the pastry is baked through, 15 to 20 minutes. Transfer them to a wire rack to cool for about 5 minutes, then arrange them on a warmed serving platter. Drizzle them with the honey, sprinkle with the nutmeg, and serve immediately.

24 blatschindas

FRUIT DESSERTS

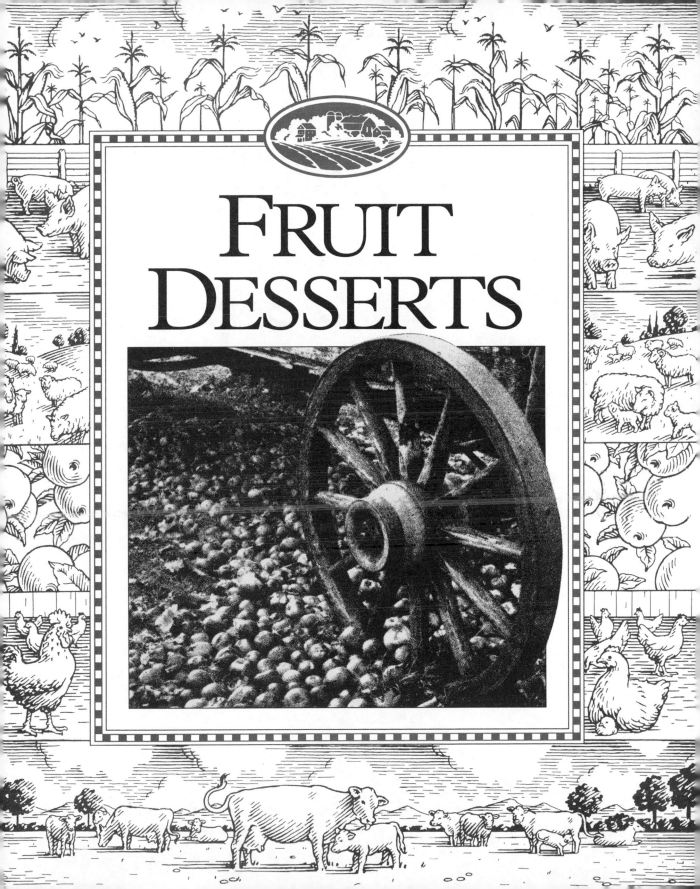

A DESSERT ASSORTMENT

Ingredients at hand figure largely in all farm cooking, and desserts are no exception. Do what farm cooks do, and let the riches of the season be your guide.

In early summer your mouth will water for rhubarb crisp. In midsummer, begin thinking of soft, ripe peaches for ice cream. Come fall, apples provide inspiration for everything from a sorbet to a fragrant charlotte.

For those in-between times of the year, when it's too early for one fruit and too late for another, there are dozens of timeless desserts to fill in: lemon or banana pudding, ginger ice cream, a compote of stewed dried fruits. Your fruit dessert can be as light or heavy as the season dictates.

MERINGUE-TOPPED BAKED STUFFED APPLES

This dish, a rather fancy variation on basic baked apples, is as fun to look at as it is delicious to eat. Don't be alarmed at the amount of sugar called for. Most of it stays in the syrup (which you can keep, tightly covered, for re-use if you like). If you plan to peel and core the apples in advance, be sure to rub a lemon all over them, to prevent them from turning brown. Try a good cooking apple here, such as Jonagold, Mutsu, or Monroe. Don't use a Granny Smith—it won't hold up in the poaching, and you'll find yourself with a mound of apple mush.

2 quarts water
3 cups plus 2 tablespoons sugar
1 vanilla bean
6 medium-size firm tart apples, cored
⅓ cup golden raisins
¼ cup dried apricots, cut into thin
    strips
¼ teaspoon ground cinnamon
3 egg whites
Pinch of salt
½ teaspoon vanilla extract
¼ cup pecans, toasted (see Note)
    and finely chopped

1 Preheat the oven to 375°F.

2 Combine the water, 3 cups of the sugar, and the vanilla bean in a large saucepan, and bring to a boil over high heat. Reduce the heat to medium-low, and cook until the sugar has dissolved, 3 to 4 minutes. (The sugar syrup can be prepared at least 1 day in advance. It will keep indefinitely in the refrigerator.)

3 Return the syrup to a boil over medium-high heat, and add the apples. Reduce the heat to a gentle boil and poach the apples, turning them occasionally, until they are softened on the outside but still somewhat firm in the center, about 20 minutes. Remove the apples from the sugar syrup and drain them well.

4 Place the raisins, apricots, and ½ cup of the apple poaching syrup in a small saucepan over medium heat. Bring to a boil, reduce the heat to low, and simmer just until the apricots have softened, about 5 minutes. Remove the pan from the heat and set it aside, leaving the fruit in the syrup.

5 Arrange the apples about ¼ inch apart in an ovenproof baking dish that is attractive enough to serve at the table. Drain the raisins and apricots of most, but not all, of the syrup, so the fruit is moist but not wet. Divide the fruit among the apples, stuffing it into the cores. Sprinkle the apples with the cinnamon.

6 Make a meringue by whipping the egg whites with the pinch of salt until they are white and frothy and beginning to stiffen. Slowly add the remaining 2 tablespoons sugar, whipping steadily, and then add the vanilla. Continue whipping until the meringue is stiff and glossy, which will take just a few minutes. Fold in the toasted pecans by hand.

7 Spread the meringue over the tops of the apples in an even layer, so it looks attractive. Bake in the center of the oven until the meringue is golden and the apples are heated through, 8 to 10 minutes. To serve, use two large spoons to cut through

the meringue. Gently lift out each apple and some of the meringue and transfer to individual dessert plates.

6 servings

Note: To toast pecans, preheat the oven to 350°F. Place the nuts in a baking pan large enough to hold them in a single layer, and toast, stirring once, until they give off a toasted aroma, about 10 minutes.

APPLE BALLS IN PINOT NOIR

This recipe comes from Ron Zimmerman, co-owner of the Herbfarm (see page 85), just outside Seattle. Ron creates and often prepares the meals at the Herbfarm's small restaurant, using only local ingredients and the extensive herb collection that grows right outside the door.

This is one of his best desserts; it takes familiar flavors and combines them in an unusual way. I love to serve these, topped with their spiced cooking liquid or over freshly made Thyme Ice Cream (page 490) or the best-quality vanilla I can find, and accompanied by a favorite cookie.

1½ cups Pinot Noir wine
¾ cup sugar
8 fresh sage leaves
1 quart cold water
1 tablespoon freshly squeezed lemon juice
4 large tart apples, such as Granny Smith or Stayman

1 Bring the wine, sugar, and sage leaves to a boil in a medium-size saucepan over medium-high heat. Reduce the heat to low, cover, and simmer for 20 minutes. Remove the pan from the heat, and discard the sage leaves.

2 Meanwhile, combine the water and lemon juice in a large bowl. Peel the apples, and using a melon baller, cut out balls and immediately place them in the acidulated water to keep them from browning. You should get about 24 balls from each apple.

3 Drain half the apple balls and place them in the saucepan with the wine mixture. Bring to a boil over medium-high heat. Reduce the heat to low, partially cover the pan, and cook at a simmer until the apple balls are softened but not mushy, about 12 minutes. Transfer the apple balls to a medium-size bowl, and repeat with the remaining apple balls.

4 When all the apple balls are cooked, add them to the bowl, pour the cooking liquid over them, and cool to room temperature. Then cover and refrigerate for at least 8 hours.

5 To serve, drain the apple balls and arrange them around a generous scoop of ice cream or in a parfait glass. Drizzle with the spiced poaching liquid, if you like.

4 to 6 servings

KEEPING APPLES

*W*hen you get good, flavorful apples, don't keep them in a basket on the counter. They look gorgeous there, but they will rapidly lose moisture, their flavor will become less pronounced, and they will get soft and, eventually, mushy. The exception is a firm, slightly underripe apple, which will mellow if kept at room temperature for a couple of days.

Ideally, apples should be kept at just above 32°F. At home, the best place to keep them is the bottom shelf of the refrigerator or in the crisper drawer, in a well-aerated plastic bag. If they get moist, wrap each one in a paper towel and return them to the plastic bag. They should keep in the refrigerator for at least 2 weeks.

CARAMELIZED PEARS WITH HAZELNUTS

This is a quick and elegant dessert for those days when the weather can't quite decide between winter and spring. You can prepare it several hours before guests arrive and warm it up before serving, or prepare it while guests relax after the main course.

Ripe (but not soft) pears are essential here. Serve Hazelnut Crisps alongside (see Index).

4 tablespoons (½ stick) unsalted butter
4 large pears, peeled, cut into
  eighths, and cored
⅓ cup dark rum
½ teaspoon ground cinnamon
3 tablespoons dark brown sugar
Minced zest of 1 lemon
2 tablespoons freshly squeezed lemon
  juice
2 to 3 pints vanilla ice cream
½ cup hazelnuts, toasted and skinned (see
  Note), coarsely chopped

1 Preheat the oven to 375 °F.

2 Melt the butter in a large skillet over medium-high heat. Add the pears in a single layer, and cook, stirring occasionally, until they are golden, about 10 to 12 min-utes. Transfer the pears to a dish or platter, and keep warm in a low (200°F) oven.

3 Add the rum, cinnamon, and brown sugar to the skillet, and cook until the mixture has thickened, about 6 minutes. Stir in the lemon zest and juice. Then re-turn the pears to the skillet, and stir until they are coated with the sauce.

4 Remove the skillet from the heat. Di-vide the ice cream among six shallow bowls, and spoon the pears over it. Sprinkle with the hazelnuts, and serve immediately.

6 servings

Note: To toast hazelnuts, preheat the oven to 350°F. Place the nuts in a baking pan large enough to hold them in a single layer, and toast, stirring once, until they give off a toasted aroma, about 10 minutes. Wrap the nuts in a kitchen towel and rub them be-tween your hands to remove the skin.

BANANA BREAD PUDDING WITH RUM SAUCE

You must be an unabashed banana fan to like this pudding because their sweet, smooth flavor is predominant. But since bananas are America's most popular fruit, I think this should fall on willing palates. The sauce is essential to the recipe—try it with the suggested rum, or with orange liqueur for a difference. (If you are baking the Fresh Banana Bread for this recipe, remember to omit the walnuts, nutmeg, and lemon zest.)

FOR THE BREAD PUDDING

2 cups milk
1 cup heavy (whipping) cream
½ cup sugar
3 large egg yolks
1 large egg
1 tablespoon vanilla extract
1 teaspoon freshly grated nutmeg
Pinch of salt
5 slices (each ½ inch thick) Fresh Banana Bread (see page 421)
3 large bananas, cut into ¼-inch-thick rounds

FOR THE RUM SAUCE

4 tablespoons (½ stick) unsalted butter
3 tablespoons dark brown sugar
2 tablespoons freshly squeezed lemon juice
½ cup rum
¼ cup water

2 cups heavy (whipping) cream, whipped to soft peaks (optional)

1 Generously butter a 12-cup ovenproof baking dish.

2 To make the custard, whisk the milk, cream, and sugar together in a large bowl. Add the egg yolks and the whole egg one at a time, whisking well after each addition. Whisk in the vanilla, nutmeg, and salt, and set aside.

3 Cut four slices of the banana bread vertically into 1-inch-wide fingers. Arrange an even layer of bread fingers on the bottom of the prepared dish, cutting and fitting them to cover the bottom. It is fine if they curve slightly up the sides of the dish. Cover the bread slices with an even layer of banana slices, and then pour enough custard over the bread and bananas to cover them. Repeat the layers of bread and bananas. Cut the remaining slice of banana bread into cubes, and sprinkle these over the bananas. Pour the rest of the custard over the bananas, press down slightly on the bread cubes, and cover. Set aside for 30 minutes.

4 Meanwhile, preheat the oven to 350°F.

5 Bake the pudding until it is almost solid through, about 45 minutes. Then remove the cover and bake until the cubes of banana bread on the top are golden, an additional 15 minutes. Remove the dish from the oven and cool it on a wire rack.

6 While the bread pudding is cooling, make the sauce: Melt the butter in a small saucepan over medium heat. Whisk in the brown sugar, lemon juice, rum, and water, and bring to a rolling boil. Cook, whisking occasionally, until the mixture begins to thicken and the sugar has dissolved, about 5 minutes. Remove the sauce from the heat and transfer it to a serving pitcher. Serve along with the slightly cooled banana bread pudding and whipped cream, if you like.

6 to 8 servings

BREAD AND BUTTER PUDDING

Warm, tender, and buttery, this scrumptious bread pudding can soothe the soul. It can peel the years away too, as one friend who tried it pointed out when she said, "Eating this makes me feel like a kid."

The pudding is based on an old-fashioned recipe in the *Thomas Jefferson Cookbook*. It's full of rum-plumped raisins, and the setting period and slow cooking give it a smooth, egg-rich, custard-like flavor and texture.

I like to serve it for either breakfast or dessert, but since it needs time to sit before baking, be sure to take that into account when you're planning the meal. Try to serve it directly from the oven, when it is puffed, slightly crisp, and golden. A caution, however: It may be too hot to eat directly from the oven, so it should cool slightly once on the table.

1 cup raisins

2 tablespoons rum

16 thin (⅜-inch) slices white bread, preferably Pepperidge Farm Distinctive White, with crusts

8 tablespoons (1 stick) unsalted butter, at room temperature

6 large eggs

1 cup sugar

1 quart milk

2 teaspoons vanilla extract

½ teaspoon freshly grated nutmeg

1 Combine the raisins and the rum in a small bowl, stir, and cover. Set aside to macerate for at least 30 minutes, or up to several hours.

2 Drain the raisins, reserving the rum. Spread one side of each bread slice evenly with butter. Line a 3½-quart heavy enamel casserole with four of the buttered slices of bread (buttered side up), overlapping them to fit in the dish. Sprinkle them with one-fourth of the raisins. Repeat the layers, using all the bread and ending with raisins.

3 In a large bowl combine the eggs, sugar, milk, vanilla, the reserved rum, and the nutmeg; whisk until thoroughly combined. Pour the mixture over the bread and raisins, cover, and refrigerate for 2 hours.

4 Preheat the oven to 300°F.

5 Place the bread pudding on a baking sheet, and bake it in the center of the oven until it is puffed and the slices on top are golden and slightly crisp, about 1½ hours. Remove it from the oven and serve immediately.

6 to 8 servings

SPICED LEMON PUDDING

This is an old-fashioned farm recipe from my grandmother's family, who homesteaded in Oregon. She passed it along to me years ago, and I've always loved the combination of mace and lemon, and the fluffy, soufflé-like texture of the pudding. This is a homey dessert, but it can also be quite elegant if you serve it in small glass dishes and garnish it with whipped cream and a sprinkling of lemon zest.

2 tablespoons unsalted butter, melted
2 tablespoons all-purpose flour
1 cup milk
Juice of 1 lemon
2 large eggs, separated
½ cup plus 1 tablespoon sugar
2 teaspoons minced lemon zest (optional)
½ teaspoon ground mace
Pinch of salt
Whipped cream (optional)

1 Melt the butter in a small heavy saucepan over medium heat. When it begins to foam, stir in the flour and cook the mixture, stirring frequently, for 2 minutes. Slowly whisk in the milk, and cook, stirring frequently, until the mixture has thickened slightly, 3 to 5 minutes. Remove the pan from the heat and let the mixture cool to lukewarm, stirring occasionally to prevent a skin from forming.

2 Preheat the oven to 350°F. Lightly butter a 6-cup soufflé dish.

3 Whisk the lemon juice and the egg yolks together in a medium-size bowl. Whisk in ½ cup of the sugar, and continue whisking until the mixture turns pale yellow and thickens slightly. Then whisk in the lemon zest and the mace.

4 Whisk the egg yolk mixture into the cooled milk mixture until thoroughly combined.

5 Whip the egg whites with a pinch of salt to form stiff peaks, adding the 1 tablespoon sugar when the whites begin to stiffen. Fold one-quarter of the egg whites into the egg yolk mixture, then fold in the remaining egg whites. Transfer the mixture to the prepared soufflé dish, smoothing it out on top.

6 Place the soufflé dish in a pan of hot water that reaches about halfway up the sides of the dish, and bake in the center of the oven until the pudding is golden and no longer loose in the center, about 40 minutes. Serve hot, with whipped cream if desired.

4 servings

RHUBARB CRUNCH

Rhubarb is a little like zucchini—when it's the season, there's so much, it comes in from every quarter. I've never minded the seasonal abundance, nor did my mother, who turned the ruby stalks into everything from stewed rhubarb for breakfast to this simple, delicious rhubarb crunch.

This is the ideal crunch in my opinion—sweet, crisp, and caramelized, with lots of tart fruit in the center. The amount of sugar added to the fruit is given in a wide range—adjust it as you like. I like rhubarb tart, so I add the smaller amount, but others differ.

If you don't have rhubarb, substitute berries, apples, or mixed fruit of your choice. Sometimes I add 2 cups of strawberries to the rhubarb, or a teaspoon of orange zest, or a few toasted walnuts. If you plan to make an all-berry crunch, use 8 cup of berries and sweeten them to taste.

1½ cups rolled oats
¾ cup plus 2 tablespoons sifted all-purpose
*   flour*
1½ cups (lightly packed) light brown sugar
12 tablespoons (1½ sticks) unsalted butter,
*   cut into 12 pieces*
4½ cups diced rhubarb
¼ to ¾ cup granulated sugar
1½ teaspoons ground cinnamon
¼ teaspoon salt
2 tablespoons water

1 Preheat the oven to 350°F.

2 Place the oats, ¾ cup of the flour, and
the brown sugar in a food processor,
and process briefly to blend the mixture.
Add the butter, and process until the ingredients are mixed. Be careful not to overmix—you want to keep the texture of the
oats. The mixture will be somewhat dusty
looking.

3 In a medium-size bowl, toss the rhubarb, remaining 2 tablespoons flour,
granulated sugar, cinnamon, salt, and water
until well mixed.

4 Place the rhubarb mixture in an 8-inch-
square nonreactive (earthenware or
glass) pan. Cover it with the oat topping,
patting it gently into place. Bake until the
fruit is bubbling up around the edges and
the topping is golden and crisp, about 45
minutes.

6 servings

AN AUTUMN
APPLE CRISP

T his is a version of Elizabeth Ryan's apple crisp, the one she makes for
herself and her husband, Peter Zimmerman, in the wintertime when
they both have time away from their orchard work and can enjoy it
(see page 482).

This dessert is very quickly
made—the longest part of it is peeling and cutting the apples—so it is
ideal to serve when unexpected visitors drop in.

1½ cups rolled oats
¾ cup all-purpose flour
1½ to 2 cups (lightly packed) light brown sugar
12 tablespoons (1½ sticks) unsalted butter, chilled and cut into 12 pieces
3 pounds apples, peeled, cored, and cut into eighths (about 10 cups)
1½ teaspoons ground cinnamon
Pinch of salt
Minced zest of 1 orange (optional)

1 Preheat the oven to 350°F.

2 Place the oats, flour, and 1½ cups of the brown sugar in a food processor, and process briefly to blend the mixture. Add the butter, and process, using short pulses, until the ingredients are mixed. Be careful not to overmix—you want to maintain the texture of the oats. The mixture will be dry looking.

3 In a large bowl combine the apples, the remaining ½ cup brown sugar (if desired), and the cinnamon, salt, and orange zest. Toss until well mixed.

4 Place the apple mixture in a nonreactive (glass or earthenware) 8½ x 12½-inch baking dish. Cover it evenly with the oat topping, patting it gently into place. Bake in the center of the oven until the topping is golden and the fruit is bubbling, about 45 minutes.

5 Remove the dish from the oven and let it cool to room temperature before serving.

8 to 10 servings

ALICE BERNER'S APPLE PANCAKE

Alice Berner, a Montana grain farmer (see page 13), whipped this up quickly, and served it as the ideal finale to a scrumptious meal of chicken and homemade noodles.

It's an old-fashioned dessert, and the way the pancake puffs is bound to create an impression on guests—it looks large and poofed enough to feed the world. It's actually light, and full of good egg flavor.

If you like, substitute pears for the apples for a change. You could also serve this for brunch instead of dessert.

FOR THE PANCAKE
4 large eggs
¾ cup milk
¾ cup all-purpose flour
3 tablespoons unsalted butter, melted

FOR THE APPLES
2 tablespoons unsalted butter
4 medium tart apples, such as Winesap or Jonagold, peeled, cored, and sliced into ¼-inch-thick slices
4 tablespoons honey, or more to taste, softened (see Note)
1½ cups plain low-fat yogurt
½ teaspoon vanilla extract
½ teaspoon ground cinnamon

1 Preheat the oven to 400°F.

2 Make the pancake: Whisk the eggs and milk together in a medium-size bowl. Then whisk in the flour a little at a time, to make a smooth batter. Whisk in the butter, and let the mixture sit for 10 minutes.

3 Pour the batter into a 10-inch oven-proof skillet, and bake in the center of the oven for 15 minutes. Reduce the heat to 350°F, and bake until the pancake puffs up around the edges of the skillet and turns golden and crisp at the edges, 10 to 15 minutes.

4 While the pancake is baking, prepare the apples: Melt the butter in a large heavy skillet over medium heat. Add the apples and cook, stirring frequently, until they are softened and golden, 15 to 20 minutes. Add 2 tablespoons of the honey, stir, and keep warm over low heat.

5 Mix the yogurt, the remaining 2 tablespoons honey, the vanilla, and the cinnamon together in a small bowl. Add additional honey, if desired.

6 Remove the skillet from the oven, and spoon the apples into the center of the pancake. Either spoon the yogurt over the apples or serve it separately. Cut the pancake into wedges, and serve immediately.

4 to 6 servings

Note: To soften congealed honey, place the jar, or a heatproof container holding the honey, in a saucepan and add water to the pan to a depth of at least 2 inches. Place the pan over medium-low heat and simmer. The honey will gradually soften.

OH, THOSE FLAVORFUL APPLES

Though Elizabeth Ryan has a graduate degree in pomology (the study of tree fruit) from Cornell University, she never wanted to grow apples. "They have a lot of pests, and you have to spray them a lot," she said. "I was more oriented to small fruits and brambles, like berries."

Yet today Elizabeth and her husband, Peter Zimmermann, are among the best-known apple growers in New York's Hudson Valley. They grow apples because they couldn't resist Breezy Hill Orchard. "We looked for a farm for a long time, and we found the perfect place," she said. "It just happened to have apple trees on it."

Elizabeth and Peter adapted easily because Breezy Hill Orchard had so much to offer. It sits on a rise, an ideal site since the cold air drains down the hill and across the valley, instead of collecting around the trees, where it might damage the fruit.

Elizabeth had never farmed before, but she wasn't entirely unfamiliar with farmlife. Every summer while she was growing up, she and her family visited relatives on the farm in Iowa where her mother had grown up. "My mother's view of the farm was that it was a horrible life," Elizabeth said with a laugh. "And I could tell even when I was young that the agricultural system wasn't working, because farmers weren't making money."

At college she took classes in agricultural economics and marketing, and then she went to Washington, D.C., to work on a public interest project involved with agriculture. "I knew after a couple of years that I wanted to be a farmer," she said. "I felt it was where my roots were. But I didn't have a lot of practical experience, because I didn't help on the farm. Girls worked in the kitchen on the farm, and I grew up never even changing a fuse."

She got some practical experience as a manager for a small vineyard in the Hudson Valley. The rest has been on her own farm. Peter, a linguist, had never worked on a farm before they bought Breezy Hill, and he is now the farm manager. "Elizabeth taught me everything I know about farming, including how to drive a tractor," he said.

FOR EVERY DISH, THERE IS AN APPLE

Elizabeth quickly recovered from her aversion to apple growing, and since buying the farm in 1984 she has become an outspo-

ken and devoted advocate. She not only describes in detail the flavor of each variety that grows on the farm, she knows their history, where they were first planted, and exactly how to cook them to their best advantage. Some of the varieties are old and obscure, like Quinte, Wealthy, and King Luscious, which Elizabeth and Peter are encouraging back into production. Others are newer and more familiar, like Golden Delicious, Empire, Jonagold, and Winesap.

Every Saturday from March through Thanksgiving, Elizabeth and Peter sell their apples at the Union Square Greenmarket in Manhattan. Customers crowd in six deep to buy new and antique varieties, and to get cooking advice. "When people ask me what apple to use, I find out what they're making, how much sugar they want to use, and what flavors they like," she said.

GETTING DOWN TO BUSINESS

▪▪▪▪▪

In Elizabeth's kitchen, apples cover every surface, and we're set to do some baking. Pale yellow, streaky red, green, and russet, they're in bushels and baskets on the floor, countertops, and tables. Several baking pans filled with apple chunks await a topping, and a huge pot of fragrant apple purée simmers on the stove.

It's a crystalline early winter day. The apples are all harvested, and pruning can't be done for another month. "It's our slow time," Elizabeth says. "I get a chance to bake for us now." On her list is an apple charlotte, apple crisp, applesauce, and an apple pie.

The baking pans contain Mutsus, Jonagolds, Winesaps, or Red Spies. "I'm trying to figure out which is best for cobbler," she says, sprinkling a generous amount of topping over each. The Mutsu cobbler comes out ahead, though they all get high marks. "The one with Mutsus is a little more tart and spicy, and it has a more aromatic flavor," she says.

For the best pies and cobblers, Elizabeth recommends a mixture of apples. "You want to balance sweet with acid, and crisp with soft," she says. "That gives more layers of flavor and makes a dish more interesting."

For a sweet pie—or a cobbler, charlotte, sauce, or tart—she recommends a combination using Golden Delicious, because their solid texture holds up well in cooking and their sweet flavor is balanced with just a bit of acid. She suggests Jonagold, Golden Delicious, and Mutsu. "Always add one or two medium- to super-tart apples for character, too, especially for pie," she says.

Rhode Island Greenings and Baldwins make up the super-tart category.

▶ ▶ ▶

They are so firm and full of tannin that when you bite into them it feels as if the enamel has been stripped off your teeth. Put them in a pie, however, and their tartness mellows and adds a flavorful edge.

Medium-tart apples with lots of character include Gravenstein, Winesap, Northern Spy, Melrose, Monroe, York, Idared, and Cortland. These are good eating apples, the kind that crack when you bite into them and fill your mouth with a sweet-tart flowery flavor.

IF YOUR CHOICE IS LIMITED

For those who don't have access to an abundance of apples, Elizabeth recommends a cooking mix such as Golden Delicious and Granny Smith. "Neither has a lot of its own flavor, or what I call character, but one is sweeter and one more tart, and you'll get more depth by combining them than by using them by themselves," she says. If apples are bland, she suggests adding lemon juice to liven them up.

One apple that Elizabeth does not recommend, for baking or anything else, is the Rome. "I know I should—we need to sell those apples—but I hate Romes. They have no flavor, and I don't want anyone to be disappointed," she says.

Though McIntosh is a widely popular apple, Elizabeth insists they're good only six weeks a year, right off the tree. "Never in my right mind would I bake with a McIntosh, or an Empire for that matter, after mid-October," she says. "They don't hold up. They get too soft and they lose their tartness, which makes them worthless. They do make spectacular applesauce in season, however."

A sugar and acid balance, along with tannin and some natural chemicals, gives apples their character. Early apples such as Yellow Transparent and Lodi, which ripen in July and August, are soft, high in acid because of summer's heat, and sour. They also tend to be watery and bland. Cooler temperatures are needed to concentrate flavor in an apple, get the sugar coursing through it, and make its flavor more complex.

"Summer apples are fine for eating, and they'll make an all right sauce, but the flavor will be thin," Elizabeth says. "They're no good for baking, because they don't hold their shape." After mid-September, when the weather cools and ripening slows, apples are at their peak of flavor and texture. Their keeping quality also improves once the weather cools.

Elizabeth sits down at the table and cuts into an apple crisp. "You know," she says thoughtfully, "apples taste different depending on where they're grown. I've tasted a McIntosh in California, and it was different from ours. I think ours are better—but then, what else would I say?"

APPLE CHARLOTTE

When I went to visit Elizabeth Ryan at Breezy Hill Orchards, she was in the kitchen baking, and apple charlotte was on her list. She had a stack of bread cut into fingers for the "crust" and a pot of aromatic apple purée simmering away on the stove. Elizabeth put it together, baked it, and when she brought it out of the oven, it was a perfect golden brown on the outside, flavorful and aromatic on the inside.

Apple charlotte is a French country dish, the peasant version of a lighter, richer, usually cream-filled dessert made with lady-fingers. In my opinion, this version is far more satisfying, and it also manages to be elegant at the same time. What's more, it is so easy to make that once you've tried it, you'll probably find yourself making it often.

There are a few secrets to the success of this recipe, and the most important is the apples you use. I recommend a combination of three different kinds, which gives it a subtlety of flavor you won't get using just one type. My favorite combination is two tart varieties and one sweet, such as a combination of Monroe, Winesap, and any Spy, or Gravenstein, Golden Delicious, and Granny Smith.

Another secret is the whole vanilla bean that cooks with the apples. It is essential.

The final secret, equally important, is to cook the apples until they are thick and quite smooth. They must be thick to hold up inside the charlotte, so it doesn't collapse when you take it from the mold. So cook them until the mixture is almost dry and the whole mass tends to move around in the pan when you stir it. There should be no juice left at all.

If you don't have a charlotte mold, use a 1-quart ovenproof bowl with a flattish bottom (you may need to adjust the amount of bread). When lining the mold, be sure it is completely covered with the bread and that the upright pieces are overlapping, so they will be strong enough to contain the filling.

FOR THE FILLING

4 tablespoons (½ stick) unsalted butter

3 pounds mixed apples, peeled, cored, and cut
into ⅛-inch-thick slices

1 vanilla bean, halved lengthwise

Minced zest of 1 lemon

1 tablespoon freshly squeezed lemon juice

½ cup sugar, or more to taste

FOR THE CRUST

8 to 10 slices firm white bread, preferably
Pepperidge Farm Distinctive White, crusts
removed

6 tablespoons (¾ stick) unsalted butter,
clarified (see page 464)

Vanilla Custard Sauce (optional; recipe follows)

1 Make the filling: Melt the butter in a
large heavy skillet over medium heat.
Add the apples in an even layer, then the
vanilla bean, lemon zest, lemon juice, and
sugar. Cover and cook, stirring occasionally,
until the apples are completely soft, 25 to
30 minutes. Remove the cover, increase the
heat if necessary for the apples to be bubbling vigorously, and continue cooking, stirring frequently, until any liquid has evaporated and the thickened apple mixture
moves around as a mass when you stir it,
about 15 minutes. It may caramelize in
spots, but watch it so it doesn't get too dark.

2 Preheat the oven to 400°F. Place a
round of buttered parchment paper in
the bottom of a 1-quart charlotte mold or
ovenproof bowl with a flat bottom.

3 Prepare the crust: Cut about 4 slices of
the bread in half to form triangles, and

then cut those triangles in half. Brush one
side of each triangle lightly with butter, and
arrange them in the base of the prepared
mold, buttered-side down, so they completely cover the bottom. If there are any
spaces, fill them in with pieces of bread that
are cut to fit.

4 Cut the remaining bread slices into
fourteen to sixteen 1-inch-wide strips,
and trim them so they are just long enough
to reach the top of the mold. Lightly brush
each one with clarified butter, and arrange
them, buttered-side out, upright along the
sides of the mold to completely line it, overlapping them slightly. Set aside the extra
bread strips.

5 Remove the vanilla bean from the apples and discard it. Spoon the apple
mixture into the mold. The apples may
mound above the edge of the mold; they
will sink during cooking. Completely cover
the apple filling with any remaining pieces
of bread, cut to fit, buttered-side out.

6 Place the charlotte mold on a baking
sheet, and bake it on the center rack of
the oven for 15 minutes. Then reduce the
heat to 350°F, and continue baking until
the bread on the top and sides is deep
golden, about 35 minutes. If the top is getting too dark, cover it loosely with aluminum foil.

7 Transfer the charlotte mold to a wire
rack and let it cool for 15 minutes.
Then, place a serving plate over the top of
the mold and carefully flip it over. The
charlotte will slide right out. Because of its

puddinglike consistency, use two large spoons to cut the charlotte. Serve it warm or at room temperature, with the custard sauce alongside.

4 to 6 servings

VANILLA CUSTARD SAUCE

■ ■ ■ ■ ■ ■

This simple custard sauce ranks as my husband's most favored dessert. It will dress up a fruit tart, a baked apple, or—especially—apple charlotte.

   When you are making this, be sure to watch carefully while the custard thickens, as even an extra 30 seconds can make the difference between a smooth, silken sauce and one that resembles loose scrambled eggs. The moment it has thickened sufficiently, transfer it to a bowl. If it is just beginning to curdle, pour it through a sieve into the bowl, and it should be just fine.

2 cups milk
1 vanilla bean, or 1 teaspoon vanilla
   extract
6 egg yolks
¼ cup sugar

1 Combine the milk and the vanilla bean, if using, in a medium-size heavy

saucepan over medium-high heat. Scald the milk by heating it just until little bubbles form around the edge of the pan. Remove the pan from the heat, cover, and set aside to infuse for 15 minutes.

2 Meanwhile, whisk the egg yolks and the sugar together in a medium bowl until pale yellow and thick.

3 Strain the hot milk into a bowl, and discard the vanilla bean, or rinse it and reserve it for vanilla sugar (see page 457). Whisk the milk into the egg yolk mixture, add the vanilla extract, if using, and return it to the saucepan. Cook, stirring constantly, over medium-low heat until the custard has thickened enough to coat the back of a spoon, 8 to 10 minutes. Be careful not to let the custard curdle.

4 Immediately transfer the custard to a bowl, so it won't continue cooking in the heat from the pan. Let it cool to room temperature, and then serve or cover and refrigerate. The custard will thicken in the refrigerator, and it will keep for 1 day.

2 cups

CANDIED PEAR SUNDAE

When pears come into season, I immediately start thinking of pear desserts. This one, inspired by a bountiful array of pears at the Union Square Greenmarket in Manhattan, teams the fruit with two of its most complementary flavors, chocolate and ginger.

FOR THE CHOCOLATE SAUCE
5 ounces bittersweet chocolate, preferably Lindt or Tobler
1 tablespoon unsalted butter
¼ cup water
½ cup heavy (whipping) cream
1 teaspoon vanilla extract

FOR THE CANDIED PEARS
3 tablespoons unsalted butter
1 pound small, not too ripe pears, such as Bosc, peeled, cored, and thinly sliced lengthwise
2 tablespoons sugar

2½ cups Ginger Ice Cream (recipe follows), frozen hard

1 Make the chocolate sauce: Combine the chocolate, butter, and water in a heavy saucepan over low heat. Cook, stirring occasionally, until melted together; make sure it doesn't burn. Whisk in the cream and the vanilla, and heat through. Keep warm over very low heat.

2 Cook the pears: Melt the butter in a large skillet over medium-high heat. Add the pears and cook until they soften and turn golden, about 10 minutes. Sprinkle the sugar over them, and shake the skillet so the pears are coated with the sugar. Continue cooking until the sugar caramelizes and turns golden, stirring and shaking the skillet constantly, 5 minutes. Remove the skillet from the heat and set it aside.

3 Spoon the chocolate sauce onto the center of four shallow bowls or four rimmed dessert plates. Mound the warm candied pears on the chocolate sauce, or arrange them in a spiral. Set a large scoop of ginger ice cream on top of the pears, and serve immediately.

4 servings

GINGER ICE CREAM

Rich, creamy, and almost hot with fresh ginger flavor, serve this ice cream with a favorite sweet cookie or the Candied Pear Sundae (preceding) for an exotically refreshing dessert.

1 piece (2 ounces) fresh ginger, peeled and minced
⅓ cup boiling water
2⅔ cups milk
½ cup heavy (whipping) cream
1 tablespoon minced candied ginger
4 large egg yolks
½ cup sugar

1 Combine the fresh ginger and the boiling water in a small bowl. Stir, cover, and let steep for 30 minutes. Then strain, pressing down on the solids to extract all the liquid. Discard the ginger and set the liquid aside.

2 Combine the milk, cream, and candied ginger in a heavy saucepan over medium-high heat. Scald the mixture by heating it just until little bubbles form around the edge of the pan. Then remove the pan from the heat, cover, and set aside to infuse for 10 minutes.

3 Whisk the egg yolks and the sugar together in a large bowl until pale yellow and thick. Strain the hot milk mixture into the egg yolk mixture, whisking constantly. Discard the candied ginger.

4 Return the milk and egg mixture to the saucepan, and place it over medium heat. Cook, stirring constantly, until it has thickened just enough to coat the back of a spoon, about 10 minutes. Watch very carefully so it doesn't curdle. The mixture will not be thick; it will resemble a custard sauce.

5 Immediately transfer the mixture to a bowl, so it won't continue to cook from the heat of the pan, and let it cool to room temperature. Stir in ¼ cup of ginger liquid. Refrigerate until the custard is well chilled, about 4 hours.

6 Stir and freeze in an ice cream maker, following the manufacturer's directions.

2½ cups (4 servings)

THYME ICE CREAM

This recipe comes from Ron Zimmerman, chef and owner of the Herbfarm in Falls City, Washington (see page 85). Ron has hundreds of herbs at his disposal to use in the dishes he serves—and use them he does. Everything from the tiny pats of butter to the tender rolls is flavored with herbs.

I love this ice cream because it is rich and smooth, the way a good custardy ice cream should be. The thyme makes it special, elegant. Try English, silver, or lemon thyme for delicate flavor nuances.

1½ cups half-and-half
2½ cups heavy (whipping) cream
⅔ cup sugar
8 sprigs (4 inches each) fresh thyme
5 large egg yolks

1 Place the half-and-half, cream, and sugar in a medium-size saucepan over medium-high heat, and stir. Add the thyme sprigs and scald the mixture by heating it just until little bubbles form around the edge of the pan. Remove the pan from the heat, cover, and set aside to infuse for 20 minutes. Then strain the milk to remove the thyme.

2 Whisk the egg yolks lightly in a large bowl. Gradually add the warm cream mixture, whisking constantly. Return the mixture to the saucepan, and place it over medium heat. Cook, stirring constantly, until it has thickened just enough to coat the back of a spoon, about 10 minutes. Watch very carefully so it doesn't curdle. The mixture will not be thick, but more like a custard sauce.

3 Transfer the mixture immediately to a large bowl and let it cool to room temperature. Then cover and refrigerate until chilled. Freeze in an ice cream maker according to the manufacturer's instructions.

1 quart

Variation: If you want to make a terrific plain vanilla ice cream, substitute 1 large vanilla bean, split lengthwise for the thyme.

LIZ CLARK'S BROWN SUGAR PEACH ICE CREAM

When my husband and I were traveling to Iowa, a friend told me about a woman who served meals for two to forty people in her home. Her food was reputed to be delicious, her clients from all over the country.

I tracked Liz Clark down in Keokuk, in the southeastern corner of the state, a town where time seems to have stood still since the 1950s.

We wound our way up a hill and into a stylish neighborhood to the given address, a small mansion overlooking the town and the Mississippi River. Liz is carefully restoring it, and she seated us in a drawing room full of antiques, the walls lined with books from another century. There we enjoyed pâté and hot goat cheese toasts until she ushered us into the dining room, where candles flickered on the wall.

All was delightfully fresh and relaxed, from the crusty homemade baguette and a garden salad showered with flower petals to this flavorful peach ice cream.

Liz grew up on a farm in Iowa, and she has an inspiring sensibility about fresh foods. She grows most of what she serves, and the rest she buys from local farmers. That is why her salad was so tender and fresh, and why this peach ice cream leapt out of the bowl with flavor.

Sweet white peaches are the best choice for this recipe. They are hard to find if you don't live in peach country, however, as they don't ship well, so use yellow peaches in a pinch. Just make sure they are bursting with perfume and juice.

1 cup (packed) dark brown sugar
1 cup water
1 tablespoon brandy
1 tablespoon freshly squeezed lemon juice
2 teaspoons vanilla extract
½ cup heavy (whipping) cream
5 medium white peaches

1 Combine the brown sugar and the water in a medium-size saucepan over medium-high heat, and bring to a boil. Lower the heat to medium and simmer until the sugar has dissolved, 4 to 5 minutes. Remove the pan from the heat and let it cool to room temperature.

2 When the sugar mixture is cooled, stir in the brandy, lemon juice, vanilla, and cream. (If you are using a hand-cranked ice cream maker, cover the mixture and chill it in the refrigerator for at least 1 hour, so it will solidify more quickly.)

3 Just before freezing the mixture, peel and pit the peaches, and purée them in a food processor. Stir them into the sugar mixture, and freeze in an ice cream maker, following the manufacturer's directions.

About 3½ cups (6 servings)

APPLE SORBET

This sorbet is particularly good in fall and winter, when apples and apple cider are at their best. And it is a refreshing accompaniment to other desserts, such as the Meringue-Topped Baked Stuffed Apples. I like it best when it is frozen to a firm slush, not completely solid.

If you can't find cider, use good-quality unfiltered apple juice. It won't have quite the depth, but it will still be very good.

1 cup sugar
1½ cups water
3 cups apple cider
1 tablespoon freshly squeezed lemon juice

1 Combine the sugar and the water in a medium-size saucepan over high heat, and bring to a boil. Reduce the heat to medium, stir, and simmer until the sugar has dissolved, about 5 minutes. Remove the pan from the heat and let it cool to room temperature.

2 Combine the apple cider and the sugar syrup, and chill, covered, until very cold, preferably overnight.

3 Stir in the lemon juice, and freeze in an ice cream maker according to the manufacturer's instructions.

About 1 quart (6 servings)

YOGURT CHEESE WITH FRESH FRUIT

W hen fresh strawberries are at their best and the first fragrant California nectarines have appeared, I can hardly resist serving them at every meal. One of my favorite ways to accompany the fruit is with yogurt cheese, which resembles a soft fresh cow's-milk cheese, yet has the unmistakable tang of yogurt. Satisfying, elegant, and refreshing, it makes a lovely dessert for those who aren't drawn by things overly sweet, and a cheerful morning dish for breakfast or brunch. Whenever it's served, there isn't much to rival it for looks.

Once when I presented the dish as a dessert, a guest commented that she thought it was a bit virtuous, while another immediately argued that there was nothing wrong with a virtuous dessert. If virtue is a problem, serve ginger or pecan cookies (see Index) alongside!

Virtuous or not, when the cheese is made from low-fat yogurt, there really isn't a more healthful dessert, though you'll be fooled by its richness. Do remember to allow enough time to prepare the cheese.

4 pounds plain low-fat yogurt
¼ cup mild honey
2 teaspoons vanilla extract
2 pounds ripe nectarines or peaches
1 pint ripe strawberries

1 Two days before you plan to serve this dessert, place the yogurt in a sieve lined with a double thickness of damp cheesecloth or a damp linen towel. Place the sieve in a bowl, cover the bowl, and let the yogurt drain for 24 hours. Check the bowl from time to time, and empty out the liquid if necessary. (It isn't necessary to refrigerate the yogurt unless it is a particularly hot day.)

2 The night before you plan to serve it, combine the drained yogurt cheese, the honey, and the vanilla in a medium-size bowl and mix well.

3 Cut half the nectarines into ¼-inch cubes. Fold the cubes into the yogurt cheese. (If you are using peaches, peel them first by submerging them in boiling water for 1 minute, draining, and peeling.) Line a

9-inch cake pan with plastic wrap, and turn the yogurt mixture into the pan, smoothing it out. Cover it with plastic wrap and chill for at least 8 hours.

4 Just before serving, cut the remaining nectarines into slices. Hull and slice the strawberries into ¼-inch-thick lengthwise slices. In a medium-size bowl, mix the

nectarines and strawberries together.

5 Turn the yogurt cheese out onto a large serving platter. Spoon the fruit over and around the cheese. Cut wedges of the yogurt cheese, which is somewhat soft, and serve it with the fruit.

6 to 8 servings

STEWED FRUITS

This compote of dried fruits will win your heart. It is spicy and rich, and long, slow cooking gives it an incomparable depth of flavor. If you have a crockpot, definitely stew the fruit in it.

You can serve this for an elegant brunch by itself or over waffles or pancakes, or for dessert over vanilla or cinnamon ice cream. Or just eat it on its own for a sweet, succulent snack.

1 pound pitted prunes
8 ounces dried apricots
8 ounces dried pears
3 cups water
½ cup sugar
½ vanilla bean
2 strips (2 inches each) lemon zest
2 tablespoons freshly squeezed lemon juice

1 Stir all the ingredients together in a large heavy saucepan. Bring the liquid

to a boil over medium-high heat, then reduce the heat to as low as possible and cook, covered, until the fruit is softened and tender, 2 hours. Stir the fruits occasionally while they cook.

If you have a crockpot, stir all the ingredients together in it and cook until the fruit is tender, 6 to 8 hours.

2 Serve the fruit warm or at room temperature.

6 to 8 servings

BIBLIOGRAPHY

Behn, Ernest. *More Profit with Less Tillage.* Des Moines, Iowa: Wallace-Homestead Book Company, 1982.

Berry, Wendell. *Home Economics.* San Francisco: North Point Press, 1987.

Bromfield, Louis. *From My Experience: The Pleasures and Miseries of Life on a Farm.* New York: Harper and Brothers Publishers, 1955.

————. *Out of the Earth.* New York: Harper and Brothers Publishers, 1948.

Burr, Fearing. *Field and Garden Vegetables of America.* Chillicothe, Illinois: The American Botanist, Booksellers, 1988.

Carluccio, Antonio. *A Passion for Mushrooms.* Topsfield, Massachusetts: Salem House Publishers, 1989.

Carson, Rachel. *Silent Spring.* Boston: Houghton Mifflin Co., 1962.

Creasy, Rosalind. *The Complete Book of Edible Landscaping.* San Francisco: Sierra Club Books, 1982.

Fukuoka, Masanobu. *The One-Straw Revolution: An Introduction to Natural Farming.* Emmaus: Rodale Press, 1978.

Jackson, Wes. *Altars of Unhewn Stone.* San Francisco: North Point Press, 1987.

Jefferson, Thomas. *Garden Book: 1766–1824.* Philadelphia: The American Philosophical Society, 1944.

Kramer, Mark. *Three Farms: Making Milk, Meat and Money from the American Soil.* Boston: Little, Brown & Co., 1977.

Larkom, Joy. *The Salad Garden.* New York: The Viking Press, 1984.

Leighton, Ann. *American Gardens in the Eighteenth Century "For Use or for Delight."* Amherst: The University of Massachusetts Press, 1986.

————. *Early American Gardens "For Meate and Medicine."* Amherst: The University of Massachusetts Press, 1970.

McGee, Harold. *On Food and Cooking: The Science and Lore of the Kitchen.* New York: Collier Books, Macmillan Publishing Co., 1984.

McPhee, John. *Giving Good Weight.* New York: Farrar, Straus & Giroux, 1975.

National Research Council. *Alternative Agriculture.* Washington, D.C.: National Academy Press, 1989.

Pellegrini, Angelo, M. *The Food-Lover's Garden.* Seattle: Madrona Publishers, Inc., 1970.

Rhodes, Richard. *Farm: A Year in the Life of an American Farmer.* New York: Simon & Schuster, 1989.

Robertson, Laurel; Flinders, Carol; and Godfrey, Bronwen. *Laurel's Kitchen.* Berkeley: Nilgiri Press, 1976.

Schneider, Elizabeth. *Uncommon Fruits and Vegetables.* New York: Harper & Row, 1986.

Scholl, Melvin. *Arnewood: The Story of an Iowa Dairyman.* Iowa City: The State Historical Society of Iowa, 1954.

Strange, Marty. *Family Farming: A New Economic Vision.* Lincoln: University of Nebraska Press, 1988.

Wood, Rebecca. *The Whole Foods Encyclopedia.* New York: Prentice Hall Press, 1988.

INDEX

Q, R